THE COLD WAR

ALSO BY DAVID MILLER

Naval
Combat Arms: Submarines
Jane's Major Warships: 1997
Modern Naval Combat
Modern Naval Warfare
Modern Sub-Hunters
Modern Submarines
Modern Submarine Warfare
Submarines of the World
The World's Navies

Land Warfare
Battlefield
Modern Land Warfare (with Chris Foss)

Strategic
Strategic Weapons Systems

Historic
A Short History of the Office of the Master-General of the Ordinance
The Wreck of the Isabella

Children's Books
Battleships
Destroyers
Frigates
People in Action: Airline Pilot
People in Action: Fighter Pilot
Soviet Navy
Soviet Rocket Forces
Soviet Submarines

THE COLD WAR
A Military History

David Miller

ST. MARTIN'S PRESS
NEW YORK

THOMAS DUNNE BOOKS.
An imprint of St. Martin's Press.

ISBN 0-312-24183-6

First published in Great Britain by John Murray (Publishers) Ltd

First U.S. Edition: November 1999

10 9 8 7 6 5 4 3 2 1

This book is dedicated to the officers, soldiers, sailors, marines and airmen of all the NATO and Warsaw Pact countries. For forty years they did their duty to their countries, and between them they ensured that the Third World War never started.

Contents

Contents

Contents

Illustrations

The author and publisher wish to acknowledge the following for permission to reproduce illustrations: 1, 3 (above), 4 (above), 4 (below), Landesbildstelle, Berlin; 2 (above), 2 (below), 3 (below), 13 (below), NATO Pictures; 5 (above), US Navy; 5 (below), 6 (above), 7, 9 (above), 9 (below), 11 (below), 12 (below), 14 (above), US Department of Defense; 6 (below), Keystone; 8 (above), Press Association; 8 (below), 90 Squadron, RAF, via Peter Green; 10 (above), 10 (below), US National Atomic Museum; 11 (above), Yarrow Shipbuilders; 12 (above), 13 (above), 16, Popperfoto; 14 (below), Ford Aerospace; 15 (above), AMX, France; 15 (below), Krauss Maffei, Germany.

MAPS

Preface

The Cold War, which seemed such an ever-present reality just a few years ago has now been relegated to history. The mighty armies that faced each other across so many borders in northern, central and southern Europe are now but shadows of their former selves. The navies which patrolled the seas have dispersed, and former enemy armies now spend most of their time on common exercises and in comforting each other about the glories that are gone. The air forces, too, are bemused by the changes that a few years have wrought; vast orders for the most complex and sophisticated machines ever invented by man have been cancelled, training is now minimal, and recruits are hard to find; indeed, some even question the need for air forces at all.

The armed forces were, however, only the public face of the international effort put into the prosecution of the Cold War. Entire industries depended upon the Cold War – tank production, warship construction, warplane manufacturing – as also did many less obvious concerns such as electronics, power-plant and machinery manufacturers. Virtually all governments involved in the Cold War ensured that their national plans revolved around preparing for, fighting and surviving a possible Third World War. Indeed, when the Cold War ended, many things came to light that show just how thorough and far-reaching the preparations had been. Buried headquarters and survival shelters, which only a very select few had ever known about, were advertised for sale. Huge strategic stockpiles of commodities such as coal, oil, sugar and flour were publicly acknowledged and sold off. Secret arsenals of weapons for use by guerrilla forces were revealed, even in ostensibly neutral countries such as Austria. But many more facets of the conflict probably remain unknown, even to this day.

The Cold War does not have two convenient dates to mark its start and finish. No troops poured across a border to open the campaign, nor did victorious armies march in triumph through the enemy's capital city to mark the end.

Many dates could be taken to mark the start of the Cold War, but the events of 1945 to 1949 are considered to be preliminary skirmishes and manoeuvring for position, and 4 April 1949, the date of signing the North Atlantic Treaty, which formalized the anti-Soviet alliance, is taken to be the most apt date.

Similarly, the end of the Cold War was publicly announced on at least ten occasions as triumphant politicians signed yet another agreement in Washington, London, Paris, Geneva or Moscow to reduce or remove tension. But the signal for the real end of the Cold War came in Berlin, the city which for forty-two years had crystallized all the issues at stake. There on one night in November 1989 an East German government official telephoned the security guard commander at the checkpoints on the Berlin Wall and ordered him to prevent East Berliners from crossing to the West. But the officer, probably no more senior than a captain, looked out the window, saw the vast crowd, sensed its determination, knew deep inside himself that the game was up, and, realizing the futility of it all, refused. Throughout the Cold War the Communist system had depended absolutely upon orders being obeyed, and with that refusal in East Berlin the entire system proceeded, with dreadful inevitability, to collapse.

The First and Second World Wars have both been recorded in great detail in a variety of government-sponsored 'Official Histories' by most of the countries involved. These histories set out the strategies and tactics of the military campaigns and record the industrial and civilian efforts to support the armed forces. Each runs into many volumes by a variety of authors, all working to an overall plan and coordinated by a managing editor. The resulting series have therefore become the standard works of reference on their subject, enabling future generations to study what went on, who was involved, and, in most cases, why the leaders acted as they did.

No such work has yet even been discussed for the Cold War, but this book is an attempt to paint an overall picture of some of the military factors involved. Perhaps it may spark interest in a proper 'Official History'.

For this author there were no heroes and no villains in the Cold War. There were definitely two 'sides', and on a political level each felt the other to be wrong, but at the military level there were just millions of officers and sailors, soldiers and airmen, the great majority of whom were doing their job as best they knew how and carrying out the orders given to them by their governments.

There were hundreds of 'incidents'. Aircraft were shot down, ships collided, and, on several occasions, tanks loaded with live ammunition faced each other across borders. But opponents 'on the other side of the fence' were never left with no way out other than humiliation; no side ever pushed the other over the brink.

In attempting an unofficial history of even just the military factors in such a complex situation stretching over forty years, not every aspect can be covered, nor can all aspects be covered in the same detail. The book ends in 1989, as did the Cold War. In addition, because the Cold War was both very long and covered a vast area, the book concentrates on events in central Europe. This is not because the author considers events on the northern and southern flanks to have been unimportant, but is necessitated by the space available. Also, central Europe best symbolizes what went on during the Cold War and is the most likely place for fighting to have started, and also, possibly, for the issue to have been decided.

Frequent mention is made of military plans prepared during the Cold War, and a word of explanation is required. Many civilians find it hard to understand why soldiers, sailors and airmen spend so much of their time analysing possible threats against them and, when preparing plans, taking the worst case. Thus, throughout the Cold War, congressional and parliamentary committees and media correspondents were regularly given the direst of predictions about the other side's numbers and capabilities. Sometimes there were genuine errors, but frequently each element in an estimate was given a pessimistic 'tweak' which, when all were put together, resulted in an overall prediction that was later proved to have been very wide of the mark indeed.

This predilection for the 'worst case' was partly due to professional caution and the desire not to be caught out. Far better, planners thought, to find the situation was not so bad after all. Partly, however, it was also due to the knowledge that if war did come it would almost certainly be of short duration and there would therefore be little chance to make good any peacetime deficiencies. Thus, by painting the gloomiest possible picture of the enemy's strengths, one's own side would be better armed to meet him should the day come. Matters were not helped, however, when politicians took the budget figure the military asked for and subtracted 10 per cent, since the military responded by adding an extra 10 per cent the next time around, on the assumption that they would lose it.

AUTHOR'S CONVENTIONS

A number of conventions have been used in this book.

National Designations
Wherever more than one nation is mentioned in a list, they are recorded in alphabetical order according to the initial letter of their name in the English

language. Such a listing does not therefore imply any order of precedence, importance, preference or merit.

Soviet Military Equipment

There is scope for confusion concerning the designation of Soviet military equipment, since the same item (e.g. an aircraft, missile, tank, etc.) could have a US designation, a NATO reporting name, a Soviet military designation and a Soviet type name – although in most cases the last two were discovered only after the Cold War had ended. In order to simplify matters for the reader, the US/NATO system is used throughout, except in the case of aircraft, where the Soviet design bureau and number are used (e.g. MiG-21, Su-27, etc.).

Military Units

In military units, confusion can be caused by differing use of formation and unit designations. A US division was some 30 per cent larger than a Soviet division; in some armies a regiment was composed of three battalions, while in others a regiment was a battalion-sized unit. The reader is referred to the Glossary, under 'Army formations and units', for more information.

Naval, Air-Force and Army Titles

A particular difficulty arises with the titles of navies and air forces, especially where the word 'royal' appears in the title. The British, for example, use the title 'Royal Navy' to apply solely to their own navy, and with foreign navies which include the word 'royal' in their titles they insert the nation's name, as in 'Royal Dutch Navy' and 'Royal Malaysian Navy'. Within those countries, however, there is no such national qualifier: to a Malaysian the 'Royal Navy' (*Tentera Laut di-Raja*) is the Malaysian navy. Further, to use national titles in the vernacular may be difficult for readers of other nationalities to understand, while to translate them literally into English may cause further confusion. The German *Luftwaffe*, for example, translates as 'Air Weapon', while the French *Marine Nationale* translates as 'National Navy'. To avoid all these problems, the convention has been adopted of referring to all navies, air forces and, for consistency, national armies simply by the national name followed by the words 'navy', 'air force' or 'army' in lower case – e.g. British air force, German navy, US air force, Soviet army and so on. Since all are treated identically, it is hoped that this will not cause offence.

Glossary

Any abbreviation is explained when it is first used in the main text. There is also a glossary at the end of the book, which explains the principal relevant military terms and abbreviations.

Preface

ACKNOWLEDGEMENTS

The author wishes to thank Wing Commander (Retired) Bruce Allcorn who proofread Chapter 7 and made many valuable suggestions. He would also like to thank Major-General Sir Robert Corbett, the last British commandant in Berlin and author of *Berlin and The British Ally: 1945–1990*, for his helpful advice on life and events in that city.

He is also most grateful to Grant McIntyre, Gail Pirkis and Caroline Westmore of the publisher, John Murray, for turning what might have been a daunting and frustrating experience into a real pleasure. Finally, he wishes to express his particular gratitude to Bob Davenport, editor extraordinary, whose eagle eye, attention to the most minute detail, wide knowledge of English language, grammar and punctuation, and apparently infinite patience have made this book a much better document than it otherwise would have been.

If, however, despite all this help there are still errors in this book, they are the responsibility of the author alone.

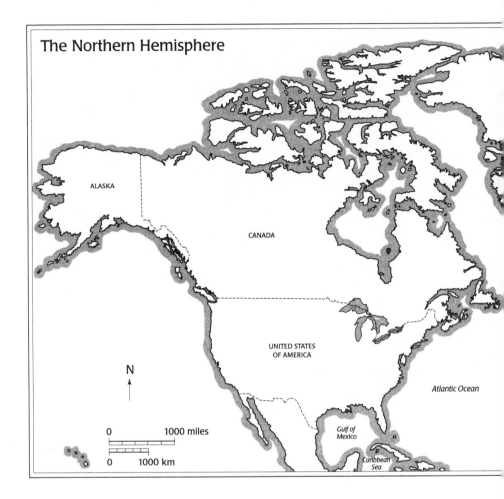

The Northern Hemisphere

ALASKA

CANADA

UNITED STATES
OF AMERICA

Atlantic Ocean

N

0   1000 miles

0   1000 km

Gulf of
Mexico

Caribbean
Sea

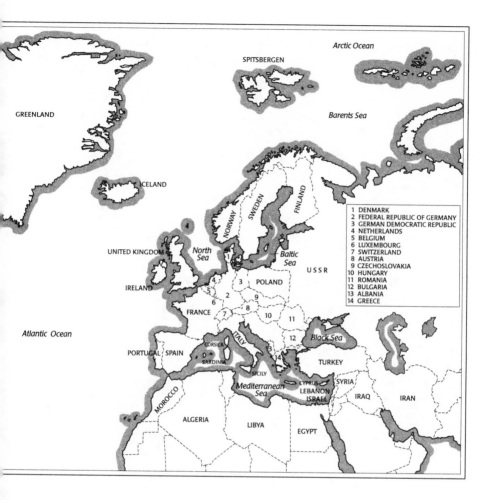

Central Europe: The Cockpit of the Cold War

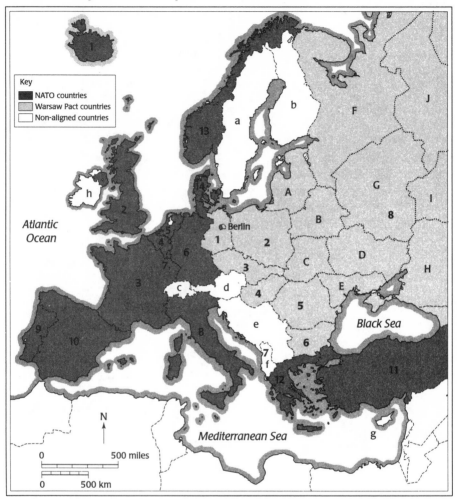

Key
- NATO countries
- Warsaw Pact countries
- Non-aligned countries

Atlantic Ocean

Berlin

Black Sea

N

Mediterranean Sea

| 0 | 500 miles |
| 0 | 500 km |

NATO countries
1. Iceland (not part of IMCS)
2. United Kingdom
3. France (not part of IMCS)
4. Belgium
5. Netherlands
6. Federal Republic of Germany
7. Luxembourg
8. Italy
9. Portugal
10. Spain (member from 1982; not part of IMCS)
11. Turkey
12. Greece
13. Norway
14. Denmark

Note: IMCS = Integrated Military Command Structure

Warsaw Pact countries
1. German Democratic Republic
2. Poland
3. Czechoslovakia
4. Hungary
5. Romania
6. Bulgaria
7. Albania (left in 1961)
8. USSR

Soviet Union military districts
A. Baltic MD
B. Byelorussia MD
C. Carpathian MD
D. Kiev MD
E. Odessa MD

F. Leningrad MD
G. Moscow MD
H. North Caucasus MD
I. Volga MD
J. Urals MD

Non-aligned countries
a. Sweden
b. Finland
c. Switzerland
d. Austria
e. Yugoslavia
f. Albania (from 1961)
g. Cyprus
h. Republic of Ireland

PART I

THE TWO GREAT ALLIANCES

1

'A Bewildered, Baffled and Breathless World'[1]

When the German surrender became official at midnight on 8 May 1945, continental Europe was in ruins. The Allied armies halted where they were and there was a limited amount of celebration, but attention rapidly switched to more pressing problems. The USA and the UK needed to send troops to the Far East for the final phase of the Japanese war, while concurrently reducing their armed forces and starting to return conscripts to civilian life. The Soviet Union needed to recover from the devastation of the war and to ensure that such an attack would never again be possible. Of the other continental European powers, the only one of contemporary significance was France, which was anxious to assert its right to take its place alongside the three major Allies, but also had a pressing need to re-establish the French state and to reassert its control over its former colonial territories.

Meanwhile, all four tried to sort out the problems of a defeated Germany: to feed the population, to restart industry, to round up prisoners of war, to try war criminals, to carry out the denazification process and to enable the people to return to some sort of normality. One of the agreements at the 1945 Potsdam Conference was that machinery and industrial equipment would be exacted as reparations, and, since most industrial facilities were in the Western zones of occupation and most agriculture in the Soviet zone, the Soviets would receive a proportion of the machinery in exchange for food to help feed the population in the Western zones. Problems then arose owing to the failure of the Soviets to supply the food (which had to be made up by shipments from the UK and the USA), coupled with their insistence on obtaining every piece of machinery they had been offered. In May 1946 the Western Allies refused to send any further reparations to the East. The Soviets objected strongly to this, and started to use their veto to block progress in the Allied Control Council, where the four Allied commanders-in-chief or their representatives met. These first significant post-war disagreements were, with hindsight, indicators of the Cold War that was to come.

3

In global terms, the war had weakened all the western European countries, eliminated Germany as a European power, and transformed the USSR into a world power. The USA, however, had become the arbiter of Western destinies, having totally displaced the UK as the most powerful non-Communist nation. Among the western European nations, however, the UK, even though it was virtually bankrupt, remained militarily the most powerful nation, primarily because of its extensive empire and the large size of its military forces. There was also the moral debt, relevant in the immediate post-war years, which Britain was owed by other countries of Europe for which it had provided a bastion of freedom and democracy – and in many cases a base for governments-in-exile and armed forces – during six tumultuous years.

In eastern Europe the Soviet Union was all-powerful. It had the largest armed forces (by a huge margin), and exerted a rigid control over the lands it occupied. In addition, it had considerable influence in the West. There were, of course, the Communist parties, which exerted a major influence in countries such as Italy and France, but, of greater importance, many non-Communists admired the performance of the Russian people in the recent war, praised their powers of resistance, especially at places like Stalingrad, and sympathized with their huge losses and undoubted suffering.

During the course of the war the Soviet Union had pushed its borders westward, so that by 1945 Estonia, Lithuania, Latvia, eastern Poland, Ruthenia, Bukovina and Bessarabia had all become integral parts of the Communist state. In addition, the Soviet Union had total control over East Germany, both by right of conquest and by inter-Allied agreement. But all this seemed to be insufficient, and in a speech on 9 February 1946 the Soviet leader Josef Stalin outlined a new Five-Year Plan, which gave absolute priority to rearmament, so that the Soviet Union could defend itself against what he termed 'encroachment and threat'.

The implementation of this policy was clear for all to see as the Soviet Union brought one east-European country after another under its domination as 'satellites': Albania (1946); Bulgaria, Hungary and Romania (1947); and Czechoslovakia (1948). Even Tito's Yugoslavia, while not a 'satellite', appeared at first to be under Soviet domination. The atmosphere of the times was well described by the former British prime minister Winston Churchill, who, in a landmark speech to students at Fulton, Missouri, on 5 March 1946, took the opportunity to warn the world of the 'iron curtain' which was descending over eastern Europe.

Undoubtedly, mistakes and misunderstandings were made between East and West, stemming, at least in part, from a difficulty that was to continue throughout the Cold War and which might be termed the 'problem of perceptions'. Thus, at the end of the twentieth century, there is some evidence that the Soviet Union may have been genuinely frightened of western

4

Europe, from whence it had repeatedly been invaded. But there is little merit in using post-Cold War hindsight to claim that Western leaders, politicians and general staffs overreacted in the late 1940s. The fact is that both sides could react only according to their reasonable perceptions at the time, tempered by their background, upbringing and experience.

EUROPE IN THE POST-WAR ERA

One of the strongest influences on contemporary perceptions was the actual state of Europe in the immediate post-war period, with Europeans finding themselves, in Churchill's words, in 'a bewildered, baffled and breathless world'. Europe, apart from the neutral countries, was physically devastated and its many peoples were mentally and physically exhausted by the war they had just been through. Industry had been wrecked, road and rail communications had been largely destroyed, and sea transport was at a virtual standstill because of wartime shipping losses.

One of the major elements contributing to a marked feeling of instability was the mass migration in which, for a variety of reasons, vast numbers of refugees were moving around Europe. It was estimated – an exact figure was impossible – that some 30 million people (known as 'displaced persons' or 'DPs') were on the move, adding to the already serious difficulties suffered by the transportation, feeding and administrative systems. For a start there were some 9 million foreign workers who had been forcibly taken to Germany from the various occupied territories to bolster the workforce during 1940–44 and who now had to be repatriated. There were large groups of foreigners who had fought on the German side and who now did all they could to resist being returned to their homelands, where they faced retribution. There were also the surviving Jews and others from the concentration camps, who no longer wished to live in Europe and thus sought to emigrate to the USA, the UK, Australia or, in the case of many Jews, Palestine.

The Soviet Union also moved a large number of people by force. A process started in 1941 was continued in the early post-war period by transporting to Siberia people from the Baltic states (Estonia, Lithuania and Latvia), the former German territory of East Prussia, the Caucasus and the Crimea. Also, in 1944–5 ethnic Finns were forced to move out of Karelia when it was ceded to the Soviet Union.

In the face of the Soviet advance, ethnic Germans living in East Prussia fled westward, mainly by sea, although many fled overland. The movement continued after the war, with some of the refugees finding temporary asylum in Denmark.

There were also large ethnic German populations living in the Danube basin, mainly in eastern Czechoslovakia (Sudetenland) and Hungary, and some of these fled, mainly to Austria, as the Red Army advanced in 1944–5. After the war's end, however, the Potsdam Conference authorized the compulsory expulsion of the remainder of these people from Czechoslovakia, Hungary and Poland – a move which rapidly got out of control and resulted in the deaths of some 3 million ethnic Germans. The vacuums created by these moves were then filled by an influx of nationals from the country concerned.

These movements were on such a vast scale and caused such massive disruption that they led to the setting up of the UN-sponsored International Relief Organization, headed by the UN High Commissioner for Refugees.

EASTERN EUROPE

Invasions from the west in 1812, 1854, 1914, 1919 and 1941 and from the east in 1902, 1919 and 1939 were etched in Russian and Soviet folk memories. It was scarcely surprising, therefore, that in the late 1940s patriotic motives should have led the Soviet leadership to defend its territory from further incursions. In addition to that, however, was a perceived need not only to protect the Communist revolution, principally by maintaining the supremacy of the Communist Party in the Soviet Union, but also to spread it.

Stalin had become obsessive about defence, and he sought to construct a series of buffer states around the Soviet Union, particularly in the west. As a first step, the Soviet Union occupied East Germany and eastern Austria; then it absorbed a number of smaller areas on its own borders. From 1946 onwards, however, Stalin progressively imposed control over other countries in what was tacitly acknowledged to be the 'Soviet sphere of influence'. In part, he achieved his objectives by a series of bilateral treaties, but where he deemed these insufficient he sought to achieve total control of what came to be termed 'Soviet satellites'.

In Albania, Enver Hoxha took power in 1945 and immediately formed a powerful centralized Communist government which, for the time being at least, was totally loyal to Moscow. Bulgaria, after the Germans left, was governed by the 'Fatherland Front' under the leadership of the Communist Georgi Dimitrov. The monarchy was abolished in 1947 and the Agrarian Party was eliminated, with its leader, Nikola Petkov, being given a show trial and then executed in September. The Communist Party was then the sole political force in the country.

The Czechoslovak government-in-exile in London negotiated with the Soviet government during the war, one outcome of which was an agreement to cede the Carpatho-Ukraine to the USSR. At the war's end the Czechoslovak government was then able to return to Prague with Edward

Beneš as president; it found the country occupied by Soviet and US troops, although these both departed in December 1945. An election was held in 1946 in which the Communists won 38 per cent of the vote and the resulting 'National Front' government was headed by the Communist leader, Klement Gottwald. One of the earliest items of business was the mass expulsion of the Sudetenland Germans, mentioned above, elements of whom had been instrumental in engineering the German occupation of Czechoslovakia in 1938. The Soviet Union then decided to bring Czechoslovakia to heel and, having banned Czech attendance at the Marshall Plan Conference in Paris in 1947, it sponsored a Communist coup in February 1948, in the aftermath of which the widely respected foreign minister Jan Masaryk died, allegedly by suicide. The trade unions responded with strikes and demonstrations which led to the Communists taking an even firmer grip on power, and when Gottwald took over from Beneš as president later that month Czechoslovakia was firmly in the Soviet camp.

Hungary fought during the Second World War on the German side, and on withdrawal of the Germans it signed an armistice with the Soviet Union which included provision for purging fascists and war criminals. Hungarian Communists returning to the country used the armistice as a mandate to eliminate unwanted democrats, and to expropriate property, not only from ethnic Germans and fascists, but also from the Catholic Church. Elections in 1945 resulted in the Small Landholders Party obtaining 60 per cent of the seats, while the Communists gained only 17 per cent, but in 1947 the Communists 'revealed conspiracies' by members of the Small Landholders Party which led to trials of some 220 members. The prime minister fled to Switzerland, but many others disappeared never to be seen again. New elections resulted in the victory of the Communist Party, and the country was forced to sign a trade pact with the Soviet Union on 14 July; thus Hungary too was firmly in the Soviet camp.

Poland had been overrun by the Red Army in 1944–5 and the Soviets stepped in quickly to install a provisional government (known as 'the Lublin Committee'), thus outwitting the government-in-exile, which was still in London. In the post-war border adjustments Poland lost its eastern territories to the Soviet Union, while its western border with Germany was moved westward to the line of the rivers Oder and Neisse. The Polish Communist Party gradually eliminated opposition parties, and Stanislaw Mikołajczyk, the leader of the most powerful opposition group, the Agrarian Party, was warned of his imminent arrest in October 1947 and fled to London, thus escaping almost certain death. By 1948 Poland too was fully under Communist control.

In Romania, the small Communist Party formed the national Democratic Front with the Socialists and the Peasant Workers Front. This coalition won 90 per cent of the votes in the 1946 election, and when the opposition sought to dispute the result it was eliminated. In July 1947 Iuliu Maniu, the leader of the National Peasant Party, was tried and sentenced to solitary confinement for life, and in December 1947 the king was forced to abdicate. The 'Unity Party', under the Communist Gheorghe Gheorgiu-Dej, then took power in early 1948.

In Yugoslavia, the Communist Tito was the predominant partisan leader, and he immediately took power in 1945. Soviet troops, which had arrived in the country in December 1944, left in March 1945. Tito's Popular Liberation Front obtained 90 per cent of the votes in the 1945 election, which was followed by widespread purging of political opponents and the nationalization of trade, industry, bank and social insurance. Yugoslavia signed a Mutual Assistance Pact with the Soviet Union in 1945 and appeared for a short time to be a firm member of the Soviet bloc, but in 1948 Tito broke with Stalin, who then, very unwisely (from his point of view), imposed an economic blockade, which forced Tito to turn to the West.

COMMUNISTS IN WESTERN EUROPE

Soviet activities were not confined to eastern Europe. Virtually all countries in western Europe had a domestic Communist party, most of which during the war had achieved a degree of respectability which stemmed in large part from their role in wartime resistance movements. There was also a widely felt admiration for the role played by the Soviet Union and its people in defeating Germany.

Perhaps the strongest Communist party in the West was in France, where it had numerous seats in the National Assembly, was very powerful in the trade-union movement, and even held four posts in the Cabinet, including that of minister of defence. The Communists managed to perform some extraordinary gyrations, one the one hand dancing to the dictates of Moscow (for example, by generating street violence in late 1947 as instructed at the Cominform meeting in mid-1947) and on the other by co-operation with General Charles De Gaulle* in opposition to the Marshall Plan and to NATO.

Italy, too, was in turmoil, with numerous political parties and former resistance groups all jostling for power – the situation being further complicated by the forcible return of 'repatriated' Italians from Yugoslavia and the colonies, and by the purging of the Fascists. The Christian Democrats

---

* When attending the dedication of France's new, nuclear-powered aircraft carrier, which is named after the general, I enquired about the correct spelling of the name. The general's son informed me that his father had wished the 'De' to be capitalized, and I see no reason not to follow this advice.

emerged as the predominant political force, but the Communist Party, led by Palmiro Togliatti, was the second most powerful.

The Greek civil war had started even before the Germans departed in 1944, and British troops were forced to intervene to restore order. After a short-lived armistice, the Communists sought to take the country over by force and initially achieved some success, not least because they were able to operate out of sanctuaries in Albania, Bulgaria and Yugoslavia. Initially, the government forces did not do well against them, their problems being exacerbated by the British withdrawal of support, for economic reasons, in 1947. But eventually the United States stepped in and ensured the government's victory.

Nowhere, however, did the issues seem to be so well delineated as in the former German capital of Berlin, which had been split between the four wartime Allies in 1945, with the Soviet Union ruling the eastern half, while the three other Allies shared the western half. In the early years, relations between the Eastern and Western occupying powers reflected their disagreements at the United Nations, but Berlin itself occupied the centre of the stage when the Berlin blockade was imposed in 1947, as is described in more detail in Chapter 32.

Efforts to achieve a comprehensive peace treaty began in Paris in July 1946 and continued through to February 1947, with a number of agreements being reached. Among these were that Italy should pay reparations, lose its colonies, and give up Trieste, which would become a free state under UN supervision, while Hungary would revert to its 1937 borders and the Soviet seizure of Bessarabia and Bukovina from Romania was made legal. Finland was treated particularly harshly, the loss of Karelia to the USSR being made permanent, while strict limits were placed on its military capabilities.

Thus the picture of Europe in this period was one of a continent where order was slowly being restored, but with poverty and misery still widespread. Tens of millions of displaced persons were on the move, requiring resettlement somewhere, and, on top of all this, the Soviet Union was progressively imposing control over eastern Europe. In this latter process, non-Communist national leaders were being ousted and, more often than not, killed, and it was clear that if the Communists won the civil war in Greece the same would happen there. Also, in almost every diplomatic forum where Soviets met Westerners, such as the United Nations and the Six-Power Conference on Germany, the Soviet representatives either caused endless difficulties or simply exercised their veto.

As if all this was not enough, Asia was in turmoil. The Chinese Civil War was at its height in the late 1940s, with the Communists appearing certain to win. In addition, a number of western European powers found themselves involved in colonial wars. The French war against the Viet Minh in Indo-China broke out in 1947, while the British war in Malaya (a so-called 'emergency') started in 1948; in both cases the enemy were Communists. In divided Korea, the Communists in the North were beginning to menace the non-Communist South. Everything seemed to confirm the widespread perception of a Communist drive for world power.

It is, therefore, scarcely surprising that in such an atmosphere Western leaders began to look to their defences – something which, with the elimination of the German threat, many had hoped to place into a state of benevolent neglect for at least a decade.

The capitals of western Europe were pervaded by a sense of impending crisis as the blows came thick and fast, and, in the face of what appeared to be an imminent catastrophe, they struggled to find some means of regional co-operation and common defence. Their initial and somewhat hesitant attempts had varied degrees of success, but all eventually came together in a major success – the North Atlantic Treaty.

THE DUNKIRK TREATY

The first major post-war treaty in western Europe was the Anglo-French Treaty of Dunkirk, which was signed on 4 March 1947. On the surface this was a fifty-year mutual-defence treaty against future *German* aggression, although both countries understood that it was really aimed against the Soviet Union. As the Soviet activities in eastern Europe continued to cause alarm, however, the British foreign secretary, Ernest Bevin, suggested that there should be a network of similar bilateral treaties between like-minded countries, but he soon changed his views and began to advocate widening the scope of the Dunkirk Treaty to include the Benelux countries.

THE BRUSSELS TREATY

Benelux was one of the first groupings to be formed after the Second World War and consisted of Belgium, the Netherlands and Luxembourg, all of which had previously tried neutrality in one form or another. Belgium had been neutral since its creation in 1839, but was overrun in both 1914 and 1940 because it had the misfortune to sit on the planned German routes into France. The Netherlands had also long been neutral, and managed to remain so in the First World War, but, like the rest of continental Europe, was occupied by the Germans in the Second World War. Unlike the other two, Luxembourg's neutrality was not voluntary but had been imposed by the Treaty of London (1867), although the country's small size and virtually disarmed status meant that the treaty proved to be totally ineffective in both world wars.

The idea of co-operation between the three countries had been mooted during the war and led, in due course, to a customs union in 1948. The countries had, however, already agreed to co-operate in foreign-policy matters, and this led to a conference in Luxembourg in January 1948 at which they agreed on a common defence policy, in which the idea of a network of bilateral agreements would be rejected in favour of multilateral regional agreements. Thus, when invited by France and the UK to join the Dunkirk Treaty, they adopted a common line that it was pointless having a treaty unless it was designed for protection against the Soviet Union, and to be effective such a treaty, they suggested, must include the USA – although this was not achieved in the short term.

Negotiations began in January 1948, and such was the pressure of events (particularly the Communist coup in Czechoslovakia) that a draft was circulated on 19 February and the new Brussels Treaty (also known as the Western Union) was initialled on 13 March and signed on 17 March 1948.

This treaty, in which the Five Powers (Belgium, France, Luxembourg, the Netherlands and the UK) agreed to collaborate in defence as well as in the political, economic and cultural fields, was unique in several ways. First, although there had been many previous peacetime alliances, this was the first to establish a permanent political and military organization in western Europe in peacetime. Second, it was formed to counter aggression in general and, unlike the Dunkirk Treaty, was ostensibly not directed against a specific threat, although there was little doubt, either then or later, that it was actually aimed at the Soviet Union. Third, it introduced a series of permanent bodies, rather than leaving the planning to sporadic liaison meetings between the relevant national military staffs.*

The negotiations leading to the signature of the Brussels Treaty did briefly consider the question of the Nordic countries, but they were quickly excluded, primarily because the five signatories considered themselves unable to offer a realistic guarantee of military protection to Scandinavia. This view was the result of contemporary military assessments coupled with a perceptible lack of enthusiasm for such a task among the Continental parties to the treaty, although for France and the UK memories of their disastrous attempt to help Norway in 1940 also played a part.

The aim of the defence organization was to provide for military and logistic co-ordination between the Five Powers and for the study of the tactical problems of the defence of western Europe. In addition, it was intended to provide the framework on which a command organization could be based in time of crisis or war. At the top of the organization was the Defence Committee, which in peacetime was composed of the defence ministers of the Five Powers; this was served by the Chiefs-of-Staff Committee and the Military Supply Board, both of which met regularly, usually in London.

---

* The official description of the defence organization is given in Appendix 1.

The Chiefs-of-Staff Committee was responsible for advising the Defence Committee on all matters affecting the defence of western Europe, although it was also required to take into account members' commitments in other parts of the world – a not insignificant requirement when, with the exception of Luxembourg, four members still had large overseas possessions. Within this broad directive the committee's special tasks were to ensure that:

- the military resources of the five member countries were organized to meet the strategic requirements of the alliance;
- the forces of the various nations were welded into an effective fighting machine;
- the combined military resources of the five nations were allotted in the best way;
- a proper balance was maintained between the conflicting requirements of the European battle, on one hand, and internal security and home defence, on the other;
- the necessary resources were assessed, prepared and distributed, in particular to the commander of the European battle, whose special task would be to make the necessary operational plans and to put them into operation.

The Chiefs-of-Staff Committee was formed on 30 April 1948 and immediately set to work. In a significant move, the United States was invited to send military observers to London to help the committee with its work, particularly on plans and the thorny problem of supplies. As a result, a US delegation arrived in London in June, headed by Major-General Lyman L. Lemnitzer (who was later to be a NATO Supreme Allied Commander Europe).

Meanwhile, the Chiefs-of-Staff Committee was hard at work, and produced its first report in the astonishingly short time of two weeks. One of its fundamental conclusions was that, in the event of war with the USSR, the Five Powers should fight as far east in Germany as possible, in order not only to protect their own territories but also to create time for the USA to intervene.

Another outcome of the Chief-of-Staff Committee's work was the creation of the Western Union Defence Organization, a permanent planning and liaison organization, which officially started work on 3 October 1948 at Fontainebleau, France. It was headed by a Commanders-in-Chief Committee chaired by the most prestigious European soldier of the day, Britain's Field Marshal Bernard Montgomery. The other members were:

- Commander-in-Chief Western Europe Land Forces – General Jean de Lattre de Tassigny (France);
- Commander-in-Chief Western Europe Air Forces – Air Chief Marshal Sir James Robb (UK);
- Flag Officer, Western Europe – Vice-Admiral Jaujard (France).

In this organization, Montgomery had two small headquarters: one in London, the other in Fontainebleau, where it sat alongside the land and air headquarters. The committee was not as powerful as appeared, however, since the land and air members became commanders-in-chief only in war, while, as was clear from his title, the 'Flag Officer, Western Europe' had no allocated naval forces. Montgomery's position also gave rise to some problems, since he was not a supreme commander but simply the chairman of a committee, and in addition to this there was a personality clash with de Lattre de Tassigny, who, like Montgomery, was a man with firm views, not least concerning his own importance.

Despite its shortcomings, the organization was a start and the United States Joint Chiefs-of-Staff were so keen to be seen to support it that, in an unprecedented move, they sent two lieutenant-colonels to Fontainebleau to work with the new headquarters as 'non-participating members'.

The Brussels Treaty had many deficiencies. Its terminology was imprecise, it did not contain an agreement to go to war automatically, nor did it give the commanders sufficient troops for the proposed tasks, and, most important of all, it did not directly involve the Americans. On the other hand, it had the important short-term benefit of demonstrating to the United States that western European countries were, at long last, prepared to co-operate and combine for the common good. It also proved to be of great utility in providing the political vehicle for the admission of West Germany to European defence in 1954. Above all, however, it proved to be the starting point for a much more significant agreement: the North Atlantic Treaty.

The seriousness of the position between East and West was emphasized when, on the day that the Brussels Treaty was signed, US president Harry S. Truman addressed a joint session of Congress. He declared the United States' full support for the treaty, but he also requested Congress to authorize the reintroduction of selective service.

A NORDIC PACT?

The end of the war had found the Soviet Union in possession of much of the Baltic littoral, including Estonia, Lithuania, Latvia and East Prussia, and in occupation of Poland and the eastern zone of Germany. The USSR had also occupied Finnmark, the northernmost Norwegian province, and the Danish-owned Baltic island of Bornholm in 1945, primarily in order to take the surrender of the German forces; both were, however, handed back peacefully, Finnmark in late 1945 and Bornholm in the spring of 1946.

Despite this, Denmark and Norway found themselves faced with a palpable Soviet threat in early 1948 and started to examine the question of a defence pact, although initially they considered only limited membership based on a 'Nordic' grouping. These countries wished to avoid becoming involved in the Great Power rivalry between the USA and the Soviet Union, and were also keen to avoid becoming embroiled in the tensions in continental Europe immediately to their south.

The most powerful and prosperous of the Nordic countries was Sweden, which had successfully maintained its armed neutrality throughout both world wars and wished to continue to do so. Thus, in the immediate post-war period Sweden performed a delicate balancing act, making a 1 billion kronor loan to the Soviet Union, but also purchasing 150 P-51 Mustang piston-engined fighters from the USA, followed by 210 Vampire jets from the UK in 1948.

Norway had been occupied by the Germans during the war, partly because of its strategic position, but also because German industry depended upon Norwegian iron-ore production. In the post-war period Norway considered the Soviet threat to be very real, and its leaders began to seek a guarantee of security which would nevertheless not antagonize the Soviet Union.

Denmark was initially well disposed towards the Soviet Union in the aftermath of the war, but became increasingly concerned by the events in eastern Europe. In the spring of 1948 the country was swept by a rumour that the Russians intended to attack western Europe during the Easter weekend. This rumour turned out to have been ill-founded, but the Danes realized that neutrality was no longer a serious option and that some form of multinational co-operation was therefore essential. During its Second World War occupation by the Germans, Denmark, unlike many other occupied countries in western Europe, had been almost totally isolated from the UK and had been forced to look to its neighbour Sweden for what little help and support that neutral country could offer. It was only natural, therefore, that in the late 1940s it should wish to explore the possibilities of an alliance with Sweden.

On 19 April 1948 the Norwegian foreign minister, Halvard Lange, made a speech in which he publicly expressed interest in a 'Nordic' solution – by which he meant one involving Denmark, Iceland, Norway and Sweden.

Finland would also have been a natural member of a Nordic grouping, but the USSR made that impossible. The peace treaty had imposed strict manpower ceilings on Finland's armed forces* and, as if this was not enough, the country was effectively neutralized by the treaty of 'Friendship, Co-operation and Mutual Assistance' that the Soviet Union had forced it to sign on 6 April.

---

* Finland was permitted 34,000 in the army, 4,000 in the navy, and 3,000 in the air force (including any naval air arm), while equipment limits included 10,000 tonnes of warships and sixty aircraft. Submarines and bombers were totally prohibited.

The Norwegian initiative was considered by the Swedish parliament, which authorized its government to consult Denmark and Norway on the subject. Throughout these discussions the basic Swedish position was that Sweden would not stretch its neutrality beyond a Nordic grouping, which would be non-aligned and strong enough to remain uncommitted to either East or West; in particular, Sweden was not prepared to participate if any other members had bilateral links to outside parties. On the other hand, the Norwegians considered that their interests would best be served by joining an Atlantic pact (i.e. one involving the United States), while the Danish prime minister sought to find common ground between the other two parties. Having established their initial positions, in September 1948 these three countries set up a Defence Committee whose task was to study the practical possibilities of defence co-operation.

At the political level, in October 1948 the Danish and Norwegian foreign ministers sounded out the US secretary of state, George Marshall, about the likely US attitude to a Nordic pact. He told them that it would be very difficult for the US government to give military guarantees to a neutral bloc, and that any supplies of military equipment would inevitably take lower priority than to formal allies.

In January 1949 the Nordic Defence Committee reported that a trilateral military alliance would increase the defensive power of the three participants both by widening their respective strategic areas and through the benefits of common planning and standardization of equipment. All this, however, could be achieved only if Denmark and Norway underwent substantial rearmament. And even if all of this were achieved, the military experts advized that the Nordic pact would be unable to resist an attack by a Great Power (by which, of course, they meant the Soviet Union).

Having received the military report, the three prime ministers and their foreign ministers met on 5–6 January 1949 and discussed a variety of topics, including how to achieve the rearmament of Denmark and Norway. Then on 14 January the US government announced publicly what it had already advised in private, namely that the priority in provision of arms would be to countries which joined the US in a collective defence agreement. The Nordic prime ministers and foreign ministers reconvened at the end of the month, and on 30 January they announced that it was impossible to reach agreement; the potential Nordic pact was thus consigned to history.

2

The Birth of NATO

At the end of the Second World War by far the most powerful of the Western Allies was the United States. There were US garrisons all over Europe, including Austria, Belgium, Berlin, Czechoslovakia, France, Germany, Italy, the Netherlands, the UK and Yugoslavia, although manning levels were rapidly reduced wherever possible. The USA was hoping for a virtually total disengagement from Europe and sought to avoid any new commitments in the area, but in February 1947 the British dropped a bombshell when their foreign secretary, Ernest Bevin, informed the US government that the UK, ravaged by war, striving desperately to administer a huge empire, in the throes of the worst winter on record and to all intents bankrupt, would be compelled to end its military assistance to Greece from the beginning of April. Indeed, Britain's true position was revealed when its government had to go cap in hand to Washington with a request for a $4.4 billion loan later in that year. Faced with the British fait accompli, the Truman administration felt it had no option but to take the British place in supporting Greece, thus initiating a policy of involvement in European affairs which has continued to this day.

The United States' most natural ally in Europe was the United Kingdom, with which it had close blood ties and with which it had been closely allied in two world wars. In the early post-war years, however, there were several stresses in the UK–US relationship, in which a variety of factors was involved. One was financial, and included problems such as the sudden termination of the provision of military equipment under the 'Lend-Lease' scheme and achieving agreement on how to work out a precise figure for the British debt incurred to the USA during the 1939–45 period. The British also felt frustrated by the US denial of access to atomic weapons, not least because British scientists had given substantial help to their development in the Manhattan Project.

Palestine was also a problem. The British administered the territory under the terms of a pre-war League of Nations mandate, and in 1946–7 British troops there were seen to be forcibly turning back Jewish refugees from Europe – something which did not go down well with the politically active Jewish community in the USA. The USA also had very firm ideas on the continued British imperial retention of the Indian subcontinent, as well as an instinctive mistrust of Attlee's left-wing government. Above all was the realization (perhaps more clearly in the United States than in the United Kingdom) that, while Britain, with its empire, had entered the Second World War Two as the strongest single power in the world, it had emerged from it as demonstrably weaker – politically, militarily and economically.

Despite these strains, the Americans and British worked closely together in many areas, particularly when dealing with the Soviet Union. Thus, when Soviet intransigence led to the break-up of the Allied Council of Foreign Ministers meeting in London on 15 December 1947 Bevin took the opportunity to outline to George Marshall a proposal for a two-tier defence system for western Europe which would include the USA. Marshall's immediate response was that any talk of a US military guarantee was premature, to say the least, but nevertheless he agreed that talks about such a treaty could start, albeit confined initially to the English-speaking north-Atlantic nations: Canada, the UK and the USA.

Meanwhile, the Soviet leaders were extending their control to countries outside the Soviet bloc. Thus, at the same time that the Communist coup was taking place in Czechoslovakia (February 1948), Stalin dispatched a formal invitation to the Finnish president to visit Moscow to negotiate a treaty of friendship, similar to those which Hungary and Romania had recently been compelled to sign. The Finnish president was seventy-eight years old, his country was small and devastated by war; there was little choice but to sign.

As these Soviet–Finnish negotiations were taking place, the Norwegian government received information from several directions that Stalin's next 'offer' of a friendship treaty would be to Norway. These sources were clearly authentic and were sufficiently serious for the Norwegian foreign minister to hold urgent talks with the American ambassador on 11 March 1948 to inform him of what he had heard. He saw the British ambassador on the same day, but, having passed on the same information he had just given to the American, he then went significantly further, telling the Briton that Norway would refuse any Soviet demands for concessions, and that if this meant that the Soviet Union would attack Norway, then so be it: Norway would resist. That said, he then formally asked the ambassador what help Norway might expect to receive from Britain if attacked. To which the ambassador could only respond that he would contact his government and await a reply.

When the Norwegian enquiry reached London, Bevin immediately communicated his views to George Marshall, describing how the possession of

Norway would turn western Europe's northern flank and give the Soviet fleet access to the Atlantic. He also admitted that, as things were, the Brussels Treaty powers were insufficiently powerful to protect themselves, let alone to make a realistic offer of help to Norway. He therefore proposed a regional 'Atlantic Approaches Pact of Mutual Assistance', in which all of the countries directly threatened by a Soviet move to the Atlantic could participate, including, the USA, the UK, Canada, Eire, Iceland, Norway, Denmark, Portugal, France and (when it had a democratic regime) Spain.

Marshall considered Bevin's message, discussed it with President Truman, and replied to the British ambassador on 12 March, suggesting that talks should begin the following week. Bevin responded on 14 March, stating that a British delegation would arrive on 22 March and suggesting that Canada should be included in these further talks, which was agreed by both Washington and Ottawa within days. The British Cabinet considered the briefing to be given to their representative at these talks on 16 March, and thus, even as the Brussels Treaty was being signed on 17 March, the talks on its supersession were already under way. This did not mean that the Brussels Treaty had been superfluous; indeed, without it the US administration and Congress could well have doubted the European ability to rally together for the common good. The tripartite talks started in Washington on 22 March, and lasted for eleven days.*

Several events in late 1948 were of considerable importance to the eventual North Atlantic Treaty. First, in October the five Brussels Treaty foreign ministers announced their complete agreement on the principle of an Atlantic treaty and invited France to produce a first draft. On 11 November this document was duly presented to the Standing Committee of the Brussels Treaty, and the final draft was agreed by all five governments on 26 November and dispatched to Washington on 29 November, where on 4 December it was considered by the British and Canadian ambassadors and the US secretary of state. Considering the novelty, scope and importance of the subject, the usually stately progress of diplomatic negotiations and the involvement of five governments, this was quite breathtaking speed.

Meanwhile, on 8 November a formal meeting took place between the Western Union Commanders-in-Chief Committee and the Commander-in-Chief, US Forces Germany. This was held at Melle, France, and considered the military aspects of a possible Atlantic treaty.

More important even than all of these, however, was the US presidential election in November, which, rather naturally, had diverted the attention of many members of the US government, not least of Truman himself.

---

* These talks were classified Top Secret, but as a junior British representative was the notorious spy Donald Maclean it seems probable that the Soviet leadership knew as much of what was discussed as did London, Ottawa and Washington.

Truman was widely predicted to have little chance of success, but one of the fruits of his unexpected victory was that most of the principal US actors in this drama remained in place, the major exception being George Marshall, who took the opportunity to retire and was replaced by Dean Acheson.

Various schemes for a new alliance were considered. The first was simply to extend the Brussels Treaty to include the USA and, perhaps, Italy. Another scheme was to have an Atlantic pact running in parallel to the Brussels Treaty; this would include only countries with Atlantic coastlines – i.e. Canada, France, the UK, the USA and, of course, Norway. Some consideration was also given to yet a third body, a Mediterranean pact, primarily as a means of including Italy.

An Ambassadors Committee comprising representatives of Belgium, Luxembourg, Canada, France, the Netherlands and the UK, chaired by the US secretary of state, also considered a number of geographical factors. In a move which has subsequently been misinterpreted, the Tropic of Cancer was adopted as the southern boundary of the treaty. This was simply meant to be a device to preclude any African, Caribbean or Latin American country from joining and not, as was subsequently believed, to place an absolute barrier on any collective planning, manoeuvres or operations south of the Tropic of Cancer in the Atlantic Ocean.

As in all negotiations, problems were encountered from time to time, but what came to be known as 'the NATO spirit' produced a feeling of mutual desire to reach a satisfactory conclusion, with the ambassadors managing to take their respective foreign ministers along with them, while the US State Department kept the Senate Foreign Relations Committee involved.

MEMBERSHIP

At the start of the Washington discussions it was clear that membership of the proposed alliance would include the Brussels Treaty powers (the Benelux countries, France and the UK), Canada and the United States, but there was some discussion over other potential members.

It was considered highly desirable that Denmark and Norway should join the proposed alliance, and, if possible, Sweden as well. These were long-established democracies and were as much threatened as any other country in Europe; indeed, in 1948–9 Norway was probably the most threatened of them all. Further, they occupied very important strategic positions. Denmark sat astride the western end of the Baltic, dominating (with Sweden) the Skaggerak and the Belts; it also owned the island of Bornholm in the middle of the Baltic. Of greater importance to the United States, however, was Danish ownership of Greenland, which was a vital stepping-stone in the air route from the United States to Europe at a time when transport aircraft had a comparatively short range. Norway was also strategically important, since it lay along the southern flank of the Soviet Union's naval routes to the Atlantic and shared (with the USSR) the island of Spitsbergen. Sweden, however, was adamant that it would not abrogate its neutrality, and its membership was not pursued.

Once talk of an Atlantic pact started, Canada, the UK and the USA all expressed a desire that Iceland should be a founder member, as did Norway when it joined the discussions. Iceland was a small, unarmed nation which found itself occupying a key strategic position in the North Atlantic. It had become independent from Denmark in 1918 and had made an immediate declaration of perpetual neutrality, although Denmark had retained responsibility for its foreign affairs until April 1940. During the Second World War Iceland had been occupied by British troops, who arrived on 10 May 1940, but in July 1941 these had been replaced by US troops, the last of whom departed in April 1947. The US had, however, negotiated the right for its aircraft to transit through Keflavik for as long as US occupation forces remained in Germany.

Iceland had been seeking its own partners, but appreciated early on that it could obtain no realistic guarantee of protection from the proposed Nordic pact. An Icelandic mission visited the USA on 14–17 March and was given an assurance that Iceland would have a special position in the alliance, that it would not be required to produce any armed forces, and that no foreign troops would be stationed in Iceland in peacetime. A very lively domestic debate eventually resulted in agreement to join.

Italy was a more difficult problem. It had emerged from the war in a weak position, having first fought as a partner with Germany and Japan in the Axis pact, before signing an armistice in 1943 and then joining the Allies as a 'Co-Belligerent'. For some years after the war Italy was not a member of the United Nations, and when discussions about a potential Atlantic treaty began there was considerable debate on whether Italy should be included or not. Internally, there was no clear support among the Italian people for such an alliance, and the Left – in particular the very strong Communist Party – wanted to declare the country neutral. Externally, there was some reluctance among other potential members who had been at war with Italy until only a few years earlier, while the United States seemed to waver: on one hand it did not want to upset other potential members, but, on the other, it did not want to upset the large Italian community in the USA. Some even argued that the northern orientation of the proposed treaty – its title had already been tentatively agreed as the 'North Atlantic Treaty' – appeared, by definition, to exclude the 'southern-tier' nations.

The United States encouraged Italy to seek to join the Western Union, but the visit of the Italian Chief of General Staff, General Marras, to the USA in December 1948 appears to have hardened the US official position in its favour. Thus, when the Ambassadors Committee, now including a representative of Norway, met in Washington on 4 March 1949 Acheson's opening speech included the statement that the United States favoured Italian membership. Ernest Bevin had included Italy in his original proposals for a Europe-wide defence treaty, but thereafter he expressed some reservations; faced with this firm proposal by the United States, however, these reservations were withdrawn and Italy was invited to join the talks on 8 March and accepted on 11 March.

Unlike other potential members, Portugal was a dictatorship, and was not invited to join the Washington talks until early 1949. Portugal stipulated that accession to the treaty would not mean that it would accept foreign troops stationed on its territory (Norway had stipulated likewise), although US bases were permitted in the strategically important Azores.

France, as usual during this period, was beset by domestic political problems. In early 1947 the government was formed from a coalition of centrist parties, and on 4 May the prime minister, the Socialist Paul Ramadier, dismissed Maurice Thorez and three other Communists from government. Despite these upheavals, France joined the United Kingdom in the Dunkirk Treaty and shared the lead with the United Kingdom in finalizing the Brussels Treaty. In 1949 the new prime minister, Henri Queuille, said that the United States must not allow France and western Europe to be invaded by the Soviet Union as they had been by Germany, and also added that the defence of western Europe must start on the Elbe (i.e. the border between the Soviet and Anglo-US zones of occupation). Not surprisingly, the French Communists were greatly opposed to the North Atlantic Treaty, but it went to the National Assembly on 17 May and was approved on 27 July.

United States' membership of a peacetime European defence pact was by no means a foregone conclusion either, and one of the key factors in any US involvement had to be the agreement of the US Congress. Here the master stroke was the decision to 'allow' the Senate to take the initiative. Thus was born the 'Vandenberg Resolution', which, like many things in NATO's birth, went through the governmental system in an exceptionally short time. Thus, the first discussions were held with Senator Arthur Vandenberg, chairman of the powerful Senate Foreign Relations Committee, on 11 April, a draft was first considered by the Foreign Relations Committee on 11 May, and it was passed by the Senate (by a majority of 64 to 6) on 11 June 1948. The resolution recommended that the president should pursue:

> progressive development of regional and other collective arrangements for individual and collective self-defense in accordance with the principle and provisions of the [United Nations] charter.
>
> Association of the United States by constitutional process with such regional and other collective arrangements as are based on continuous and effective self-help and mutual aid, and as affect its national security.

Contribution to the maintenance of peace by making clear its determination to exercise the right of individual or collective self-defense under Article 51 [of the UN Charter] should any armed attack occur affecting its national security.[1]

Several other countries were considered for membership during the original negotiations, but their cases were either postponed or rejected for one reason or another. It was recognized from the start that West German membership would be inevitable, but would not be appropriate in the first instance. Similarly, it was always intended that Greece, Turkey and Spain would eventually become members.

There was some discussion of the NATO guarantee of mutual defence being extended to cover Belgian, British, Dutch and French overseas possessions. The countries concerned allowed this suggestion to be quietly dropped, except that the 'Algerian Departments of France' were included in Article 6 and Danish membership was always understood to include Greenland.

The Republic of Ireland had remained neutral throughout the war and had denied the Allies the use of any facilities such as ports and airfields. In spite of this, the UK was keen for Eire to join the proposed Atlantic pact, and the Irish government was invited to attend the negotiations in mid-1948. When, however, the Irish government replied that it would join the discussions only if the UK promised to transfer the Six Counties (the predominantly Protestant North) to the Republic of Ireland, the matter was immediately dropped and was never reopened.

The treaty was signed on 4 April 1949, following which the member countries secured national endorsement, which, as is made clear from Table 2.1 was obtained by overwhelming majorities, auguring well for the success of the resulting North Atlantic Treaty Organization.*

The armed forces of the twelve NATO powers at the start of the Alliance in 1949 were not impressive, however. The vast American and British wartime fleets had been drastically reduced, with large numbers of ships either scrapped or placed in low-readiness reserve. The air forces numbered less than 1,000 operational aircraft, most of which were obsolete Second World War piston-engined machines, with small numbers of modern jet-engined aircraft concentrated in the British and US air forces. On land there were some twenty nominal divisions, most of which were involved in occupation duties and were poorly equipped and organized for modern war.

Despite these military shortcomings, the Alliance had made a sound start. The Europe of the period was in an extremely agitated state, and both political and military leaders had more than enough problems to deal with, both domestically and, in many cases, abroad. Despite this, the whole process of

---

* The full text of the North Atlantic Treaty is given in Appendix 2.

Table 2.1 The Voting Record for Ratifying the North Atlantic Treaty[2]

Country	Legislative body	Date of vote (1949)	Votes			
			For	Against	Abstentions	Absentees
Belgium	Chamber of Deputies	4 May	139	22*	1	
	Senate		127	13		
Canada	Parliament	30 April	Unanimous			
Denmark	Folketing (Lower House)	24 March	119	23	1	5
	Landsting (Upper House)	25 March	64	8		4
France	National Assembly	27 July	395	189†	22‡	
	Conseil de la République	29 July	284	20		
Iceland	Althing	30 March	37	13	2	
Italy	Chamber of Deputies	21 July	323	160*	8	
	Senate	30 July	175	81	1	
Luxembourg	Chamber of Deputies	31 May	46	5		
Netherlands	States-General – Lower House	19 July	65	7*		28
	States-General – Upper House	3 August	29	2*		
Norway	Storting	29 March	130	11§		7
Portugal	National Assembly	27 July	80	3¶		
United Kingdom	House of Commons	12 May	333	6		
United States	Senate	21 July	82	13		

* All 'nays' were Communists.
† Included 168 Communists and 'fellow-travellers'.
‡ Mostly from Overseas Departments.
§ Nine Communists; two Labour.
¶ Opposed only to register a protest at the exclusion of Spain.

setting up NATO was achieved with a certainty of common purpose, a deftness of diplomatic and political touch, and a generosity of spirit which can only be viewed with admiration. The speed with which decisions were taken was extraordinary, as was the way in which normal diplomatic procedures were brushed aside in order to achieve results.

3

The Development of NATO: 1949–1989

THE DIPLOMATIC SCENE

Once the euphoria resulting from signing the treaty on 4 April 1949 had died down, NATO's most senior body, the North Atlantic Council, met at foreign-minister level in September and established a number of permanent bodies, including the Defence Council and the Military Committee, as well as regional planning groups to cover the Alliance area. The momentum was maintained by the Defence Council, which in December 1949 agreed to a strategic concept and in the following April to the first draft of a medium-term defence plan.

The invasion of South Korea by the Communist North in June 1950 caused considerable anxiety in western Europe and seemed to prove the case for the existence of the Atlantic Alliance. As a direct result, in September 1950 NATO formally adopted the concept of 'forward defence' (i.e. as far to the east as possible) in order to resist similar aggression in Europe. Such a strategy could only be implemented in western Europe by troops stationed in West Germany and, although it had been discussed informally for some time, the question of rearming West Germany was raised formally.

Repeated reorganizations eventually resulted in the appointment of the first Supreme Allied Commander Europe (SACEUR) in 1950, and of the first Secretary-General, Supreme Allied Commander Atlantic (SACLANT) and Commander-in-Chief Channel (CINCHAN) in 1952. That year also saw the first expansion, when Greece and Turkey were brought into the Alliance, thus extending its coverage to include all of the Mediterranean and bringing the Alliance face to face with the USSR on the Soviet–Turkish border. With the inclusion of Turkey, NATO now included an Islamic nation, which was to prove significant in later years, although the traditional hostility between

Greece and Turkey caused repeated complications, and required a very delicate balance to ensure that neither party felt that the other was being given any form of preferential treatment.

In these first few years the Alliance concentrated on three areas: increasing its defence potential, getting its organization structure right and rearming Germany. The original proposal to solve the 'German question' was the creation of a European Defence Community in which West Germany could participate, but this was negated when the French National Assembly voted against such an organization in August 1954. This setback caused a new round of diplomatic activity, which involved both West Germany and Italy joining the Western Union (Brussels Treaty) and was finally resolved in the Paris Agreement of 23 October 1954, under which:

- the Federal Republic of Germany (FRG) – West Germany – was declared a sovereign state;
- American, British and French forces in the FRG ceased to be there by right of occupation but remained at the invitation of the government of the FRG;
- the FRG joined NATO;
- the UK and the USA undertook to maintain forces in continental Europe for as long as might be necessary;
- the Western Union was renamed the Western European Union.

The FRG acceded to the NATO alliance on 5 May 1955, and on 14 May the Soviet Union announced the establishment of the Warsaw Pact (see Chapter 6). Despite the resulting furore, however, with some treaties being torn up and new ones being signed, the four Second World War allies were still able to sign the Austrian Peace Treaty on 15 May, ending the military occupation of that country.

A Four Power summit was also held in Geneva to discuss a possible peace treaty with Germany, but two sessions – the first in July, the second in October – failed to reach a satisfactory conclusion. The year ended with the Soviet announcement of a policy of 'peaceful coexistence', but any optimism generated in NATO was dashed in 1956 by two major events. The joint Anglo-French invasion of Egypt was the first crisis to create serious strains within the Alliance, while the major external event was the Soviet invasion of Hungary, which once again demonstrated the Soviet Union's determination to maintain its hegemony in eastern Europe. The threat was further enhanced by Soviet progress in the 'space race', where a number of successes, such as the launch of the first space satellite in October 1957, showed a capability with major repercussions for the arms race.

In the spring of 1960 the Soviet Union suddenly announced that it had shot down a US 'spy plane' on a flight over its territory and had captured the pilot, who had parachuted to safety. US president Dwight D.

Eisenhower had little alternative but to admit that the USA had been conducting espionage flights, and announced that they had been suspended forthwith, but his Soviet opposite number, First Secretary Nikita Khrushchev, refused to accept this and stormed out of the 16 May Geneva summit conference in protest.

NATO's momentum increased as members realized that it was a source not only of military but also of political strength. The 'Athens Guidelines', issued in 1962, gave a broad outline of the circumstances under which NATO would consider using nuclear weapons and what political discussions might be feasible in a crisis. Later in 1962, however, the Cuban Missile Crisis, when the Soviet Union attempted to place nuclear missiles on the Caribbean island, overshadowed everything that had gone before. The USA and the USSR confronted each other in the western Atlantic. NATO was essentially on the sidelines, although the Alliance issued a formal endorsement of the US actions. One of the outcomes of the Cuban crisis was that in 1963 the USA and the UK assigned some of their existing nuclear forces to NATO, but a related proposal for a NATO-owned and -operated nuclear force came to naught.

In 1963 US president John F. Kennedy paid an extremely successful visit to Europe, which included his famous '*Ich bin ein Berliner*' speech in West Berlin. His assassination later in the year came as a major shock to NATO, although there was muted relief when it became clear that this was not the result of some Soviet plot. Then in 1964 Khrushchev was ousted in a bloodless coup and, on 16 October, China exploded its first atomic bomb.

The year 1966 saw a succession of problems with France culminate in the announcement that French forces would be withdrawn from the integrated command structure (see Chapter 4). A corollary was that NATO had to remove all installations not under French command from French soil, which caused a major exodus of headquarters to the Low Countries, and of US military facilities to West Germany and the UK.

In 1967 the Military Committee conducted NATO's first major strategic review since 1956, proposing a change from the 'tripwire' strategy* to 'flexible response' which was approved at a December 1967 ministerial meeting.†
Under this new concept, NATO devized a multitude of balanced responses, both nuclear and conventional, which, in the event of Warsaw Pact aggression, could be implemented in a balanced fashion, depending upon the prevailing circumstances.[1] That year also saw the publication of the 'Harmel

---

* The 'tripwire' strategy, which had been promulgated in the USA by President Eisenhower on 12 January 1955 and was endorsed by NATO the following year, involved instant massive retaliation in response to any Soviet aggression.
† This also happened, by chance, to be the first ministerial meeting at NATO's new headquarters in Brussels, where it had moved to from Fontainebleau.

Report' on *Future Tasks of the Alliance*, which restated the principles of the Alliance, stressed the importance of common approaches and greater consultation, and drew 'particular attention to the defence problems of the exposed areas e.g. the South-Eastern flank'.[2]

In 1968 Communist eastern Europe suffered yet another of its periodic upheavals, this time in Czechoslovakia, leading to an invasion by Warsaw Pact forces, which, while NATO took no overt military action, did cause the Alliance to review its responses to aggression. NATO also issued a warning about the dangers inherent in the Soviet advocacy of the right to intervene in the affairs of a fellow member of the 'Socialist Commonwealth', a somewhat elusive body whose existence was not recognized by the United Nations. However, by doing nothing to interfere with the invasion of Czechoslovakia, NATO members appeared to give at least tacit acknowledgement to the existence of a Soviet 'Great Power sphere of influence' in which the rules which normally governed the behaviour of smaller states did not apply.

The following two years saw important diplomatic initiatives. In late 1969 the first of the Strategic Arms Limitation Talks (SALT) was held in November; this was followed in December by the launch of the West German government's *'Ostpolitik'*. Chancellor Willy Brandt's strategy proved very fruitful and resulted in a German–Soviet Treaty in August 1970 and a German–Polish Treaty four months later, and these were accompanied by direct talks between West and East Germany, which started in March 1970. In addition to all these, France, the UK and the USA took a separate initiative by starting talks with the USSR on Berlin.

The NATO proposal for talks on Mutual and Balanced Force Reductions (MBFR), which had first been made in 1968, finally elicited a Soviet response in 1971. Other talks also bore fruit in 1971, with the signing not only of the Quadripartite Agreement on Berlin – the first such written agreement since 1949 – but also of an agreement between West and East Germany on civil access to the city. Then, in the following year, both the Anti-Ballistic Missile (ABM) Treaty and the Strategic Arms Limitation Treaty Round I (SALT I) were signed, and discussions on SALT II started.

This series of successes in the early 1970s gave rise to one of a periodic series of feelings of optimism, which led in May 1972 to the adoption of a NATO proposal for a Conference on Security and Co-operation in Europe (CSCE), to be held in Helsinki. The preparatory round of CSCE talks ended in June 1973 and the conference proper began in July, attended by representatives from thirty-three European states (Albania was the only one refusing to attend), plus the United States and Canada. The feeling of real progress continued with the opening of the MBFR talks in Vienna in January 1973.

This apparently new era in East–West relations, coupled with unprecedented economic well-being in most NATO countries, inevitably led to a lessening in the cohesion of NATO, but the Alliance continued. A salutary lesson from outside Europe came in October 1973, when the Egyptians carried out a major attack across the Suez Canal which took the Israelis completely by surprise – an ominous warning of what might happen in Europe if NATO lowered its guard. In addition, the Arab–Israeli war dragged in both the USA and the USSR, both of which made threatening gestures, including placing at least part of their nuclear forces on a higher alert status. Although direct confrontation was averted, the events reminded NATO members of the dangers of a sudden crisis – a reminder which was emphasized by evidence of a continuing Soviet military build-up in eastern Europe.

NATO reached its twenty-fifth anniversary in 1974 with a feeling of cautious optimism. Diplomatic negotiations were going well, the German Democratic Republic – East Germany – had been recognized by the Western countries, the two Germanies had been admitted to the United Nations in September 1973, Soviet first secretary Leonid Brezhnev had visited both Berlin and Washington, also in 1973, and the MBFR talks were firmly under way.

The following years were a continuation of these processes, and détente seemed almost to have attained a degree of permanence until on 27 December 1979 the Soviet Union invaded Afghanistan. This event had a major impact on NATO, since it appeared that behind the Soviet offers of arms control and reductions in East–West tension there still lurked the inherent aggressiveness which had caused NATO to be formed thirty years previously. The apprehension caused by the invasion of Afghanistan was increased by the threat of a Warsaw Pact invasion of Poland as the 'Solidarity' trade-union movement gathered pace, culminating in the takeover of power by General Wojciech Jaruzelski on 19 October 1981. On 13 December this was followed by the declaration of martial law, which led to wide-scale arrests, imprisonment and deaths.

The early and mid-1980s were characterized by a roller-coaster effect as relationships between East and West seemed to alternate abruptly between improvement and deterioration. The Alliance believed that the strategic balance of forces was tipping ever more in the favour of the USSR, and 1981 saw the first issue of a US-government unclassified report titled *Soviet Military Power*, a well-produced, illustrated and relatively detailed publication which was subsequently issued annually.[3] The Soviet Union made an immediate response by publishing its own glossy assessment of the balance of power, titled *Whence the Threat to Peace?*[4] NATO then decided to join in this 'documentary war', publishing its own, somewhat less glossy, assessment of the balance in 1982.[5]

Spain's membership of the Alliance had first been discussed in the preliminary talks in Washington in 1948, and had been raised periodically thereafter, but it finally became reality in December 1981. Although Spanish delegates immediately took part in Alliance decision-making, however, some years were to pass before Spain decided to join the integrated command structure.

Throughout this period the problem of intermediate-range nuclear forces (INF) was rumbling on, sparked by the Soviet decision to deploy SS-20 missiles in eastern Europe, which is described in greater detail in Chapter 4.

The US presidential elections in 1980 resulted in victory by Ronald Reagan, who on taking power in January 1981 immediately brought a new sense of direction to both US and Alliance discussions. One of his early moves was the 1983 announcement of the start of the Strategic Defense Initiative (SDI), which was intended to provide a guaranteed defensive shield against incoming missiles and to be superior to a strategy depending upon a heavy counter-attack. The Soviet Union became extremely agitated about SDI, since it threatened to negate the value of its vast stocks of inter-continental and submarine-launched ballistic missiles (ICBMs and SLBMs). Also in 1983 NATO, having failed to persuade the Soviet Union to stop deploying SS-20s, started to deploy Pershing II missiles in West Germany and ground-launched cruise missiles (GLCMs) in the UK and the FRG.

In 1984 NATO approved SACEUR's new concept known as 'Follow-On Forces Attack' (FOFA). Soviet operational plans were known to be based on sudden attacks by in-place forces (i.e. those already in position in eastern Europe in peacetime), which were designated 'first echelon forces' by NATO. The Soviets intended that this first echelon would keep going for as long as possible, but that, if it was halted by NATO forces, they would then pass through fresh, previously uncommitted forces, designated the 'second echelon', to restore the momentum of the attack. FOFA was concerned with conventional operations to locate, attack and destroy Warsaw Pact second-echelon forces before they were committed; it required target-acquisition means that were not only more effective but operated at much greater depth than existing systems, allied to more rapid information processing, and improved means of conventional attack on targets deep in the enemy's rear areas.

The remainder of the 1980s seemed like a helter-skelter ride as one agreement followed after another, particularly following the appointment of Mikhail Gorbachev as general secretary of the Communist Party of the Soviet Union (and hence leader of the USSR). Progress in many areas of East–West discussions, such as the MBFR and CSCE talks, started to improve, and became even better following the Reagan–Gorbachev meeting in Reykjavik in October 1986, even though that meeting itself did not result in any firm agreements.

The INF Treaty on the reduction of tactical nuclear weapons was signed in December 1987, and the Soviet army began its withdrawal from Afghanistan in May 1988, completing it in February 1989. Also in February 1989 the Soviet Union and all Warsaw Pact members except Romania announced troop reductions as a prelude to the opening of the Conventional Armed Forces in Europe (CFE) talks in Vienna in March. But, far away from these high-level discussions, though inspired by the atmosphere of change they engendered, the people of East Germany were taking matters into their own hands. Thus in the second half of 1989 East Germans started to escape to West Germany via Czechoslovakia, with the Czech government doing virtually nothing to help its Warsaw Pact comrade-in-arms. Then in November the popular pressure on the East German government became intense and, having realized that, on this occasion, they would receive no assistance from the Soviet army, the East German authorities opened the checkpoints in the Berlin Wall. There were many diplomatic formalities to follow, but in essence the Cold War was over and NATO had achieved the aim for which it was founded.

INTERNAL PROCESSES

The perceived threat from the Soviet Union caused the European nations and those of North America to draw together through NATO in a way which had never previously proved possible, even in the face of war. Thus, at the political level, there was regular consultation both through ministerial meetings and through the permanent representatives in Brussels, and, while they always remained sovereign nations, NATO members nevertheless sacrificed a degree of independence through membership of the Alliance. Even the most powerful nation of all, the United States, regularly consulted its NATO colleagues before the rounds of various discussions with the USSR, and as regularly reported on the outcome.

NATO did not have its own parliament, but the 188–member North Atlantic Assembly fulfilled at least some of the tasks of such a body.* The Assembly existed outside NATO, was funded by member nations (plus a small grant from NATO itself), and met twice a year, for three days in the spring and five days in the autumn. Its task was to provide a forum where matters of current concern could be discussed by representatives of the national legislative assemblies (government ministers were ineligible for

---

* The number of members was based (approximately) on population: Belgium 7; Canada 12; Denmark 5; France 18; Federal Republic of Germany 18; Greece 7; Iceland 3; Italy 18; Luxembourg 3; Netherlands 7; Norway 5; Portugal 7; Spain 12; Turkey 12; UK 18; USA 36.

membership), and it then produced two types of document: *recommendations*, which were sent to the North Atlantic Council urging a particular action, and *resolutions*, which were sent to member governments and were essentially expressions of opinion.

NATO's bureaucratic infrastructure was vast. The political and diplomatic International Staff was divided into five divisions, covering political affairs; defence planning and policy; defence support, infrastructure logistics and civil-emergency planning; scientific affairs; and international affairs.

The International Military Staff (IMS) was also large, with tentacles spread throughout the Alliance, most of its tasks being to make plans for war, to provide co-ordination on military matters, and to service a multitude of international committees and working groups. These were the forums at which national representatives provided the views of their defence ministries to NATO and took back the views of the committee or working group to their capitals. The committees and working groups covered a vast range of subjects, ranging from weapons standardization, through data systems inter-operability, to the specifications for the fuel to be used in military aircraft.

NATO also had a variety of executive functions. At NATO Headquarters itself, the IMS divisions covered intelligence; plans and policy; operations; logistics and resources; communications and information systems; and armaments and standardization. There were also a number of bodies responsible for the management of NATO-owned systems, such as the NATO Airborne Early Warning Programme Management Agency (NAPMA), which managed the NATO airborne-early-warning force of E-3A Sentry aircraft at Geilenkirchen in West Germany, the Central European Pipeline Office (CEPO), which managed NATO's fuel pipeline and storage system, and the NATO Communications and Information Systems Agency (NACISA).

NATO owned and operated several training centres, which included the NATO Defence College in Rome, the Supreme Headquarters Allied Powers Europe (SHAPE) Training Centre at Oberammergau in West Germany, the Long-Range Reconnaissance Patrol School in southern Germany, and the NATO Communication and Information Systems Training Centre at Latina, in Italy. Research facilities included the SACLANT Undersea Research Centre at La Spezia, Italy, and the SHAPE Technical Centre, which provided scientific and technical advice and support to SHAPE from its base in The Hague.

4

Stresses and Strains

In such a vast organization which endured over such a long period and was composed of such disparate nations, most of whom had fought each other at least once in the twentieth century, there were inevitably a number of stresses and strains. Never once, however, did they lead to a member leaving the Alliance, either of its own volition or as a result of expulsion.

FRANCE

The most critical of these strains involved France's departure from the integrated command structure. The reasons for this were grounded in recent French history. France had been totally humiliated by the rapidity with which the German forces overran the country in 1940. These problems were exacerbated by the split between the Vichy government, headed by Marshal Philippe Pétain, and the Free French, headed by General Charles De Gaulle. Although the latter participated in the Allied successes in 1944–5, it was always as a junior partner to the USA and the UK; but in the final days of the war De Gaulle's personality was so strong that he managed to secure a French zone of occupation both in western Germany and in Berlin.

Following De Gaulle's resignation as president in January 1946, France suffered from a succession of governments in the late 1940s, from a substantial degree of antipathy between former Vichyists and those who had served in either the Free French forces or the resistance, and from a powerful Communist party. Despite these problems, the French rebuilt their armed forces rapidly (with substantial aid from the USA and, to a lesser extent, from the UK), and they also reimposed control over their colonial empire.

The French quickly appreciated that, if their country was to regain its position as a Great Power, it had to possess its own atomic-energy programme. The British had come to the same conclusion, but France was in an infinitely worse industrial position than the UK and, unlike the British, its scientists had not been involved in the United States' Manhattan Project during the war. Nevertheless, the Commissariat à l'Énergie Atomique (CEA) was established as early as October 1945 and, in an essentially civil programme, the first nuclear reactor went critical in December 1948.

The French military monitored CEA's progress, but it was not until the early 1950s that they began to take a serious interest in building a bomb. Their interest was increased by two events in the middle of the decade. The first of these was the disastrous war in Indo-China, which culminated in the siege of Dien Bien Phu (December 1954 to May 1955), where a remote French garrison was surrounded and cut off by the Communist Viet Minh. With disaster staring them in the face, the French appealed to their American allies for help in the form of a bombing raid against the Viet Minh forces surrounding Dien Bien Phu, preferably involving the use of atomic weapons. Congressional leaders stipulated that they would support such a US operation only if it had British support, but this was not forthcoming, the proposal was dropped, and the French garrison was defeated.

Two years later came the Anglo-French fiasco at Suez, where France was the junior partner in an ill-fated attempt to wrest control of the Suez Canal back from the Egyptians. The two allies drew opprobrium down upon themselves from both the United States and the Soviet Union, and were forced into an ignominious and humiliating retreat.

These two events convinced the French that they must become self-sufficient in defence, develop their own nuclear weapons, and reduce their dependence on allies to the absolute minimum; this led to setting up the Comité des Applications Militaire (CAM) under the CEA in 1956. Matters were proceeding with a fair degree of priority, but when De Gaulle returned to power in May 1958 he gave new impetus to the programme, although the date of the first successful atomic explosion (February 1960) had been set well before his re-election and development of France's strategic bomber, the Mirage IV, had already been started on 11 April 1958.

Between 1958 and 1962 President De Gaulle made several proposals to both the USA and the UK with a view to enhancing the French role in NATO, but when these were rejected he turned his attention to a 'French' solution, which involved the gradual reduction of French participation in NATO's affairs and which would, as he saw it, liberate France from possible subjection to foreign decisions. Accordingly, in 1966 the French government gave its NATO allies notice that it intended to withdraw its forces from NATO's integrated command structure and requested that NATO should move all headquarters and installations not under French control from French soil.

This demand involved NATO in considerable expenditure. Numerous headquarters had to be completely uprooted and moved, most of which had been originally located in France either at France's direct request or to satisfy French sensibilities. Thus, SHAPE moved to Mons in Belgium and Allied Forces Central Europe (AFCENT) to Brunssum in the Netherlands, while the NATO Defence College moved to Rome.

US armed forces were even more severely affected and were forced to undertake Operation Freloc (France Relocation). Under this, the greater part of the logistic system supporting US forces in Germany had to be reoriented from a west–east axis through the French Atlantic ports to a north–south axis through West German North Sea ports. This not only involved the US in considerable expense but also meant that the supply chain for US forces in the FRG would be much more vulnerable in the event of war. Equally serious was that the US nuclear depots had to be located in West Germany, which meant that if the Warsaw Pact carried out a surprise attack these depots might be overrun before their weapons could be out-loaded. Other elements were moved to the UK, including most of the logistic facilities not moved to West Germany, as well as a number of squadrons of USAF aircraft.

Despite causing all this upheaval, the French most definitely did not leave the Atlantic Alliance, but they were highly selective as to which parts they chose to participate in. Because it remained a member of the Alliance, France took part in the meetings of the North Atlantic Council and played a full part in the Economic Committee, the Council of National Armaments Directors and the Science Committee, among other bodies. Having left the integrated military structure, it no longer participated in top-level bodies such as the Defence Planning Committee, the Military Committee and the Nuclear Planning Group, nor did it contribute to the Military Agency for Standardization or the NATO Integrated Communication System. On the other hand, it still participated in the NATO Air Defence Ground Environment and the Allied Command Europe communications system, known as ACE HIGH, and, by some curious anomaly, it continued to participate in NATO's civil-defence programmes. The French armed forces established liaison missions with those NATO headquarters with which they might become involved in the event of war, such as Central Army Group (CENTAG) and Northern Army Group (NORTHAG).

The one task to which France remained totally committed was the occupation of Berlin and the arrangements for its defence, where it never wavered for a second in its commitment to the Allied position. It should be noted, however, that everything to do with Berlin was totally outside the NATO structure.

Some elements of the post-1966 French position were quite clear: for example, no NATO units were allowed on French soil without specific permission, nor was there any automatic Allied access to French airspace. Other areas were more ambiguous – perhaps deliberately so. France always maintained that it had total freedom of action where its nuclear forces were concerned and such co-operation as it was prepared to offer concerned only conventional forces.* France also maintained that the commitment of French forces could never be assumed, and that any forces committed in support of NATO allies would always remain under French command. Thus, at least in public, it was always open to question as to whether or not the First French Army, located in south-west Germany, would participate in the defence of the Federal Republic.

It was, of course, implied in the 'no automaticity' concept that France might have remained aloof from a European conflict, provided there was no perceived threat to French national territory or sovereignty, although this did not exclude action if the approaches to French territory were considered to be under threat. It was a matter of French policy to avoid giving explicit definitions of a variety of terms, including what could be regarded as the country's 'vital interests' and the specific circumstances in which the French government would sanction the use of nuclear weapons.

Unlike the United Kingdom, the French had scarcely any domestic opposition to the possession of nuclear weapons. Even the Socialist François Mitterrand, who in earlier days was, at best, lukewarm about such weapons, became an ardent supporter once he was in power, and during his presidency he did more than any almost any of his predecessors to ensure that France's *force de dissuasion* remained strong and up to date. In fact there was a remarkable national consensus on the issue of nuclear weapons, and the French Catholic bishops even published a pastoral letter, in November 1983, in which they declared that nuclear deterrence was totally consistent with the Catholic Church's doctrine of the 'just war'. Indeed, they went so far as to state that an argument for 'peace at any price' would result in a situation in which the West would not have the means to defend itself, thus effectively encouraging aggression.†

It is a splendid contradiction, but it was the very fact of NATO's existence that enabled France to leave it. Had the Warsaw Pact forces been standing on the other bank of the Rhine, as was the case in 1914 and 1939, then France would perforce have had to seek allies. But the existence of West Germany and its strong buffer of NATO troops on the line of the river Elbe gave France that element of physical security that enabled it to act semi-independently. Further, by holding the Alliance at arm's length and refusing to commit themselves, instead of being just one among fifteen or sixteen

---

* This was the public position. There are, however, strong reasons for believing that there was a degree of covert co-operation. France, the UK and the USA, for example, would have needed to ensure that their ballistic-missile submarines' patrol areas did not clash.
† Earlier in the year (18 April 1983) Catholic bishops in West Germany had issued a similar pastoral letter, in which they stated that nuclear weapons were a necessary but regrettable method of maintaining peace in Europe.

allies, the French were always treated as a special case and were constantly courted by those seeking their support. This especially applied to the question of the First French Army, where both CENTAG and NORTHAG competed for its support as a counter-attack force.

OTHER INTERNAL TENSIONS

NATO proved exceptionally able to contain numerous strains between its members. The Anglo-French attack on the Suez Canal caused considerable debate within the Alliance, as some other members felt very strongly that they should have been consulted, but there were many other tensions. The traditional hostility between Greece and Turkey made their relationship in NATO difficult at the best of times, although matters became even more tense when Turkey invaded northern Cyprus in 1974. There were also numerous disputes between the two countries in the Aegean, both at sea and in the air.

The UK and Iceland were involved in a short, bitter (and ultimately pointless) fisheries dispute (known as the 'Cod War') in 1974.

NATO, founded as a bastion of democracy, managed to accommodate a number of military *coups d'état* among its members. General António Spínola led a military takeover in Portugal in 1974, while in Greece Colonel Georgios Papadopoulos seized control in 1967 and kicked out the king six months later. There was also a mutinous seizure of power by a group of French generals in Algeria in 1956, which almost led to a military coup in Paris.

NATO AND THE HUNGARIAN CRISIS

The Hungarian uprising in 1956 (see Chapter 6) inspired much vocal support in the West, especially from newspapers and American-run radio stations in Europe. This, however, was the limit of the support the Hungarians received, and when the North Atlantic Council convened in December of that year all it could say was that it had:

> followed the course of events in Hungary with shock and revulsion. The brutal suppression of the heroic Hungarian people stands in stark contrast with Soviet public professions. The Council reaffirmed the conviction of its member governments that the United Nations should continue its efforts, through the pressure of world opinion, to induce the Soviets to withdraw their forces from Hungary and to right the wrongs done to the Hungarian people . . .[1]

In other words, NATO did nothing.

NATO AND THE CZECH CRISIS

Although NATO took certain low-level precautionary steps, the Alliance's reactions to the 1968 Czechoslovak crisis (see Chapter 6) were again mainly vocal. Advance signals of a probable invasion were received in the West for many months before the event. In early May, Western intelligence services, using radio monitoring, aircraft equipped with long-range optical and electronic devices, and satellites, detected signs of troop concentrations on such an ominous scale that the Federal German foreign minister informed the Federal Cabinet and issued a press statement on 22 May. The Warsaw Pact troops conducted an exercise called *Böhmerwald* in Czechoslovakia, but Western observers then discovered that route signs leading towards the Czechoslovak border and within the country itself had been left in position, and that some of the Soviet troops taking part in the exercise had remained inside Czechoslovakia instead of leaving.

Then in late July a considerable amount of detailed information became available, reporting large troop movements in the southern part of East Germany, in southern Poland, and along those parts of Poland and the USSR bordering on Czechoslovakia. In an effort to try to discover more, USAF SR-71 Blackbird spy planes were brought in from the United States to fly along the line of the Inner German Border to observe the activity up to 100 km beyond the 'Iron Curtain'. Another valuable intelligence source was the Allied missions to the Soviet commander-in-chief,* and the British mission reported on 22 July that the Soviet army's 71st Artillery Brigade and 6 Motor Rifle Division had completely vacated their usual barracks at Bernau and that an East German army barracks at Halle was similarly empty, while on 29 July one of their patrols saw the Soviet 19 Motor Rifle Division actually deploying from its barracks.[2]

Even without such classified sources, the Federal German News Service was able to establish that by the end of July some twenty Warsaw Pact divisions were lining the Czech frontiers and that their plan was to drive a wedge straight across the country, with the aim of dividing the fourteen divisions of the Czech army into two.

The evidence of a probable invasion accumulated rapidly, and on 18 August Western radio monitoring units reported that all Warsaw Pact units near the Czechoslovak border had gone on to radio silence – usually an accurate portent that something was about to happen. Then, at 2311 hours precisely on Sunday 20 August, Western radar monitors detected that Prague airspace had suddenly been blanked out on their screens by artificial

---

* In 1946 the three western Allied commanders-in-chief exchanged liaison missions with their Soviet opposite number. Such missions continued until the end of the Cold War.

'snow'.* The situation was made worse for the West because the whole of eastern Europe was also being protected naturally by a dense and widespread layer of cloud, which could not be penetrated by the sensors aboard US spy satellites.

A major external factor, which affected the US forces in western Europe closely, was the situation in South Vietnam, where the war was at its height; the US armed forces had some 530,000 troops deployed there, and suffered 14,437 deaths during 1968. That year was the year of the Communist Tet offensive (30 January to 29 February), which was subsequently shown to have been a major Communist defeat, but at the time it had a very adverse political and public-relations impact in the United States. Having failed at Tet, the North Vietnamese mounted a second, short-lived, offensive in May, and then a third, which involved attacks all over South Vietnam, on 17 August. That this came just four days before the Warsaw Pact invasion of Czechoslovakia may well have been more than mere coincidence. However, the fact was that in Washington the attention was predominantly on events in Vietnam, while in western Europe many individuals and units had been withdrawn from the US Seventh Army to serve in Indo-China.

NATO appears to have ignored all these warnings; for example, SACEUR (General Lemnitzer) departed to visit exercises two days before the invasion and was in Greece on the day it took place. One possible alternative, supported by unconfirmed rumours at the time, is that the commander of the Warsaw Pact operation, Soviet general I. G. Pavlovsky, warned Western commanders of the forthcoming operation and gave them a believable assurance that there was no hostile intent towards the West.

Even if this report were true, the fact is that some forty Warsaw Pact divisions were on the move; had they simply kept moving and rolled across the Czechoslovak border into the Federal Republic, NATO was in no position to have resisted. NATO troops in western Europe were on the lowest stage of alert, and it would have taken US reinforcements several weeks or more to have reached Europe from the USA, by which time the fighting might well have overrun the airfields they were intending to use.†

Publicly at least, the NATO reaction was merely one of words, with the North Atlantic Council, for example, stating in November 1968 that:

---

* 'Snow' is a form of radar jamming created by a combination of electronic means and aircraft dropping short strips of metal foil.
† The author was serving in Germany at the time and well remembers that virtually every unit was at a very low state of readiness, since August was, by custom, the period when summer holidays were taken. Most units were thus down to the absolute minimum manpower permitted under NATO rules, and many of the troops theoretically 'present' on duty had been sent away on official training and would have taken several days to return to barracks before starting deployment.

World opinion has been profoundly shocked by this armed intervention carried out against the wishes of the Government and people of Czechoslovakia. . . . The contention of the Soviet leadership that there exists a right of intervention in the affairs of other states deemed to be within the so-called 'Socialist Commonwealth' runs counter to the basic principles of the United Nations Charter, is dangerous to European security and has inevitably aroused grave anxieties . . .[3]

Internally, however, NATO carried out a serious and deep analysis of its failings. It revised its crisis-management procedures, both within the organization itself and in the national capitals. It also reviewed its force structure, its force strengths and its mobilization and reinforcement procedures. It also had to face a major change in the Warsaw Pact's deployments, because a number of Soviet divisions remained in western Czechoslovakia, where there had been none before.

THE SS-20 ISSUE

The INF (intermediate-range nuclear forces) crisis was one of the most important ever to hit NATO. It started in about 1974, when NATO members began to see a steady build-up of a new Soviet intermediate-range ballistic missile,* the SS-20. This was seen to be a major attempt by the USSR to alter the balance in this field in its favour and thus pose a major threat to western Europe. In consequence, the Alliance reacted with a vigour some had begun to doubt it possessed; indeed, the SS-20 played a key role in the eventual demise of the Soviet Union and the Warsaw Pact.

Intermediate-range nuclear forces had not been a major issue up to that time. NATO itself had deployed some US IRBM systems in Europe between 1959 and 1965, comprising sixty Thors in the UK and sixty Jupiters, thirty of which were based in Italy and thirty in Turkey. Their operational lives were, however, very brief, since all were phased out in 1965: the British Thors because they were sited in the open and were too vulnerable to a Soviet first strike, while the withdrawal of the Jupiters from southern Europe was part of the Cuban Missile Crisis settlement.

The Soviet IRBMs remained, however, and throughout the 1960s and 1970s NATO seemed tacitly to accept the existence of a large number of IRBMs sited in the USSR's western military districts and clearly targeted on NATO countries. These missiles were of two types, the older being the SS-4, which entered service in 1957 and carried a single 1 MT warhead,[†]

---

* An intermediate-range ballistic missile (IRBM) was a land-based missile with a range between 1,500 nautical miles (2,780 km) and 3,000 nautical miles (5,560 km).
† A 1 MT (1 megaton) warhead is equivalent to 1 million tons of TNT; a 1 kT (1 kiloton) warhead is equivalent to 1,000 tons of TNT – see Chapter 7.

while the SS-5 entered service in 1961 in two versions: Mod 1, with a single
1 MT warhead, and Mod 3, with three 300 kT warheads. Most of these were
deployed in missile fields just to the east of the Soviet–Polish border, and at
their peak in the late 1960s some 700 were in service, reducing to approximately 400 in the mid-1970s. The SS-4 had a range of some 2,000 km, while
that of the SS-5 was 4,100 km, which enabled both missiles to cover the
whole of western Europe, although their relative inaccuracy (the SS-4 had
a CEP (see Chapter 7) of 2.4 km, while that of the SS-5 was 1 km) meant
that they could be targeted only against cities or other area targets.

The existence of two new missiles, the SS-16 and the SS-20, became
known in the West in the late 1960s. Both could be launched either from silos
or from wheeled transporter–erector–launcher (TEL) vehicles, but there was
an even more significant relationship between the two, since they shared two
identical missile stages. The SS-20 was a two-stage missile with a range of
5,000 km and carrying three 150 kT warheads with an accuracy (CEP) of 400
m. The SS-16 carried a single 1 MT warhead and was essentially an SS-20
with an additional third stage, giving it a range of 9,000 km. This range meant
that the SS-16 was classified as an ICBM and was covered by the SALT
treaty, whereas the SS-20 was an IRBM and thus was not covered by SALT.

The SS-20 was road-mobile, using a single twelve-wheeled TEL vehicle,
housed in a purpose-built shelter with a split roof which could be opened to
allow the missile to be launched. Later, when they signed the INF Treaty in
December 1987, the Soviets admitted that they had deployed 650 SS-20
missiles, plus a further forty-two for training. These had been operated by
ten missile divisions: six in the western USSR and four in Asia. These divisions included forty-eight regiments, each with its own operating base,
which included a number of individual missile shelters with a number of
pre-surveyed launch sites in the surrounding area.

These two missiles posed three problems for NATO. US concern centred
on the fact that it would be possible for the Soviet Union to manufacture
two-stage missiles (i.e. SS-20s) and, quite separately, to also manufacture
and store third stages. The verification measures then under discussion
would not have been able to differentiate between them, meaning, so the US
argued, that at a time of crisis it would be possible to bring these two elements together to create SS-16 ICBMs and thus directly threaten the USA.
Following intense discussions in the SALT II negotiations, the agreement
included the termination of both testing and deployment of SS-16s.

As a separate issue, however, the SS-20 posed a new and serious threat to
western Europe: first, its launcher was highly mobile and thus difficult to
detect and destroy; second, it had three accurate MIRV warheads, which
could be targeted against military targets; and, third, it increased the
number of Soviet warheads from some 400-odd on SS-4s and SS-5s to 1,950
on 650 SS-20s.

To deal with this threatening situation, and in an attempt to avert an arms race in Europe, in 1979 NATO agreed on two new approaches to the problem. It decided, first:

> to modernize NATO's LRTNF [long-range tactical nuclear forces] by the deployment in Europe of US ground-launched systems comprising 108 Pershing II launchers which would replace existing US Pershing IA, and 464 Ground-Launched Cruise Missiles [GLCM], all with single warheads. All the nations currently participating in the integrated defence structure will participate in the programme; the missiles will be stationed in selected countries and certain support costs will be met through NATO's existing common funding arrangements . . . Ministers agreed that as an integral part of TNF modernization, 1,000 US nuclear warheads will be withdrawn from Europe as soon as possible. Further, Ministers decided that the 572 LRTNF warheads should be accommodated within that reduced level, which necessarily implies a numerical shift of emphasis away from warheads to delivery systems of other types and shorter ranges.[4]

In parallel with this, however, in what was known as the 'twin-track' approach, NATO ministers also:

> fully support[ed] the decision taken by the United States, following consultations within the Alliance, to negotiate arms limitations on LRTNF and to propose to the USSR to begin negotiations as soon as possible . . .[5]

The diplomatic track included three major offers to the USSR: a reduction in strategic-nuclear-force levels within the SALT framework, and new initiatives in both the MBFR and the CSCE processes. The military track involved fielding ground-launched cruise missiles and Pershing IIs.

The timing of the problem coincided with a general resurgence of public concern in Western countries over defence matters. This involved increased interest in some countries, but there were also small but highly vocal groups which were opposed to most forms of defence and to nuclear weapons in particular. When they found themselves faced with Soviet rejection of the 'diplomatic' element of the 'twin-track' approach, NATO members were therefore faced with a difficult choice. But, despite many predictions that they would lack the nerve, they went ahead and authorized the fielding of the new counter-systems in 1983.[6] The greatest opposition came from Denmark, where the parliament not only voted against deployment of Pershing II or GLCMs there, but also voted to withhold that element of Denmark's contribution to NATO which would have gone towards the infrastructure costs of such missiles. In the UK there were repeated demonstrations against deployment of GLCMs in southern England, but the government brushed these aside. Helmut Schmidt, the West German chancellor, faced greater resistance from within his own Social Democratic Party than from the official opposition and threatened to resign if the parliamentary vote went against him. (He won the vote on 26 May 1981.)

Despite the opposition, US-operated GLCMs began to arrive in western Europe in November 1983, whereupon the Soviet Union withdrew from the INF Treaty negotiations in Geneva. Several weeks later it also effectively withdrew from the SALT and MBFR talks, as well.

NATO's response to the Soviet threat posed by the SS-20 centred on the BGM-109 GLCM, a Mach 0.7* missile which carried a variable-yield nuclear warhead (10–50 kT) over ranges up to 2,500 km. It flew at very low altitude, using a computer-controlled navigation system, and was extremely accurate, with a CEP of some 30 m. Four missiles were carried on a single TEL and were launched at an angle of 45 degrees. In this demonstration of NATO solidarity in the face of the SS-20 threat, no less than 116 launchers (464 missiles) were deployed to Europe, starting in November 1983 and with deployment completed in 1988. The bases were in Belgium (12 launchers), Germany (24), Italy (28), the Netherlands (12) and the UK (40).

The other element of the NATO deployment was the Pershing II missile. The Pershing IA had been deployed in West Germany since the 1960s, with 108 operated by the US army and 72 by the West German air force.[†] The Pershing IA had a maximum range of 740 km and carried a 400 kT nuclear warhead with an accuracy (CEP) of 400 m. The Pershing II used the same launcher and appeared generally similar, but was quite different internally. The main difference was in its warhead, which not only was much more accurate (with a CEP of 45 m), but had a special 'earth penetrator' which could drive through most types of soil to a depth of some 30 m before detonating its 250 kT nuclear weapon, thus destroying most types of command bunker. This warhead, coupled with its range of 1,500 km, posed a major threat to Soviet and Warsaw Pact buried headquarters, including those in the western military districts of the USSR.

It appeared that the Soviet authorities thought that the West would not have the nerve, solidarity or popular support necessary to achieve these deployments, because they continued with their SS-20 programme, which by late 1985 had reached a total of 441 launchers with 1,323 warheads.[7] When General Secretary Konstantin Chernenko died in March 1985, however, he was succeeded by Mikhail Gorbachev, and the atmosphere immediately began to change. Diplomatic progress became more rapid, and in December 1987 the INF Treaty was signed, under which not only would 670 Soviet missiles (including 405 SS-20s) and 400 US systems be

---

* Mach 1 is the speed of sound, which is approximately 1,200 km/h at sea level, but varies with temperature and pressure.
† Pershing I, the original version, was carried on a tracked launcher. The Pershing IA system consisted of the same missile but mounted on a wheeled launcher, enabling it to be carried in a C-130 Hercules transport aircraft.

withdrawn and destroyed, but the whole destruction programme would be subject to on-site verification by the opposite side.

The treaty laid down a three-year period for the elimination of all inter-mediate-range weapons and launchers (GLCM, Pershing, SS–20, SS–12 and SS–4), in two phases: deployed warheads were to be reduced to 180 on each side within twenty-nine months, with total elimination after three years; shorter-range nuclear weapons were to be totally eliminated within eighteen months. The treaty also included on-site inspections between twenty and ninety days after signature, to verify numbers, with further inspections up to the year 2000.

5

NATO's Military Organization

From its inception NATO was involved in delicate juggling acts to balance a frequently bewildering variety of requirements. The overriding aim was to field forces which would deter an attack by the Soviet Union and Warsaw Pact, since anything else the Alliance attempted was wasted if it could not achieve that. But this had to be balanced against what was both politically acceptable and economically affordable to the members – requirements which were not always mutually compatible. Then, too, the command structure needed to share out the posts to achieve a balance between the United States, which was not only the most powerful single member but also met a very large proportion of the bills, and the remaining nations, who wished to ensure that their national aspirations were seen to be met. Finally, the organization as a whole needed to present a good public image, and to produce solutions which would not offend public opinion in any member nation too greatly.

At the top of the military organization was the Military Committee, on which all nations were represented by their chiefs-of-staff and which normally met three times a year.* Since the chiefs-of-staff were based in their national capitals, there was a need for some permanent representation at NATO Headquarters to conduct day-to-day business, and this was originally provided by the Standing Group, which consisted of just three members – France, the UK and the USA – with all other nations except Iceland appointing a 'permanent national liaison officer'. The title of the group changed to the 'Military Representatives Committee' in 1950, and to the 'Military Committee in Permanent Session' in 1957. When France withdrew from the

---

* The chief-of-staff was the senior serving military officer in the national armed forces – i.e. Chairman of the Joint Chiefs-of-Staff (US), Chief of the Defence Staff (UK), etc. When the chiefs-of-staff attended in person, the committee was designated the NATO Military Committee in Chiefs-of-Staff Session.

integrated military structure in 1966 this top-level body was reorganized again, being expanded to include a permanent 'national military representative' at three-star level (i.e. lieutenant-general or equivalent) from all nations except France and Iceland, although the title remained unchanged.*

Originally, the chairmanship of the Military Committee in Chiefs-of-Staff Session rotated annually between members, but a separate chairman of the Military Committee in Permanent Session was appointed in 1958, and from 1963 onwards the same officer chaired both committees. Designated the Chairman of the NATO Military Committee, this officer was in effect the senior military officer in NATO, and since the post was created in 1958 he has always been a European, thus balancing the US influence in other senior posts in the Alliance.†

THE COMMANDS

On the establishment of NATO, a series of regional planning groups (RPGs) was set up, each comprising those nations with a strategic interest in the particular area:

- Canada/US RPG – Canada, USA;
- Western Europe RPG – Benelux, Canada, France, UK, USA;
- North Atlantic Ocean RPG – Canada, Denmark, France, Iceland, Norway, Portugal, UK, USA;
- Northern Europe RPG – Denmark, Norway, UK, USA;
- Southern Europe/Western Mediterranean RPG – France, Italy, UK, USA.

These RPGs were not, however, the only forums where discussions were taking place, and there were a number of bilateral links, of which by far the most important was that between the United States and the United Kingdom. These two countries not only had strong traditional and cultural ties, but also had forged a close alliance during the war under the Allied Combined Chiefs-of-Staff (CCS) organization. This CCS mechanism continued to be used after the war, and during 1945–9 it produced a variety of combined war plans to counter possible Soviet aggression. The link continued with the setting-up of NATO, and was used by them, as the two predominant military powers in the new organization, for private discussions on the command arrangements for the Alliance.‡

---

* The top rank structure and the NATO 'star' system are explained in Appendix 4.
† A full list of NATO and Warsaw Pact commanders-in-chief is in Appendix 5.
‡ To this day (1998) there is a large UK military staff in Washington and a slightly smaller US staff in London who continue to provide this unique 'Anglo-Saxon' link.

The RPGs produced a variety of organizational proposals, but, despite external pressures such as the explosion of the first Soviet atomic bomb, the Communist takeover in China and the outbreak of the Korean war, the discussions dragged on through the whole of 1950 and 1951, and it was not until early 1952 that a full structure was in place.

Naturally, a hierarchy of command appointments were needed, and these were designated as follows:

- major NATO commands (MNCs) – the most senior appointments, at four-star level, normally designated 'Supreme Allied Commander . . .' (SAC); e.g. SACEUR (Supreme Allied Commander Europe);
- principal subordinate commands (PSCs) – the next level down, headed by a commander-in-chief (CINC) at either three- or four-star level; e.g. CINCENT (Commander-in-Chief Allied Forces Central Europe);
- major subordinate commands (MSCs) – these were usually at four-star level, headed by a commander; e.g. COMCENTAG (Commander Central Army Group).*

It was clear that one supreme allied commander would be required for Europe (SACEUR), that he would be an American, and that he should be the most prestigious military officer of the day. Thus, General Dwight D. Eisenhower took up this appointment on 2 April 1951, with Field Marshal Bernard Montgomery, the British former military head of the Western Union Defence Organization (Brussels Treaty) forces, as his deputy. They established Supreme Headquarters Allied Powers Europe (SHAPE) at Fontainebleau in France, and quickly agreed on a command structure, which was in place in November 1951. This consisted of:

- Allied Land Forces Central Europe (AFCENT) – a four-star land command covering Benelux, France and West Germany;
- Allied Air Forces Central Europe (AIRCENT) – a four-star air command, covering the same geographical area as AFCENT;
- Allied Forces Northern Europe (AFNORTH) – a four-star, joint (i.e. navy, army, air force) command, covering Denmark and Norway;
- Allied Forces Southern Europe (AFSOUTH) – a four-star joint command, covering Italy and the western Mediterranean, and including the US Sixth Fleet;
- Flag Officer Western Europe (FOWE) – who provided naval representation to SHAPE, but commanded only the French, UK and US Rhine flotillas.

---

* As always, there were exceptions to every rule. Thus, Commander UK Air Forces was actually known (incorrectly) as CINCUKAIR and, although an MSC, reported direct to SACEUR and not through a PSC. Similarly, Commander-in-Chief Channel (CINCHAN), although nominally a PSC, was actually treated as an MNC – an anomaly which ceased after the end of the Cold War.

It was, however, significant that the British refused to place the land or air defences of the United Kingdom under NATO. As a result, the land defence of the UK remained a national responsibility throughout the Cold War, although, as will be discussed later, the air defence eventually did become a NATO responsibility.

If SACEUR's demesne was agreed without much disagreement, the same cannot be said of the Atlantic, where the two basic issues were the subdivisions of the command and the fact that both the Americans and the British wanted to provide the sea-going commander. The matter was not just a question of national prestige, however: it also included important factors of wartime strategy, with the United States being concerned about troops and supply convoys crossing the Atlantic in a west–east direction in war, while British concerns centred on south–north trade routes, including that for oil. Many meetings were held and a large number of alternative plans were discussed, with the naval discussions not being helped when the issue entered the British political arena in 1951, with Churchill, at that time the leader of the opposition, attacking the socialist government (led by Clement Attlee) for agreeing to a US officer as SACLANT. The problem was also complicated by disagreements over command in the Mediterranean and in the southern part of NATO's Atlantic area, which had already been designated IBERLANT.

In the autumn of 1951 a British general election put the problem on hold, and when Churchill again became prime minister, on 26 October, the question of NATO naval commands featured high on his list of priorities. Churchill went to Washington in January 1952, and after a round of fierce arguments he eventually gave way, although a British admiral was to be appointed Deputy SACLANT. The principle agreed, the navy planners then set up a complicated organizational system which involved numerous situations where an officer held two appointments (known as 'double-hatting') or even three ('triple-hatting'), although the problems inherent in such an arrangement were alleviated by having separate staffs for the various functions.

The problems did not go away, however, and among the knotty issues was the question of the US navy's aircraft carriers. The control of atomic weapons aboard these carriers was governed by the US McMahon Act, which stipulated that control could not be passed to another power, and this raised a major hurdle when the US Navy's Strike Fleet Atlantic (STRIKE-FLTLANT) was operating in the Eastern Atlantic area, where the NATO commander was Commander-in-Chief Eastern Atlantic (CINCEAST-LANT), a British officer. There were also problems over IBERLANT, which were eventually solved by placing Commander IBERLANT, a British officer, under CINCEASTLANT.

After much argument, the naval organization in the Atlantic settled down in late 1952:

- SACLANT (US) and his deputy (UK) were in the headquarters at Norfolk, Virginia;
- STRIKEFLTLANT remained under the command of SACLANT, regardless of its position in the Atlantic;
- CINCWESTLANT (US) exercised command over most of the northern Atlantic, with two sub-area commands: US Atlantic Sub-Area and Canadian Sub-Area;
- CINCEASTLANT (UK) controlled four geographical sub-areas – Central (UK), Northern (UK), Biscay (French) and IBERLANT (UK) – with a fifth functional command (Commander Submarines Eastern Atlantic (COMSUBEASTLANT)), being a British officer.

One notable difference between the American and other command systems concerned the air. Under the US system the naval commander controlled all his air assets, since the US navy had assumed responsibility for long-range maritime patrol aircraft from the (then) US Army Air Force in 1943. Under the British and French systems, however, land-based air support was provided by the air force, as a result of which there were two commanders of equal rank – one navy, one air force – at EASTLANT and at the geographical sub-areas.

Similar difficulties faced the planners in the Mediterranean. The British had considerable interests here: they regarded the sea lines of communication (SLOC) as vital to their wartime requirements; they were strongly involved in Gibraltar, Malta, Cyprus and Egypt; and they had a predominant interest in the security of the Suez Canal. They had also, as they pointed out, been the predominant naval power in the region for some 150 years, and maintained a sizeable Mediterranean Fleet, based in Malta. The French also had strong interests here, since they had colonial ties with Morocco and Tunisia, while Algeria was legally a *département* of France, and they needed to secure the north–south SLOC to metropolitan France. The US Sixth Fleet was permanently based in the Mediterranean, but, since it carried atomic weapons, its command, was subject to the McMahon Act. Italy also had a major interest, as the largest power bordering the Mediterranean and with a rapidly growing navy. Allied to all this was a totally new factor – the imminent entry of Greece and Turkey into the Atlantic Alliance, with a concomitant need to accommodate the geographically adjacent but traditionally hostile countries into the command structure.

A further and novel factor was added to the situation when the British posted Admiral Earl Mountbatten as commander-in-chief of the British Mediterranean Fleet. This was seen as slightly underhand by some Americans, although it was part of such a senior officer's normal career progression. Nevertheless, the British could not deny that such a thrusting, charismatic and successful officer – he had previously served as Supreme Allied Commander South-East Asia Command from 1943 to 1945, as viceroy of India in 1947 and as governor-general of India in 1947–8 – might not have some influence on the situation.

A series of plans was proposed by the tri-national Standing Group at NATO Headquarters, by SACEUR and by the various nations involved, but every one of them met with a fundamental objection from one or several of the parties concerned. Eventually, however, a compromise was reached in which:

- Commander-in-Chief Allied Forces Mediterranean (CINCAFMED) (UK) reported direct to SACEUR;
- geographical subordinates were Gibraltar (GIBMED) (UK), Occidentale (MEDOC) (French), Central (MEDCENT) (Italian), South-East (MEDSOUEAST) (UK), Eastern (MEDEAST) (Greek), and North-Eastern (MEDNOREAST) (Turkish);
- there were also three functional commands: US Patrols Mediterranean (USPATMED) (US),* Submarines Mediterranean (SUBMED) (UK) and Submarines North-East (SUBMEDNOREAST) (Turkey).

Admiral Mountbatten duly set up his NATO headquarters in Malta in December 1952,† but without STRIKEFORSOUTH – the US Sixth Fleet – which remained under CINCAFSOUTH, an American four-star officer with his headquarters in Naples, Italy.

These examples from the very early days of NATO show one of the underlying strengths of the Alliance: not that bureaucratic conflicts – which might today be termed 'star wars' – were avoided, but that they were always resolved. It would have been too much to expect that the various national susceptibilities would not have resulted in some bruising discussions, but somehow the will was always there to find a solution.

The organization did not, of course, remain static: it changed to meet altered circumstances in national organizations and to match political and military developments within the Alliance. Thus the national 'share' of appointments had to be adjusted to include the Germans in 1955, again in 1966 to cover the departure of the French, and yet again in 1982 to accommodate Spain, although Spain did not enter the integrated command structure.

In the late 1960s two events increased yet further the importance of the UK to the Alliance. The first was the move of many USAF air bases from France to the UK as a result of General De Gaulle's diktat; the second was the adoption in 1967 of the strategy of 'flexible response'. As a result the

---

* This command was intended to be the operational headquarters for US navy long-range anti-submarine warfare (ASW) aircraft, which would be allocated in war.
† It did not become fully operational until March 1953.

British Isles became of major significance as a base for offensive and defensive operations, and their security became a matter of great concern to the Alliance. A new NATO command was therefore established on 10 April 1975, when Commander UK Air Forces (CINCUKAIR) took post at High Wycombe, England. CINCUKAIR was 'double-hatted' as Commander-in-Chief RAF Strike Command, and, although only a major subordinate commander (MSC), he reported directly to SACEUR.* This brought British airspace firmly under NATO's control in war, but failed to cause the sort of political and public reactions which had made the decisions on the naval commands in the Atlantic and Mediterranean so difficult in the 1950s.

When NATO was set up there were two principal subordinate commands (PSCs) on the Continent: Land Forces Central Europe and Air Forces Central Europe. The air-force headquarters was subsequently disbanded, but was resurrected in 1975 as Allied Air Forces Central Europe (AAFCE), although a directive by NATO's Defence Planning Committee that it should be moved from Ramstein in southern Germany and collocated with AFCENT at Brunssum was successfully resisted by the air forces until well past the end of the Cold War.[1]

Physical moves were also made. As has already been described, the French decision to leave the integrated military structure also involved a large-scale movement of NATO facilities from France to Belgium, Italy, the Netherlands and the United Kingdom. For different reasons HQ IBERLANT was transferred from Gibraltar to Lisbon, Portugal, in 1966, and HQ Allied Naval Forces Southern Europe (NAVSOUTH) from Malta to Naples in 1971.

TELECOMMUNICATIONS

As an alliance involving numerous capitals and many major military headquarters spread over a wide geographical area, NATO was worth little if all these could not communicate with each other over routine matters, in crises, when implementing contingency plans and, ultimately, in war. Great emphasis was therefore placed on telecommunications systems, which, in the 1950s and 1960s, and in keeping with the technology of the times, were provided primarily by a huge network of landlines leased from the various PTTs,† combined with a number of point-to-point radio links.

This resulted in a somewhat fragmented and haphazard system, and the

---

* UKAIR was also unusual in that it was the only single-service (i.e. all air force), single nation MSC.

† PTT (Post, Telephone, Telegraph) was the generic term for the telecommunications agencies, which almost to the end of the Cold War were government-owned – e.g. the Bundespost (West Germany) and the General Post Office (UK).

next step was to bring this under control, which resulted in a NATO-wide communications system linking NATO Headquarters in Brussels with the capitals of all the member nations and to each of the major NATO commanders. The requirement for this system – designated the NATO Integrated Communications System (NICS) – was identified in 1965; the system was approved in 1971 and entered service in manageable segments from the mid-1970s onwards, becoming the largest infrastructure-funded project* undertaken by the Alliance, having been estimated to have cost some £500 million by 1985.

The backbone of the NICS was provided by a number of different communications systems, of which the most dramatic were based on satellites. Indeed, NATO was one of the earliest major organizations to use satellites, thus refuting the widely held image of its being a slow-reacting organization which was almost always behind the times. NATO first trialled mobile ground stations operating to a US satellite in a system known as NATO I in the 1960s, and then the Alliance's first wholly owned satellites were launched in 1970–71 (the NATO II programme), followed by four more in 1976, 1977, 1978 and 1984 (NATO III).[†] The ground elements comprised two transportable earth stations in NATO I, twelve static earth stations in NATO II, and twenty-one static and a number of mobile stations (for use in contingency plans) in NATO III.

These telecommunications systems provided numerous facilities for the Alliance, including fully automated telephone and telegraph systems covering the entire NATO area, but there were many other systems at lower levels, one example being the Allied Command Europe's ACE HIGH system, which was installed in the late 1950s to provide the circuits necessary to carry alert messages and to provide the links necessary to enable SACEUR to implement his 'tripwire' retaliation strike plan. The backbone of the system comprised forty-nine long-range radio links, with a further forty line-of-sight microwave links providing access into national systems. The system extended from northern Norway through central Europe to eastern Turkey, and, while NATO controlled the overall system, each nation was responsible for providing the manpower and administrative support for the stations within its boundaries.[‡] In addition, both MNCs had their own signal groups – e.g. the Central Region Signals Group (CRSG), which served AFCENT – to provide NATO telecommunications.

---

* Infrastructure-funded projects were paid for out of a commonly agreed annual NATO budget; the only alternative source of funding was national.
† A NATO IV system was ordered in the late 1980s but did not come into service until after the Cold War had ended.
‡ ACE HIGH was built at a time when France was part of the integrated military structure and several stations were, therefore, on French territory. The French continued to provide a full service at these stations through to the end of the Cold War and beyond.

There were two significant features of these large communications networks. First, the commitment of large sums of money indicated the extent to which the nations relied on the Alliance. Second, the multinational manning of the units providing the system showed that soldiers, sailors and airmen of the different nations could work together both efficiently and amicably at unit level.

6

The Warsaw Pact

It is scarcely surprising that in the early post-war years the Russians, and through them the remainder of the Soviet Union, should have been apprehensive at the prospect of a rearmed Germany. They had been invaded three times from the west in the previous forty years, and the German occupation had not been a pleasant experience. Then, in the aftermath of victory in 1945, Stalin thought he perceived the rise of yet another anti-Soviet coalition, led by the Unites States, the richest and most powerful nation in the world, and – at that time – the sole possessor of the atomic bomb.

Stalin therefore set about creating a Soviet-controlled bloc in eastern Europe, which, by combining a series of 'class brothers', would form a protective shield for the USSR. Accordingly, the defence arrangements of each of these countries were linked to the USSR in a series of bilateral treaties which were imposed on each of them in turn, while their armed forces were trained in the Soviet manner and armed with a mixture of outdated Soviet equipment (including US and British equipment supplied under Lend-Lease) and captured German stocks. Marshal Konstantin Rokossovsky, an ethnic Pole who had risen to the highest ranks in the Red Army, was appointed minister of national defence in Poland in 1949, and other Soviet officers were placed in similar positions of responsibility in other 'satellite' armies.

The formation of NATO in 1949 undoubtedly came as a shock to the Soviet Union, but little was changed in the Soviet-bloc military arrangements until the death of Stalin in 1953. The new leadership then placed the forces of the Soviet Union and the satellites on a much more organized basis, and was looking for some overall co-ordinating vehicle when the Western powers decided to admit a rearmed Federal Republic of Germany first to the Western European Union and then to NATO.

The latter event spurred a quick reaction from the Soviet leadership, and on 14 May 1955 a conference was held at Warsaw, where Albania, Bulgaria,

Czechoslovakia, the German Democratic Republic (GDR), Hungary, Poland, Romania and the Soviet Union joined together to form the 'Warsaw Pact'. The members' commitment was set out in Article 4:

> In the event of armed attack in Europe on one or several States that are signatories of the Treaty by any State or group of States, each State that is a Party to this Treaty shall in the exercise of the right to individual or collective self-defence in accordance with Article 51 of the Charter of the United Nations Organization, render the State or States so attacked immediate assistance . . . by all the means it may consider necessary, including the use of armed force.*

At the diplomatic level, establishing the Warsaw Pact achieved a number of significant Soviet goals. The pact was publicized, in the first instance, as a direct reaction to the admission of West Germany to NATO by a group of nations who had every reason to fear German rearmament. On the diplomatic and propaganda fronts, however, it also established a treaty organization in eastern Europe which paralleled NATO in the west, and, as was to be seen, it also led the USSR to believe that it had a legitimate right to exercise control over the countries of eastern Europe.

The Warsaw Pact agreement itself did not cover the stationing of Soviet forces in non-Soviet countries; this was subsequently the subject of separate bilateral treaties signed later (and amended from time to time):

- Czechoslovakia – there was no treaty originally, as there were no Soviet troops stationed there, but one was signed on 16 October 1968 following the suppression of the 'Prague Spring';
- East Germany (GDR) – 12 March 1957;
- Hungary – 27 May 1957;
- Poland – 17 December 1956;
- Romania – April 1957;
- Albania and Bulgaria had no Soviet forces stationed on their territory and did not require an agreement.

The signatories of the Warsaw Pact went on to establish a joint command of their armed forces, although the participation of the East German armed forces in the joint command was not included in the original treaty, possibly because they were already a virtually integral part of the Soviet forces stationed in their territory. Soviet domination of the Warsaw Pact forces was absolute, and the commander-in-chief was always a Soviet army officer, with his headquarters in Moscow.† The deputy commander-in-chief and the chief of the Joint Staff were also Soviet officers, as were the three deputies who served as commanders-in-chief for the joint naval, air and air defence forces.

---

* The text of the Warsaw Treaty is given in Appendix 3.
† A full list of both Warsaw Pact and NATO commanders-in-chief is given in Appendix 5.

The highest elements of non-Soviet national representation within the military framework were the various ministers of national defence (all military officers, on the Soviet model), who ranked as deputy commanders-in-chief. But, to ensure compliance with Soviet requirements yet further, Soviet officers, usually of colonel-general rank, were integrated into the defence ministries in each of the Pact countries, under the title 'senior representative of the commander-in-chief'.

The suppression of the 1956 Hungarian uprising was a purely Soviet affair, but the operation had a substantial effect on the Warsaw Pact. Viewing this in conjunction with earlier actions against riots in East Berlin and Poland, it was clear to the 'northern tier' of countries (Czechoslovakia, East Germany, Hungary and Poland) that, unless the leadership policies in the Soviet Union changed dramatically, they would never be allowed any significant independence from Moscow. On the other hand, Moscow was pressed into making some meaningful accommodations, including revisions to the bilateral treaties on the stationing of troops, while the numerous senior Soviet officers who had been imposed on many of the satellite armies since the end of the war were at last removed and returned to the USSR.

Further changes to the Warsaw Pact, which had been under discussion for some years, were implemented following the suppression of the 'Prague Spring' in 1968. These included the creation of a Council of Ministers of National Defence and of a Military Council, and the reorganization of the higher staffs to include greater representation from non-Soviet countries. There was also an increase in the number of personnel exchanges between the various armed forces. Above all, however, there was evidence of a greater willingness on the part of the Soviet officers to be more co-operative with their partners in the Pact and to work together more closely. Nevertheless, and despite pressure from countries such as Romania, the most senior posts remained firmly in Soviet hands, although it could be argued that, while NATO included many non-US posts at the second-tier level, the top command posts such as SACLANT, SACEUR and Commander-in-Chief Allied Forces Southern Europe (CINCSOUTH) remained equally firmly in US hands.

Although the non-Soviet Warsaw Pact armed forces used predominantly Soviet equipment, some nationally designed and developed equipment was produced. All member countries used Soviet tanks and combat aircraft, for example, but Czechoslovakia produced much of its own artillery, while Polish shipyards produced landing ships not only for Poland's navy but for the Soviet navy as well. Soviet strategy and Soviet military doctrine remained supreme, however, which gave rise to discontent in the higher echelons of the national armies and in the national governments, who felt that they had no control over the missions likely to be undertaken by their national armies. There were periodic moves to place a non-Soviet general as commander-in-chief of the Pact forces, particularly when Marshal I. I. Yakubovsky died in post in 1976, but these never came to anything.

The Warsaw Pact also embraced a number of non-military organizations. Such bodies included the Technical and Scientific Committee, set up in 1969 to co-ordinate military and civil research, and the Committee of Foreign Ministers, which was established in 1976.

One significant feature which differentiated the Warsaw Pact from NATO was that at no time during the Cold War did the Soviet Union ever provide atomic or nuclear weapons to the other members of the Pact.

Despite the overwhelming power of the Soviet Union and the tight grip it imposed on its 'satellites', the Warsaw Pact suffered from repeated internal problems. Also, unlike NATO, the military forces of the Pact were used on at least one occasion to bring recalcitrant members back into line.

HUNGARY: 1956

There were riots in East Berlin in June 1953 and in Poznán, Poland, in June 1956, both of which were put down by direct intervention by Soviet troops. These were, however, fairly localized affairs, but the Hungarian revolt in 1956 was a nationwide event, and its brutal repression by the Soviet Union was a turning point for both the Soviet Union and NATO.

Hungary had fought on the German side in the Second World War and was overrun by the Soviet army in 1944. Elections then established a coalition government, but with a substantial Communist minority. The Hungarian Communists then followed a similar pattern to that of their 'socialist comrades' in the other satellites and steadily removed their opponents until they won the next elections in 1949, principally because there were no other candidates. The Communists, headed by Secretary-General Mátyás Rákosi, then implemented the usual policies of collectivization of farms and rapid expansion of industry, thus sowing the seeds for their ultimate defeat.

In the aftermath of Stalin's death in 1953 Rákosi was instructed by the Soviet leadership to install Imre Nagy as prime minister, but after a short period in office Nagy suffered a heart attack in 1955 and had to be replaced.

The situation in Hungary deteriorated rapidly in early 1956, largely due to a general feeling of discontent with Communist rule, to which there were four contributory factors. First, there was a widespread feeling that the leadership itself was irresolute and uncertain as to the way forward, and Hungarian dissidents had taken heart from a visit by Soviet leaders to Yugoslavia in June 1955, which appeared to accord an air of respectability to Tito's form of nationalist Communism, independent of Soviet control, and from Khrushchev's de-Stalinization initiative in January 1956. Second, due to the ineptitude so frequently displayed by Communist regimes, the economy was manifestly failing. Third, Soviet armed suppression of the Polish revolt in Poznań encouraged Rákosi to take even more repressive measures in Hungary, but a visit to Budapest by Soviet Politburo member Anastas Mikoyan in July 1956 resulted in a shake-up of the government, with the deeply hated Rákosi being dismissed and replaced by Erno Gero. Finally, even further encouragement to the dissidents came in October 1956, when widespread unrest in Poland resulted in a relatively popular figure, Władysław Gomułka, being released from jail (he had been found guilty of 'Titoism') and appointed as first secretary.

This was taken as a signal that a national form of Communism would be acceptable to the Soviet leadership, and a student rally in Budapest on 22 October produced a fourteen-point manifesto demanding a similar system for Hungary. Next day a rally in support of the Poles started peacefully but got out of hand in the evening when an aggressive speech on the radio by Rákosi led to a confrontation between the crowd and the AVH (state security police), who eventually shot into the crowd.

Revolutionary councils immediately sprang up all over the country, advocating three policies: nationalism, neutrality and the withdrawal of Soviet troops. The Soviet leadership, which regarded Hungary as an essential element of its defensive strategy, was alarmed, while the Hungarian Politburo tried to cover all eventualities by calling for Soviet troops and also reappointing the ailing Nagy as prime minister, even though he was opposed to Soviet intervention. When the Soviet tanks began to roll into Budapest in the early hours of 24 October they only made matters much worse, and a number were quickly destroyed by petrol bombs. Two representatives of the Soviet Politburo, Mikoyan and Mikhail Suslov, visited Budapest on 24–26 October and swept the Communist old guard aside, confirming Nagy's appointment and replacing Gero by János Kádár. Nagy announced his new government on 27 October, the Soviet tanks left on 29 October, and Mikoyan and Suslov returned to Budapest on the 30th to announce that Hungarian sovereignty would be respected.

This Soviet activity was in reality an elaborate camouflage, however, and military forces were massing for the invasion. But at this point external events intervened. On 29 October the Israelis attacked Egypt, and the British and French governments issued an ultimatum to the two sides to withdraw from the Suez Canal and sent an amphibious task force from Cyprus and Malta (30 October). This diverted world attention from events in Hungary, and the Soviet army used some 250,000 troops and 2,500 armoured vehicles to surround Budapest on 1 November. After apparently granting concessions (whose only purpose was to give its troops time to 'shake out' into battle order), the Soviet Union struck at midnight on 3/4 November.

Budapest then became a violent and bloody battlefield as Hungarian freedom fighters tried to destroy the Soviet tanks and to kill or demoralize the Soviet troops. But, despite showing great courage and exhibiting considerable ingenuity in their methods of attack, the Hungarians were slowly but inexorably beaten by the organized might of the Soviet army. The main fighting was over by 14 November, and all resistance had crumbled by 30 November. About 25,000 Hungarians and 7,000 Soviet soldiers had been killed in the fighting, but the result was a foregone conclusion.

CZECHOSLOVAKIA: 1968

The Warsaw Pact invasion of Czechoslovakia in August 1968 exhibited precisely what was meant by the new Brezhnev doctrine of 'Socialist Commonwealth'. In the aftermath of the Second World War the Czechoslovak people as a whole were grateful to the Soviet army for their liberation from German occupation, while many still retained bitter memories of being 'sold down the river' by Britain and France in the Munich Agreement of 1938. As a result, the long-established Communist Party did well in the 1946 elections and took part in the subsequent coalition, providing the prime minister and the minister of police. Unlike in most other countries of eastern Europe, the Soviet army did not retain any troops in Czechoslovakia once the Germans had been defeated.

The Communists gradually expanded their influence, and from February 1948 they provided an uninspiring and inefficient government for some twenty years, but growing popular unrest resulted in the appointment in January 1968 of Alexander Dubček as first secretary of the Czechoslovak Communist Party.

Dubček promised reforms, especially of the political and education systems, and this, coupled with the suspension of censorship and a rapidly increasing Western influence, resulted in a euphoric period known as the 'Prague Spring'. These developments were, however, viewed with considerable disfavour by the other Eastern-bloc leaders, particularly those in East Germany and the USSR, who saw the events in Czechoslovakia not only as a major strategic threat to the Warsaw Pact, but also, if the freedom virus were to prove infectious, as a challenge to their own positions. The only exception was Romania, which not only gave vocal support for the 'Czechoslovak experiment' and resolutely declined to become involved in any concerted action, but also signed a Treaty of Friendship and Co-operation with Czechoslovakia in the week preceding the eventual invasion.

The Soviet leaders, instead of going it alone, as they had done in Hungary, made extensive use of the Warsaw Pact consultative machinery, initially in an endeavour to find a non-violent solution. Thus a Pact meeting in Warsaw in June resulted in a formal letter of warning being sent to the Central Committee of the Czech Communist Party. This was followed by a meeting between the Politburo of the Soviet Communist Party and the Central Committee of the Czechoslovak Communist Party in late July, and the crisis then appeared to have been defused.

Meanwhile, however, the Soviets had also been using the Pact machinery to plan co-ordinated military action, in which East German, Hungarian, Polish and Soviet units would all take part. Several major Warsaw Pact exercises were held in the summer of 1968 – far more than had been the case in the previous few years, which should have been seen as a classic signal of an imminent invasion. In any invasion, the major problems for commanders and their staffs are command-and-control, telecommunications and logistics, together with transport, movement control and supplies. The first overt exercise, called *Böhmerwald*, involving Soviet, Czech, East German and Polish troops, was a command-post and telecommunications exercise which took place from 20 to 30 June in Czechoslovakia and was a none too subtle warning to the Czechoslovak leadership. More ominous, however, was the major logistics exercise (*Nyemen*) held between 23 July and 10 August. This included calling up reservists in the four western Soviet republics, and led immediately into another command-post, telecommunications and air-defence exercise ('*Skyshield*') between 11 and 20 August. This was clearly meant to cover the assembly and 'shaking out' of the Soviet, East German and Polish troops taking part in the invasion, since it led straight into the invasion itself on the night of 20 August, which was a Sunday and traditionally the time of least resistance to military force.

Just after 2300 on 20 August a Soviet *spetsnaz* (special forces) battalion landed at Prague Airport and took it over with great speed. This was closely followed by 103 Guards Airborne Division, which flew in and then raced into the city to take over the vital points. Meanwhile the ground troops rolled over the border:

- The Soviet 1st Army,* normally stationed in East Germany and consisting of four Soviet divisions and the East German 11 Motorized Infantry Division, headed south. It passed through Karlovy Vary (Karlsbad), Márianské Lánzě (Marienbad) and Plzeň (Pilsen) until the leading elements had reached České Budějovice (Budweis), where they halted and faced westward, sealing off Czechoslovakia's border with the Federal Republic of Germany and covering any possible reaction by NATO.
- The Soviet 20th Army, consisting of four Soviet divisions and the East German 7 Armoured Division, headed along two axes from Poland and East Germany. The two columns joined up outside Prague and then

---

* Note that Soviet 'armies' were equivalent in size and combat power to a NATO 'corps'.

moved into the city, where they relieved the 103 Guards Airborne Division.

- A Polish army of four divisions entered the country from the north, between Hradec Králové and Ostrava.
- Two Hungarian divisions, with Soviet units in support, moved northward into the south of the country.
- Five Soviet divisions moved into eastern Czechoslovakia from southern Poland and the western USSR.
- Some twenty air regiments of the Soviet 24th Air Army occupied all the airfields in the country.*

The whole operation consisted of three phases. In the first, some twenty Warsaw Pact divisions totalling some 250,000 men, complete with their associated weapons and supplies, invaded Czechoslovakia from north, south and east, occupying all places of any strategic significance. The second phase, concurrent with the first, involved the movement of ten Soviet divisions from the western Soviet military districts into the positions in East Germany and Poland vacated by the Soviet divisions that had invaded Czechoslovakia. In the third phase, many of the divisions that had invaded Czechoslovakia in the first phase redeployed to the western end of the country, facing the border with the Federal Republic of Germany, in an area previously occupied by Czechoslovak divisions. The net result was that the Soviet Union had not only restored its control over Czechoslovakia, but had also greatly strengthened its front line against NATO. From a purely military perspective, it was a masterly manoeuvre.

The Czechoslovak people and their national army were completely defeated by this use of overpowering force. The Czech population was united in its opposition to such use of force, but there was no armed resistance, as there had been in Hungary, and *force majeure* triumphed once again. The Czechs were deeply embittered by the experience. They felt badly let down by the West, as they had done after the Munich Agreement. They also felt let down by the Hungarians and Poles, whom they had considered to be fellow sufferers under the Soviet yoke. But most of all they deeply resented the return of Germans in uniform after the bitter years of occupation between 1938 and 1945.

One curious feature of the invasion of Czechoslovakia was that, although it involved numerous non-Soviet formations and clearly used the Warsaw Pact co-ordinating machinery, it was actually commanded by the commander-in-chief of the Soviet armed forces and not by the commander-in-chief of the Warsaw Pact.

---

* All Warsaw Pact aircraft taking part in the operation had red stripes around their rear fuselage and on their wings, to differentiate them from Czech aircraft.

THE POLISH CRISIS: 1980–81

Poland has been fought over and partitioned on numerous occasions during the past two centuries, but in the aftermath of the Second World War it took on a new role as the supply route between the USSR and Soviet forces confronting NATO across the Inner German Border. Despite the presence of a Soviet garrison numbering some 40,000, it proved to be a troublesome ally, due in part to historical factors, the most recent being the Red Army drive on Warsaw in 1920, the partitioning of Polish territory with Nazi Germany in 1939, and the murder of some 15,000 of Poland's political and military elite in the Katyn Forest in 1940.

The first major unrest came in June 1956. It started with factory workers in Poznań protesting about low pay and standards of living, but then, like the Berlin uprising in 1953, turned into a more general protest against the Communist government. A Soviet delegation, headed by Nikolai Bulganin, arrived in Warsaw in July, but the Polish leaders stood up to them and matters simmered until October, when disagreements within the upper echelons of the Polish Communist Party resulted in a visit by another Soviet delegation, this time headed by First Secretary Khrushchev, on 19 October. The Polish Communist leader, Gomułka, warned the Soviets of the dire consequences of military intervention, and, following Khrushchev's return to Moscow, a meeting of the Central Committee of the Polish Communist Party resulted in the defeat of the anti-reform group, elected Gomułka as first secretary, and dropped Marshal Rokossovsky from the Politburo.* Faced with strong support for the new regime from the mass of the Polish people and in the absence of any suggestion that Poland should abandon the Warsaw Pact or evict the Soviet army garrison, Khrushchev telephoned Gomułka to inform him that the USSR had no further objections to his limited reforms.

There was more trouble in December 1970, when shipyard workers in Gdańsk rioted. This time it was Gomułka who was ousted, being replaced by Edward Gierek, who once again tried to resolve the workers' grievances. There was further trouble in 1976, when food prices were increased, but after several riots the government backed down and the prices returned to their previous level, while Gierek negotiated a large Soviet loan to enable him to meet some of the workers' demands.

In July 1980 the government once again raised meat prices and, as before, this quickly led to riots, which started on this occasion at a tractor factory in Warsaw. Unrest spread quickly, and in August 50,000 workers came out on

---

* Rokossovsky had been imposed as minister of national defence by the USSR in 1949. Following his dismissal in 1958 he was replaced by a Polish general and then returned to Moscow and retirement.

strike, including those at the Gdańsk shipyard. By now the demands had increased to include political and trade union reform, and the agreement reached between the government and the Gdańsk shipworkers included the right to form non-Communist trade unions, resulting in the official establishment of the 'Solidarity' union. Gierek was replaced by Stanisław Kania as the crisis deepened, but the new man seemed equally unable to find a solution, and the civil disturbances increased.

Kania was visited by no less than three separate delegations of senior Soviet officials between January and March 1981, and the tempo of Warsaw Pact exercises increased, all of which bore a disturbing resemblance to events in Czechoslovakia in 1968. So, too, did the next development: a letter from the Central Committee of the Communist Party of the Soviet Union (CPSU) in mid-September, which drew Kania's attention to the widespread Polish criticism of the USSR and its soldiers, and expressed an earnest hope that the Polish leadership would take resolute steps to stop this.

By October Soviet patience was beginning to run out, and on 28 October 1981 the minister of national defence, General Wojciech Jaruzelski, was appointed first secretary of the Polish United Workers Party – the only soldier ever to be appointed to such a post in any east-European Communist party. Jaruzelski first banned all strikes for a period of ninety days and then on 13 December imposed martial law under the control of a newly created 'Military Council'. The crisis was now effectively over – at least for the time being.

Throughout these events the threat of a repeat of the Warsaw Pact invasion of Czechoslovakia hung over the country, and Marshal V. G. Kulikov, the Pact's commander-in-chief, was a frequent visitor to Poland. He called on First Secretary Kania in February 1981 and on the new first secretary, General Jaruzelski, once just before the ban on strikes was imposed in November and again on the day that the martial-law decree was issued in December.

As during the earlier Czechoslovak crisis, the number of Warsaw Pact exercises had increased, with no less than fourteen being held between September 1980 and December 1981, when the crisis ended. One of the largest was a major command and staff exercise lasting from 17 March to 7 April 1981; designated *Soyuz-81*, this involved Czechoslovak, East German and Polish troops, including a large number of reservists from all participating countries. A similar exercise, designated *Zapad-81*, followed in September.

There can be no doubt that planning for an invasion went much further than just staff preparations. Western intelligence detected major troop concentrations around the Polish borders in early December and expected the actual operation to begin on 8 December. One piece of evidence was the use of a huge building at Prora on the Baltic island of Rügen as a transit camp for several thousand East German troops assembling for the operation (although they returned to their peacetime locations once the operation had been cancelled).[1] Erich Honecker, the East German leader, wrote to Soviet first secretary Brezhnev on 26 November, strongly urging him to press for Warsaw Pact intervention at the forthcoming Pact meeting on 5 December. Numerous Western leaders urged Brezhnev not to do so, however, and this, coupled with the firm measures being imposed by General Jaruzelski, appears to have had an effect, since when the leaders met in Moscow they decided not to invade.[2]

The armies of the 'southern tier' of the Warsaw Pact (Bulgaria, Hungary and Romania) did not take part in any of these activities and were not included in the plans to invade Poland.

General Jaruzelski has consistently declined to give any details of events during this period, but there can be little doubt that Poland would have been invaded either by the Warsaw Pact or by Soviet forces alone had he not taken over and pacified his country. Poland was vital to Soviet strategic plans in a way that neither Czechoslovakia or Hungary had been, since all the supply routes to East Germany ran through the country.* Further, such an invasion would have been strenuously resisted not only by the Polish people, but also, in all probability, by large elements, if not the entirety, of the Polish army. Such resistance would have been even more violent had troops from the GDR joined their 'class comrades' of the Soviet army, and it is just possible that the West might have been dragged in, although it was physically separated from Poland by East Germany. The alternatives to Jaruzelski were therefore extremely dire, and it may well be that he actually saved his country from a bloody fate and was not the villain he has been made out to be.

THE FIRST MAVERICK – ALBANIA

Albania, with a population of some 3 million and the poorest country in Europe, was the smallest state to join the Warsaw Pact. Following a civil war in 1944 the Communists, headed by Enver Hoxha, seized power and established a 'people's republic' in January 1946. The regime was initially friendly with Yugoslavia, but when Stalin and Tito split in 1948 Hoxha aligned with the Soviet Union, and in return he received considerable economic and military assistance. Albania was one of the founder members of the Warsaw

---

* In 1982 the Soviets and East Germans started work on a totally new port at Neu Mukran on Rügen island. This was intended as a safeguard against future disruption of the overland route through Poland; however, such a sea route would have been disrupted by ice in winter and would have been very vulnerable to hostile action in war.

Pact, although one of its few major contributions was to provide the Soviet navy with a base on the island of Sazan (Saseno) in the Gulf of Vlorës, in return for which the Soviet Union cancelled Albania's considerable debt, made large credits available, and also supplied much military and naval equipment, including two submarines and a variety of surface vessels.

Hoxha was a strict Stalinist and reacted very strongly to Khrushchev's denunciation of the former Soviet dictator in a speech to the Twentieth Party Congress in February 1956. As relations cooled, the Soviet and other east-European governments reduced Albania's line of credit, making its finances still worse, and Hoxha developed relations with the only other 'Stalinist' power: Communist China. China's relations with the Soviet Union also worsened, and the Soviet leaders started to condemn China's new friend, Albania, as a means of disguising their real target: China itself. As a result, in December 1961 Albania severed all relations with the USSR and left the Warsaw Pact. The Albanians also seized all Soviet facilities in the country, including the naval base on Sazan, where their haul included two Soviet submarines which happened to be in port.

Thereafter, Albania remained a maverick. It maintained close relations with China for some years until the Chinese cut off their aid in 1978, after which Albania carried on alone. In effect, however, its only role of even marginal significance in the Cold War was its relatively brief membership of the Warsaw Pact and its provision of berthing facilities to the Soviet navy within the confines of the Mediterranean.

THE SECOND MAVERICK – ROMANIA

During the Second World War Romania provided two armies which fought alongside their German allies on the Eastern Front, losing some 173,000 troops in the battle of Stalingrad. By 1944 national support for the war had waned, and in early 1944 King Michael deposed the dictator General Ion Antonescu and surrendered unconditionally to the advancing Soviet armies. On 30 December 1947, however, the king was compelled to abdicate and Romania became a 'people's republic', and in 1948 Georghe Georghiu-Dej, a long-time Communist, was appointed first secretary of the Communist Party at Moscow's insistence.

Georghiu-Dej controlled Romania until 1965 and originally supported the Soviet line, especially over the Soviet army's quelling of the Poznán riots and the Hungarian uprising. Such support played a key role in the Soviet decision to withdraw its troops from Romania in 1958, but it now appears that Georghiu-Dej was playing a double game. In 1963 the Romanian ambassador to the United Nations held a meeting with US secretary of state Dean Rusk in which the Romanian referred to the recent Cuban Missile

Crisis and explained that his country had opposed the Soviet moves and would never support the USSR in wars outside the immediate area of the Warsaw Pact. In return for a promise of this, he asked for, and was later given, an assurance that the USA would not target missiles on Romania.[3]

Nikolae Ceauşescu was carefully groomed to succeed Georghiu-Dej, and took over as first secretary (later changed to general secretary) in 1965. He adopted an increasingly nationalist position, and his relationship with the Warsaw Pact was ambivalent, to say the least.

Ceauşescu openly opposed the invasion of Czechoslovakia and flatly refused to allow Romanian troops to take part; indeed, he even ordered a limited mobilization to protect his country's northern border with the USSR. Following this, in 1972 at Ceauşescu's behest the National Assembly passed a law which banned military operations outside Romania's borders, leading to a national strategy in which regular troops would fight delaying actions in border regions, buying time for a *levée en masse*, following which the invader would be faced with a prospect of a people's war.

On the other hand, the Romanian armed forces maintained a large contingent at the Warsaw Pact Joint Headquarters in Moscow, and a Soviet staff remained at the Romanian Defence Ministry throughout the Cold War. Romania also remained on the Warsaw Pact's infrastructure committees and commissions. Other contradictions included Romania's refusal to permit any Warsaw Pact troop deployments on its territory,* while allowing its air force to be integrated into the Warsaw Pact air defence system.

The Romanian armaments programme was another curious affair. Parts of the army were well equipped, particularly the mountain troops, while others, such as the armoured corps, had much outdated equipment. Considerable national resources were devoted to building a Romanian-designed destroyer† and frigates, although in any conflict against their only possible enemy, the infinitely more powerful Soviet Black Sea Fleet, their operational careers would have been very brief. Indeed, there were indications that the megalomania which seems to have afflicted Ceauşescu's later career even prompted him to take an interest in the acquisition of nuclear weapons, although how far this developed has yet to be revealed.[4]

FINIS

In the end, the collapse of the Warsaw Pact was not due to external interference, because, whatever they may have been doing clandestinely, the Western powers and NATO demonstrated time and again that they were not

---

* There were occasional command-post exercises in the mid-1980s.
† It was classified by the Romanian navy, with typical exaggeration, as a 'battlecruiser'.

prepared to intervene openly. Thus the East Berlin and Poznań rioters and the street fighters in Budapest and Prague were never going to receive physical support from NATO, and they knew it. Instead, the Pact imploded, partly due to Gorbachev's reluctance to maintain its hegemony by force when he became general secretary of the CPSU, although its own internal contradictions also played a role. Deep down, however, only a handful of people in each member country were actually devoted Communists, and even fewer looked to the Soviet Union as their natural ally against the West. Allied to this was the implacable opposition of the Roman Catholic Church in Czechoslovakia, Hungary and Poland, where being Christian really did matter and gave many of the anti-Communists the strength to hold on.

The major events affecting the end of the Cold War were:

- the dismantling of the Berlin Wall began (22 December 1989);
- the Romanian regime collapsed following Ceauşescu's flight, capture, trial and death (25 December 1989);
- Soviet troops began to withdraw from Czechoslovakia (February 1990) and Hungary (March 1990); both withdrawals were completed by 19 June 1991;
- West and East Germany were reunified (3 October 1990); East German armed forces were disbanded;
- Lech Wałesa was elected president of Poland (9 December 1990);
- the Baltic states declared their independence (Lithuania on 11 March 1990; Estonia on 20 August 1991; Latvia on 21 August 1991);
- the western republics of the Soviet Union declared their independence (Belorussia (now Belarus) on 24 August 1991; Moldova (formerly Moldavia) on 27 August 1991; Ukraine on 5 December 1991).

In the middle of all these momentous events, the quiet, almost furtive, dismantling of the Warsaw Pact's military and political apparatus on 31 March 1991 passed unmourned and almost unnoticed.

PART II

STRATEGIC ISSUES

7

The Nature of Nuclear War

Hanging over every political and military decision throughout the Cold War was the threat of atomic and, later, of thermonuclear attack. This dreadful prospect faced politicians, the military and civil populations alike, and as much in neutral countries as in those involved in any possible conflict. As with many such issues, however, the majority were aware only of an appalling, but vague, Doomsday threat; indeed, as will be shown, even the so-called 'experts' could make only imprecise forecasts of what it would involve. It is therefore necessary to identify the major characteristics of nuclear weapons and to highlight some of their possible effects, in order to place the subsequent chapters in perspective.*

NUCLEAR EXPLOSIONS

A nuclear explosion releases energy on a scale vastly greater than that of conventional high explosives, its yield being expressed in terms of its equivalence to the detonation of TNT;† thus a 1 kiloton (1 kT) nuclear weapon is equivalent to 1,000 tons of TNT, a 1 megaton (1 MT) weapon is equivalent to 1 million tons of TNT, and so on. Some comparisons will place the figures in perspective:

- During its strategic bombing campaign in Europe between mid-1942 and May 1945, the United States' Eighth Air Force dropped approximately 700 kT of bombs. In the 1970s a single USAF FB-111 fighter-bomber could carry six B61 bombs with a total yield of 3 MT.
- The largest known single detonation of high explosives occurred on 27 November 1944 at a British underground ammunition store at Hanbury, Staffordshire, when approximately 4 kT of aircraft bombs of

---

* A list of nuclear-weapons 'firsts' is given in Appendix 6.
† Trinitrotoluene (TNT) is the 'standard' chemical high explosive.

various sizes exploded at a depth of some 27 m. The resulting crater was 274 m long, 244 m wide and approximately 24 m deep, and, although in a sparsely populated farming area, the explosion killed seventy people and wounded another twenty. In the 1960s a single W33 203 mm howitzer nuclear shell had a yield of 10 kT.

- The atomic bomb dropped on Hiroshima on 6 August 1945 had a yield of about 15 kT, while that dropped on Nagasaki three days later had a yield of 22 kT.
- The largest known nuclear explosion was a Soviet 58 MT weapon, exploded in a 3,700 m airburst at the Novaya Zemlya test site on 30 October 1961.
- The most powerful US nuclear test took place on 28 February 1954. A surface test on Bikini Atoll, it was expected to produce a yield of 6 MT, but actually produced 15 MT, gouging a crater 1,830 m in diameter and 73 m deep.[1]

Nuclear explosions release energy in five forms which affect humans: flash (light), blast (shock and sound), thermal radiation (heat), initial nuclear radiation and residual nuclear radiation (fallout). The proportions vary according to the height of the burst, but, in a typical airburst, blast and thermal radiation account for some 85 per cent of the energy output, initial radiation approximately 5 per cent and residual radiation some 10 per cent. Nuclear weapons also release two forms of energy which affect electronic equipments only: electromagnetic pulse (EMP) and transient radiation effects on electronics (TREE).

Types of Burst
The effects of a nuclear explosion depend to a large degree on the height of the burst.

An 'airburst' takes place where the fireball just fails to touch the surface of the earth.* In a 1 MT weapon, for example, the fireball is 1,700 m in diameter, meaning that an airburst for such a weapon would have to be at an altitude greater than 870 m. In an airburst nearly all the shock energy leaves the fireball as blast, while the thermal radiation travels long distances, but there is no ground crater. Initial radiation also travels long distances, although it decreases more rapidly with the distance from the explosion, but there is no residual radiation. Technically, there are two types of airburst: endo-atmospheric (i.e. within the atmosphere), which takes place at a height of less than 30 km, and exo-atmospheric (i.e. outside the atmosphere), which takes place at a height greater than 30 km. In practice, an exo-atmospheric burst has only one effect of any military significance – EMP – and 'airburst' is normally taken to mean an endo-atmospheric burst.

---

* For practical purposes, this means that the bottom edge of the fireball is 20 m above ground level.

One aspect of airbursts is that, if it is decided to replace a single large warhead with a number of smaller warheads but with the same overall yield (e.g. replace a single 3 MT warhead by six, each with a yield of 500 kT, and provided they are detonated so that their blast patterns do not overlap), then the total damage inflicted will increase greatly. In general terms, therefore, airbursts would have been used where maximum blast effect and minimum fallout were required (e.g. to destroy cities, airfields, oil refineries), with the height of burst optimized to ensure that the desired blast effect covered the target.

Nuclear bursts which take place either on the surface or sufficiently low above it that the fireball will touch it are known as 'groundbursts' or 'surface bursts'. Much of the energy appears as air blast and ground shock, but part is expended in creating a surface crater. Fallout from such a burst is much greater than immediate radiation. Thus a groundburst would have been used either to optimize blast against a pinpoint target such as a missile silo or a hardened building, or to generate fallout to attack rural populations.

A 'subsurface burst' is one in which the explosion occurs at some depth underground or underwater. Here most of the energy is dissipated in shock, although some may also be released as air blast. Due to the contamination of the surrounding earth or water with radioactive products, the residual radiation will be significant. 'Subsurface' bursts would be used for anti-submarine warfare at sea or to demolish buried headquarters on land.

Flash

The first evidence of a nuclear explosion is a very intense flash of light, which covers a large geographical area. It is of major significance to people in the open, and particularly to those who happen to be facing the explosion, in whom it will cause temporary flash blindness and eye damage, including retina burns. Its effect is enhanced at night, when those facing the explosion could be dazzled for up to ten minutes. The effects of flash are, however, reduced by cloudy weather and rain.

Blast

Most of the material damage caused by a nuclear explosion is due – directly or indirectly – to the pressure wave, which has two components: blast wave through the air and shock wave through the ground. The blast wave travels outwards from the centre of the explosion at a speed of some 305 m/s with both speed and intensity decreasing rapidly with distance. Blast is defined in terms of 'overpressure' – i.e. the pressure in excess of the ambient pressure.*

An overpressure of 0.2 kilograms-force per square centimetre (0.2 kgf/cm^2)

---

* Ambient pressure is approximately 1 kgf/cm^2.

(equivalent to a wind of 161 km/h) would collapse wooden houses, but brick-built houses would probably survive, although windows, doors, floors and ceilings would be seriously damaged; the remains of such houses might be used for survival, but not for 'living' as currently understood. Industrial premises would be damaged, but the stronger the structure, the less the damage. Within the 0.2 kgf/cm² area about 10 per cent of the population would die.

An overpressure of 0.4 kgf/cm² (equivalent to a wind speed of 322 km/h would cause both wooden-framed and conventional two-storey, brick-built houses to collapse, and would render most industrial premises unusable, destroy oil storage tanks, collapse steel-truss bridges, and uproot some 90 per cent of trees. Within this 0.4 kgf/cm² overpressure area, approximately 80 per cent of the population would die – some from direct exposure to the blast, but most from injuries resulting from collapsing buildings and flying debris. Fire would also be a major hazard, but would probably not be of great significance compared to the devastation and deaths already caused.

One strong possibility is the creation of a firestorm. In this, once the blast had spread outward, there would be a negative pressure at the centre, resulting in winds blowing inward towards ground zero,* fanning the fires and in turn increasing the wind, as happened in the Second World War in the conventional bombing raids on Hamburg, Dresden and Tokyo. This has a curious and contradictory effect, in that the wind towards the centre tends to limit the spread of the fire outward, but ensures that the fire destroys virtually everything at the centre.

Thermal Radiation (Heat)

A nuclear explosion generates heat as intense as that at the centre of the sun. This heat travels outward at a speed of some 300 million metres per second, and in a groundburst it will vaporize most substances within the fireball and for distances up to 5 km from ground zero, while many substances will spontaneously ignite at greater distances. Fifty per cent of people caught in the open suffer will flash burns, the severity depending upon the distance from ground zero; a 1 MT airburst, for example, would cause third degree burns at 11,000 m and second degree burns at 13,000 m.

Anything which throws a shadow will provide protection, and a British study in the 1960s showed that in the UK in peacetime in daylight some 10 per cent of the population (approximately 5 million people) was in the open at any one time, but that 75 per cent (3.75 million) of these would always be offered at least some protection by buildings. If adequate warning of an impending nuclear strike had been given, however, it would have been reasonable to expect that the numbers in the open would be substantially reduced.

---

* Ground zero (GZ) is the point on the earth's surface vertically above or below the centre of a nuclear explosion. At sea, the equivalent is surface zero (SZ).

Initial Nuclear Radiation

A very powerful pulse of initial nuclear radiation (INR) is released within the first minute of an explosion. INR expands in a circular pattern and is relatively short-ranged: the lethal range for a 1 MT weapon, for example, is 2,600 m. INR consists, in the main, of neutrons and gamma rays which penetrate the body and react with bone marrow, but these are substantially attenuated by dense materials such as concrete, steel or earth, so that people inside a building, in a steel vehicle (such as a battle tank or an armoured personnel carrier) or in an underground bunker receive varying degrees of protection.

People in the open are very vulnerable to INR, and the majority of radiation victims at Hiroshima and Nagasaki suffered from this initial radiation rather than from fallout. With high-yield nuclear weapons, however, the blast effect has a greater lethal range than INR, so that above a yield of about 100 kT INR ceases to be significant.

The 'enhanced radiation warhead' (popularly known as the 'neutron bomb') was designed to optimize the effects of INR, by using low-yield weapons in low airbursts over a target such as a company of tanks. The INR would have penetrated the armour and inflicted high radiation doses, while the low blast effect would have caused little serious damage to vehicles or buildings.

Residual Nuclear Radiation

Residual nuclear radiation is caused by materials which are vaporized in the initial heat and then sucked up as dust into the fireball, where they are irradiated and then fall back to earth as radioactive fallout. Larger particles return to earth within a few hours, but the remaining, increasingly small, particles may take weeks, or even months, to return to earth. The area covered lies downwind of ground zero and is generally elliptical in shape, giving rise to its colloquial name of the 'fallout plume'.

Radiation is measured in *rads*, and accumulated doses have the following effects:*

- 5,000 rads and above: death in up to two days;
- 1,000 to 5,000 rads: death within fourteen days, although the lower the dose the more protracted the period;
- 600 to 1,000 rads: 90–100 per cent deaths over a period of up to six weeks;
- 200 to 600 rads: 0 to 90 per cent deaths over a period of 2 to 12 weeks;

---

* Two units are used to measure radiation: the *roentgen* measures exposure and the *rad* measures absorption. For the purposes of this book, the two are essentially synonymous (i.e. 1 roentgen = 1 rad) and the rad will be used. The absorbed radiation can be expressed either as a dose rate (rads per hour) or as an accumulated figure (total rads over a specified time). To confuse matters further, NATO recently redesignated the *rad* as the *Grey*, but, since it was the term commonly used throughout the Cold War, the term rad will be used here.

- below 200 rads: no long-term effects, although there will be a period of several weeks' convalescence from effects of radiation such as skin burns etc.

Table 7.1 Examples of Lethal Effects of a Nuclear Explosion[2]

		10 kT		1 MT	
Effect	Criterion	Airburst	Groundburst	Airburst	Groundburst
Blast	0.4 kgf/cm^2	1,400 m	1,000 m	6,500 m	4,600 m
Burns	Third-degree	1,900 m		11,000 m	
Radiation burns	450 rads		1,300 m		2,600 m

Ionization of the Atmosphere
Nuclear explosions cause ionization of the atmosphere, which affects radio and radar systems whose waves pass through the disturbed areas. The period of disruption may be brief (a few seconds) or lengthy (several hours), and the severity will depend upon the yield of the nuclear explosion and its height, as well as upon the characteristics of the equipment itself. Systems which depend upon reflected waves, such as radars, tropospheric scatter systems and high-frequency radios, would be particularly affected.*

Electromagnetic Pulse (EMP)
EMP is an extremely powerful short-duration burst of broad-band radio energy generated by a nuclear explosion. This could affect electronic equipment, such as telephone systems, radio and television equipment, radars, computers and power supplies. As far as is known, it is harmless to man and animals.

EMP travels with the speed of light and radiates over 360 degrees and out to the line of sight from the source; thus, the higher the altitude of the burst the wider the area covered, until the point is reached where an exo-atmospheric burst would be intended primarily as an anti-electronic-systems weapon. An explosion at an altitude of 80 km would cover a circular area of 966 km radius, while an explosion at a height of 320 km would cover the whole of the contiguous United States and most of Canada.[†] In a similar manner to lightning, EMP tends to home in on and then travel along con-

---

* The main NATO communications system in Europe, designated ACE HIGH, used tropospheric scatter, whose value in the aftermath of a series of nuclear explosions would have been questionable, to say the least.
† In a well-documented event, the street lighting on the Hawaiian island of Oahu suffered thirty separate and serious failures due to the EMP from a test which took place at Johnson Island, some 1,300 km distant.[3]

ductors such as overhead or buried communications-cable runs, power cables, railway tracks and aircraft fuselages, and is particularly effective against transistorized equipment.

In aircraft, for example, EMP can cause computer malfunctions, inject energy into the aircraft wiring looms (resulting in unwanted signals to the equipment), and cause power surges which can result in system or component burn-out. This problem can be alleviated by shielding and filtering.

On the ground, protection against EMP is provided by careful planning of systems and good detailed design of equipments, including the use of efficient grounding (earth) and appropriate components. The EMP threat was taken very seriously in the West, particularly in the latter half of the Cold War, and vast sums of money were spent in developing and installing 'nuclear hardening' and in testing the results. Protection was also necessary against the EMP effects of weapons released by one's own side; this might have included switching equipments off before an explosion.

Transient Radiation Effects on Electronics (TREE)

Although TREE occurs at the same time as EMP and has a similar source, it is a different phenomenon, caused by the initial nuclear radiation acting on electronic components. With high-yield nuclear weapons the range of TREE is probably less than that of damage caused by heat or blast, but it is of considerably greater significance in low-yield weapons, particularly those with enhanced-radiation warheads. Although the actual phenomenon is of very brief duration (typically a fraction of a second) the effect on electronic equipment may be long-lasting, if components are destroyed. Again, protection is achieved by good design and the use of filters.

NUCLEAR ATTACKS ON CENTRES OF POPULATION

A detailed assessment of the effects of nuclear weapons in a particular situation needs to take account of a wide variety of variable factors. In considering urban areas, for example, these include the location, density and distribution of the population in peacetime, as well as ambient conditions such as wind (which dictates the direction of the fallout plume), rain and temperature, all of which will affect the velocity and deceleration of the blast wave. The time of day is also relevant, not only because it will affect the ambient conditions, but also because the population distribution may be different between daytime and night-time, while the blinding effect of the light flash will be much more serious in the hours of darkness. Terrain also has an effect: for example, the blast wave will behave differently in hilly country compared to a plain.

Further differences arise according to whether the population has been warned of an impending attack, and, if so, whether it has been told to stay put (as in the UK), to disperse to the countryside (as in the USA) or to go to shelters (as in Sweden and Switzerland). The outcome will be further affected according to whether, having received the relevant instructions, the population has actually obeyed them. The availability of protective clothing – especially respirators – will also affect the outcome, as will the post-strike availability of the essentials of life such as food, water and fuel. House construction methods also have to be taken into account, since these vary not only between countries, but also between regions within a country and between areas in a city (for example, between poor and wealthy districts).

In interpreting nuclear-casualty tables, it is important to note that casualties and damage are not necessarily cumulative from the different causes. Thus, for example, people within the danger zone for radiation may well have already been killed by blast or fire, and they can only die once! Similarly, a communication link in the area susceptible to TREE or EMP might well not be functioning because its antenna mast has already been blown down by blast.

A PRE-EMPTIVE ATTACK ON MILITARY TARGETS

One of the concerns of both sides in the Cold War was of being subjected to a pre-emptive attack against their military forces. Most troop concentrations (such as barracks) either are in urban areas or form large population centres equivalent to urban areas. The effect of a nuclear strike on such troops would depend on whether they had received adequate warning of an attack, enabling them to disperse to rural areas and, once there, to take adequate protective measures.* It would also depend on the distribution of the troops: in the former USSR, for example, troops deploying from an urban area likely to be a nuclear target would have been well advised to take up a position generally west of the city, since that would have placed them upwind of the fallout plume (the prevailing wind is westerly), although this might have placed them downwind of a strike on another city.

There were, however, yet more considerations for the military. It was possible that troops might have survived the attack only to discover that the city where their families had remained had been devastated. Depending upon the prevailing state of discipline, such troops might then have given priority to aiding the civil population rather than to taking part in any continuing military operations.

---

* In the NATO Central European Command, for example, all military units were required to make and to practise plans to deploy from their peacetime camp to a 'survival location' at some distance from their barracks. Such emergency deployments were to be implemented on receipt of a codeword (originally 'Quicktrain', later 'Active Edge').

Airfields were somewhat different, since they covered large areas, while their population was concentrated in a small part of this. Most front-line airfields were essentially unprotected until the mid-1970s, when many of the facilities were given 'nuclear hardening' and fitted with filters.* Such airfields would have been high-priority targets for the opposing side, although in some cases aircraft and their support facilities could be deployed away from the large static airfields; for example, the Swedish and German air force used highways as runways, while the British deployed their V/STOL (vertical/short take-off and landing) Harriers to greenfield sites.

Damage to ships from either an airburst or a groundburst would be primarily caused by the shock wave. A powerful weapon at close range could have caused the hull to rupture, or even made the ship roll over, while a more distant weapon might have damaged the superstructure and deck equipment without actually sinking the ship. From the 1970s onwards most new warships in the major navies were fitted with 'NBC-proof citadels' – proof against nuclear, biological and chemical weapons – giving the crew protection against immediate radiation and fallout, while wash-down systems provided effective decontamination.

As far as is known, no tests were conducted against submerged submarines. The usual method of destroying a submarine is by a depth charge, which is used to generate a large pressure near to the submarine with the aim of puncturing the pressure hull. A nuclear weapon would have served a similar, but very much more powerful, function, although its effect would have diminished with distance.

SECONDARY EFFECTS

Nuclear explosions give rise to consequential effects which are not a direct result of the explosion itself. For example, human casualties would have been far more likely to be caused by fires started by thermal radiation, or by flying debris (e.g. from falling buildings) and explosions (e.g. from ruptured gas mains), rather than by the blast effect itself. Similarly, in the post-strike period many deaths would have occurred from starvation and thirst (due to contamination or destruction of food stocks and water supplies), from exposure to cold climates (due to the destruction of buildings and clothing stocks), and from general debility and despair. There would also undoubtedly have been massive epidemics of diseases such as typhoid and cholera.

---

* Such facilities included 'crisis management centres' (operations rooms), 'hardened aircraft shelters' (HAS), 'hardened equipment shelters' (HES), pilot briefing facilities (PBF), etc.

RURAL AREAS

Consideration of the effects of nuclear weapons usually concentrated on urban areas, where the human casualties would have been highest and the devastation most obvious. There would, however, have been many effects in the countryside. Even under non-nuclear conditions, grasslands, heathlands, forests and some crops are extremely vulnerable to fire, especially during the dry season, and nuclear explosions would have been much worse. Indeed, since it was unlikely that human agencies would have been available to extinguish them, such fires could have raged over wide areas and for long periods. In addition, fallout would have affected both humans and animals in the rural areas, and, as in the urban areas, diseases would have spread rapidly.

Urban-population dispersal to the countryside, whether as government policy or as a panic measure, would inevitably have affected the rural areas and population. The sudden and unplanned arrival of large numbers of city-dwellers, ill-prepared both mentally and physically for rural life in a nuclear environment, would quickly have caused problems over accommodation, but in the mid-term the problems would have centred on food, water and disease.

LONG-TERM EFFECTS

A major unknown factor in assessing the long-term effects of nuclear war was that, apart from the very limited examples of Hiroshima and Nagasaki, there was no precedent for what would happen. There was a degree of agreement over the types of consequences of a nuclear strike, such as cancers and genetic abnormalities (certainly among women pregnant at the time of the nuclear war, and possibly also hereditary), but there was no agreement on the scale. The US Office of Technology Assessment, for example, estimated in 1980 that following a general nuclear war, long-term radiation might possibly affect between 3.5 and 25 million people in the USA, 16 to 44 million in the USSR, and 11 to 37 million in the rest of the world. The very wide ranges resulted from the extreme sensitivity of the estimates to the assumptions made – at one extreme, that all factors were favourable to the defence; at the other extreme, that all factors were unfavourable.

NUCLEAR TESTS

All known nuclear powers (the USA, the USSR, the UK, France and China) carried out long-running programmes of tests, while India conducted just one test. The majority of these tests were conducted in order to check that the devices would function properly, but many – particularly those conducted before the signing of the Partial Test Ban Treaty in 1963 – were also used to try to establish the effects of nuclear explosions on buildings, aircraft, ships and so on.

Table 7.2 Nuclear Weapons Tests[4]

Dates*	Environment	USA	USSR[†]	UK[‡]	France	China	India	Totals
16 July 1945 to	Atmosphere	212	212	21	4	0	0	449
5 August 1963	Underground	114	0	2	4	0	0	120
	Underwater	5	3	0	0	0	0	8
6 August 1963	Atmosphere	0	0	0	41	23	0	64
to 1990	Underground	598	464	20	134	13	1	1,230
	Underwater	0	0	0	0	0	0	0
Totals		929	679	43	183	36	1	1,871

* The Partial Test Ban Treaty was signed on 5 August 1963.
† Soviet figures for 1945 to 5 August 1963 are based on information made public in 1990.
‡ All British tests from 1962 were conducted jointly with the USA at the Nevada Test Site.

One particular shortcoming of the testing programme was that, because of the fallout problem, only a very small number of the atmospheric tests carried out (see Table 7.2) were properly monitored groundbursts, the remainder being airbursts and high-altitude bursts or underground tests. This meant that assessments of the effects of groundbursts had to be based upon mathematical models, which might or might not have been accurate.

Another significant unknown was the effect of multiple explosions. At Hiroshima and Nagasaki and in all known subsequent tests, only one nuclear weapon was ever detonated at a time. Thus the possible effect of tens or even hundreds of more or less simultaneous nuclear explosions over a relatively small geographical area such as Germany or the western USSR was simply not known, and there could have been cumulative effects which were unforeseeable.

Another unknown was the behaviour pattern of people. In general terms, during the Second World War the mass of people contradicted what was thought to be the 'lesson of Guernica'[§] and stayed put in their cities. Indeed,

§ During the Spanish Civil War (1936–9), the small town of Guernica was heavily bombed by German aircraft operating in support of General Francisco Franco. This was the first example in Europe of 'modern' bombing, and led to many false conclusions about the effect of such bombing on civil populations.

instead of rioting and bringing massive pressure to bear on governments to surrender, as had also been predicted, not only did they remain passive, but in many instances the attacks actually increased their determination to resist. Attacks by V-1 and A-4 (V-2) missiles on cities such as London and Antwerp gave rise to slightly greater degrees of panic than did manned bombers, but not on the scale the Germans had expected. The threat from nuclear weapons was, however, different by many orders of magnitude, and included not only immediate damage on an almost unimaginable scale but also the certainty of long-term suffering for those who survived. How people might have responded to that threat was simply impossible to predict.

It must therefore be borne in mind throughout this book that the fore-casts of the effects of individual nuclear weapons, especially groundbursts, and the predictions of the outcomes of nuclear wars were essentially 'best guesses'. They were also very sensitive to the assumptions on which they were based, and it was by no means unknown for officials and academics (in both East and West) to 'fine-tune' their assumptions in order to produce out-comes favourable to the case they were trying to make.

8

Nuclear War–Fighting Systems

THE SECOND WORLD WAR LEGACY

Among the many military legacies of the Second World War, two of the most significant were land- and sea-based ballistic missiles,* which quickly enabled the two superpowers to threaten each other directly. The German A-4 (V-2)† rocket entered service in 1944 and carried out attacks on the UK, Belgium and the Netherlands in a programme unique in the annals of warfare, the concept, delivery system, propulsion, guidance and method of deployment all being totally new.

Because it was developed by the army as a form of very-long-range artillery, the A-4 was highly mobile, using a simple transporter–erector, while its size was the maximum that could be transported through a standard European railway tunnel. The missile had a range of approximately 320 km, and the warhead contained 910 kg of high explosive (Amatol). Some 4,320 A-4s were launched in anger, the principal targets being London and, later, Antwerp. The A-4 caused the Allies severe problems in the last months of the war, because there was no known defence against it, other than over-running the launching sites on the ground.

The German missile designers' sights were aimed at even more distant targets, and presaged the intercontinental-missile era with two plans for

---

* A ballistic missile is one launched by a motor which then cuts off, so that for the rest of the flight the missile follows a trajectory in which the predominant forces are gravity and aerodynamic drag.
† The German Second World War missiles had both a designer's designation and a *Vergeltungswaffen* (Vengeance Weapon) designation. The V-1 (Fieseler Fi-103). was a pulsejet-powered, winged missile. (Fieseler was a German aircraft design and manufacturing company). The V-2 (Aggregat A-4) was a rocket-powered long-range missile. (All ballistic missiles designed at the Kummersdorf and Peenemünde development centres had an '*Aggregat*' or 'model' number, starting with the A-1 in the early 1930s.)

ballistic-missile attacks on the continental USA.* The first of these envisaged mounting an A-4 missile in a submerged container/launcher which would be towed across the Atlantic behind a submarine – the embryo of the concept of submarine-launched ballistic missiles (SLBMs), which were to appear in the late 1950s. The second was for a two-stage missile with a 5,000 km range; this would have been launched against New York from sites in western France – the precursor of the intercontinental ballistic missile (ICBM). Both projects were technically feasible, but, fortunately for the Allies, the Germans ran out of time before either could be implemented. As a result of the success of the A-4, however, the Americans, Russians and British captured as many A-4s as they could, and took as many sample missiles, designs and designers as they could lay their hands on back home to develop new versions of these 'terror weapons'.

Such missiles, coupled with the most significant weapon of all, the atomic bomb, also brought into the realms of possibility the destruction of the civilized world in what US president Jimmy Carter once described as 'one long, cold, final afternoon'. The atomic bomb gave military planners new destructive power, far in excess of anything that had gone before, with one bomber or missile able to carry a warhead more powerful than thousands of its predecessors. Not surprisingly, these new weapons and new delivery means required novel strategic concepts for their use, one of the most important – and contradictory – elements of which was that they would truly fulfil their function only if they never had to be used.

THE BACKGROUND TO STRATEGY

Nuclear strategy and nuclear-weapon targeting in the Cold War were very complicated businesses, not least because all those involved were venturing into the unknown. The USA declared itself wedded to the concept of deterrence, whose fundamental proposition was that a rational opponent would not attack if the risks of retaliation outweighed the predicted gains of the attack. Caspar Weinberger, secretary of state for defense under President Reagan, stated that, to be effective, deterrence had to meet four tests:

- Survivability: our [i.e. US] forces must be able to survive a pre-emptive attack with sufficient strength to threaten losses that outweigh gains;
- Credibility: our threatened response to an attack must be credible; that is,

---

* There was also a third plan, which involved mounting a V-1 missile in a container atop the hull of a diesel-electric submarine, which would surface for the launch. This was the forerunner of the cruise missiles which were operational for a short time in the 1950s and 1960s, and again from the 1980s onwards.

of a form that the potential aggressor believes we can and would carry it out;

- Clarity: the action to be deterred must be sufficiently clear to our adversaries that the potential aggressor knows what is prohibited; and
- Safety: the risk of failure through accident, unauthorized use, or miscalculation must be minimized.[1]

In other words, an aggressor who was considering a first strike would be deterred from carrying out an attack on the enemy's population centres if he considered that the enemy would retain both the capability and the will to attack the aggressor's population in turn.

At least in public, the Soviet Union was very dismissive of the doctrine of deterrence, but such a concept seems to have been at the heart of Marshal V. D. Sokolovskiy's statement in 1975 (in what may be assumed to be a close reflection of the Kremlin's views) that:

> Nuclear rocket attacks by strategic weapons will have decisive primary significance on the outcome of a modern war. Mass nuclear attacks on the strategic nuclear weapons of the enemy, on his economy and government control system, with simultaneous defeat of the armed forces in theatres of military operations, will make it possible to attain the political aims of a war in a considerably shorter period of time than in past wars.[2]

Sokolovskiy then went on to say that:

> The basic aim of this type of military operation is to undermine the military power of the enemy by eliminating the nuclear means of fighting and formations of armed forces, and eliminating the military–economic potential by destroying the economic foundations for war, and by disrupting governmental and military control. The basic means for attaining these ends are the Strategic Rocket troops equipped with ICBMs and IRBMs with powerful thermonuclear and atomic warheads, and also long-range aviation and rocket-carrying submarines armed with rockets with nuclear warheads, hydrogen and atomic bombs. These ends can be achieved by attacks on selected objectives by nuclear rocket and nuclear aviation strikes. The most powerful attack may be the first massed nuclear rocket strike with which our Armed Forces *will retaliate against the actions of the imperialist aggressors who unleash a nuclear war* [my italics]. In making nuclear rocket and nuclear aviation strikes, military bases (air, missile and naval), industrial objects, primarily atomic, aircraft, missile, power and machine-construction plants, communications centres, ports, control points, etc. can be destroyed.[3]

In other words, the Soviet Union would have responded to a Western first strike with a massive counter-attack, directed against both military and military–industrial targets.

There were three important elements in the strategies of both sides. The first was that each side needed to have an accurate knowledge and understanding of the opponent's value system, especially when judging what would be considered 'unacceptable' and 'credible'. Second, peacetime discussions and war gaming were inevitably conducted in 'ivory-tower' conditions. The third factor in the strategic area was whether or not it was feasible to use what were termed 'tactical nuclear weapons' on the battlefield or at sea without escalating immediately to strategic nuclear warfare.

One of the fundamental requirements of deterrence, at least as discussed within the United States, was that commanders and planners needed to be certain about what the rational planner on the other side would find to be totally unacceptable. The problem was, of course, that perceptions of unacceptability can differ widely. The Russian people have been notable during many centuries for their stoic resistance to suffering; during the Second World War, for example, the western part of the USSR suffered dreadfully, with at least 20 million deaths. Nevertheless, the Soviet Union recovered remarkably quickly after the war. Further, in a state such as the USSR, where one group dominated a number of disparate groups, it seems possible that a nuclear strike in the Ukraine or Kazakhstan might not have been considered 'unacceptable' to an ethnic Russian in a command bunker in Moscow, while a nuclear attack on Moscow might have had little relevance in Siberia.

The countries of western Europe also had experienced suffering. Germany had incurred tremendous losses among its young male population, and the state had been almost totally destroyed twice in the space of thirty years, but the recoveries had been both rapid and complete. France had been occupied and had its territory fought over twice, while the British had been bombed but not occupied. British, French and German post-war planners might therefore have had some, albeit differing, perceptions of the Russian wartime suffering and what Soviet leaders might have deemed to be 'unacceptable damage'. A US planner, brought up in a country which had never suffered a direct major attack, would have had a different perception still. On the other hand, despite the openness of Western society, the Soviets may not have had sufficient knowledge and understanding of Western countries to be able to judge correctly what the United States or western Europeans would consider unacceptable losses.

An additional hazard was the distinct danger that, if a real war had started, time would have been so short that one side or the other might well have escalated rapidly to the highest level in order not to be caught out by its opponent. This was in many ways a modern equivalent of the mobilization timetables which so influenced general staffs in 1914 and were so inflexible that the generals brought enormous pressure on their governments to call up the reserves and start the railways moving in order to complete national deployment before the prospective enemy could do so.

In addition to these weighty factors, there were many other issues which were new to war planning. For example, if side A's aim was to force side B into negotiating, then it made little sense to destroy B's political and military leadership, which was precisely the group required to conduct such negotiations. Also, while A might gain some short-term military advantages by destroying B's communications systems, such destruction would only prevent B's leadership from communicating with the attackers to negotiate a cessation of hostilities. A further factor was that the loss of communications would prevent B's leadership from exercising control over its subordinates, giving rise to the possibility that the junior echelons might then act in a totally unpredictable and irrational manner. This could possibly escalate the war well beyond what A's leadership had planned and force B into escalatory retaliation, to which A then felt it necessary to respond, and so on. Thus, while in virtually all previous wars, up to and including the Second World War, it had been a traditional aim to destroy the enemy's capital city and communications systems, in a Third World War it might have proved more effective and symbolic to leave them alone, while destroying other cities.*

Another novel factor, of growing importance during the Cold War, was that in earlier eras it had been assumed that war and military matters in general were best left to the military, and that academics, if they insisted on meddling, should confine their attentions to military history. To be sure, an occasional civilian commentator might use either newspapers or books to publish his views, but defence matters were considered the province of admirals and generals, who in turn consigned the detail to the commanders and colonels. One of the significant innovations during the Cold War, however, was the increasing interest taken by sections of the academic community, particularly in matters of nuclear strategy, and an enormous volume of articles, theses and books appeared. Such academics, particularly in the United States, sometimes also achieved positions of great influence in the government.

One contradiction these academics could not escape was that if they had 'inside' official information it was invariably so highly classified that they could not use it, while if they did not have such information their arguments were unavoidably based on information available in the public sector, which was frequently out of date, incomplete or, in some cases, just wrong. To take just one example, in the mid-1950s various books were published based on the hypothesis that H-bombs could never be reduced in size sufficiently to fit on the front end of an ICBM, the authors being quite unaware that, even as they wrote, such 'miniaturized' warheads were actually under test.

A further problem facing the population at large was that public pronouncements by senior service officers (especially when appearing before congressional or parliamentary committees) were almost always gloomy. Their equipment, they claimed, was at best obsolescent, and the shining new

---

* This explains why Moscow was a 'withhold' in most US nuclear plans.

equipment which had been introduced into service the previous year with such ceremony was now completely outclassed by something just introduced by the enemy; and, in any case, the manpower was insufficient. But they would always claim that, given more money, new equipment, greater resources and more men – and provided these were given to the admiral's or general's own service or branch of service – all would be solved.*

Indeed, there were frequently two quite different agendas, especially in the United States. On the one side there was the public rhetoric, which was frequently designed to meet political or even bureaucratic aims – e.g. congressional appropriations or the aims of national (sometimes even local) politics and even inter-service rivalries. On the other side were the real policy and the actual governmental plans for the employment of the nuclear arsenal in a real-world conflict.

A particular case was the concept of the triad, a term which originated in the US Department of Defense and which was used to describe – and justify – a threefold order of strategic forces, consisting of sea-based missiles, land-based missiles and bombers. In reality it was not so much a philosophical concept – although it certainly had a fine Hegelian ring to it† – as an attempt to rationalize a situation which already existed and to continue to procure new systems to equip all three legs, such as bombers, which might not otherwise have been sustainable.

TYPES OF ATTACK

Various types of attack were envisaged. *First strike* (also known as a 'pre-emptive strike') was the most feared, in which one superpower would launch an attack on its opponent's strategic weapons with no preliminary warning and no sign of a build-up. In such a case the target superpower might have received about thirty minutes' warning of weapons being launched from the opponent's home territory, although it was always possible that some weapons might be launched from closer in (e.g. by Soviet Yankee-class nuclear-powered ballistic-missile submarines (SSBNs) patrolling off the US coast, or US Pershing missiles located in West Germany), when the warning would have been of the order of four minutes.

One of the possible responses to an incoming first strike was *launch-on-*

---

* Extensive research by the author has failed to unearth a single example of a general or admiral proposing that his own service or branch of service should be reduced in size since national defence would be better served by an increase elsewhere.
† Hegel postulated that all progress is the outcome of a conflict of opposites, or that thesis and antithesis interact to produce a synthesis. From this some twentieth century thinkers have suggested that everything is organized in a threefold system: e.g. earth, air, water.

warning, in which the victim launched its ICBMs in the minutes available between detecting the strike and its actual arrival. The main problem with this was that the aggressor would almost certainly have retained a reserve of ICBMs and it seemed unlikely that, in the time available, the victim would have been able to establish which silos the incoming missiles had been launched from and thus which silos remained occupied and so were worth attacking. It appeared logical, therefore, that a launch-on-warning aimed at enemy ICBM silos and thus hitting many empty silos would have been largely wasted and that such a strike would more profitably have been aimed at 'other military targets' (see below).

US strategists discussed a possible Soviet strategy known as '*pin down*', which postulated that Soviet SLBMs might be launched from SSBNs close to the US coast to prevent a launch-on-warning by US ICBMs. It was at least theoretically possible that such SLBMs could have been aimed and timed in such a way that they exploded among the US ICBMs as they lifted off from their silos, thus either destroying the US missiles or seriously affecting their accuracy.

Another form of Soviet strike which caused concern to US planners was the development of the *Fractional Orbital Bombardment System* (FOBS), which involved launching a missile into a low (approximately 160 km) orbit and then, after less than one complete orbit, firing retrorockets to make the warhead descend rapidly and steeply on to the target. This would have greatly reduced the warning time and, because the missiles would have approached the continental USA from a hitherto unexpected direction (south-east), it forced the USA to build a new radar station at Eglin Air Force Base in Florida. The Soviets tested both SS-9 and SS-X-10 missiles in this role, but neither was ever deployed operationally.

At the lowest end of the strategic nuclear ladder was the use of a very small number of nuclear weapons in an *exemplary* (or *demonstrative*) attack, intended to show determination either to use nuclear weapons on a large scale, if pushed any further, or to attack certain types of target. Such an attack would have had to be either preceded or accompanied by a specific warning to make it clear to the other side what was intended, but there was an argument that such an attack would invite retaliation in kind, in which the other side would launch a similar number of warheads against similar types of target. Indeed, the other side might well have felt compelled to make a response-in-kind even if it intended to take matters no further.* Thus the originator of an exemplary attack needed to expect similar losses and casualties to its opponent's, which (at least in theory) would not have been

---

* In *The Third World War; August 1985*, the war depicted by General Sir John Hackett culminates in a single Soviet strike on the British city of Birmingham, to which the USA and the UK immediately respond by launching two missiles each at the city of Minsk.[4]

escalatory. Contingency plans for such 'demonstrations' were included in NATO nuclear planning, and were certainly part of the Berlin plans.*

One step higher on the ladder of nuclear escalation was a *limited-objective attack*. Attacks on numerous types of target fell into this category, such as Soviet strikes against one or more US carrier groups, US strikes against Soviet naval surface-action groups, and strikes against bases such as Pearl Harbor or Plesetsk. The Soviet Union was considered more likely than the USA to undertake such strikes, although the USA needed to have the capability in case it was required for a response-in-kind. The conduct of such attacks would have required elaborate command-and-control facilities, and it could well have been very difficult for the victim to distinguish between tactical and strategic weapons (if, indeed, such a distinction retained any relevance once war had started).

Massive counter-military attacks also covered a wide spectrum of possibilities, ranging from a strike at the opponent's strategic offensive forces to an all-out attack on all military forces, logistics installations, military-oriented research establishments and military–industrial facilities. Targets for such an attack would have been selected from a list of some 10,000 such targets in the USSR and some 5,000–7,000 in the USA. Such an attack could not avoid collateral damage to urban centres and would, at least in theory, have been deterred by a city-attack capability.

Throughout the Cold War both sides intended to maintain a reserve of weapons as an *urban–industrial reserve*, which was to be used as a last resort, when all else had failed, against the enemy's vitals. Thus US plans for a response-in-kind following a Soviet first strike against ICBM sites could only have been carried out using weapons which were not part of the urban–industrial reserve. There was a point, certainly in US planning in the 1970s, where targeting enemy cities simply in order to kill people changed to a more precise form of targeting in which specific military, economic and political targets were selected with the intention of inhibiting the enemy's post-war recovery.

All US plans, and presumably the Soviets' too, enabled the plan to be implemented with the exclusion of either a specific target or targets, or of a category of target. In US strategic jargon, these were known as '*withholds*'. Thus communications systems were withholds, in some US plans, while Moscow was a withhold in a US attack on major cities.† The Reagan plans, however, specifically instructed that weapons were to be retained to attack such 'withholds', presumably on the semantic ground that if a target was omitted from a plan but no weapons were left to attack it, it was an 'exclusion' rather than a withhold.

---

* See page 337.
† It should be noted, however, that a withhold in a US nuclear plan might not also have been withheld in British, Chinese or French national targeting plans.

Response-in-kind was designed to attack the same character of target and to inflict casualties of the same order of magnitude as the attack being replied to. To be credible it had maintain the same character of engagement, although it was foreseen, at least in the USA, that it could be escalatory if force assymetries existed such that the opponent could not counter-escalate.[5]

Nth-country reserve was a concept in which a superpower retained a reserve of strategic weapons to deal with another country, apart from the opposing superpower. At the height of the Cold War this might have been China in the case of the USA, and France and the UK in the case of the USSR.

TYPES OF TARGET

The USA divided targets into three major categories: counter-force, counter-value, and other military targets.

Counter-force targets were the enemy's strategic nuclear forces, which comprised ICBM silos, bomber bases and SSBNs in harbour. The category also included political and military nuclear command-and-control centres, and their relevant communications systems. Such targets were given progressively greater protective 'hardening' as the Cold War progressed, and their destruction depended increasingly upon the power and accuracy of the warheads.

Counter-value targets were cities and industrial complexes. In the late 1980s the USA had 162 cities with populations greater than 100,000, of which thirty-five exceeded 1 million inhabitants. In contrast, the USSR had 254 cities of over 100,000, of which only thirteen exceeded 1 million inhabitants. Western Europe had some exceptional concentrations, including eight areas with over 2.5 million inhabitants. For the USA and the USSR, cities were the targets for their SLBMs and the less accurate ICBMs.

Other military targets covered a collection of low-collateral-damage, high-military-value targets, including barracks, nuclear storage sites, nuclear production facilities, and headquarters. According to US sources there were about 2,000–3,000 such targets in the USSR and approximately 1,000 in the USA, although Soviet target analysts could well have included more in the USA.

WARHEADS

In the original ballistic missiles, such as the German A-4 and its immediate derivatives, the warhead was an integral part of the missile. From the mid-1950s onwards, however, the warhead separated from the missile in space and descended on an independent, unpowered trajectory to the target; the missile itself thus became simply a means of transportation. Initially, such re-entry vehicles (RVs) contained one warhead each, but by the early 1960s US and Soviet strategic planners found themselves faced by many more targets than they had missiles. One possible solution was to build vast numbers of missiles, but this would have required an equal number of silos, plus the associated command-and-control facilities, and would have been extremely expensive.

The first practicable solution was the use of multiple re-entry vehicles (MRVs), in which several RVs were placed on one missile and, like the shot from a hunting gun, were all aimed at the same target, thus increasing the chance of a kill. A variation on this theme was to aim the MRVs at several targets within the same small area, and the three MRVs on the Soviet SS-9 Mod 4, for example, were aimed to impact with the same spatial dispersion as the three silos in a US Minuteman complex.

Technology moved on quickly, and it then became possible to target each warhead independently on to separate targets. This was achieved by mounting them on a post-boost vehicle (PBV, also known as a 'bus'), which, under computer control, dispatched its RVs one at a time according to the targeting programme. Such warheads were known as 'multiple independently targeted re-entry vehicles' (MIRVs), and eventually missiles were carrying as many as fourteen. Unfortunately, radar observation was able to determine how many such devices were being launched by a particular missile bus by counting the number of course alterations (known as 'dips'), so the RVs were equipped with decoys and 'penetration aids' which matched the real RVs' radar and thermal signature, to confuse the defences.

Single warheads, MRVs and MIRVs all followed ballistic trajectories, which could be rapidly and accurately predicted by the defence, but as the Cold War came to an end a new type of warhead, the Manoeuvrable Re-entry Vehicle (MaRV), was under development, although it did not attain operational status.

THROW WEIGHT

The maximum missile payload was termed the 'throw weight', and during the SALT II negotiations this was defined as the sum of the weights of the RVs, the post-boost vehicle and any anti-ballistic-missile penetration aids, including the devices to release the RVs. Throw weight was thus a function of the power of the missile's propulsion system, and increased steadily over the years. In any one missile the amount of fuel was fixed, so the only way to alter the range was by varying the payload – i.e. by reducing the number of RVs, 'penaids' or decoys.

One of the significant elements of throw weight was that it showed the potential for future improvements, since existing throw weight could be fractionated to provide a greater number of smaller warheads, thus increasing the war-fighting capability. As designers became more able to reduce the size of warheads, however, throw weight became less important, and it was in any case never an indication of a system's ability to destroy targets at the far end of the flight.

ACCURACY

The accuracy of missile RVs is expressed as the circular error probable (CEP), which is defined as the radius of a circle, centred upon the *mean point of impact*, within which 50 per cent of the warheads aimed at the target will fall. The size of the CEP is determined by a combination of computer calculations and empirical data obtained from the testing programme, and is normally understood to apply to the missile's maximum range. When fired to less than that range, the CEP reduces in proportion.*

Of greater importance is the distance between the mean point of impact and the target itself, which is termed *bias*. This is similar to the deflection of a rifle bullet by wind, and in the case of a missile is a result of the cumulative effect on the trajectory of the missile and the RV of system errors such as uneven erosion of the ablative shield† during re-entry and errors in components such as the on-board accelerometer, as well as unforeseeable events such as the weather over the target.

TIMING

Timing was, for both sides, a critical consideration. In launching a first strike, for example, there was a host of weapons to be co-ordinated, including:

- home-based ICBMs;
- SSBNs – some close to enemy shores, some in transit and some at their bases;

---

* Thus, if a missile with a maximum range of 10,000 km with a CEP of 1 km is fired at a target 8,000 km distant, the CEP will be $1 \times (8,000 \div 10,000) = 0.8$ km. It should be noted, however, that the CEP has always been a fairly uncertain figure, not least because neither the USA nor the USSR was keen to reveal the CEP of its own warheads with too great a degree of precision.
† The ablative shield is designed to ease the RV's re-entry into the atmosphere and is constructed of materials which are intended to erode.

- medium -range ballistic missiles (MRBMs) with shorter flight times (e.g. US Pershing MRBMs based in West Germany);
- bombers.

In addition, the USA had to consider:

- US navy carrier groups at sea;
- British and French nuclear forces;
- European-based NATO aircraft;
- airbases around the world with aircraft with roles in the US missile attack plans.

'FRATRICIDE'

There were also many technical restrictions. It was discovered in the 1970s, for example, that an attack by several warheads on a single target – or a simultaneous attack on an entire missile field – would inevitably lead to 'fratricide', in which the explosion of the first warheads to arrive would either destroy the subsequent warheads or knock them off course. This effectively reduced the number of warheads that could attack any one target to two within a few seconds of each other, followed by a gap of some ten to twenty minutes before a further attack could be undertaken.

9

Intercontinental Ballistic Missiles

Snark and Navaho

In the immediate post-war years the feeling in the United States was that ballistic missiles offered the best long-term solution for strategic warfare, but that the technology of the time did not appear to make it possible to build a missile with the necessary range (9,300 km) and capable of carrying a nuclear payload, which at that time was large and heavy, weighing some 3 tonnes. The Convair company flight-tested the intercontinental-range MX-774 missile in 1948, but the newly independent US air force decided to follow the path pioneered by the German V-1 'flying bomb' and to develop cruise missiles* instead.

The first of these was the N-69 Snark pilotless bomber, which was much larger than the V-1 and had a range of 10,200 km, cruising at a height of some 12,000 m and using a star tracker to update its inertial navigation system. Its speed of 990 km/h meant, however, that, at its extreme range, it took some eleven hours to reach the target. The nose-cone carried a 5 MT (later 20 MT) nuclear warhead, and the missile could approach the target from any direction and at any height, while its very small radar cross-section made it difficult to detect. The Snark entered service in 1957 but was retired in 1961, when the Atlas ballistic missile became operational; its main significance was that it was the first operational missile to bring one superpower within attacking range of the other.

Snark was due to be succeeded by the SM-64A Navaho, a vertically

---

* A cruise missile flies within the earth's atmosphere, using aerodynamic lift to overcome gravity and an engine/motor to overcome drag. It is essentially an aircraft with some form of guidance system to replace a human pilot.

launched, winged cruise missile, which travelled at Mach 3.25 (3,500 km/h) at a height of 18,300 m. Navaho would almost certainly have proved a highly effective strategic weapon, but it never reached production, as the USAF had already transferred its attention to ICBMs.*

Redstone and Jupiter

Development of long-range ballistic missiles in the United States in the immediate post-war years was erratic, to say the least. The US army had obtained the plans for the A-4 (V-2) and assembled a number of former German scientists, including Werner von Braun, at the Redstone Arsenal. Their first product was the Redstone short-range (400 km), land-mobile, liquid-fuelled, nuclear-armed missile, which was in service from 1958 to 1963. Next the army started to develop the Jupiter, which was again a land-mobile missile system, but this time with a range of 2,400 km. This was midway through development when, in late 1956, the secretary of state for defense ordered that the US air force was to assume responsibility for all missiles with a range greater than 200 nautical miles (370 km). Development was completed by the USAF, and Jupiter subsequently saw limited service with the air force.

Thor

Having been concentrating on long-range cruise missiles, the USAF now had to make up for a lot of lost ground. Despite having been handed the perfectly acceptable Jupiter by the army, it initiated a very expensive crash programme for its own IRBM, leading to the Thor. This did nothing that Jupiter could not already do, but operated from a fixed base, rather than from a mobile platform. Thor's 2,700 km range, however, was insufficient for the missile to be launched against the USSR from the continental USA, so it was handed over to the UK air force, which deployed sixty missiles between 1959 and 1964.

The entire Thor storage-and-launch complex was above ground in unprotected shelters, and the missile had be towed out to the launch pad, raised to the vertical, fuelled, prepared, and then launched, the whole process taking fifteen minutes. This was all done in the open, on concrete hard-standing, at well-documented sites, and was very vulnerable. No cost-effective measure to reduce the reaction time could be found, so the missile was phased out after only five years of service.

---

* The specifications of German and US land-based strategic missiles are given in Appendix 7.

Atlas

Meanwhile, the USAF's major development effort had turned to the Atlas missile, which was much larger and was a true ICBM, with a range of 14,000 km. Atlas benefited from much of the technology which had been developed for the Navaho cruise missile, and entered service in 1960.

The first USAF squadron equipped with the Atlas missile used an almost identical siting system to Thor, with six above-ground shelters and each missile having a thirty-minute launch countdown, but the next squadron's nine missiles were in three separated groups of three, with individual shelters having a split roof, enabling the missiles to be raised to the vertical *in situ*, thus saving several minutes of launch time. The next three squadrons had similarly dispersed sites, but this time the missiles were housed in semi-hardened bunkers, recessed into the ground and with even greater separation. The final units were housed in hardened underground silos.

Titan

Titan I, which had a range of 10,000 km, was, like the final Atlas, located in silos and raised to the surface for launch; however, it had a new and much faster fuelling system, enabling it to be launched some twenty minutes after the countdown started. There were five Titan I sites, one with eighteen missiles and four with nine each, but the system had only a brief period of service, becoming operational in 1961 and being replaced by Titan II from 1963 onwards, the process being completed in 1966.

Despite its name, Titan II was almost totally different from Titan I, not least because of a 50 per cent increase in range, to 15,000 km. Again, the missiles were sited in squadrons consisting of three widely separated groups of three, with two squadrons at each of three bases, but the new system introduced a completely novel launch system, with the missile being launched from inside the silo. Two other advances in this missile were the use of an inertial guidance system and the use of storable liquid fuel – i.e. the fuel was already loaded in the missile, thus cutting out the time needed to fuel the earlier missiles. In combination these developments resulted in a launch time of just sixty seconds. Fifty-four missiles were deployed, being operational from 1963 to 1987.

Minuteman

By now, the future obviously lay with solid-fuelled missiles, which were safer and more reliable, and in simpler, cheaper and more survivable siting and launch systems. A rail-mobile system was considered for Minuteman I, but the silo option won.

The two-stage Minuteman I was deployed from 1962 onwards in individual unmanned silos, which were scattered over large areas. Ten silos were grouped into a 'flight', five flights in a 'squadron', and squadrons into 'wings'; there were four squadrons in each of four wings, while the fifth wing had five squadrons. The overall total was 800 missiles.

Minuteman II was longer and heavier than Minuteman I, with extended range (12,500 km compared to 10,000 km) and a more accurate warhead. It entered service in 1966, and by 1969 it had replaced all Minuteman Is. Of the 450 deployed, ten were subsequently reconfigured to carry the Emergency Rocket Communications System (ERCS) and thus no longer carried nuclear warheads.*

Minuteman III introduced a third stage and was also the first US ICBM to carry MIRVs, but its basing and launch systems were the same as those of Minuteman II.

Peacekeeper (MX)

The Missile, Experimental (MX) programme was one of the longest and most controversial in the Cold War, with much of the argument centring on the question of basing. Indeed, MX consumed money at a prodigious rate and gave rise to an industry of its own for many years before it began to make any contribution to Western deterrence. The programme started in the early 1970s, and eventually resulted in the fielding of just fifty Peacekeeper missiles in 1986. After all the argument on different basing systems, these were placed in Minuteman III silos. Peacekeeper had a range of 9,600 km and carried ten W-87 warheads, each with a yield of 300 kT and an accuracy (CEP) of 100 m, giving them an extremely high lethality. During the Cold War these would almost inevitably have been targeted on both Soviet leadership bunkers and 'superhardened' ICBM silos.

SOVIET ICBM DEVELOPMENT[†]

The first official rocket-propulsion laboratory in the Soviet Union was opened in 1921, but attention was concentrated on short-range artillery missiles until after the Second World War, when the USSR produced a copy of the German A-4, known under the NATO system as the SS-1, 'Scud'.[‡] The SS-2, 'Sibling', was similar, but with Soviet advances to increase range and reliability, while the SS-3, 'Shyster', was the first to carry an atomic warhead.

---

* ERCS involved placing a communications package on the missile in place of the warhead. The missiles could then be launched to provide communications relay facilities between national command posts and nuclear forces in the event that all other means of communication had been lost.

† The specifications of Soviet land-based strategic missiles are given in Appendix 8.

‡ This missile served in the Red Army for many years, and developed versions are still in wide-scale use in the 1990s in Middle Eastern and Asian armies.

SS-6

In the 1950s the USSR found itself without a strategic bomber force to counter the B-36s, B-47s and B-52s of the USAF, and the quickest way to produce an answer was an ICBM. The technology of the time was, however, comparatively crude: warheads were heavy, and the sum total of the components, the payload and the fuel needed for intercontinental range came to well over 200 tonnes. Nevertheless, the USSR, which was never deterred by the size of a project, pressed ahead to produce the huge SS-6, 'Sapwood', which first flew on 3 August 1957. The necessary thrust was obtained by using a basic missile surrounded by four large strap-on boosters, the main missile and each booster having a 102,00 kgf thrust rocket motor. Thus, the device had a launch weight of no less than 300 tonnes, but was powered by motors with a total thrust of 510,000 kgf.

As a strategic weapon the SS-6 was less than successful: it had a poor reaction time, due to the need to load huge quantities of cryogenic fuel,* it was far too big to be put in a silo, its electronics were crude and unreliable, and it was very inaccurate, with a CEP of some 8 km. The knowledge that the USSR had such a powerful launch vehicle had a major psychological impact on the USA, but no more than four SS-6s were ever deployed operationally as ICBMs. The SS-6 was, however, used for space launches for many years, since it could lift the heavy weights needed for programmes such as Sputnik, Luna, Vostok, Voshkod, Mars and Venera.

SS-7/SS-8

The first really successful Soviet ICBM was the SS-7, 'Saddler', of which 186 were deployed from 1961 until it was withdrawn in 1979 under the terms of SALT I. The SS-7 was the first Soviet missile to enter service using storable liquid fuel. It had two stages giving it a range of some 11,500 km, and was therefore the first Soviet ICBM to pose a realistic threat to the continental USA, although its relative inaccuracy (it had a CEP of 2.8 km) restricted it to counter-value targets.

It was long a feature of Soviet military philosophy that an ambitious programme was backed up by a much less demanding and technically safer system, which in this case was the SS-8, 'Sasin'. Only twenty-three SS-8s were ever deployed, and they had a limited life from 1965 to 1977.

SS-9/SS-10

The SS-9, 'Scarp', was the first of the second generation of Soviet ICBMs: a heavy, silo-based missile which became operational in 1966. Numbers

---

* Cryogenic fuels are liquified gases which need to be kept at low temperatures and are therefore difficult to handle.

peaked at 313 in 1970, remaining at this level until 1975, when retirements began, the last of the type being withdrawn in 1979. Four versions were known: the first to enter service was Mod 1, which had a 20 MT warhead, while Mod 2, the principal production version, had a 25 MT warhead – by far the most powerful warhead ever to achieve operational status in any country. The Mod 3 was a special version which was used to test the Fractional Orbital Bombardment System (FOBS), which was designed to attack the USA from the south-east; it caused considerable concern in the Pentagon. Mod 4 carried three MRVs, which impacted with the same spread as a typical USAF Minuteman missile complex, although it never actually entered service, the mission being allocated to the SS-11 Mod 3 instead.

The SS-10, 'Scrag', was the insurance against the failure of the SS-9. This huge missile, which used cryogenic fuels, was shown at the 1968 Red Square parade but never entered service.

SS-11

The two-stage SS-11, 'Sego', used storable liquid propellant and entered service in 1966, eventually serving in three principal variants. Mod 1 had a single 950 kT warhead, Mod 2 had increased range and throw weight, as well as penetration aids and a more accurate warhead, while Mod 3 carried three 200 kT MRVs, the first such system to be fielded by the USSR, with a footprint virtually identical with that of Minuteman silos. The SS-11 had a long life, with just over half being replaced by the SS-17 and SS-19 in the late 1970s, while the balance of 420 remained until 1987, when they were replaced progressively by the road-mobile SS-25.

SS-13

Developed concurrently with the SS-11, the SS-13, 'Savage', was the first solid-fuel Soviet ICBM, and had an unusual construction with three stages linked by open Warren-girder trusses – a configuration matched only by the earlier SS-10. There were claims in the early 1970s that the SS-13 was being used in a mobile role, but these were never substantiated. The USSR claimed that the SS-25 was a modified version of the SS-13 (which was permitted under SALT II), and flew two missiles in 1986 to demonstrate that this was the case to the USA. Only sixty SS-13s entered service, and the production and maintenance of such a small number must have been very expensive. However, it must be assumed that it played a useful role in the Soviet nuclear force, as the SS-13 remained in service from 1972 until past the end of the Cold War.

SS-17

The SS-17, 'Spanker', which used storable liquid propellant, was developed in parallel with the SS-19 as a replacement for the SS-11 and was in service from 1975 to 1990. It was the first Soviet ICBM to be launched by using a gas generator to blow the missile out of the silo, with ignition taking place only when the missile was well clear. Known as the 'cold-launch technique', this method minimized damage to the silo and enabled it to be reused. This caused considerable alarm in the United States, as it was seen to indicate a plan for a nuclear war lasting several days, if not weeks. The second innovation was that several versions carried MIRVs, the first operational Soviet ICBMs to do so: Mods 1 and 3 carried four 200 kT MIRVs, but the Soviets, as always, hedged their bets, and the SS-17 Mod 2 carried a single 3.6 MT warhead.

SS-18

The SS-18, 'Satan', the successor to the SS-9, was by far the largest ICBM to be fielded by either of the two superpowers, and its throw weight of 8,800 kg was the greatest of any Cold War missile. Starting in 1975, it was deployed in former SS-9 silos, which were modified and upgraded to take the new missile. Mods 1 and 3 both had a single large 20 MT warhead, while Mods 2 and 4 each had ten 500 kT MIRVs. The SS-18 was described by the USA as 'extremely accurate' and 'designed to attack hard targets, such as US ICBM silos'. Also, according to US sources, the SS-18 force was capable of destroying '65–80% of the US ICBM force, using two warheads against each. Even after such an attack, there would still be over 1,000 SS-18 warheads available for further strikes against US targets.'[1]

SS-19

The SS-19, 'Stiletto', was developed in parallel to the SS-17 and entered service in 1971, with a peak deployment of 360; it was the most widely used Soviet ICBM of its generation. It was a hot-launch missile, although it was housed in a canister which reduced silo damage. Various versions of the missile were developed, but the service version was the Mod 3, with six 550 kT MIRVs, each with a CEP of 400 m, which, again according to US sources, meant that 'while less accurate than the SS-18, [it had] significant capability against all but hardened silos. It could also be used against targets in Eurasia.'[2] It would therefore appear safe to assume that the SS-19 was targeted against counter-force targets, such as reasonably hardened military targets, but not against ICBM silos, which were the task of the SS-18.

SS-24

The SS-24, 'Scalpel', was fielded in two launch modes, the Mod 1 being rail-mobile, while Mod 2 was silo-based. The actual missiles in each variant were virtually identical, being ten 500 kT MIRVS with a range of 10,000 km and a CEP of 200 m. Mod 1 was deployed in trains with three launchers each, with three rail garrisons, all in Russia; there were four trains each at

101

Kostromo and Krasnoyarsk and three trains at Bershet. Fifty-six of the silo-launched version (Mod 2) were deployed, split between one site in Russia (ten silos) and one site in the Ukraine (forty-six silos).

SS-25

The SS-25, 'Sickle', was the last Soviet ICBM to be fielded during the Cold War. It was a single-warhead missile, carrying one highly accurate 550 kT warhead, and entered service in 1985. At the end of the Cold War 288 missiles were split between nine sites, with further missiles being deployed up to 1994. The missile was road-mobile, but was normally housed in a garage with a sliding roof which could be opened for an emergency launch. Given the necessary warning, however, the fourteen-wheel TELs were deployed to pre-surveyed sites in forests, where they were raised on jacks for stability during launch.

The SS-25 missile was contained in a large cylindrical canister, and the system was reloadable, highly survivable and capable of rapid retargeting. This led US sources to speculate that it was designed for use in a protracted nuclear war as a reserve weapon, when it would ride out the first wave of US attacks on the Soviet nuclear arsenal and then retaliate against surviving targets, which could be selected and set into the warhead at the time. It was during the flight testing of the SS-25 that the Soviets first used encryption on their telemetry down-links, which caused the US to claim that they were acting in contravention of the SALT II agreement.

BASING

The original German A-4 missile employed a brilliantly simple road-mobile system, in which the missile was carried on a four-wheeled trailer known as a *Meillerwagen*. When the missile was to be launched, the *Meillerwagen* raised it to the vertical and then lowered it on to a small launch platform. Each site had a crew of 136 men, with many more men and vehicles in the logistics chain.

The Germans also gave active consideration to launching the A-4 missile from a train. According to a 1944 plan, each train would carry six ready-to-use missiles, and include an erector–launcher car, seven fuel-tanker cars, a generator car, a workshop, a spares car and several cars for the crew. On top of this, however, the train would also carry all the vehicles normally associated with a missile battery, in order that the unit could dismount from the train and operate independently of it, which brought the whole battery up to the unwieldy total of seventy to eighty freight cars, probably requiring at least two separate trains. Separate logistic trains were planned to bring further supplies of fuel and missiles. Prototype trains were running before the end of the war, but the system was not a practicable proposition in view of the air supremacy of the Allies, for whom all trains were a high-priority target.[3]

ICBM forces were originally built to threaten the opponent's civil population, which in itself was not a difficult task: the warheads were relatively inaccurate, but the cities were large and the warheads powerful. It was obviously highly desirable, from both political and military viewpoints, to defend the population from this threat, in the same way that bombers had been opposed by a mixture of fighters and anti-aircraft guns during the recent war. It was not feasible at the time to intercept incoming ICBMs, so the only defence was to attack the ICBMs at their source, which could be done only by conducting a pre-emptive strike with other ICBMs. Thus the position was rapidly reached where the ICBMs' principal target was the other side's ICBMs, moving on to other missions only when that first battle had been decided. It was therefore necessary to optimize the attacking potential of one's own missiles while ensuring their survivability in the face of an opponent's first strike. There were four possibilities:

- superhardened silos, which would withstand even the most powerful incoming warhead;
- using a greater number of silos than missiles, so that the opponent would waste warheads on empty silos;
- making the missiles mobile, as the Germans did, so that the enemy could not locate them;
- using anti-ballistic-missile (ABM) defences.

The essence of the problem can be illustrated by a simplified example in which the aggressor (A) has 100 ICBMs, each with ten warheads, while the other side (B) has 500 ICBMs, each with three warheads. (For the purpose of this example, all missiles and warheads are perfectly available and reliable, and each warhead will kill one silo.) Thus A is capable of destroying 1,000 silos, and if he carries out a pre-emptive strike he requires to use only fifty missiles, leaving B with no missiles. A still has fifty missiles and is clearly the winner. If, however, B builds another 500 silos, but no more missiles, and spreads his 500 ICBMs randomly among the 1,000 silos, A, not knowing which silos are occupied, must attack all 1,000. Both sides then end up with zero ICBMs, which is a better outcome for B than the first, but is unsatisfactory from a military point of view. But if B now builds a total of 2,000 silos, half his missiles (i.e. 250) must survive the attack.

Silos
The first missiles, such as the early Atlas and Thor, were located in a shed, primarily for protection from the weather, and were taken out to enable them to be raised to the vertical for fuelling and launch. The missiles were also

located close to each other. Both factors together made the missiles extremely vulnerable to incoming missiles, which did not need to be too accurate to achieve a kill.*

The next step was to place the missiles in semi-hardened shelters and to separate these shelters so that one incoming warhead could not destroy more than one missile. In addition, the shelters had split roofs, so that the missile could be raised, fuelled and launched without wasting time moving it out on to a launch pad. As the perception of the threat increased, the spacing between individual missiles increased yet further and the shelters became bunkers, recessed into the ground.

The next step was to mount the missile vertically rather than horizontally, and to put it in a hole in the ground. The USAF, however, adopted a 'halfway' system with the Atlas and Titan I missiles, in which the missile stood upright in a silo which, in the case of Atlas, was some 53 m deep and 16 m in diameter, resting on the launch platform, which was counterbalanced by a 150 tonne weight. The launch procedure involved fuelling the missile in the silo and then using hydraulic rams to raise the entire launch platform and missile to the surface, where the missile was then launched. Titan I had a super-fast fuelling system and a high-speed elevator which reduced reaction time to approximately twenty minutes, while the silo and all associated facilities were hardened to withstand an overpressure of 20 kgf/cm^2.

A completely new launch system was introduced with Titan II, in which the missile was launched direct from the silo. There was, however, considerable concern about the effects of the rocket efflux on the missile during the few seconds that the missile was still inside the silo, so the missile rested on a large flame deflector, which directed the efflux into two large ducts exhausting to the atmosphere a short distance from the silo. Each missile complex was 45 m deep and 17 m wide and occupied nine levels, which housed electrical power, air conditioning, ventilation, and environmental protection, as well as hazard sensors and the associated corrective devices. At the centre was the launch duct, in which the missile was suspended in an environmentally controlled atmosphere. A walkway extended from the missile silo to a blast lock which provided controlled access between the silo and the tunnels leading upward to the above-ground access and laterally to the launch-control centre (LCC). The LCC was a three-level, shock-isolated cage suspended from a reinforced-concrete dome and housed two officers and two enlisted men. As with the Titan I silo, the Titan II silo was hardened to 20 kgf/cm^2.

When it learned that the Soviets were launching direct from the silo, the

---

* This explains the brevity of Thor's operational life with the UK air force.

USAF followed suit and the Minuteman I missile became the first US missile to use the 'hot launch', in which the missile rose from the silo surrounded by the flames and smoke from the rocket motor. The next Soviet innovation was the 'cold launch', in which a gas generator within the silo produced a pressure sufficient to propel the missile some 20–30 m clear of the silo before its first-stage motor fired. This protected the silo from damage, enabling it to be reused within a fairly short space of time. It was used by the Soviets from the SS-17 onwards, and by the USAF in Peacekeeper (MX).

Following their introduction in the mid-1960s, underground silos became increasingly complicated and expensive structures. Ideally they were located at a relatively high altitude, to improve the missiles' range, and in springy ground, to absorb as much as possible of the shock waves from incoming warheads. The silo was a vertical, steel/reinforced-concrete tube, housing an elaborate suspension and shock-isolation system which supported the missile as well as providing further insulation to minimize the transfer of shock motion from the walls and floor of the silo to the missile. The top third of the silo housed maintenance and launch facilities, which were known as the 'head works' in USAF parlance. Finally, the missile tube was capped by a massive sliding door, which provided protection against overpressure by transmitting the shock caused by the explosion of an incoming warhead to the cover supports rather than to the vertical tube containing the missile; it also provided protection against radiation and EMP effects. The door was designed to sweep the area as it opened, to prevent debris falling into the silo tube and possibly interfering with the launch process.

Individual silos were grouped together for control purposes, but were sited sufficiently far apart to ensure that one incoming warhead could not destroy more than one missile. Control was exercised by an underground command centre, manned by a small crew of watchkeepers, whose functions included operating the dual-key safety system in which launch could be authorized only by two officers acting independently. This command centre was linked to its superior headquarters and to the individual silos under its control by telecommunications and by systems-monitoring links. This introduced a further problem: the vulnerability of these links to blast and, in particular, to electromagnetic pulses (EMP). Making these links survivable against the perceived threats (known as 'nuclear hardening') became an increasingly complex and expensive undertaking as the Cold War progressed.

The protection factor ('hardness') of a silo was measured by its ability to withstand the overpressure resulting from the blast effects of a nuclear explosion, and was expressed in kilograms-force per square centimetre (kgf/cm^2) or pounds per square inch (psi) (1 kgf/cm$^2 \approx 14.2$ psi). In the

USA, the Atlas, Titan I and Titan II silos were constructed with a hardness of 20 kgf/cm² (300 psi), while the Minuteman I silos (mid-1960s) were built with a hardness of some 85 kgf/cm² (1,200 psi). Finally, in the 1970s, Minuteman III/Peacekeeper silos were built with a hardness of 140 kgf/cm² (2,000 psi). By this time, however, the silos were so expensive that, despite reports that the Soviets were 'superhardening' their silos to resist over-pressures of 425 kgf/cm² (6,000 psi), Congress repeatedly refused to authorize any further hardening of US silos.

The Soviet programme of silo building, refurbishment and hardening was more successful. The earliest silos, built before 1969, were hardened to withstand an overpressure of some 7 kgf/cm² (100 psi), with the next generation built to 20 kgf/cm² (300 psi). Those built in the early 1970s for the SS-18 could withstand 425 kgf/cm² (6,000 psi), which was achieved using concrete reinforced by concentric steel rings.

Alternative Basing Schemes
Although most of their ICBMs were always sited in silos, both the USA and the USSR repeatedly examined alternatives, both to increase survivability and, perhaps of greater importance in the USA than in the USSR, to reduce costs. In the USA, environmental factors also became an increasingly important consideration.

One of the US schemes was called Multiple Protective Structures (MPS) and consisted of a number of 'racetracks', each about 45 km in circumference and equipped with twenty-three hardened shelters. One mobile ICBM, mounted on a large wheeled TEL, would have moved around each racetrack at night in a random fashion, with decoy TELs and missiles adding to the adversary's uncertainties. Basic MPS involved 200 missiles moving between 4,600 shelters covering an area of some 12,800 km², but a more grandiose version envisaged 300 missiles moving around 8,500 shelters.*

An enhanced version of MPS was proposed in the early 1980s, in which a new Small ICBM (SICBM) would have been deployed in fixed, hardened silos distributed randomly among the 200 racetracks of the MPS system, thus adding to the aiming points for the Soviet ICBM force. It was intended that the SICBM would be 11.6 m long and weigh 9,980 kg, have a range of 12,000 km, and carry a single 500 kT warhead; it would have been launched by an airborne launch-control centre. SICBM would have been housed in a

---

* It was estimated that among the requirements of the racetrack scheme would be: cement – 600,00 tonnes; sand – up to 48 million tonnes; liquid asphalt – 954 million litres; petroleum fuels – 568 million litres; water – 81.3 billion litres. In addition, thirty-five federal laws would have impacted on the land-acquisition process, and the scheme would have required the fourth largest city in Nevada to be built from scratch and then maintained.[4]

tight-fitting container placed in a vertical silo hardened to approximately 530 kgf/cm², and it would have required an exceptionally accurate incoming warhead to destroy such a target. Various other launch methods were also considered for SICBM, including a road vehicle, normal silos, airborne launch from a transport aircraft, and (possibly the only time this was ever considered for an ICBM) from a helicopter.

Another scheme was based on the racetrack principle of MPS, but this time with the TELs running inside shallow tunnels, 4 m in diameter. The TELs would simply have kept moving, thus avoiding the need for shelters, and would have had large plugs fore and aft to protect against nuclear blast within the tunnel. If required to launch, the TEL would have halted and used hydraulic jacks to drive the armoured roof upwards, breaking through the surface until the missile was raised to the vertical.

Deep Basing (DB) involved placing the ICBMs either singly or in groups deep underground, where they would ride out an attack and then emerge to carry out a retaliatory strike. One of the major DB schemes was the 'mesa concept', in which the missiles, crews and equipment were to be placed in interconnecting tunnels some 760–915 m deep under a mesa or similar geological formation.* Following an enemy nuclear strike, the crews would have used special machines to dig a tunnel to the surface and then brought the launcher to the open to initiate a retaliatory strike. This scheme's disadvantage lay in its poor reaction time and the difficulty it posed for arms-control verification. From the practical point of view it would have been necessary to find rock which was both fault-free and sufficiently strong to resist a Soviet nuclear attack, but which could nevertheless be drilled through in an acceptable time and without the machinery becoming jammed by debris. On top of all that, a second incoming nuclear strike when the drilling machine was near to the surface would have caused irreparable damage. A related project (Project Brimstone) examined existing deep mines, but also proved unworkable.

A totally different approach, known as Closely Based Spacing or 'Dense Pack', was also considered. This suggested that, instead of spacing missile silos sufficiently far apart to ensure that not more than one could be destroyed by one incoming warhead, 100 MX missiles should be sited in superhardened silos placed deliberately close together. The idea was that this would take advantage of the 'fratricide' effect in which incoming warheads would be deflected or destroyed by the nuclear explosions of the previous warheads. A spacing of the order of 550 m was suggested, and it was claimed that in such a scheme between 50 and 70 per cent of the ICBMs would have survived.

---

* A mesa is a type of high, rocky tableland with precipitous sides, found in certain parts of the USA.

Mobile basing

All the basing methods discussed above were either static or involved limited movement in a closed circuit, but the question of mobile basing was often considered as well. As described earlier, the German A-4 was designed as a road-mobile system, but an alternative rail-based option was also considered, and a similar scheme was designed and tested during the development phase of the Minuteman I. The plan was to have fifty trains, each of some fourteen vehicles, which would have included up to five TEL cars, each carrying a single missile, together with command-and-control, living-accommodation, and power facilities. The scheme was examined in great detail, and a prototype 'Mobile Minuteman' train was tested on the public railway. Although the scheme proved feasible, it was dropped in favour of silo deployment.

A similar proposal was considered during the long development of the Peacekeeper (MX) system, and very nearly became operational. This version would have consisted of twenty-five missile trains, each carrying two missiles. Each train would have consisted of the locomotive and six cars: two missile launch cars; a launch-control car, a maintenance car, and two security cars. In peacetime the trains would have been located in a 'rail garrison' sited on an existing Strategic Air Command base, which would have contained four or five shelters (known as 'igloos'), each housing one train. These garrisons would each have covered an area of some 18–20 hectares, with tracks leading to the USA's 240,000 km national rail network. On receipt of strategic warning the trains would have deployed on to this national network, where they would have rapidly attained a high degree of survivability. This scheme was under active development from 1989 until its cancellation in 1991.

As we have seen, the Soviet SS-24 Mod 1 was actually fielded in the rail-mobile mode. There were three rail garrisons, all in Russia, with four trains at two sites and three trains at the third. The trains had one launcher each, with two further cars for launch control, maintenance, and power supply.

The Soviets also fielded a road-mobile ICBM, the SS-25, which was also the last Soviet ICBM to enter service during the Cold War. This single-warhead missile was carried on a fourteen-wheeled TEL, which was raised on jacks for stability during the launch. The TEL and its missile were normally housed in a garage with a sliding roof which would be opened for an emergency launch. Given the necessary warning, however, the TELs deployed to pre-surveyed sites in forests.

One US proposal was the 'continuous patrol aircraft', in which a packaged missile was carried inside a large, fuel-efficient aircraft. On receipt of verified launch instructions, the missile would have been extracted by a drogue parachute, and once it was descending vertically its engine would have fired automatically, enabling the missile to climb away on a normal trajectory. Tests were carried out using a Minuteman I missile transported by a C-5 Galaxy and were completely successful. Large numbers of aircraft would have been needed to maintain the number required on simultaneous patrol. It would have been very difficult for a potential enemy to track them and even more difficult to guarantee the destruction of every airborne aircraft in a pre-emptive strike, but the main weaknesses of the scheme were the vulnerability of the airfields, the enormous operating costs, and, to a lesser degree, the decreased accuracy of the missile.

10

Submarine-Based Missiles

During the Second World War German submarines in the Atlantic brought the United Kingdom very close to collapse before they were ultimately defeated, while US submarines in the Pacific achieved a mastery which played a significant part in Japan's defeat. However, only a tiny handful of people foresaw a potential marriage between submarines and the newly developed missiles, and once again this occurred in Germany. The original suggestion came from a visitor to the German rocket-development site at Peenemünde, who proposed that the A-4 (V-2) missile, in addition to being launched from land, might also be launched from a submersible barge towed by a submarine. With such a device, he suggested, the Germans would be able to bombard New York. The suggestion was seized upon by the staff at Peenemünde, but the land-based missile was given higher priority and only one barge was completed before the surrender in May 1945. A separate proposal to mount V-1 cruise missiles in submarines for use against New York was considered in 1943, but was rejected due to a lack of suitable submarines.

The nuclear-powered missile submarine (submarine, ballistic, nuclear – SSBN) and its weapon, the submarine-launched ballistic missile (SLBM), formed a truly innovative weapon system. It was in essence a missile base, but with the immense advantage over land-based ICBMs that not only was it mobile, but it could use that mobility to hide in the vastness of the oceans.*

US SYSTEMS

Regulus
Some of the V-1 and A-4 missiles obtained by the US forces in 1945 were allocated to the US navy, together with a number of the German scientists

---

* The specifications of US and Soviet sea-based strategic missiles are given in Appendix 9, and of US and Soviet strategic submarines in Appendix 10.

who had been involved in their development. These missiles were immediately seen as having a seaborne role against land targets, and, of the two, the V-1 cruise missile seemed to offer the greater promise in the short term. As a result, two fleet submarines were converted by installing a watertight hangar abaft the sail with a stern-facing take-off ramp – an installation similar to that used by the Japanese navy for its aircraft-carrying submarines, of which the US navy captured a number in 1945. The submarines had to surface to launch the missiles, and the first of many test flights took place in February 1947. The navy also conducted trials with the A-4, including the first launch of a ballistic missile at sea, from the flight deck of the aircraft carrier USS *Midway* on 6 September 1947. Numerous tests were conducted with both types of missile until the programme ended in 1950, but it was a start.

Meanwhile, two exceptionally far-sighted submarine-launched cruise-missile programmes were initiated, one for Rigel in 1947 and the second for Triton in 1952, although both were eventually cancelled. A less ambitious cruise-missile programme named Regulus did, however, reach service. Powered by a turbojet, the subsonic Regulus I had swept wings, and served operationally aboard submarines from 1954 to 1964. It was armed with a nuclear warhead, but was relatively inaccurate and was targeted against large cities within 650 km of its submarine launch position, such as Beijing. A second cruise missile, Regulus II, was greatly superior to Regulus I and carried a nuclear warhead at speeds in excess of Mach 2 to ranges of 1,610 km. Although it was proving very successful, the programme was cancelled in 1959, as the concurrent Polaris programme held out greater promise.

Polaris
The United States' first SLBM and SSBN programme – known collectively by the missile's name, Polaris – was one of the most successful defence projects ever undertaken. It was a huge undertaking, which incorporated an astonishing range of innovations in two parallel but interlocking programmes. On the missile side, these included solid-fuel propulsion, cold-gas launch from a submerged submarine, lightweight ablative re-entry vehicles, and small nuclear warheads. Alongside this was the submarine programme, which involved cutting a nuclear-propelled attack submarine under construction in two and inserting a 39.6 m 'plug' containing sixteen vertical missile tubes. The submarine system also involved new launch-control and communications systems, as well as novel systems for submarine navigation. This very ambitious programme was steered to completion by Rear-Admiral William Raborn of the US navy.

When the first Polaris submarine entered service, in 1960, it revolutionized strategic warfare. The Polaris A-1 missile carried a single 500 kT warhead over a range of 2,600 km and, using inertial guidance, achieved a

111

CEP of some 1,830 m. Polaris A-2 also had single warhead, but this was both more powerful (800 kT) and more accurate (CEP = 1.2 km), while Polaris A-3 carried three RVs, each with a 200 kT yield and a CEP of 850 m. The Polaris A-3 also became the first (and so far the only) SLBM to be supplied to a foreign nation, when it was sold to the United Kingdom to arm that country's Resolution-class SSBNs.

Poseidon
The Poseidon C-3 two-stage missile started life as an evolutionary development of the earlier missile (its initial designation was Polaris B-3) and, although having a greater diameter, it was able to use the same launch tubes by eliminating the guide-rings used on Polaris. The first Poseidon was launched in August 1968, and the system entered service in 1971. The most important innovation was that it was armed with MIRV warheads, of which a maximum of fourteen could be carried, though this was limited to ten 100 kT warheads under the SALT I agreement with the USSR. The potential accuracy of the MIRVs could have given them a counter-force (hard-target) capability, but, since this ran counter to contemporary US strategists' view of SLBMs as a survivable, second-strike, counter-value (i.e. anti-city) system, the proposed high-precision stellar-inertial navigation system was not authorized by the Department of Defense.

At its peak Poseidon armed thirty-one SSBNs. Conversion of twelve of these boats to carry the Trident missile started in 1984, however, and by 1990 only ten Poseidon boats remained in service.

Trident
Development of Trident I began in 1972, the missile being essentially a Poseidon C-3 with a third-stage motor added to give a greatly increased range of 7,400 km – that range enabling the SSBNs to obtain more sea room. The Trident design was a much more efficient design than earlier SLBMs, maximising its use of the volume available, and making use of all the fuel. The designers were also able to include the stellar navigation package which had been forbidden Poseidon, thus enabling the warhead to be extremely accurate, with a CEP of 463 m. Trident I (C-4) was put into production even though it was known that Trident II (D-5) would become the definitive system, and it armed twelve SSBNs which had originally carried Poseidon as well as the first eight Ohio-class SSBNs.

Next came Trident II (D-5), which was the same diameter as Trident I but 3.6 m longer, giving it a range of 12,000 km and nearly double the throw weight of the earlier missile. As the Cold War ended, Trident II was coming into service aboard the twenty-four-missile Ohio-class SSBNs. Trident II was fitted with NAVSTAR satellite receivers, giving mid-course navigational updates to the inertial system, resulting in a CEP of 90 m, making this a genuine hard-target attack system, with a range enabling it to hit any target in the world from anywhere in any ocean.

Tomahawk

In the late 1980s the US navy introduced the Tomahawk cruise missile into service, thus turning the wheel full circle, since the navy had started its Cold War development with a cruise missile – the Regulus – some forty years earlier. This missile was, however, much superior in performance, range and accuracy, delivering a 200 kT warhead to a maximum range of 2,500 km with an accuracy of 280 m. It was also smaller and lighter, being capable of being launched from a standard 533 mm diameter torpedo tube.

SLBM Launching

One of the keys to success of the US SLBMs was the use of a gas-operated system which blew the missile out of the launch tube towards the surface, thus avoiding the rocket-motor ignition taking place in the tube, with its attendant dangers to the submarine. In some missiles the first-stage motor to drive the missile up into the atmosphere fired below the surface, while in others (e.g. Trident) it fired when clear of the surface. The missiles were launched in sequence, Poseidon missiles being launched at a rate of one every fifty seconds.

US SUBMARINES

The original submarines used by the US navy in the 1946–7 V-1 programme were standard Second World War diesel-electric fleet submarines with large cylindrical hangars abaft the sail, with a short, sloping launching rail. The next step was the Regulus I and II programmes, which involved five submarines. The first two of these were converted fleet submarines with cylindrical aft-facing hangars, but the other three were purpose-built, with the missiles stored in a large hangar in the bows, two of them being diesel-electric-powered and the third, *Halibut*, nuclear-powered. All ceased to operate Regulus when the system was discontinued in 1964 and were then employed on different missions.

Led by Rear-Admiral Raborn, the Fleet Ballistic Missile System (FBMS) programme started in the mid-1950s, and the first submarine, *George Washington*, complete with sixteen operational Polaris A-1 missiles, entered service on 15 November 1960 – an astonishing technical, manufacturing and managerial achievement.

To save time, the George Washington class was created by taking five Skipjack-class attack-submarine hulls currently under construction, cutting them in two, and adding a missile section containing sixteen vertical tubes abaft the sail. There were, of course, many minor changes, including the addition of missile control and launch systems, special navigation systems, and new communications. The system introduced many new concepts which subsequently became standard practice, including the sixty-day operational cycle, using two crews, designated Blue and Gold, one of which was at sea, the other ashore on rest, leave, training and, finally, preparing to take over for the next operational cruise.

The George Washington class was very quickly followed by five Ethan Allen-class boats, completed between 1961 and 1963, which were very similar to the George Washington class, but with the advantage of being designed as SSBNs from the start.

The range of Polaris (A-1 – 2,600 km; A-2 – 2,800 km; A-3 – 4,630 km) meant that all these SSBNs had to operate relatively close to Russian shores to meet the requirement to hit Moscow. So, in order to reduce transit times, the boats were forward based at Holy Loch (Scotland), Rota (Spain) and Apra Harbor (Guam). None of these ten SSBNs could be converted to take the Poseidon missile, and in 1980–81 all were either converted to nuclear-powered attack submarines (SSNs) by deactivating the missile tubes or were decommissioned.

The first of the Ethan Allen class had not even been completed before the next class was being laid down, and thirty-one Lafayette-class SSBNs joined the fleet between 1963 and 1967.* All thirty-one entered service with Polaris missiles (the first eight with Polaris A-2, the remainder with A-3), and a further four were planned to bring the grand total of Polaris-armed boats to forty-five. These last boats were never built, and the thirty-one Lafayette-class were converted in 1970–78 to take the Poseidon missile. Twelve were later converted yet again to take Trident C-4 (1978–83), with the first of these, *Francis Scott Key*, sailing on its first patrol on 20 October 1979.

Finally came the Ohio class, the largest US submarine and the most powerful single weapons platform ever built – 171 m long, displacing 16,964 tonnes and carrying twenty-four missiles. Like most other strategic programmes, the Ohio-class programme was surrounded by doubts, and in particular by concern over its costs, but eventually the first submarine sailed on its initial patrol on 11 November 1981. The first eight, which entered service between 1981 and 1986, were armed with Trident I (C-4) missiles, and the remaining ten (completed in 1988–97) with Trident II (D-5).

Missile Numbers

When the first SSBN was being designed there was a major investigation into the optimum number of missiles. The minimum cost-effective number

---

* There were, in fact, three sub-groups, with relatively minor differences between them: the Lafayette class (nine boats), the James Madison class (ten boats) and the Benjamin Franklin class (twelve boats).

was twelve, but the maximum depended on the money available. The number of sixteen was simply the number that fitted in the largest submarine the US navy felt that it could persuade the Pentagon and Congress to pay for, and the majority of SSBNs subsequently built for both the US and foreign navies have been equipped with this number of tubes. There is, however, nothing magic about the figure of sixteen, and SSBNs have been built with twelve tubes (Soviet Yankee class), twenty tubes (Soviet Typhoon class) and twenty-four tubes (US Ohio class).

Availability

Availability of the later missiles aboard SSBNs remains classified, but in a US navy Polaris submarine fourteen missiles were available for 100 per cent of the time, while all sixteen were available for 95 per cent of the time.

Typical of its generation, the US navy's Lafayette class usually spent sixty-eight days on patrol with the Blue crew, followed by a thirty-two–day refit before starting the next patrol with the Gold crew. There was also a sixteen-month yard overhaul every six years, giving an overall availability for each hull of 55 per cent. The Ohio class, however, offered a considerable increase in availability, with seventy-day patrols, followed by twenty-five-day refits, and with a twelve-month yard refit every nine years, increasing overall availability to 66 per cent.

ALTERNATIVE US SEA SYSTEMS

As with land-based missiles, there were repeated attempts in the USA to discover a form of sea-borne basing that was either less expensive or more survivable – or, preferably, both. Designs took a variety of forms.

In the immediate post-war period the USA examined the German plan to launch A-4s from submersible barges, and carried out some tests, using ex-German A-4s and US-built barges. The result was always that the rocket efflux destroyed the barge, resulting in a somewhat erratic launch. Nevertheless, the idea was re-examined in 1961–5 as a possible alternative to Polaris, under the code-name Project Hydra, and was looked at yet again in the early 1980s as an alternative to both Trident and the Peacekeeper (MX) ICBM. Project Hydra showed that the technique was perfectly feasible, although it found that the most effective way of launching was simply to put the missile in the water without any form of protective container. The missiles needed to be waterproofed, and those with a specific gravity greater than 1.0 needed a flotation collar to make them float, the collar being shed on launch. The plan was for such missiles to be taken to sea aboard a converted merchant ship and lowered into the water, where they would be left until they were activated and the launch command was signalled from a headquarters ashore.

The 1970s plan was for thirty fast merchant ships, each capable of rapid changes in appearance, to operate out of two bases, one on the Atlantic and one on the Pacific. Each ship would have carried ten missiles, and two plans were considered: one to offload the missiles into the sea in peacetime, the other to offload them only in a crisis. In fact the project foundered on the deployment issue, as the system was judged to be far too vulnerable and susceptible to accidents, but there was never any doubt as to its technical feasibility.*

There were a number of proposals in the late 1970s to use small diesel-electric submarines, operating on or near the continental shelf. One proposal involved a design displacing some 450 tonnes, based on the West German-designed Type 209; another was for a larger boat displacing between 500 and 1,000 tonnes. Such submarines would have carried two (or, in some proposals, three) Minuteman III missiles in external, horizontally mounted containers, from which the missile would have been floated out, brought upright by its ballasted rear end, and then 'wet launched' as with Project Hydra. Force levels varied between 100 and 138, with manning figures ranging between five and fifteen men per submarine. The most serious drawbacks were that, being diesel-electric powered, slow and with relatively short range, the submarines would have needed protection by a strong ASW force, while if they operated within the limits of the continental shelf they were vulnerable to attack by a relatively small number of Soviet missiles.

The Hydra plan was for surface ships to place missiles in the sea for a water launch, but there were other plans to use the surface ships themselves as launch platforms. The most serious of these was the 'Multi-Lateral Force' (MLF) proposed by President John F. Kennedy in 1961. This proposal was for a fleet of twenty-five surface ships to be built in west-European yards, each armed with eight Polaris A-3 missiles, supplied by the United States. Both ships and missiles would have been jointly owned by the nations concerned and jointly manned (as, for example, happened later for the E-3 Airborne Warning and Control System (AWACS) force).

One curious event, possibly linked to the MLF proposal, was associated with the Italian cruiser *Giuseppe Garibaldi*. This ship underwent a major refit in the early 1960s and emerged in 1962 as a guided-missile cruiser, its principal weapons being US-supplied Terrier anti-aircraft missiles. It was, however, also equipped with four vertical launch tubes for Polaris A-3 missiles. Dummies were successfully tested, but real missiles were never

---

* In the mid-1990s a Russian agency was marketing the 'Surf' system for civil use; this involved a missile being taken to sea in an amphibious ship and then dropped into the sea for a 'Hydra'-type launch. Using a combination of SS-N-20 and SS-N-23 missiles with new fourth and fifth stages, it would place a 2,400 kg payload into a 200 km near-earth orbit.

embarked, nor were live Polaris missiles ever made available to the Italian navy.[1]

The most significant feature of the MLF proposal was that the warheads would have been under NATO control, with release authorized by a NATO body to be set up for that purpose, and signalled over a NATO-owned 'permissive link' to the ships. The MLF never came about, but the question of NATO control over nuclear weapons led to the setting up of the Nuclear Planning Group.

There was also a proposal for a NATO-operated ballistic-missile submarine force. This was, however, quickly scotched, since the US would not reveal its nuclear-propulsion secrets and a diesel-electric submarine would have lacked the essential stealth.

SOVIET SYSTEMS

SS-N-1

On capturing German material in 1945, Soviet leaders were quick to see the potential importance of sea-borne long-range missiles, and their first attempt was to develop a towed-container system.[2] Several hundred were built in the late 1940s, but the system does not appear to have become operational and attention soon switched to launching missiles from the submarine itself. Soviet army SS-1 (NATO = 'Scud') missiles were converted for naval use, and a Zulu-class diesel-electric submarine was adapted to house a single missile in a tube which stretched from the keel to the top of the sail. The first successful launch took place on 16 September 1955, and this system, designated SS-N-1 by NATO, entered service in 1959; its range was a meagre 150 km. Two missiles were carried in each of five converted Zulu-class submarines (Zulu V), and may also have been carried for a short time by the newly built Golf-class submarines, as well.

With a range of 150 km and an anti-ship role, SS-N-1 was not, however, a strategic missile; its significance here is as a 'proof-of-concept' system leading to strategic missiles.

SS-N-4

Having proved the concept, the Soviet navy was quick to follow up with the more advanced SS-N-4 missile, which first went to sea in 1961. The system replaced the SS-N-1 aboard the Zulu V, but its principal platforms were the Golf-class diesel-electric and the Hotel-class nuclear (SSBN) submarines, which carried three missiles each. The SS-N-4 was a large missile for its time, with a launch weight of 13,750 kg, and carried a single 1 MT warhead, although contemporary reports credited it with a 5 MT warhead. Its range was 650 km. This was a surface-launched missile, and the submarine could

117

travel at up to 15 knots and in conditions up to Sea State 5, although the submarine had to be on an even keel at the moment of launch.

SS-N-5/SS-N-6

The SS-N-5, 'Sark', which was deployed aboard later Golf- and Hotel-class submarines, was the first Soviet SLBM which could be launched while the submarine was submerged, the limits being a maximum depth of 60 m and surface conditions not exceeding Sea State 5. Of even greater significance was the SS-N-6, 'Serb', which enabled Soviet designers to switch from a few sail-mounted missiles to the same sixteen-tube, internally mounted layout as in Western SSBNs. It entered service in 1967 embarked aboard Yankee I-class SSBNs. The SS-N-6 had a relatively short range (2,400 km for Mod 1 and 3,000 km for Mods 2 and 3), which meant that the submarines had to deploy close to the Atlantic and Pacific coastlines of the USA. This made them vulnerable to US home-based anti-submarine measures, but, on the other hand, they threatened very rapid attacks on targets such as US ICBM fields – a threat which caused serious concern to US strategic planners.

SS-N-8

The pace of Soviet naval missile development was maintained by the SS-N-8, 'Sawfly', which started test flights in 1971, demonstrating a range of 7,800 km. This caused considerable alarm in the West, as it exceeded, by a very considerable margin, the range of any other US or Soviet SLBM, and the alarm only increased when the Mod 2 version went on to demonstrate a range of 9,100 km. The long range was necessary because the SS-N-8 was designed for deployment aboard the new Delta-class submarines, which would operate from 'SSBN bastions' in Soviet-dominated waters (see page 122). Accuracy was improved by using a stellar-inertial navigation system, although later reports suggested that this was frequently much less accurate than was believed in the West at the time.

SS-N-17

The SS-N-17, 'Snipe', was embarked in one submarine only (the sole Yankee II), which was in service from 1977. It was the first Soviet navy SLBM to be powered by solid fuel, and also the first to carry a post-boost vehicle – in this case used for only a single re-entry vehicle. This system demonstrated a Soviet practice which tended to confuse Western observers, where a 'one-off' system was put into extended operational service – something which almost never happened in the West, as such a practice was very expensive in terms of procurement, training and logistic support. Even if, as was suggested at the time, the SS-N-17 might serve some special strategic purpose, there were inevitably protracted periods when the submarine was in refit, when the entire system was unavailable.

SS-N-18

The SS-N-18, 'Stingray', which entered service in 1977, was a direct development of the SS-N-8 and was the first Soviet SLBM to carry MIRVs. It was installed in the Delta III-class SSBNs, which, owing to the missile's greater length, had an even higher 'hump' abaft the sail than in the Delta I and II. The SS-N-18 continued the Soviet preference for storable-liquid propulsion.

SS-N-20

The SS-N-20, 'Sturgeon', was specifically developed for use aboard the Typhoon-class SSBN and carried up to ten 100 kT MIRVs with a CEP of 500 m. This gave them a relatively low lethality (by nuclear standards), but was sufficient for the Typhoons' wartime second-strike role (see below). Although it was the second Soviet SLBM to use solid fuel, it was the first such to be produced in quantity. The SS-N-20 entered service with the Typhoon in 1982, and was deployed only in that class of SSBN.

SS-N-23

The SS-N-23, 'Skiff', was the successor to the SS-N-18 and became operational with the Delta IV class in 1985. Unlike the solid-fuelled SS-N-20, it used storable-liquid propulsion, possibly because the Soviet navy had found such a system preferable to solid fuel over many years of service. The SS-N-23 was originally thought to be operating with ten MIRV warheads, but was later learned to have only four. The US also expected that it would be retrofitted into Delta IIIs, but this did not happen.

SOVIET SUBMARINES

Zulu

Zulu-class diesel-electric submarines were built in the early 1950s and, after one had been used to launch an SS-N-1 missile, five were converted and were then known to NATO as Zulu V, fitted first with two SS-N-1s and later with two SS-N-4s. The launching procedure was complicated, to say the least. The missile was fuelled and prepared while the submarine was submerged and, when all was ready, the submarine then surfaced and the two missiles were raised by lifts until they were clear of the sail, where they were held in position by four brackets. The missiles were then aligned with the target, the motors were started, and (presumably using nice judgement) the missiles were launched when the submarine was upright.

Golf, Hotel

The Zulu class was followed by two classes of purpose-built missile submarines, but, with typical Soviet caution, one class was diesel-electric-powered, while the other had nuclear propulsion. Fifteen of the diesel-electric boats – designated Golf class by NATO – entered service between 1959 and 1962 fitted with three sail-mounted SS-N-4s, using the same surface-launch techniques as the Zulu V. Thirteen of these were later converted to take the SS-N-5, which was launched submerged. The Hotel-class nuclear-powered submarines were developed concurrently with the Golf class and had very similar missile arrangements, with three SS-N-4s mounted vertically in the sail.

Yankee

An important development came in 1967, when the Yankee I-class SSBNs entered service. These were the first Soviet SSBNs with sixteen missile tubes and the first to house the tubes in the pressure hull, as with the US Polaris submarines. Thirty-four were built between 1969 and 1972. Like the earlier classes, these boats patrolled off the US coast, but the greater range of the SS-N-6 missile enabled them to threaten targets much deeper inland. One boat, the sole Yankee II, was built to test the SS-N-17 missile, and a number of Yankee Is were converted as cruise-missile carriers.

Delta

The Delta class proved to be a very successful project for the Soviet navy, and the design remained in production from the late 1960s in four major versions: Delta I (eighteen built), Delta II (four built), Delta III (fourteen built) and Delta IV (seven built). The Delta I was built around the SS-N-8 missile and made maximum use of the well-proven Yankee design, enabling the Soviet navy to get it into service quickly, although, since the SS-N-8 was considerably larger than the SS-N-6, the 'hump' was higher and only twelve missiles could be accommodated. The Delta II, however, was longer, to enable the number of missiles to be increased to sixteen to match Western SSBNs. The fourteen Delta IIIs were the only Soviet SSBNs to carry the SS-N-18 missile, which was even longer than SS-N-8, thus requiring an even higher 'hump'. Last of the class were the Delta IVs, commissioned between 1985 and 1992, which carried sixteen SS-N-23 SLBMs. All four Delta classes were designed to operate in the two Soviet 'SSBN bastions', their probable role being to deliver the first wave in a second strike.

Typhoon

The first Typhoon hull was laid down in 1977, and when it was first revealed in the West in the early 1980s it caused a greater stir than almost any other weapon system in the Cold War. Western intelligence had become aware of something unusual three years previously, when First Secretary Leonid Brezhnev told President Gerald Ford that he would go ahead with Project Typhoon if the US would not agree to drop the Trident programme. Later, US reconnaissance satellites took pictures of components being assembled at Severodvinsk which were so large that it was assumed that they were for another long-awaited project, an aircraft carrier. What eventually appeared, however, was the largest submarine the world has ever seen: its submerged displacement of 25,000 tonnes far exceeds that of the US navy's Ohio-class SSBN (16,964 tonnes), while its length of 171 m is a little greater than that of a US navy Ticonderoga-class cruiser.

The Typhoon was innovative in many ways apart from its sheer size. The outer casing conceals no less than five interconnected pressure hulls, and the twenty SS-N-20 missiles are mounted forward of the sail – a feature unique among SSBNs.

The Typhoon was designed to provide a platform which would spend most of its very long patrols lying on the seabed beneath the Arctic ice cap. It would sit out a nuclear exchange and surface through the ice to launch its missiles only when the adversary was taking the first steps towards post-nuclear recovery. In the original concept it was planned that each Typhoon would spend as much as a year on patrol, and one of the reasons for its huge size was the need to provide good habitability and adequate recreation possibilities for the crew. Internally, the Typhoon is exceptionally spacious, with extensive facilities including saunas and a swimming pool, all designed to ease the burden of protracted periods at sea. Six of these unique submarines were built between 1977 and 1989.

ALTERNATIVE SOVIET SEA SYSTEMS

As far as is known, the sole Soviet alternative to SLBMs was a 1.5 m diameter torpedo developed in the late 1940s, which would have been launched from a single bow tube at a range of some 30–40 km from the target, usually a port. The missile travelled at approximately 55 km/h, and with a payload of some 3.6 tonnes it would have delivered a nuclear warhead with a yield of approximately 1 MT.*

SOVIET SSBN STRATEGY

In the early years of the Cold War the Soviet Union found itself in a position where US missile and airbases, some operated by the USA and others by NATO allies, directly threatened the Soviet land mass. On the other

---

* At around the same time, in the early 1950s, the British were working on a similar concept, in which a miniature submarine (known as an 'X' craft) delivered a nuclear mine to the entrance of a Soviet harbour. Several 'X' craft were built, but the idea was then abandoned.

hand, the Soviet Union did not have a long-range air capability equivalent to the USAF's Strategic Air Command with which to pose a corresponding threat to the USA, and it thus turned to missile-armed submarines as the quickest way of obtaining such a capability. The early missiles had a short range (650 km for the SS-N-4, for example) and the submarines would have been vulnerable to very active ASW activity by the USA. In particular, submarines armed with the surface-launched missiles (SS-N-1 and SS-N-4) would have been extremely vulnerable during their lengthy launch preparations.

At that time the primary purpose of the nuclear force was to pose an anti-city threat, and there were large numbers of important urban concentrations down the east and west coasts of the USA within the range of those missiles. When the Yankee SSBNs first started to patrol off the US Pacific and Atlantic coasts in the late 1960s, armed with their counter-value SS-N-6s, they too were targeted at large area targets, such as cities, government facilities, military bases and airfields. All these early SSBNs – including the Yankees – also brought another factor to the threat to the USA, since their missiles would have had a very short time of flight (possibly between four and five minutes), compared to the thirty minutes' warning the USA expected to receive of a trans-polar missile attack. For the Soviet navy, these new types of submarine and missile also had the advantage that, apart from increasing the capability of the navy, they also helped to increase the experience of its officers and ratings.

The Delta-I/SS-N-8 combination, however, represented a complete change in strategy, since the long range of the missiles enabled the submarines to operate in what came to be known as the 'SSBN bastions'. There were two of these – the Barents Sea in the west and the Sea of Okhotsk in the east – where the SSBNs had plenty of room for submerged patrols, while the sea around them and the airspace above them were patrolled and defended by Soviet naval and air forces. In particular, the Soviet SSBNs were defended against attacks by US and British SSNs, one of whose primary roles was to try to destroy Soviet SSBNs before they could launch their missiles. One consequence of this strategy was that Soviet war plans allocated increasing surface and air forces to the defence of the bastions, which reduced the assets they could assign to attacking NATO naval forces elsewhere.

Delta-II/SS-N-8 and Delta-III/SS-N-18 continued this pattern, but the Delta-IV/SS-N-23 and Typhoon/SS-N-20 combinations, which were produced simultaneously in the 1980s, introduced a new dimension. They were intended for different missions, the Delta IV being intended for use early in a nuclear campaign, possibly even in the first strike, but from the Arctic region, rising though relatively thin ice to fire its missiles from the surface. Typhoon, on the other hand, was intended to submerge under the deep ice cap for a protracted period, possibly as long as a year, and then break through thicker ice in order to carry out a final strike on the USA as it attempted to recover from the effects of a nuclear war.

LOCATING THE SSBNS

Both sides considered it necessary to be aware of the movements of the other side's SSBNs, first to establish routine patterns and then to detect any variations from the routine – such as, for example, an increase in the number of SSBNs at sea, which might indicate possible preparation for war. The start points for all SSBN missions – their bases – were well known to both sides, and the most vulnerable part of an SSBN's voyage was its departure from its base.

The bases were closely monitored by satellite and, at least in the case of the Western bases, visually as well, but there were also more covert means of surveillance. Knowledge of the submarines' operational cycles enabled the sailing and return dates of SSBNs to be predicted with a fair degree of accuracy, and in the early days the other side's SSNs would wait outside bases to monitor SSBN movements using their on-board sensors. This was countered by giving departing SSBNs an ASW escort of aircraft, surface ships and SSNs, which in its turn was countered by using attack submarines to place sensors on the seabed. The British, for example, built a specialized and very complex ship, *Challenger*, at very considerable expense, specifically to locate and remove such devices from the approaches to the nuclear-submarine base in the Clyde.*

Once at sea, the SSBNs would make fairly rapid, but careful, transits to their operational area, where they would then cruise at about 3 knots, varying their depth to take maximum advantage of oceanic conditions, to make detection as difficult as possible.

---

* Unfortunately, after the ship had undergone a very protracted development period, the Soviet navy changed its surveillance system, making *Challenger* completely redundant.

11

Strategic Bombers

Strategic bombers exercised a major influence over the first half of the Cold War, principally because in the 1940s and 1950s they were the only practicable means of delivering the very heavy atomic and hydrogen weapons over intercontinental ranges.* Allied to this, bombers had played a major role in the recently concluded Second World War, with the Allied bombing campaigns against Germany and Japan giving the appearance of a war-winning strategy. Indeed, the war had been brought to a close by the two USAAF (United States Army Air Force) B-29 bombers which dropped atomic bombs on Hiroshima and Nagasaki.

There were also bureaucratic reasons for the fierce advocacy of the bomber, however. The US air force finally became independent of the US army in 1947 and was extremely keen to prove itself to be the war-winning arm in the Cold War. In the UK, which found itself facing the reality that it was now only the second most powerful nation in the West, membership of the exclusive 'nuclear club' appeared to be the only way to retain superpower status, and, in the short term, bombers were the only feasible way of achieving that. On the Soviet side, the air force realized that it had never produced a bomber force to match those of the USA and UK, and was desperate to rectify this. Thus, from 1945 into the mid-1960s, the strategic bomber armed with nuclear weapons was the symbol of global power.†

US AIRCRAFT

B-29/B-50
The original atomic bomber – and, after fifty years, still the only aircraft to have dropped atomic bombs operationally – was the piston-engined Boeing

---

* The first operational H-bomb, the US Mark 17, weighed 19,050 kg.
† Specifications of US and Soviet strategic bombers are given in Appendix 11.

B-29 Superfortress, which entered service in 1943 and was the USA's front-line bomber in the last year of the war against Japan and, with Strategic Air Command (SAC), in the early years of the Cold War. The early atomic bombs were large and very heavy, and the B-29 carried two, but with a range of 5,250 km it could not reach all parts of the USSR from bases in the United States. Thus, in the early Cold War period it was regularly deployed overseas, particularly in the UK, Okinawa and Guam. The B-29 was also provided to the UK air force from 1950 to 1958 (as the Washington B.1), albeit only as a conventional bomber. The B-29 was replaced in US (but not in British) service by an upgraded and more capable version, the B-50.

B-36
The Convair B-36 was the largest bomber ever to enter service. Its design had started in 1939–40, when it appeared possible that the UK would be overrun by the Germans and there was a perceived requirement to bomb targets in western Europe from bases in North America. Once it became clear that the UK would survive, however, the B-36 was given a lower priority, and it did not enter service until 1948. It was powered by six piston and four turbojet engines, which gave it the unprecedented unrefuelled range of 13,000 km.

B-47
The first major all-jet bomber was the Boeing B-47, which entered service in 1950; by the end of the decade, 1,260 B-47s were in front-line service with twenty-eight SAC bombing wings. At that time the traditional bomber was large, slow, powered by four piston engines, manned by a crew of ten to twelve men, and defended by numerous gun turrets, but the B-47 completely changed all that. It had swept wings and tail, was as fast as contemporary fighters, was powered by six jet engines in neat pods under the wings, carried a crew of three, operated 3,000 m higher than previous types, and was defended only by a single, remotely controlled turret in the tail. The problem was its relatively short range of 5,800 km, which again was partially compensated by forward deployment (e.g. to the UK) and partly by the large-scale introduction of air-to-air refuelling.

B-52
The mainstay of SAC's bomber force for most of the Cold War was the Boeing B-52, which was designed in the late 1940s, entered service in 1955, and was still in front-line service at the end of the Cold War. When it entered service the B-52 set new standards for strategic bombers in almost every respect, including the carriage of eight nuclear bombs or up to 40,000 kg of conventional bombs over ranges of up to 12,900 km. In all, 744 were built, many of which were rebuilt several times to keep the force up to date. Although the B-52 started its career as a nuclear bomber, it changed from a

high-level to a low-level role, while from the mid-1980s onwards it became a missile launch platform – a less demanding role and more suited to the venerable age of the airframes.

B-58

The most dramatic bomber to serve with SAC was the tailless, delta-winged Convair B-58, with a Mach 2 speed and 8,250 km range. Air-to-air refuelling enabled the B-58 to undertake long flights (e.g. from Tokyo to London), loudly advertising its wartime capabilities. The aircraft used a unique system in which a large pod under the fuselage housed both the nuclear weapon and the fuel for the outward flight; it was dropped complete, enabling the aircraft to make a very rapid getaway before returning to base on its internal fuel supply. Although generally successful, the B-58 was very expensive to operate, even by US standards, and was retired after just ten years' service, without replacement.

FB-111

Every development after the B-52 proved to be controversial, and the FB-111 was no exception. The original concept, known as the Tactical Fighter Experimental (TFX), was for one basic design which would meet the needs of the US air force, navy and Marines, as well as selling widely to US allies. In the end only the US and Australian air forces bought it, although the UK's nearly did so, after the cancellation of its own strike bomber, the TSR-2. Almost inevitably, the widely disparate requirements could never be satisfied, although a very effective low-level strategic bomber was eventually produced, with 437 of various marks entering service. FB-111s could carry a maximum of six Short-Range Attack Missiles, each with a 200 kT nuclear warhead, or six gravity nuclear bombs. The greatest significance of the FB-111 was its ability to operate at very low levels at high speeds, and aircraft based in the UK were targeted on heavily defended, large area targets in the western USSR.

XB-70

One of several abortive attempts in the 1960s to produce a new strategic bomber was the XB-70 Valkyrie, a six-engined behemoth and the largest bomber ever built. The B-70 was intended to fly for long periods at Mach 3 at high altitude, but its extraordinary performance was paralleled by its enormous costs, and after a spectacular crash in which one of the two prototypes was destroyed the whole project was cancelled.

B-1

The US air force's final Cold War bomber was the B-1, which had a very protracted gestation, its official designation of AMSA (Advanced Manned

Strategic Aircraft) being misinterpreted by cynics as 'America's Most Studied Aircraft'. One particularly strong argument in the early 1960s against the project was simply to question the need for a new manned bomber at all, since vast sums were already being spent on ICBMs, on upgrading B-52s for the air force, and on building new SSBNs and SLBMs for the navy. Even those who supported the need for a new bomber could not agree on what sort of aircraft was needed, but in 1971 the air force placed an order for an initial quantity of four B-1As, a four-engined, swing-wing aircraft, capable of Mach 2 at high altitudes. The first prototype flew in 1974, but when the Carter administration assumed power in January 1977 it gave high priority to an antagonistic examination of the project, which led to its cancellation, virtually in its entirety, that June. When the Reagan administration took over in 1981, however, the air force proposed a new version of the aircraft, optimized for low-level, stealthy penetration, which emerged as the B-1B. An order for 100 was placed, and they entered service from 1985 onwards.

In the low-level penetration role the B-1B flew at Mach 0.85 at a height of about 60 m. The B-1B defended itself partly through very sophisticated electronic-warfare equipment, but also through 'stealth' design, it being claimed that the B-1A had a radar cross-section (RCS) one-tenth that of a B-52, while the B-1B had an RCS one-tenth that of the B-1A. Payload comprised various combinations of Air-Launched Cruise Missiles, Short-Range Attack Missiles and nuclear gravity bombs.

SOVIET AIRCRAFT

Tu-4

At the start of the Cold War the Soviet Union saw itself as threatened by the long-range bombers of the USA but without any effective means of retaliation. For some years the Soviet air force depended upon a copy of the B-29, which had been reverse-engineered (i.e. copied) from three USAAF aircraft which had landed and been interned at Soviet airbases during the Second World War. Designated the Tupolev Tu-4 (NATO = 'Bull'), large numbers served with the Soviet air force and thirteen were passed to the Chinese air force, which also used them for a time as nuclear bombers. The Tupolev bureau designed improved and larger versions of the Tu-4, but the Soviet leadership decided not to develop piston-engined bombers any further and to concentrate on the development of turboprop and turbojet designs.

Tu-16

The first Soviet design to enter service, in 1954, was the Tupolev Tu-16 (NATO = 'Badger'), which was similar in capability to the US B-47 and the

British Valiant (see Chapter 12), but with only two engines. Unlike those American and British designs, however, the Tu-16 remained in service for many years, with over 2,000 being built, of which the majority were still in service at the end of the Cold War. There were numerous versions, but the nuclear version carried two nuclear bombs in an internal bomb bay, and 287 of this strategic-bomber version remained in service as late as 1987. The Tu-16 was capable of carrying its maximum load of two nuclear weapons over a range of some 4,800 km at a speed of 780 km/h, which enabled it to threaten targets in Europe, Alaska and Japan, but not in the continental USA.

Tu-22

As the US progressed to the Convair B-58, so too did the Soviet air force develop supersonic bombers: the Myasishchev M-4 (NATO = 'Bounder'), which progressed no further than the prototype stage, and the Tupolev Tu-22 (NATO = 'Blinder'). The Tu-22 was a large and sophisticated aircraft, with highly swept wings and two massive turbojets in the tail, giving it a dash speed of Mach 1.4 at 12,000 m. Payload was either two nuclear gravity bombs carried internally or a 'Kitchen' cruise missile. Combat radius at high altitude was 2,250 km, with a 400 km supersonic dash over the target (or less at low level).

Tu-20/Tu-95

The Tupolev design bureau also produced the Tupolev Tu-20 (NATO = 'Bear') – a remarkable design, which first flew in 1955 and entered service in 1956. To the astonishment of Western observers, this aircraft combined swept wings with turboprop engines, and, despite its undoubted success, it remains the only aircraft to combine these two features. The Tu-20 had the immense range, without air-to-air refuelling, of 14,800 km with a payload of at least four nuclear bombs. It was regularly underrated by Western observers, especially in the Pentagon, despite regular non-stop flights by both military and civil versions from the USSR to Cuba. A variety of versions were still in wide-scale service at the end of the Cold War.

Strategic versions were the Bear-A bomber, carrying two nuclear gravity bombs, the missile-carrying Tu-95 Bear-B, carrying a huge AS-3 (NATO = 'Kangaroo') cruise missile with an 800 kT nuclear warhead and a range of some 680 km, and the Bear-H attack version, which carried four AS-15 'Kent' cruise missiles, with a range of 3,000 km. All types of Bear regularly carried out training missions against NATO countries, approaching to within some 80 km of the US and British coasts. On an operational sortie against the USA, however, it would have had to fly at medium and high altitudes to obtain maximum range, which would have made it vulnerable to US and allied fighters.

M-6

Contemporary with the US B-52 was the Myasishchev M-6 (NATO = 'Bison'), a large swept-wing strategic bomber, powered by four turbojets, rather than the Tu-20's turboprops. The large number of M-6s dreaded by the West never materialized, as their performance – particularly the range and the size of the bomb bay – never quite met the operational requirement, and the M-6 was then used for reconnaissance and electronic-intelligence tasks; however, it was symptomatic of the atmosphere of the time that its appearance in 1955 caused much excitement in the United States and led to a great increase in the production rate of the B-52. Like the Bear, the M-6 would have had to approach the USA at medium to high altitudes.

Tu-22M / Tu-26

In 1969 US satellites began to return photographs of a new Soviet bomber on the apron at the new aircraft factory at Kazan. This turned out to be a swing-wing version of the Tupolev Tu-22, designated Tu-22M (NATO = 'Backfire'). Subsequently, a virtually new aircraft with some external similarities to the Tu-22M appeared and was put into production as the Tu-26 (NATO = 'Backfire-B'). (The relationship between the Tu-22M and the Tu-26 was probably similar to that between the American B-1A and B-1B.)

Three versions of the Tu-26 entered service, one of which carried nuclear weapons for use in the land-attack role. There were, however, repeated arguments between the United States and the Soviet Union over the role of this bomber, with the former stating and the latter denying that it was a strategic bomber. This became a major issue in the SALT II negotiations, and President Brezhnev eventually ordered that the aircraft's flight-refuelling probes be removed to prove that it did not have the ability to reach the USA, although since these could have been replaced in less than thirty minutes this was only a token gesture. The Tu-26 entered service in the mid-1970s and was produced at the rate agreed under SALT II – thirty per year – with service numbers peaking at about 220.

Tu-160

Finally came the Tupolev Tu-160 (NATO = 'Blackjack'), which flew for the first time in 1981 and just eighteen entered service from 1987 onwards. With a maximum take-off weight of 275,000 kg this was the heaviest combat aircraft ever built, and it carried a payload of 16,330 kg. The Tu-160 was fitted with swing wings and powered by four very powerful turbojets, giving it a range of 14,000 km at a height of 18,300 m, with a cruising speed of 850 km/h and a dash speed of Mach 1.9. The Tu-160 was also capable of low-level attack. Two large bomb bays could house nuclear gravity bombs, short-range missiles, or air-launched cruise missiles. Ironically, this remarkable aircraft – one of the finest bombers ever built, which at long last gave the

Soviet Union the strategic bombing capability it had always sought – appeared just as the Cold War came to an end.

Bomber designers and the tacticians fought an unending war against the potential defenders in an effort to ensure that the bomber would get through to its targets. In the late 1940s the major threat came from radar-directed anti-aircraft guns, which had reached a considerable degree of sophistication, and the bombers' first response was simply to fly higher than the effective ceiling of the guns. The next threat was air-defence fighters, and here again the bombers responded by flying higher and faster – there were numerous reports of British and US reconnaissance flights over the USSR in the early 1950s in which the Soviet fighters simply could not reach the same altitude as the intruder.

Second World War bombers were fitted with machine-guns in a variety of positions – including the nose, the waist, above and below the fuselage, and the tail – but these were rapidly reduced to just the tail, the elimination of the others saving considerable weight and enabling the aircraft to fly higher and faster. Also in the Second World War, bombers had been escorted by fighters, particularly on the USAAF's daylight raids; but the strategic ranges now being flown were far in excess of anything a fighter could undertake. So in the 1950s the US air force trialled the idea of the B-36 bomber taking a fighter with it, with the latter being carried on a retractable cradle from which it could be launched in mid-air to deal with enemy fighters, then being recovered for the return to base. A special miniature fighter, the McDonnell XF-85 Goblin, was tested, as was the RF-84K, a modified version of the full-size F-84 Thunderjet fighter, but, although launching proved feasible, recovery did not, and the idea was not pursued.

Electronic countermeasures (ECM) were always used, becoming increasingly sophisticated as time passed. Thus electronic jamming was used to confuse enemy radars, as was 'chaff' (strips of metal foil cut to the wavelength of the radar), which was dropped in large quantities, either by the bomber or by specialized escorting aircraft.

One of the earliest devices to help the bomber get through was the US air force's ADM-20 Quail, which resembled a miniature unmanned aircraft and was dropped over enemy territory, where it flew for some 400 km, using its on-board ECM devices to confuse the enemy as to the strength, direction and probable targets of the incoming bomber force. A maximum of three Quails could be carried by a B-52, and the device was in service from 1962 to 1979.

The main emphasis then turned to stand-off missiles – a concept which, like so many others, had its genesis in Germany, where V-1 missiles had been launched from Heinkel He-111 bombers in 1944–5. The Cold War missiles carried a nuclear warhead and were designed to be launched from the bomber while still outside the range of the enemy air defences. One of the first was the US Hound Dog – a slim missile with small delta wings, and powered by a turbojet – which entered service in 1961. Two Hound Dogs, each with a 1 MT nuclear warhead, were carried beneath the wings of a B-52. The missile could be set to fly at any height between about 50 m and 16,000 m, and had a range at high level of 1,140 km, less at low level. The guidance system was capable of high- or low-level approach, with dog-legs and jinxes to confuse the defence.

Next came the unhappy saga of Skybolt, which was an attempt to use a bomber to launch a ballistic missile, which would have given longer range and, of greater importance, a much shorter flight time. The UK air force joined the project, but the incoming Kennedy administration unilaterally cancelled it in December 1961 – greatly to the indignation of the British, who used the issue as a lever to obtain Polaris missiles and SSBN technology to replace its V-force bombers (see Chapter 12).

The Short-Range Attack Missile (SRAM), which entered service in 1972, was a rocket-propelled missile with a 170 kT nuclear warhead and a speed of Mach 3. SRAMs could fly either a semi-ballistic, a terrain-following or an 'under-the-radar' flight profile, the latter terminating in a pull-up and high-angle dive on to the target. The range depended on the height, and was from 56 km at low level to 170 km at high level. B-52s normally carried twenty SRAMs, while the FB-111A carried six and the B-1B twenty-four.

The Air-Launched Cruise Missile (ALCM) entered service with the US air force in 1982. This weapon had folding wings which extended when it was dropped from the carrier aircraft, and was powered by a small turbojet engine. Designed exclusively for low-level flight, the ALCM used a radar altimeter to maintain height and a map-matching process known as terrain comparison (TerCom) to give very precise navigation. The nuclear-armed version (AGM-96B) had a 200 kT warhead, a CEP of 30 m and a range of some 2,500 km. The AGM-96C was conventionally armed, with a high-explosive warhead, and this version demonstrated its effectiveness and accuracy when thirty-five were launched by B-52s during the Gulf War. B-52s could carry up to twelve and B-1Bs twenty-four.

Soviet stand-off missile development followed a similar pattern and time-scale, although in the early stages of the Cold War the missiles tended to be much larger and less effective than their US counterparts. Indeed, the first missile designed for use by strategic bombers, the AS-3 (NATO = 'Kangaroo') remains the largest air-launched missile to go into service, with a length of some 15 m, a wingspan of 9 m and a weight of 11,000 kg; only one could be carried by a Tu-95 (Bear-B). It did, however, have a useful range (650 km) and a high speed (Mach 2), and with an 800 kT warhead it was targeted against large area targets such as cities and ports.

The AS-15 (NATO = 'Kent') was much smaller and generally similar in size, performance and role to the US Tomahawk; sixteen could be carried by the Tu-95 Bear-B and twelve by the Tu-160 Blackjack. It carried a 200 kT nuclear warhead and flew at high subsonic speeds over a range of some 3,000 km at a height of 200 m, with an accuracy (CEP) of 150 m.

STRATEGIC AIR POWER IN THE COLD WAR

Manned aircraft offered certain unique advantages. First, they possessed inherent flexibility, in that they could be launched on receipt of strategic warning and then be held in the air, diverted to airfields outside the threatened area, or recalled to base. The fact that men were aboard and in control meant that targets could be changed during flight, that moving targets or even targets of opportunity could be engaged, and that orders could be altered or countermanded. Also, unlike with SSBNs, there were excellent communications between the command centres and the airfields, and between the ground and the aircraft. Finally, the bomber-delivered gravity bomb was the most accurate of any nuclear delivery system.

Among their disadvantages, however, was the bombers' vulnerability to air defences and their absolute dependence on airfields with large runways and extensive maintenance facilities. Every airfield capable of taking strategic aircraft was known to both sides throughout the Cold War, and there can be no doubt that they were primary targets for both conventional and nuclear strikes.

At the start of the Cold War all that the strategic bomber had to do was to fly high and reasonably fast to reach its target, and even if it was picked up by enemy radar there was little that the enemy could do about it. Thus, throughout the late 1940s and most of the 1950s, bombers of Strategic Air Command could quite safely overfly almost anywhere on earth, since anti-aircraft guns could not fire high enough and contemporary fighters' ceilings were too low to threaten them. That changed, however, in the mid/late 1950s as the performance of Soviet fighters improved, and in particular when they were fitted with airborne radar, enabling them to find and track targets in the dark and in bad weather. At first, bombers sought to counter this by flying even higher and faster, but then yet better fighters and in particular the fielding of air-defence missile systems caused different solutions to be sought.

The advantages offered by bombers over missiles depended upon the aircraft getting airborne in the first place, and in the worst-case situation of an 'out-of-the-blue' missile attack the bombers might only receive some seventeen minutes' warning in the USA (less if the missiles were launched from Yankee-class SSBNs off the US coast) and four minutes in western Europe. Western bombers were therefore placed on a high-readiness status, known as Quick Reaction Alert (QRA). In the UK's V-force, for example, this was introduced in early 1962 and involved one aircraft in each squadron being at fifteen minutes' notice twenty-four hours per day, 365 days per year. Bomber Command stipulated that, apart from the aircraft on QRA, 30 per cent of the available aircraft (i.e. those not on major servicing or overseas) should be ready to deploy after four hours, rising to 100 per cent after twenty hours.[1]

Bomber fleets are almost always listed by total numbers, but this is misleading and nothing like that number would have reached the target in an unexpected crisis. A proportion would always have been in deep maintenance or rebuild, while others would have been simply unserviceable at the time they were required. In addition, it was not unknown for major problems to be discovered en route to the holding position which would prevent the aircraft proceeding to its target. Finally, at least some would have been either shot down or damaged by air-defence missiles, fighters and, on low-level missions, anti-aircraft artillery.

Deployment

SAC's bomber force was for a long period the most powerful single strategic military force in the world, with vast numbers of the most modern bombers deployed at bases across the continental United States. The first overseas protracted deployment was to the UK in July 1948, in response to the Berlin crisis (see Chapter 32), when three British airfields were made available to six squadrons of SAC's B-29s, although these were not, as was reported at the time, atomic bomb carriers (which were known as 'Silver Plate'). What was originally described as a temporary deployment rapidly became permanent, and, when the NATO Treaty was signed, the number of SAC bases in the UK increased from three to seven, then to eight, and Silver Plate B-29s arrived for the first time. Their targets at that time were in the southern USSR, their routing being over France and then along the northern Mediterranean and across the Black Sea and into the Ukraine and southern Russia. Other SAC bases were in Alaska, the Azores, Guam, Libya, Morocco, Okinawa and the Philippines, although SAC aircraft also made temporary deployments to many other friendly countries.

Targeting

For all their advantages, strategic bombers inevitably took many hours to reach their targets. This was not a serious drawback when they were the only means of attacking the enemy, but when ICBMs and SLBMs entered the nuclear plan, with their flight times of approximately thirty minutes, bombers were perforce relegated to the second wave. Their missions could include non-time-urgent targets or simply 'filling in the gaps' which malfunctioning missiles or warheads left in the missile targeting plan.

A map of planned US strategic attacks on the Soviet Union which was prepared in the early 1950s as part of Operation Dropshot shows SAC bombers attacking from bases in the continental USA, Alaska, Okinawa, Guam, Egypt, Aden and the UK. The mission was to:

> initiate, as soon as possible after D-day, strategic air attacks with atomic and conventional bombs: against Soviet facilities for the assembly and delivery of weapons of mass destruction; against LOCs [lines of communication], supply bases and troop concentrations in the USSR, in satellite countries and in overrun areas, which would blunt Soviet offensives; and against petroleum, electric power and steel target systems in the USSR.[2]

Tankers

One of the most significant developments was the introduction of air-to-air refuelling, which extended the bombers' range very considerably. The Boeing KC-97E tanker entered service in the early 1950s, and the Soviets, British and French all subsequently introduced similar systems.* The US and French air forces used a 'flying-boom' system, in which an operator in the tanker steered a boom into a receptacle on the upper surface of the receiving aircraft. The British, however, used a 'probe-and-drogue' system, in which the tanker streamed a rubber hose from a drum and the pilot of the receiving aircraft manoeuvred until the probe on his aircraft engaged in the drogue at the end of the hose. The Soviets initially used a third method on their Tu-16 Badgers, which involved connecting a hose between the wing-tips of the two aircraft, but this was later replaced by the 'probe-and-drogue' method.

Various aircraft were pressed into use as tankers. The US air force policy was to manufacture tanker versions of civil airliners, with the KC-97 Stratotanker being based on the Boeing Stratocruiser, the KC-135 on the Boeing 707, and the KC-10 Extender on the Douglas DC-10. The British, who came to the tanker scene a little later than the Americans, tended to convert service or civil aircraft which had been made redundant from their existing tasks. The first two (Valiant and Victor) were converted from bombers, while the latter two (VC-10 and Tristar) were converted from airliners.

One-Way Flights

Strategic bombers did not necessarily have to return to the bases from which they had been launched, and, in order to obtain the maximum range, many

---

* Specifications of various tanker aircraft are given in Appendix 12.

nuclear missions were planned in which the aircraft would have recovered to a distant base. Thus, for example, a bomber which took off from the continental United States might have flown over the Arctic, launched its missiles or dropped its bombs on targets in the USSR, and then carried on to land in Turkey or Pakistan.

There were, however, frequent (but never confirmed) reports that at least some missions were planned as 'one-way', with the best that the crew could hope for being a parachute drop into enemy territory. The respected aviation author Bill Gunston, writing about French Mirage IV bomber, states that: 'Even with tanker support, many missions have been planned on a no-return basis . . .'[3] There were similar reports about RAF Canberra bombers based in Germany.

Operation Linebacker II

Although perhaps not typical of a nuclear attack, the bomber raids carried out by US forces on North Vietnam during Operation Linebacker II give an illustration of the 'state of the art' in the early 1970s. The USA made great use of air power throughout the Vietnam War, and particularly of its large force of B-52s, which were in the inventory for nuclear operations, but also had a very effective conventional capability. The North Vietnamese developed a very sophisticated air-defence system, using mostly Soviet radars, guns, missiles and aircraft, but with some Chinese equipment as well.

Operation Linebacker II took place when President Richard Nixon decided to use air power as a reprisal when the North Vietnamese abandoned the Paris peace talks on 13 December 1972. In the first raid, on 18 December, 121 B-52s attacked targets in and around Hanoi, supported by ECM aircraft, F-111s attacking North Vietnamese fighter bases, and F-4 Phantoms sowing chaff corridors. The North Vietnamese launched over 200 surface-to-air missiles (SAMs), fired much anti-aircraft ammunition, and flew fighter sorties, bringing down three B-52s and damaging two others. The following night no US aircraft were lost, but on 20 December six B-52s were downed. US tactics were then amended, reducing losses on the next four days, and there was then a thirty-six-hour 'Christmas truce' before 113 B-52s in seven waves struck targets in and around Hanoi, Haiphong and Thai Nguyen during a fifteen-minute period. The defences were overwhelmed, and only two B-52s were shot down. The operation continued for another three days, and then the North Vietnamese signified their willingness to return to the negotiating table.

During the eleven days of Linebacker II 729 B-52 missions were flown and 49,000 bombs (13,605 tonnes) were dropped on thiry-four discrete targets. Fifteen B-52s were lost and nine damaged, all to SAMs.

12

The Other Strategic Nuclear Powers

In the immediate post-war years, the evidence of Hiroshima and Nagasaki was clear for all to see: the most powerful weapons in the world were the new atomic bombs, and only those who possessed them would be in the 'top league' of strategic powers. The corollary was that a non-nuclear power would be helpless if threatened by a nuclear power. Faced by this inescapable logic, the efforts to restrict the spread of nuclear weapons has never proved successful.

THE UK

Bombers
The history of the British V-bombers is worth studying in some detail, since it shows the complex issues faced by a smaller power in obtaining a viable nuclear force, and the never-ending effort and expense in keeping it operationally viable.*

For over a century the British were the most powerful single power in the world, but at the end of the Second World War they found themselves in a very weak position. The UK was virtually bankrupt, owed vast sums to the United States, and faced a major problem in rebuilding both industry and society at home. To complicate matters, it still had major overseas commitments in continental Europe, as well as responsibilities around the world with its colonial territories. On top of all this was the looming Soviet threat and a continuing desire to remain in the 'top league'.

It thus became inevitable that the British would develop their own atomic bomb, although their programme was seriously hindered for a while by the

---

* Specifications of British nuclear bombs and bombers are given in Appendix 13.

refusal of the United States to make atomic information available to the United Kingdom, under the terms of the McMahon Act. This was something which the British found especially galling as they had assisted very substantially in the US Manhattan Project. Nevertheless, after much high-level consideration, the British programme was eventually given Cabinet approval on 8 January 1947,[1] and, after brief consideration of ballistic and cruise missiles, it was concluded that the programme must be based upon delivery by long-range manned bombers.

The UK was thus faced with setting up a very large programme. First was the work on the bomb itself, which included the full range of development activity and the construction of a wide range of facilities, including testing establishments, factories to produce the weapons, and storage sites once they had been completed. Second was the delivery system, which had been established as a manned bomber, powered by the then new turbojet engines. Third came the organization in both the government and the UK air force to operate, store, maintain and, in the ultimate, to use the weapons, which required new headquarters, procedures and communications systems.

Despite the complexity and expense, this was all achieved, and the first British atomic device was exploded on the Pacific island of Trimouille on 3 October 1952 and the first atomic bombs were delivered to the air force in November 1953. Meanwhile, technology had progressed from the atomic (A-bomb) to the thermonuclear (H-bomb) weapon, and the British development programme continued, resulting in the first British thermonuclear explosion, a bomb which was dropped from a Valiant bomber over Malden Island in the Pacific on 28 April 1958.

The British programme proceeded through a series of exotically named weapons, starting with Blue Danube, the original British A-bomb, with a 20 kT yield. This was followed by Violet Club, just five of which were produced and which served very briefly in order to give the air force a 'megaton' capability at the earliest opportunity. Violet Club was, however, described as a 'rather delicate' weapon; it had to be assembled on the bomber base itself by staff from the Atomic Warfare Research Establishment, and once assembled it could be transported only between the assembly point, the storage building and the aircraft. Doubtless all concerned were very relieved when the definitive weapon, Yellow Sun Mk 1, entered service in 1960.

Britain developed its own nuclear weapons to overcome the ban on information from the USA, and it was therefore somewhat contradictory that one of the consequences of that development was that the USA then felt able to release both information and weapons to the UK. Thus, in a programme known as 'Project E', the USA supplied a number of nuclear weapons to meet the air force's requirements until such time as sufficient British 'megaton weapons' were available; these US weapons reached the UK air force in October 1958 and remained operational until 1962. The weapons were stored on British air bases, but, by US law, had to protected and maintained by US air-force personnel, and could be transferred to British custody only on direct orders from the US president. The British found that the US custodial arrangements created many complications, especially as the survivability of the V-bombers required them to be deployed rapidly to dispersal airfields in the face of an imminent threat – a factor which the inflexible US custodial and release procedures were not designed to cope with. There was therefore considerable relief when the British-made weapons became operational, enabling the remaining 'Project E' weapons for the V-force to be returned to the USA. (US weapons for British aircraft assigned to SACEUR remained until 1968, however.)

The British aimed to field a force of 144 V-bombers in the 'Medium Bomber Force', and, in a move which even today causes surprise, they developed four, radically different, designs, of which three actually entered service. During the early years the mainstay of this force was the Vickers Valiant, of which nine squadrons were formed between 1955 and 1957. The Valiant was superseded in Bomber Command by Avro Vulcans and Handley-Page Victors, although the Valiant continued in service as a bomber assigned to SACEUR, and as a strategic reconnaissance and tanker aircraft.

Having worked hard to get the V-force into service, the British then had to work as hard to keep it up to date. The aircraft were designed to meet a requirement for dropping gravity bombs from a high level, out of range of a defender's anti-aircraft artillery; they were thus optimized for cruising and bombing at 12,000 m. The rapid development of Soviet missile defences, however, made it clear that such high-flying aircraft were extremely vulnerable, and the V-bombers had to be re-roled to a low-level approach, which, because of the resulting increased fuel consumption, had the immediate effect of restricting their radius of action, in turn reducing the number of potential targets. It also increased the loads on the airframes, as was discovered when Valiants were found to be suffering from metal fatigue, which led to the abrupt grounding of the entire fleet in December 1984 and its early retirement a month later.

Meanwhile the front line was maintained by the Vulcans and Victors. The delta-winged Vulcan became operational in March 1957, armed with Blue Danube, with twelve aircraft converted for a short time (1958–9) to carry the 'interim megaton weapon' (Violet Club). All Vulcans then carried Yellow Sun or Red Beard nuclear gravity bombs, until, finally, thirty-three were converted to take the Blue Steel stand-off weapon. The Victor, which featured a 'crescent' wing, entered service in 1958, and, like Vulcan, carried first Blue Danube and later Yellow Sun or Red Beard (but not Violet Club). Then, too, twenty-three were converted to take Blue Steel.

Blue Steel, which entered service in 1962, represented a different way to solve the problem of countering the enemy air defences. Carrying a 1 MT warhead and flying at Mach 2, it was originally designed for high-level delivery, at which it had a range of 280 km, but when converted to the low-level role this was reduced to 35–42 km.

Several attempts were made to extend the effectiveness of the V-force, the main one being purchase of the US air force's proposed Skybolt air-launched ballistic missile. This was intended for launch from Vulcans, and would have had a range of 1,760 km if launched from 12,000 m and of 460 km if launched from 300 m. The missiles would have been fitted with British nuclear warheads, but, to the intense embarrassment of the British, the project was abruptly terminated by the USA in December 1962. In the end, the vaunted V-force was replaced by the British navy's Polaris submarines on 30 June 1969.

When the British air-force nuclear deterrent became operational there was an obvious need for co-ordination with the Americans, so the British held discussions with the US Strategic Air Command (not, significantly, with the Joint Service Targeting Staff). At the initial meetings in 1957 it was discovered that every British target was also covered by the SAC's list, and, in addition, that both air forces had 'doubled up' their intended strikes, to ensure success.[2] This was resolved by a combined plan in which the British were allocated 106 targets, including sixty-nine cities of governmental or military significance, seventeen Soviet air-force airfields with nuclear roles, and twenty elements of the Soviet air-defence system. Full tactical co-ordination was achieved by joint planning of routes, timing and ECM tactics.

For the British, however, there was a separate consideration, in that the V-force was an 'independent deterrent': its purpose was to be used not only in allied operations with US and NATO forces, but also, as a last resort, in national plans. As a result, once the co-ordinated plan with SAC had been devised, a second national targeting plan was prepared which listed '131 Soviet cities whose population exceeded 100,000; from these 131 cities, ninety-eight were chosen which lay within about 3,000 km of the UK and they were graded in order of priority according to population, administrative importance, economic importance and transportation'.[3] This British national list became operational in November 1957, and was updated in June 1958.

Land-Based Missiles

The British also started to develop an IRBM. Designated Blue Streak, this was a liquid-fuelled ballistic missile, with a range of 2,800 km – the same as that required of the V-bombers – and a 3 MT warhead. Blue Streak was designed to be emplaced in an underground silo, but raised to the surface for fuelling (which took twenty minutes) and launch. The project was started in 1955 but was abruptly cancelled in 1960, just before the (successful) first flight.

Sixty US-owned Thor IRBMs were deployed by the British air force between 1958 and 1963, each armed with a 1 MT warhead. These missiles were treated as part of the V-force, and their targeting was controlled by the Bomber Command Operations Centre, although since the warheads were supplied and controlled by the USA it is to be presumed that their targeting was fully integrated with US plans. Further, like the 'Project E' weapons supplied for use by the V-bombers, they were not available for UK national strike plans.

Submarines*

When President John F. Kennedy and Prime Minister Harold Macmillan met in Bermuda in December 1962, one of the subjects discussed was the replacement of the US Skybolt missile, which had just been cancelled by the USA. Prime Minister Macmillan managed to persuade the president to allow the British to participate in the Polaris programme. Since the British navy had traditionally worked very closely with that of USA, the programme went remarkably smoothly, being completed on schedule, with HMS *Resolution*, the first British SSBN, concluding its first patrol in June 1968. The submarine was created by inserting a sixteen-missile plug into a Valiant-class attack-submarine design, while the Polaris A-3 missiles were designed and built in the USA but had British warheads and re-entry vehicles. The number of missiles was set at sixteen simply in order to ensure maximum commonality with the US Lafayette design.

The British originally planned to build five Resolution-class SSBNs, but, although the Labour government which took power after the 1964 general election decided to continue the programme, it reduced the overall numbers to four boats. With one boat always in refit, one working-up and one in port, the British could only guarantee to have one submarine at sea at a time, with two for some of the time; the average was 1.44.

The general British philosophy of counter-value strikes was carried over from the bomber era to the submarines. The general principles were spelled out by the British admiral Sir Ian Easton in discussing the British purchase of the Trident SLBM system:

> The nuclear destruction of a number – say, some dozen – of Soviet cities with a population of over 100,000 would be a traumatic blow to the Soviet Union. Among these cities might be Moscow, Leningrad, Kiev, Kharkov, Gorky and Stalingrad. The enormous loss of population and industry, the disruption of services critical to the life of the country, and the likely destruction of a proportion of the central bureaucracy of a centrally-organized state, could be expected to markedly weaken the vitality of the nation and the will of its people, and, perhaps, of its armies.[4]

The original British SLBM was the Polaris A-3, whose British 'front end' carried three 200 kT MRVs. These were all aimed around the same target,

---

* Specifications of British, Chinese and French SSBNs are given in Appendix 14.

with a spread between impact points of some 16 km. When the advent of Soviet ABM defences around Moscow using the Galosh missile called the effectiveness of the MRVs into question, the USA offered to supply Poseidon, whose MIRVs were designed to outwit such defences. The British, however, opted for a programme of their own, Project Chevaline, which was based in outline on a US programme called Antelope. In Chevaline, the two warheads and a large number of penetration aids were mounted on a manoeuvrable penetration-aid carrier which deployed the various elements of its payload on separate trajectories, all of which were aimed at the same target, and was designed so that, having dispensed its payload, it then appeared to be and acted like a warhead itself. There were two warheads and three dummy warheads, all of which were enclosed in metallic balloons, with, to confuse the defences even further, a number of empty balloons as well. As the balloons entered the atmosphere they burned away, and the six objects then began a series of planned manoeuvres designed to mislead enemy ABM defences, before all impacting in the same general area. Thus, in effect, Chevaline depended upon disguising the warheads as dummies during the space phase, and disguising dummies as warheads during re-entry. Submarines began patrols with Chevaline in 1982.

In addition to the front end, the main Polaris missile was the subject of several refurbishment programmes. Most noteworthy was the replacement of the engines, which was carried out by the manufacturer in the United States, although the technology was by then so dated that the company had to re-employ retired workers, since the skills required were no longer available.

The Resolution-class submarines were designed to last for twenty years (i.e. 1968–89), but this was subsequently extended to twenty-five years and later to thirty years. In the event this was not achieved, and towards the end of their lives they were showing distinct signs of age, with reports of cracking in the coolant circuits, while *Resolution*'s final refit lasted five years – two years longer than had been taken to build it in the first place. Fortunately for the UK, these problems occurred at the end of the Cold War. The Polaris force served until past the end of the Cold War, being replaced by a force of four new submarines armed with Trident II (D-4) missiles in the 1990s.

FRANCE

Bombers*

Like those of other countries, the first French atomic weapons were carried by a bomber, in this case the Mirage IVA. This was created by scaling up the

---

* Specifications of French nuclear weapons are given in Appendix 15.

very successful Mirage III fighter, adding an extra seat for a navigator/ systems officer, and replacing the single engine by two more powerful ones. The first prototype flew in June 1959 and the complete system became operational in 1964, the twenty-four-hour nuclear alert actually starting on 1 October 1964. In its original form, Mirage IVA was a supersonic, high-level bomber carrying the AN 11 gravity bomb, but from 1967 onwards it was converted to the low-level role, using an AN 22 retarded bomb.*

The original deployment consisted of thirty-six front-line aircraft, together with an integral force of Boeing KC-135F tankers which were located at nine widely separated bases, but in 1976 this was changed to thirty-two aircraft at six bases, with the KC-135Fs concentrated rather than dispersed. The number of Mirage IVAs gradually reduced, until the last squadron was disbanded in 1988.

Meanwhile, the Mirage IVP (P = *Pénétration*) entered service in 1986, at the same time as updated tankers (now designated KC-135FR) were being received. Eighteen Mirage IVAs were reworked to Mirage IVP standard, with improved navigation and electronic equipment to enable them to operate the ASMP (*Air–Sol Moyenne Portée*), a Mach 2.5 missile with a range of 300 km and a single 300 kT thermonuclear warhead, which was intended for stand-off attacks against heavily defended targets such as air-fields and command-and-control centres. The Mirage IVP served through the end of the Cold War, until 1997.

The unrefuelled range of the Mirage IVA/P was insufficient for it to attack targets in the Soviet Union and return to airbases in France, and so the plan was for it to be refuelled over the Baltic or the North Sea, increasing the range from 2,500 km to some 3,800 km. This had two consequences. First, while the ability of the Mirage IVA/P to scramble was excellent, the critical factor was actually how long it took the heavily laden and much slower KC-135F/FR tankers to get to the first refuelling point. Second, the two aircraft were acutely vulnerable while they were refuelling, which limited how closely they could approach Warsaw Pact-dominated airspace. Nevertheless, at least some of the force should have got through to attack targets as far east as Moscow, although how many might have returned was open to question.

Land-Based Missiles

In establishing its strategic forces, France determined that they should parallel, in concept if not in size, those of the USA and the Soviet Union by consisting of a triad of land-, sea- and air-based systems. Thus, work began in the 1960s on a *Sol–Sol Balistique Stratégique* (surface-to-surface ballistic

---

* A 'retarded' bomb deploys a small braking parachute to delay its fall, thus enabling the aircraft to fly clear before the nuclear weapon explodes.

strategic missile – SSBS) system. Originally it was intended to deploy fifty-four missiles, but this was reduced first to twenty-seven and then to the eighteen which were actually deployed. Each missile was located in a hardened silo, with at least 3 km between silos, on the Plateau d'Albion in Haute-Provence in south-east France, which was selected for the nature of its soil, its sparse population and its height (some 1,000 m), which enhanced the missiles' range. Each nine-missile site had its own command post (each of which could also launch the missiles at the other site). In Condition Blue all missiles could be launched within five minutes of the order being issued, while in Condition Red this was reduced to one minute.

The original missile was the SSBS S2, a two-stage missile with a range of about 3,300 km and carrying a single 120 kT warhead. This was in service from August 1971, but in 1980 it began to be replaced by the SSBS S3D (D = *durci*: hardened), with a range of 3,500 km and a 1 MT warhead hardened against the effects of EMP. One group of nine S2 missiles was replaced in June 1980, the second in January 1983.

It was very easy for any potential enemy to locate each of France's eighteen SSBS silos and thus to target them precisely, which made them very vulnerable to a first strike. Indeed, some pragmatic French politicians made a virtue of necessity, postulating that an enemy would be compelled to make its intentions obvious by attacking the SSBS sites, thus giving France justification to launch its other strategic weapons.

Submarines

The third leg of the French strategic triad was the ballistic-missile submarine, designated *Sous-Marin Lance Engins* (SNLE) in French service, the first of which became operational in 1972. Unlike the first SSBN designs in the USA and the UK, the French SNLEs were designed as such from the start and were not created by cutting an SSN in two and inserting a missile section. The British, faced with similar problems to the French, built a force of four SSBNs of which one was guaranteed to be on patrol at all times, whereas the French built five boats, of which two were guaranteed to be at sea, and then in 1983 they increased the at-sea figure to three. Availability increased yet further when the sixth SNLE, of an improved design, joined the fleet in 1985.

The first French SLBMs, the two-stage, solid fuel MSBS M1 and M2,* had ranges of 2,500 km and 3,000 km respectively, and carried a single 500 kT warhead with a CEP of approximately 1,000 m. The M1 entered service in 1971 and was in service until 1974, when the M2 took its place. In 1977 the M2 was itself replaced by the M20, which carried a single 1 MT

---

* MSBS = *Mer–Sol Balistique Stratégique* (sea-to-land ballistic strategic missile).

warhead, together with penetration aids and decoys, to a range of 3,000 km. The final Cold War missile was the three-stage M4, which entered service in two variants: M4A, with a range of 4,000 km, and M4B, with a range of 5,000 km. Both carried six MIRVs (six TN 70s on the M4A and six TN 71s on the M4B), and one set of sixteen M4As and three sets of sixteen M4Bs were rotated between five SSBNs.

In March 1989 (i.e. close to the end of the Cold War) the French navy completed its two-hundredth deterrent patrol. Each of these had lasted seventy days, with a twenty-one-day break between patrols for cleaning, minor servicing and crew changeover at the SNLE base on the Île de Longue, off the port of Brest.

The original SNLEs were restricted by the range of the M1 and M2, and thus probably carried out their deterrent patrols in the Norwegian Sea. The increased range of the M20 enabled them to operate from the east Mediterranean and north Atlantic, while the M4 enabled them to operate from most parts of the north Atlantic, including close to the French coast, where they could take advantage of protection, particularly against Soviet ASW forces, by shore-based ASW aircraft.

Targeting

The general French position towards deterrence was given in 1964 by President De Gaulle, who stated that:

> But, once reaching a certain nuclear capability and as far as one's own direct defence is concerned, the proportion of respective means has no absolute value. In fact, since a man and a country can die but once, deterrence exists as soon as one can mortally wound the potential aggressor and is fully resolved to do so, and he is well convinced of it.[5]

The declared French policy throughout the Cold War was to target Soviet cities, even when the increasing accuracy of French warheads seemed to make a counter-force strike a possibility. Thus the possibilities with the MSBS M4 were: to concentrate all six MIRVs on one target, to use three each against two targets, to use two each against three targets, or to use one on each of six targets. French officials even argued against increasing the SNLE force to fifteen, as proposed by the Gaullists, because that would have created spare capacity in the anti-city targeting, thus enabling military targets to be engaged and, in effect, 'diluting' the French deterrent.

CHINA

The People's Republic of China (PRC) was not a direct participant in the Cold War, but its nuclear forces became an increasingly important factor in both Soviet and US calculations of the strategic balance. As in France and the UK, the government of the PRC which took power in 1949 quickly decided that a nuclear armoury would be essential if the country was to achieve the world status it deserved. The correctness of this decision was supported in Chinese eyes by the various crises involving the PRC and the USA in which the latter, either implicitly or, in some cases, explicitly, threatened the use of nuclear weapons against the PRC.

The Chinese programme appears to have started in 1955, and during the following five years Soviet scientists and military officers played a major role in helping the PRC to establish a nuclear research, development and production infrastructure. This massive help – unprecedented between a nuclear and a non-nuclear power – ceased abruptly with the political rift between the two countries in 1960, which set the Chinese programme back several years. Even so, the first atomic-bomb test took place on 16 October 1964, when a 22 kT device was exploded, followed by a second in May 1965 and a third in May 1966, while in October 1966 a missile was launched carrying a nuclear warhead which successfully detonated on arrival at the Lop Nor test site. The first H-bomb was successfully tested in June 1967, less than three years after the first atomic-bomb test – a considerably shorter gap than has been achieved by any other country.

Despite the Soviet help in the 1950s, the PRC's rapid ascent to the status of a nuclear power was a truly remarkable achievement. It must be remembered that at the time of the Communist takeover in 1949 China was, in industrial terms, a very backward country, with very little modern infrastructure, and most of the little that did exist had been damaged in either the Second World War or the Civil War. On top of that, there were no established aircraft-construction or shipbuilding industries, no electronics industry, and only a limited weapons industry. Almost everything, therefore, had to be created from nothing.*

Bombers
The only aircraft with a strategic capability to enter service with the Chinese air force was the Hong 6, a licence-produced version of the Soviet Tupolev Tu-16 Badger. An elderly twin-jet design, it could carry a single nuclear weapon to a range of some 3,000 km. Some 120 were produced and, at least at the end of the Cold War, there were no known plans to produce a successor.

Land-Based Missiles
The Soviet Union supplied the PRC with two SS-1 missiles in 1956. These were direct copies of the German A-4, and were followed by fourteen of the

---

* Specifications of Chinese ballistic-missile submarines are given in Appendix 14 and of Chinese missiles in Appendix 16.

improved SS-2 missile between 1957 and 1960. The latter was placed in production as the Dong Feng 1 (DF-1; 'Dong Feng' means 'East Wind') and carried a high-explosive warhead; it was primitive, but it gave the People's Liberation Army experience of working with missiles. Meanwhile, a serious domestic research-and-development programme had been set in train, with the intention of producing a family of land-based missiles for use against US targets. The DF-2 was the first and was based on the Soviet SS-3, 'Shyster'. The missile was road-mobile and was launched from an erector–launcher, although its liquid fuel required a long and hazardous preparation time.

Next came the DF-3, which was much larger, but still road-mobile, although the use of storable liquid propellant resulted in a much reduced preparation time. Deployment peaked at some 120 in the early 1980s but reduced to approximately seventy by the late 1980s. The DF-3 carried a 3 MT thermonuclear warhead and had a range of 2,650 km, enabling it to threaten the US bases then located in the Philippines. A number of DF-3s, reported to be thirty-six, were exported to Saudi Arabia, although it is claimed that these were armed with high-explosive and not nuclear warheads.

The series continued with DF-4, in which a DF-3 first stage was mated to a new second stage; fuel was again storable liquid. With a range of 4,500 km, the DF-4 could attack the US facilities on Guam with a 3 MT warhead, and some fifteen to twenty were deployed. The final missile in this series was the DF-5, which in its DF-5A version delivered a 5 MT warhead over a 13,000 km range.

The PRC has used a wide variety of basing methods for its ICBMs. Both the DF-2 and the DF-3 were road-mobile, but their successor, the DF-4, was originally planned to be silo-based, although once the vulnerability of such a scheme had been appreciated alternative basing methods were sought. A rail-mobile scheme was considered and tested in 1975, but it was finally decided to install part of the DF-4 force in silos and part in caves. The silos are similar those used by the first-generation US ICBMs, with the missiles sitting in the silos atop large elevators which raise them to the surface for fuelling, final preparation and launch (as with the US Atlas missiles in the 1960s). The remaining missiles are mounted on mobile erectors located inside modified caves with blast-proof doors; the missiles would be brought out and erected before launching.

A range of further possibilities was considered for the DF-5s, including rail-mobility and imaginative schemes such as false bridge towers, narrow gorges, mock civilian houses and even barges on the Yangtze river.[6] In the end it was decided to base them in hardened underground silos among a large number of dummy silos.

The effectiveness of the Chinese basing policy was endorsed by the US Joint Chiefs-of-Staff, who stated that:

China views its strategic missile force as an effective nuclear deterrent because its deployment strategy of mobility, hardening, and concealment poses targeting problems for any potential aggressor. This strategy enhances the survivability of some portion of the missile force for a significant retaliatory strike.[7]

Indeed, even after the end of the Cold War it was generally admitted that not even US or Soviet satellites had been able to identify anything approaching all the Chinese missile sites; thus China had achieved what neither the USA nor the USSR had ever been able to do.

Submarines

Just before their split, the Soviet Union supplied the PRC with the plans and components for a Golf-class, diesel-electric-powered, ballistic-missile submarine, which was completed at Lüda in 1964. This was originally fitted with three vertical launch tubes in the sail, as in the Soviet original, but in 1974 it was modified by removing all three launch tubes and replacing them with two of greater diameter to enable it to test Chinese SLBMs.

The submarine element of the force was the Daqingyu-class SSBN, one of which was launched in 1981 and completed in 1987. This was powered by a single pressurized-water nuclear reactor and was armed with twelve Ju Lang 1 SLBMs.

The Ju Lang 1 ('Ju Lang' means 'Great Wave'), like the US navy's Polaris, used solid fuel, rather than the liquid fuel of the land-based ICBMs. The first launch was from a submerged barge in April 1982, followed by a launch from the Golf-class trials submarine on 12 October 1982 and from a Daqingyu-class SSBN in 1988. The missile carried a single 250 kT warhead to a range of 1,700 km, and by the end of the Cold War it served in one twelve-missile SSBN.

Targeting

The PRC's initial intention was to target US military facilities in the Far East and, eventually, the USA itself. Thus the DF-2 was intended for US facilities in Japan, the DF-3 for US bases at Subic Bay and Clark Field in the Philippines, the DF-4 for the airbase on Guam island, and the DF-5 for Hawaii and the west coast of the continental USA. With the deterioration of the relationship with the USSR and, in particular, the border clashes in 1969, the PRC completely reoriented its strategic force to target the Soviet Union – the only example of such a move during the entire Cold War. Thus the DF-2 and the DF-3 were retargeted against Soviet cities in the Far East and Central Asia, while the DF-4 brought Moscow and the large cities and military–industrial facilities in the Urals and Siberia within range. The DF-5, however, could reach any target in the Soviet Union and western Europe.

One of the unusual aspects of the Chinese nuclear forces is that they have been fielded in remarkably small numbers: the maximum numbers of land-based missiles to be deployed, for example, were 120 DF-3s, twenty DF-4s and four DF-5s. The capacity undoubtedly existed to produce and deploy many more, but the Chinese leadership appears to have taken the view that its strategic needs would be adequately met by possessing a nuclear force capable of delivering an effective retaliatory strike if attacked by nuclear weapons – i.e. an assured and effective second-strike capability against population and military–industrial centres.

13

Civil Defence

The ultimate threat that each side in the Cold War posed to the other was to the civil population, but, despite this, governments' attitudes to protecting their own populations were rather ambivalent. In most countries, policies seemed to follow a seven- to ten-year cycle, varying from, at worst, almost total uninterest to, at best, a grudging and lukewarm enthusiasm. The figures speak for themselves: as a proportion of the defence budget, the USSR spent just under 1 per cent on civil defence, while the USA spent approximately 0.1 per cent, and the figure in most other countries was even less.

The difficulty was that, if it was to be taken seriously, the scale of the problem was huge and the costs were enormous. Further, the measures could, of necessity, only be passive: protective shelters for the population to take refuge in, respirators and protective suits to resist biological and chemical attack, fire engines to extinguish fires, and a proper organization to make it all work. Very few countries proved willing to undertake such measures on the necessary scale, particularly if they were achievable only at the expense of cuts in the more active part of the national defence budget.

It was generally accepted that even a counter-force strike (i.e. against military targets such as ICBM silos, airfields, naval ports and nuclear command-and-control centres) would result in massive civilian casualties – the so-called 'collateral damage'. One major study suggested that both the USA and the USSR would suffer casualties of the order of 12–27 million deaths from a counter-force strike, while the estimated deaths from a counter-value strike (i.e. against cities and industrial complexes) would be 25–66 million in the USA and 45–77 million in the USSR.* In both cases (i.e. counter-force and counter-value), further large numbers would have

---

* The wide ranges resulted from taking a variety of assumptions for the attack pattern and for weather and other environmental factors at the time of the attack.

suffered longer-term radiation-caused cancers. The study report also stated that, in addition, there would have been many further deaths and injuries from indirect consequences of the nuclear attacks, such as riots, sickness, disease and starvation, whose numbers were impossible to calculate.[1]

Civil-defence measures potentially consisted of four elements: a system to detect an incoming attack and warn the civil population; a policy for the orderly evacuation of urban areas; the construction of shelters; and plans to achieve national survival after an attack. Different countries gave differing emphases to these, although towards the end of the Cold War there appeared to be a growing consensus that even the most all-embracing and expensive civil-defence policies would be of little use in the face of a heavy, all-out, counter-city attack. After all, ran one argument, what value would there be in surviving in a shelter only to emerge to a world that had been totally destroyed?

Warning systems were designed to enable the general population to seek protection against heat flash, blast and, to a certain extent, fallout. The USA and the USSR would normally have received between seventeen and thirty minutes' warning of approaching missiles, but, like countries in western Europe, could have received as little as four minutes, which would have given very little time for the public to be alerted.

To be effective, an evacuation plan would have had to be implemented well in advance of an attack, but evacuation was a course fraught with difficulty. A general evacuation of the big cities would bring national life and much of industry to a standstill, and could not be sustained for a long period. Evacuation of a large city would be a lengthy, complicated and difficult operation, and if the missiles arrived while vast convoys of trains, buses and cars were stuck on the railroads and highways the nation concerned would actually suffer the worst of both worlds. Also, it would be difficult to predict in advance which refuge areas would be safe, and the arrival of large groups of townspeople in rural areas would cause enormous feeding, accommodation, medical, health, sanitation and morale problems. Finally, the opposing side might interpret the evacuation as a sign that the country concerned was conducting it as a prelude to launching its own strike, and use this as a pretext to strike first.

THE USSR

The USSR treated civil defence more seriously than most other countries, with the central headquarters being an integral part of the Ministry of Defence. One of the deputy ministers of defence was specifically responsible for civil defence, and there was a chain of command running through the council of ministers in each of the fifteen republics of the USSR down to full-time officials at town and large-factory level. The Ministry of Defence also controlled a nationwide network of civil-defence schools, where training courses were run for both military and civilian personnel.

The civilian organizations were backed up by a military Civil Defence Corps, some 50,000 strong, which was trained in basic military skills as well as civil-defence skills such as operating engineering equipment, traffic direction, and first aid. Other Ministry of Defence bodies, such as the Construction Troops, the Railway and Road Construction Troops and the Transport Organization Service, were also called upon to perform civil-defence tasks, including building shelters.

In and near the major cities, the USSR constructed hardened command posts which were designed to accommodate approximately 100,000 people in what was termed the 'leadership category' – which, by definition, meant Communist Party officials and military officers. There was also a shelter programme for the people, and by 1981 there were some 20,000 shelters, capable of accommodating approximately 13 million people, which amounted to approximately 10 per cent of the population of cities with over 20,000 inhabitants. The rate of building continued for several years after that, but it failed even to keep pace with the increase in population numbers and by the late 1980s the programme was moribund.

The remainder of the urban population would have had to rely on evacuation, and the occasional small-scale exercise was conducted. Whether the system would have coped with transporting, housing and feeding millions of city-dwellers eager to reach the countryside, particularly in the depths of a Russian winter, can only be a matter for conjecture.

The other Warsaw Pact countries had generally similar organizations, with a department in the national ministry of defence, usually headed by a lieutenant-general, responsible for civil defence.

THE USA

In the USA the responsibility for civil defence originally lay with the Department of Defense, but it was passed to the newly established Federal Emergency Management Agency (FEMA) in 1979. FEMA plans assumed that the primary Soviet strategic mission in a first strike would be against counter-force targets, and its crisis relocation plans were based on the high degree of mobility inherent in the United States, with an extensive highway system and widespread automobile ownership. Whether the gasoline would have been available for such a mass movement, whether the huge numbers of travellers would have been amenable to control, and whether the rural areas could have accepted and sustained the numbers involved was never put to the test.

THE UK

The British system made the civil authorities* responsible for civil defence, with the military in support. A large Civil Defence Corps was established in the early 1950s, consisting mainly of volunteers, backed up by a small cadre of full-time staff. This corps was trained and equipped for both heavy and light rescue, and operated in conjunction with the police, the fire services and the military, but it was disbanded in the early 1960s.

On several occasions during the Cold War the British government considered the idea of a large-scale shelter programme for the general population, but the idea was always rejected on the grounds of the enormous cost, a 1980s assessment putting the price at some £1,300 per head. As a result, the actual plan – known as the 'Stay-Put Policy' – depended upon providing a warning system and the use of TV, radio, newspapers and mailshots to tell the population to remain where they were in the event of war. The education of the population in protective measures would have been implemented only when war appeared inevitable.

Actual warning of a nuclear attack and reporting post-strike developments was the responsibility of the UK Warning and Monitoring Organization (UKWMO), which consisted of a very small number of full-time officials and some 10,000 men and women volunteers of the Royal Observer Corps.† The national nuclear-attack warning was disseminated using a cascade system, which originated with the detection of an incoming strike at the Ballistic Missiles Early Warning Station (BMEWS) at Fylingdales, Yorkshire. BMEWS passed the warning to the UK Regional Air Operations Centre, where an UKWMO cell activated some 250 carrier control points (CCPs) located throughout the UK in major police stations. On receipt of the signal, these CCPs would, in their turn, pass the warning to some 11,000 lower-level warning points (selected industrial premises, smaller police stations, fire stations and UKWMO monitoring posts) as well as activating some 7,000 powered sirens to alert the general public. In the post-strike period, UKWMO was responsible for plotting the national fallout patterns, using input from its network of some 870 three-person monitoring posts spread across the whole of the UK.

---

* In the United Kingdom, civil-defence responsibility was split: the Home Office (equivalent to an interior ministry in most other countries) was responsible for England and Wales, while the Scottish Home and Health Department and the Northern Ireland Office covered civil defence in their particular areas.
† The Royal Observer Corps was established during the Second World War to spot, identify and report approaching enemy aircraft; it converted to its nuclear-war role in the early 1950s. Its personnel wore a distinctive uniform, but were part-time, unpaid volunteers.

The UK governmental organization for the aftermath of nuclear war involved setting up a network of 'regions', each divided into a number of sub-regions, which were themselves divided into a number of counties. There was a headquarters at each level, consisting of elected representatives, civil servants, and officials of the military, police and fire services, together with support staff. Each command level, down to and including counties, had a purpose-built, heavily protected bunker; these bunkers, together with a small number of central-government and military bunkers, comprised the total national stock of nuclear-proof accommodation. There were also extensive preparations for a post-strike, military-run, country-wide communications system, which would have provided government communications until the civil system had been restored.

Finally, there was a Home Defence College, run by the Home Office, whose task was to provide training in civil-defence duties for officials and elected members. The government also maintained stockpiles of strategic commodities such as fuel, sugar, salt and flour.

OTHER COUNTRIES

Other NATO countries' policies were generally similar. The NATO policy was that 'The deterrent posture of the strategic concept of flexible response can only be fully realized if military preparedness is complemented by credible civil preparedness.'[2] Civil emergency planning was essentially a national function, but NATO policy was co-ordinated by the Senior Civil Emergency Planning Committee, which met in Brussels twice a year in peacetime but would have gone into permanent session in war.

Shelter policies were debated in most countries throughout the Cold War, as it was clear that shelters would provide protection from most of the effects of a nuclear war. In West Germany, legislation ensured that all new housing included a cellar built to government specifications. The Swedish system potentially housed some 70 per cent of the population, the Swiss some 90 per cent.

Norway was one of the NATO countries to take civil defence very seriously, with a civil-defence organization run by the Ministry of Justice. The civil-defence force had a permanent staff of 500 and a mobilized strength of 70,000, with some 33,000 more in an industrial-defence organization. In 1990, with a population of approximately 4.2 million, the country had sufficient shelters to accommodate 2.6 million people (62 per cent of the population), of whom about 2.3 million would have been in private shelters built to government standards and about 276,000 in public shelters. The government also had plans to evacuate some 500,000 people from cities, towns and areas close to military installations.[3]

A NON-CREDIBLE SYSTEM

There was no doubt that the two measures which might have been effective were shelters and evacuation. The former would, however, have been enormously costly, while the latter would have involved major problems of control and reception arrangements. There was also the major question of whether the general population, faced by the prospect of imminent nuclear attack, would actually have been amenable either to reason or even to a degree of coercion. It is certainly arguable whether the inhabitants of major cities such as London, New York, Washington DC, Paris, Cologne, Moscow or Leningrad, knowing that their cities must be on the enemy's target list, would have remained in their homes, and there must have been at least a possibility that a fairly large number would have fled, probably with increasing degrees of panic, to the countryside.

The general picture, however, was one of governments doing the bare minimum for the civil population and begrudging any expenditure on preparations for civil defence. Curiously, many countries did this against a background of a network of government bunkers which would have ensured that those making the 'no evacuation/no shelter' policies would themselves have dispersed and survived.

14

Assessing the Balance

For civilians, the media and academics, the most obvious way of assessing the nuclear balance was by simple numerical comparison of missiles, warheads, bombers, bombs, submarines and so on. Known as 'static' measures, these could be very misleading, but they were (and still are) all that was possible without access to the full range of facts and to computers with the processing power necessary to run the comparisons.

The raw yield of a nuclear weapon is expressed in terms of its equivalence to the energy released by high explosive (TNT). Raw yield is, however, not an accurate expression of the weapon's effect, and to compare the total raw yields of weapons held by different nations is virtually meaningless. The first refined expression of war fighting performance is therefore *equivalent megatonnage* (EMT), which reflects a weapon's potential to damage 'soft' or area targets.

For yields of 200 kT and above: $\text{EMT} = \text{yield}^{2/3}$

For yields of less than 200 kT: $\text{EMT} = \text{yield}^{1/2}$

Table 14.1 Equivalent megatonnage

Raw yield	Formula	EMT
10 kT		0.10
20 kT	$\text{Yield}^{1/2}$	0.14
100 kT		0.32
200 kT		0.45
1 MT		1.00
2 MT	$\text{Yield}^{2/3}$	1.59
10 MT		4.64
20 MT		7.37

Table 14.1 shows a 'law of diminishing returns' operating, where, for example, a tenfold increase in raw yield from 1 MT to 10 MT results in less than a fivefold increase in EMT.

EMT does not, however, make any allowance for accuracy (CEP), which is an important consideration when attacking pinpoint targets such as missile silos. This requires a more sophisticated measure to assess weapon *lethality* or *counter-military potential* (CMP):

$$\text{counter-military potential} = \frac{\text{yield}^n}{\text{CEP}^2}$$

where $n = 2/3$ for yields of 200 kT and above

$n = 4/5$ for yields of less than 200 kT

and   CEP is measured in nautical miles.

Thus the greater the accuracy (i.e. the smaller the CEP), the greater will be the CMP; in fact the lethality increases much more rapidly with accuracy than it does with yield.

It follows from this that the ability of a country to destroy an opponent's missiles in their silos is the product of the CMP and the total number of warheads:

i.e.   total CMP = CMP × number of warheads

AVAILABILITY

The simple fact that a missile existed was not, however, the whole story, and two further factors came into play in assessing whether or not a missile was likely to achieve its purpose: availability and reliability.

Availability was an assessment of whether or not a weapons system would be 'ready to go' at the moment it was required, and was a function of factors such as a missile's having been taken 'off-line' for maintenance, or removed altogether either to be modernized or for the silo to be rebuilt to meet greater hardness criteria, and so on. If a missile was unavailable, then so too were its warheads, making a difference of one potential target in the case of a single-warhead missile, but of up to ten or even fourteen where the missile was fitted with multiple warheads (MRVs or MIRVs).

One factor which could have increased the number of missiles available was the use of at least some of the apparently non-operational stocks. Thus an SSBN in port undergoing a short refit between patrols might have been brought up to operational status within forty-eight hours and could either have put to sea rapidly or, in the worst case, have fired its missiles while still lying alongside. Some navies also operated trials submarines (e.g. the French *Gymnote* and the single Chinese Golf-class) which could have launched missiles in a wartime emergency.

Land-based test centres existed to test prototypes and, at least in the US case, were also used for routine testing of operational missiles. They thus obviously had full-scale launch facilities which could be used to generate additional missile launches in war. The US Vandenberg Air Force Base in California, for example, was capable of launching up to sixteen missiles,[1] while there were launch facilities for Chinese DF-4s at various test centres in China, for Russian missiles at similar sites in the USSR, and for four French SSBS S3D missiles at the Centre d'Essais des Landes (CEL) test facility for land-based missiles, in south-west France.

RELIABILITY

Reliability, on the other hand, was an assessment of the probability that available systems would function correctly from the moment of issuing the launch instruction to the arrival of a warhead at the target. The general approach to determining the probability of success for a complex operation was to break it down into a sequence of discrete events and to determine the probability of the successful outcome of each one, normally expressed as a percentage. All these probabilities were then multiplied together to give the overall probability of success – i.e. the probability that the missile would accomplish its mission. Thus, for example, a missile with ten discrete functions (first stage motor fires, missile leaves silo, second stage motor fires, second stage separates from first stage, and so on), each with a 98 per cent probability of success, has an overall reliability factor of $(98 \div 100)^{10} = 82$ per cent.

One problem with the reliability equation was that it was impracticable to test the missiles on their operational flight paths. US test flights, for example, were in either south-easterly or south-westerly directions or due south, whereas the operational flights would have been to the north, north-west or north-east. Similarly, Soviet test flights were not in the direction required for operational flights, although the huge land mass of the USSR enabled Soviet strategic rocket forces to carry out regular missile testing using live missiles fired from their operational silos, whereas US ICBMs had to be taken to Vandenberg Air Force Base. Thus it was possible that, had they ever been launched in anger, missile guidance systems might have been influenced by some unexpected factor, such as a minor variation in the earth's magnetic field, for which no allowance had been made. This might well not have had a significant effect on a counter-value mission, but could have caused just sufficient variation in a counter-force mission to make the difference between success and failure.

157

Although SSBNs frequently launched SLBMs with inert heads, there was only one known example of a fully operational SSBN/SLBM launch with a nuclear warhead. Designated 'Frigate Bird', this took place in the Pacific Ocean on 6 May 1962, when USS *Ethan Allen* (SSBN-608) launched a Polaris A-2 missile with a W47 warhead. The test, which was successful, involved a flight of 1,890 km from the submerged launch, culminating in an airburst over Christmas Island.

Numerous operational examples occurred to show that missiles were neither as available nor as reliable as may have been thought. The US navy's Poseidon C-3 had severe reliability problems in the early 1970s, and there were several reports that missiles had failed to fire during routine tests. A significant number of Poseidons' W68 warheads were also reported to have been defective, due to degradation of the high-explosive element, one effect of which could have been the failure of the detonator.[2] Although unconfirmed at the time, the US navy subsequently tacitly endorsed these reports by stating that the Trident II C-4 had a 'much better reliability record' than the Poseidon C-3.

In an incident in 1986, an unarmed Soviet navy SS-N-8 was test-fired by a Delta II SSBN in the Barents Sea and aimed at the missile test range on the Kamchatka Peninsula, but landed near the Amur river on the Sino-Soviet border, some 2,400 km from its target. Since missile are always carefully checked and prepared for test flights, such a major deviation from the intended flight path caused considerable concern at the time.[3] Another incident, much publicized at the time, occurred in October 1986, when a Soviet Yankee-class SSBN suffered serious structural damage as a result of an explosion in one of the missile tubes, presumably involving the highly volatile liquid fuels. In another incident a Soviet Delta IV-class SSBN attempted to launch sixteen SS-N-23 missiles one after another in the White Sea on 7 December 1989. The third missile failed very soon after launch and fell back on to the submarine (which presumably was on the surface) and thirteen men were injured.

According to Russian sources, the SS-N-4 SLBM was in service between 1961 and 1973, and during that time 311 test launches were made. Of those launches, there were 38 missile failures, 38 failures due to other known causes, and 10 due to unknown causes. In other words, only 72.3 per cent (225) of the missiles were successful, and that was without a live warhead, which would have introduced yet another element of uncertainty.[4]

SINGLE-SHOT KILL PROBABILITY

Single-shot kill probability (SSKP) is an expression of the probability that one warhead of specified reliability will destroy a hardened target. Thus it can be calculated that a single warhead of 0.5 MT yield, a CEP of 260 m and a reliability of 85 per cent, attacking a target capable of withstanding an over-pressure of 146 kgf/cm^2, would have an SSKP of 54 per cent. In other words, the warhead has a marginally better than 'evens' chance of success.

CAPABILITIES

As explained earlier, a true assessment of the nuclear balance would require a detailed analysis of a vast array of variable factors, and would need to include allowances for factors such as availability, reliability, differing prac-tices in SSBN sea-time, the weather at both launch sites and targets, and so on. It would also need to take account of each side's targeting plans, includ-ing how many warheads might be allocated to the first and second strikes, how many might be classified as 'withholds', how many might be retained as strategic and 'nth-country reserves', and so on. Determining such a balance would also require individual missile systems to be split between counter-value and counter-force targets.

With so many factors to be taken into account, a powerful computer would be needed to calculate the final result, which would need to be accom-panied by long and detailed explanations. However, Tables 14.2 to 14.4 show a general picture of the situation by taking three 'snapshots' of the situation in 1970, at which time the missile race was really under way, in 1990, at the end of the Cold War, and in 1980, halfway between the two.*

Table 14.2 The Strategic Balance – Missiles*

Missiles	1970		1980		1990	
	USA	USSR	USA	USSR	USA	USSR
ICBMs	1,054	1,465	1,039	1,330	990	1,710
SLBMs	656	229	576	937	624	930
Total	1,710	1,694	1,615	2,267	1,614	2,640

Table 14.2 shows the balance in numbers of missiles. The number of ICBMs shows the total number of land-based missiles, which (ignoring dummy silos) was also the majority of targets the enemy would have needed to destroy in a pre-emptive strike (the others being a relatively small number of command-and-control sites). In ICBMs, both sides showed a fairly steady figure, the 1990 reduction in US ICBMs being due to the retirement without

---

* The figures in Tables 14.2 to 14.4 are derived from the detailed tables in Appendix 17.

replacement of the Titan II. In SLBM numbers, the USA had already peaked in numbers by 1970 and retained a reasonably steady state thereafter, while the USSR grew rapidly from 35 per cent of the US figure in 1970 to 163 per cent a decade later, as the many Delta-class SSBNs entered service.

Table 14.3 The Strategic Balance – Warheads

Warheads	1970		1980		1990	
	USA	USSR	USA	USSR	USA	USSR
On ICBMs	1,054	1,465	2,139	4,388	2,440	6,955
On SLBMs	656	229	4,880	1,897	5,376	3,162
Totals	1,710	1,694	7,019	6,285	7,816	10,117

Table 14.3 shows the number of warheads on the missiles, and is an indication (ignoring dummy silos) of how many targets could have been attacked, bearing in mind that pinpoint targets would probably have been targeted by two warheads. When compared with Table 14.2 it shows that, whereas there was little prospect of a successful pre-emptive strike in 1970, both sides had obtained such a capability by 1980. The table also shows that the increase in numbers of warheads on the US side was greatest on SLBMs, while in the USSR the growth was greater on ICBMs, and that by 1990 the Soviet Union possessed a marked advantage in overall warhead numbers.

Table 14.4 The Strategic Balance – Counter-Military Potential (CMP)

CMP	1970		1980		1990	
	USA	USSR	USA	USSR	USA	USSR
ICBMs	12,909	3,420	49,490	62,745	182,123	143,814
SLBMs	914	138	37,901	1,407	89,737	4,245
Totals	13,823	3,538	87,391	64,152	271,860	148,059

Table 14.4 takes the balance a stage further and compares the CMP of the two forces. From this it is clear that the power of the missile forces of both sides increased greatly during the period: by a factor of twenty for the USA and of forty-two for the USSR. The table also shows that the Soviet counter-military potential was concentrated in its ICBM force, leaving the counter-value role to the submarine-based missiles. It is also clear, however, that neither side had an advantage over the other.

PART III

NAVAL WARFARE

15

The NATO Navies

Command of the seas was at least as important in the Cold War as it had been at any time in history. Indeed, for both the USA and the USSR it became more important than ever with the development of nuclear-powered submarines carrying long-range ballistic missiles with the ability to deliver strategic weapons of devastating power against land targets anywhere in the world. In terms of surface warfare, however, the Cold War had a different importance to the two alliances, since NATO depended on the sea, while the Warsaw Pact did not.

The USA was able to deploy aircraft carriers, with their increasingly potent air wings, to any part of the world, while for NATO the Atlantic Ocean was the sea line of communication (SLOC) along which huge numbers of men and vast quantities of heavy military equipment would travel to support Europe in time of war. The sea was also the means by which many NATO forces would be deployed or redeployed, particularly to the flanks, depending upon the Soviet threat; thus the great majority of reinforcements for Norway, Denmark and Turkey were all scheduled to arrive by sea. In addition, western Europe would have required vast amounts of oil – much more in war than in peace – which would have had to continue to be brought to European oil terminals.

For the Warsaw Pact, naval surface warfare was of considerably lesser importance, since it was not essential for survival. Thus Warsaw Pact nations with access to the sea maintained only small navies – with the sole exception of the USSR, which built up a sizeable fleet, but principally in order to provide a counter to US naval might.

The opening balance between NATO and Soviet naval forces is shown in Appendix 18.

THE US NAVY

The United States navy emerged from the Second World War as the largest, most efficient and best-equipped navy in the world. The Japanese

163

navy had been the only force able to challenge US naval power in the Pacific, but it had now ceased to exist, as had the German and Italian navies across the Atlantic. The UK, on the other hand, had entered the war as the world's strongest naval power and its navy had expanded rapidly between 1939 and 1945, but, even so, it had failed to match the phenomenal growth of the US navy. As a result, in the early post-war years the British found that, while they were still strong, they had nevertheless been relegated to second place – a position they initially found hard to accept, as the row over the demand that a British admiral be SACLANT in the early 1950s showed. The traditional friendship between the US and UK navies, which had become even closer during the war, did, however, make the change in status less unpleasant than it might otherwise have been and, once the British had adjusted, the two navies continued to enjoy a very close relationship.

The US navy found itself in 1946 with a role that was not very clear-cut and a huge surplus of warships, many of them less than three years old. The active fleet was reduced dramatically, building programmes were cut to the bone, many ships were transferred to allies or scrapped, and the remainder – still a large number – were placed in reserve. Development work continued, including detailed examination of German designs and many tests of captured German equipment, particularly missiles and submarines, but it was the emergence of the Soviet threat, particularly in Europe, that first provided a post-war focus for the fleet.

The establishment of NATO, coupled with the military weakness of the west-European nations, made it inevitable that the United States would become involved in any conflict in Europe and that the majority of its help would go by sea. Maintaining the sea lines of communication across the north Atlantic thus became a major commitment, taking two forms: anti-surface operations against Soviet navy surface groups and anti-submarine operations.

The United States' position in the world also meant that the navy had to undertake missions in the Third World in support of the national policy of containing Communist expansion. This involved active naval operations in Korea and Vietnam, as well as in numerous minor conflicts, such as in Lebanon. The major confrontation throughout the Cold War period, however, was with the Soviet navy, where the US navy saw its potential enemy grow from a relatively minor coastal force to the second greatest navy in the world.

In the late 1940s and early 1950s the main emphasis was placed on carrier groups which would carry bombers to attack the Soviet navy's ship and air bases supporting the Northern, Baltic and Black Sea fleets. The growing numbers of Soviet submarines were countered by a variety of means. There were large numbers of Second World War destroyers and frigates still available which were capable of accommodating the anti-submarine-warfare sensors and weapons of the time, as well as large numbers of ASW aircraft. Also, in the late 1940s a new type of 'hunter/killer' submarine was developed, which was equipped with large and highly sensitive sonars and whose intended mission was to wait off Soviet naval bases and to attack enemy submarines as they deployed; it was, however, not a success, and attention returned to more traditional designs. The US navy also devoted considerable funds to the Sound Surveillance System (SOSUS), a series of microphones lying on the seabed across choke points such as the Greenland–Iceland–UK gap and linked by seabed cables to control centres ashore, which gave advance warning of submarine deployments.

One of the key developments was the introduction of nuclear propulsion for both submarines and surface ships, which was masterminded by one of the most remarkable figures of the post-war era in any navy: Admiral Hyman Rickover.* He applied nuclear propulsion to submarines and later to aircraft carriers and cruisers, producing ships whose endurance was limited only by that of the crew, although the nuclear carriers still needed to be replenished with fuel, weapons and ammunition for the air wing.

The Vietnam War was a major preoccupation for the US navy for over a decade, but the absence of any significant naval opposition meant that naval air and surface power could be used almost totally in support of the land battle. Despite its many commitments in the Pacific and other areas, however, the north Atlantic was the principal concern of the US navy throughout the Cold War, and virtually all US ship designs were judged against their value in a potential Atlantic conflict against the Soviet navy.

For many years the 'massive retaliation' and 'tripwire' strategies meant that any war in Europe would escalate fairly rapidly to a nuclear conflict. This, almost by definition, would be of relatively short duration; thus war stocks of ammunition, fuel and supplies in western Europe were relatively small, and there would have been little point in fighting expensive convoy battles across the Atlantic. Once the strategy changed to that of 'flexible response', however, it became possible that the war would be much longer and that fresh supplies of both men and *matériel* would have to be transported to Europe across the Atlantic.

In the 1970s, therefore, the US navy faced up to the new requirement, setting itself a goal of a '600-ship' navy. Large-scale building plans were initiated, and the programme was well under way when the Cold War came to an abrupt halt. The plans were then very quickly adjusted downwards, with

---

* Rickover (1900–86) was on the verge of retirement as a captain in 1946 when he joined the atomic-energy programme. He subsequently became chief of the Nuclear Power Division of the US navy. An extremely influential figure, with many friends in Congress, he eventually retired at the age of eighty-two, with the rank of four-star admiral.

orders cancelled, building slowed down, and many older vessels scrapped before the scheduled end of their operational lives.

Throughout the Cold War, one of the key components in the US navy's ability to deploy overseas was its under-way replenishment force. This comprised a large number of specialist vessels which could resupply warships with all their needs, enabling them to undertake operations anywhere in the world's oceans and for an almost unlimited time. The most sophisticated of them, the Sacramento class, carried 177,000 barrels of fuel oil, 1,950 tonnes of munitions, 225 tonnes of dry stores and 225 tonnes of refrigerated stores, and had a speed of 26 knots, enabling them to keep pace with a carrier task group.

One of the great achievements of the US navy during the Cold War was that it posed a very direct threat to any Soviet war plans. It could sustain movement along the transatlantic SLOC; it threatened the Soviet navy's fleet of SSBNs, even in their bastions; its carrier groups threatened attacks against major naval bases; its SSBNs threatened the very survival of the USSR; and the amphibious-warfare groups threatened landings on the Soviet flanks. Finally, the US navy possessed two intangible assets in its prestige as one of the major victors in the Second World War and in its ability to deploy large and impressive ships anywhere in the world. The combination of these factors led the Soviet Union to undertake a major naval expansion and building programme, which proved not only to be extremely costly but also to be one of the key components in its eventual collapse.

The predominance of the United States navy in the Cold War was beyond anything that had gone before – except, perhaps, the British navy at the height of its influence in the late Victorian era. Between 1945 and 1990 the US navy produced ships of a size, complexity and sophistication far beyond the capability of any other navy, and in numbers which no other nation could match. To take just four examples: thirteen supercarriers were built, thirty-one Spruance-class destroyers, sixteen Ticonderoga-class cruisers and thirty-eight Los Angeles-class SSNs, all of them world-leaders in their types.*

OTHER NATO NAVIES

All NATO nations except Luxembourg and Iceland contributed naval forces to the Alliance. These navies were of varying sizes and degrees of sophistication, and were developed and organized according to each nation's perceptions of its requirements. A degree of standardization was achieved in areas

---

* A further eleven Ticonderoga-class cruisers and sixteen Los Angeles-class SSNs were completed after the end of the Cold War.

such as station-keeping, weaponry, communications, data links, replenishment techniques and some equipment, although the basic ship designs and
tactical deployments were a national responsibility. Standardization was also
achieved as a consequence of international programmes, particularly those
involving ships procured under US aid programmes.

Belgium

Belgium's allotted NATO maritime roles included the defence, in conjunction with its allies, of the North Sea, the English Channel and the Western
Approaches. The early post-war expansion programme was based on ex-US
and ex-British warships, but four Belgian-designed frigates were constructed in the 1970s and ten 'Tripartite' (Belgium, France and the
Netherlands) minehunters in the 1980s.

Canada

The Canadian navy expanded from very small beginnings in 1939 into a
sizeable and efficient force by 1945, and it endeavoured to maintain a large-
ship capability in the early post-war years, operating an aircraft carrier and
two cruisers, all of British design. The financial and manpower costs were,
however, too great, and the two cruisers were paid off in the 1960s and the
aircraft carrier in 1970. Thereafter the navy concentrated on its NATO-
assigned ASW mission in the North Atlantic, for which it built a series of
escort vessels of unique design and pioneered the use of ASW helicopters
from small warships. The Canadians also operated a small number of submarines and some minesweepers.

Denmark

Denmark had virtually no navy at the war's end in 1945, but on joining
NATO in 1949 it was allotted the role of Baltic defence, in which it was
joined by West Germany when the latter became a NATO member in 1955.
Denmark's second naval task was the mining of the Kattegat and the Belts
to deny the Soviet fleet an exit into the North Sea. The navy also had the
national task of patrolling Greenland waters.

   To fulfil these missions, the Danish navy maintained a small number of
frigates, all designed and built in Denmark, together with three unusual
corvettes (Nils Juel class), and also provided a small number of submarines
and fast-attack craft. To meet its minelaying commitment the Danish navy
was equipped with a number of dedicated minelayers.

   The Danish navy found itself facing a major re-equipment problem in the
1980s, which unfortunately coincided with a general domestic feeling of
opposition to defence (it was the time of NATO's 'twin-track' approach to
the Soviet SS-20 programme). As a result, the navy produced a novel type
of warship, the Stanflex 300 (Flyvefisken class), which employed a single

basic hull constructed of fibreglass and a common propulsion system, but with changeable weapon and sensor containers, which enabled the ships to be employed and equipped for either fast attack, minelaying, mine counter-measures (MCM) or ASW duties.

France

The French navy started the post-war era with a mixture of pre-war French warships, war-built British and American ships, and German and Italian prizes, which were used to re-establish France as a naval power – a process which was aided by the acquisition of two aircraft carriers from the UK and a third from the USA. The fleet also included two battleships: *Richelieu*, which had taken part in the war, and *Jean Bart*, which had lain incomplete throughout the war and was eventually completed, at very considerable expense, in 1949.

France was a founder member of NATO, but, while committing a substantial part of its naval forces to the Alliance, which involved the construction of large numbers of escorts, the navy also retained substantial colonial responsibilities and in 1947–54 was heavily committed to the war in distant Indo-China.

The Mediterranean was also of particular importance to France, which had a large number of dependent territories along the southern littoral, and, as a result, the US and, to a lesser extent, British domination of the NATO command structure in the Southern region caused deep resentment. Matters came to a head when General De Gaulle returned to power in 1958, and when a French request for a greater share of the command appointments was turned down he removed the French fleet from the NATO command structure – an act which led eventually to the complete withdrawal of all French forces. Thereafter the French navy acted independently, although there was still a degree of co-operation with NATO and with the US navy.

The navy also played a key role in De Gaulle's aspirations for French strategic power, and he placed an increased priority on its nuclear weapons programme, which had been in place for some years. This enormous undertaking was successful, but at the expense of other naval programmes, and very few other warships were built in the 1960s. Indeed, the nuclear development programme coupled with the operations of the submarine force absorbed a growing proportion of the available naval funds for the remainder of the Cold War, rising to some 37 per cent in 1990.

French naval aspirations also led France to develop a nuclear aircraft carrier to replace the two Clemenceau-class carriers. Although the new carrier, *Charles De Gaulle*, was completed some years after the end of the Cold War, the expense of the ship and its associated aircraft was having an effect on the rest of the fleet from the early 1980s onwards.

The economies necessary to fund these programmes included keeping ships in service longer than had been planned, delays in construction of surface ships, and the construction of a very unsophisticated 'colonial corvette', the Floreal class (designated an *'aviso'* or *'fregatte de surveillance'* in French service). In addition, the two Clemenceau-class carriers, commissioned in 1960–61, were required to operate to the end of the 1990s, as were their aircraft, including the F-8 Crusader and Étendard naval fighters and the Alizé early-warning aircraft.

West Germany

The West German navy (*Bundesmarine*) was created in 1956 and from then on was firmly integrated within NATO, its principal tasks being the defence of the Baltic and North seas, in conjunction with other NATO navies. Initially the ships were a mixture of surplus US and British types, with a few German-built ships which had been transferred to the Allies as war reparations being returned as well, but the warship-building industry was rapidly restored.

The largest units were destroyers, of which the first six were ex-US Fletcher-class ships, supplemented in the mid-1960s by four German-designed and -built ships. Next to be acquired were three US-designed Adams-class destroyers and then eight frigates based on a Dutch design. The German navy also provided a large number of fast-attack craft and mine-countermeasure vessels (MCMVs), but, not surprisingly in view of its history, one of its main strengths lay in its U-boats. These were all of German design, and by the 1970s eighteen 500-tonne-displacement Type 206s were in service. West Germany also proved particularly successful in exporting submarines, which helped to sustain its design and construction capability at times when there were no domestic orders.

Greece and Turkey

The Greek and Turkish navies operated in the Aegean and eastern Mediterranean, but, unlike Greece, Turkey also had major commitments in the Dardanelles and the Black Sea. Although their countries were traditional enemies, the two navies were of similar size and followed very similar development patterns during the Cold War, largely because assistance from the USA and other NATO allies had to be demonstrably even-handed to ensure that neither felt the other was being favoured.

Both navies operated large numbers of ex-US destroyers until the early 1980s, when Greece acquired two ex-Dutch Kortenaer-class frigates. The Turkish navy did not buy any Kortenaers, but when it started to acquire German-designed MEKO frigates the Greek navy followed suit.

Both navies also operated large submarine forces, and here again they used ex-US boats of Second World War vintage, until they both started to acquire German Type 209s in the early 1970s. Both also operated a number of landing ships, since much of their maritime rivalry revolved around the islands in the Aegean.

Italy

The Mediterranean was a very important area both to NATO and to Italy, with a substantial Soviet threat. There were Soviet air and naval bases on the Black Sea and a steadily growing naval squadron in the Mediterranean itself. In addition, the Soviet navy maintained a submarine base in Albania until the diplomatic split in December 1961, and also operated naval and air bases in Egypt (until 1976) and in Libya. The Italian navy had ended the Second World War with a fleet consisting almost entirely of Italian-built vessels, but some of the best of these were lost when they were allocated to former Allied powers under the terms of the 1949 peace treaty.

During the Cold War the Italian navy built up a substantial force of large, fast and well-armed cruisers and destroyers, and also built the *Giuseppe Garibaldi*, a highly effective carrier for V/STOL aircraft, displacing 13,850 tonnes. These were all Italian-designed and -built, and the first generation of post-war submarines which were provided from US navy surplus stocks were also steadily replaced by Italian-designed boats. The Italian navy also maintained a substantial number of corvettes and fast patrol boats for operations close to the Italian coast, particularly in the Adriatic and in the Strait of Messina.

The Netherlands

The Dutch navy was rebuilt after the war with help from both the USA and the UK. On the establishment of NATO, the Dutch were given two tasks: helping in the provision of ASW forces in the eastern Atlantic and in the anti-submarine and anti-mine defence in the North Sea. Three large ships were operated for some years: the ex-British carrier *Karel Doorman* (acquired in 1948) and two large Dutch-built cruisers which had been laid down in 1939 and were completed in 1953. All three proved too expensive, however, and the carrier was sold in 1969, while the cruisers lasted until 1973 and 1976.

The Dutch navy provided a task group for employment in the north Atlantic, comprising a flagship (a Tromp-class destroyer), a number of frigates and a replenishment ship, all Dutch-designed and -built. The Dutch also operated a small number of diesel-electric submarines and a large MCM force.

Norway

Norway occupied a particularly important place in NATO's maritime strategy, since it lay alongside the only route by which ships and submarines of the Soviet Northern Fleet could sail out into the Atlantic. The Norwegian navy was far too small to challenge the large Soviet surface action groups, and it concentrated instead on anti-submarine warfare, particularly in its many fjords. Its equipment included a number of frigates built to a US design in Norwegian shipyards (the Oslo class), and sixteen small diesel-electric submarines (the Kobben class), which were designed and built in Germany. Replacement of the latter by the new Ula class (also German-built) was just beginning as the Cold War ended. Norway also operated some coastal-attack craft and MCMVs.

Portugal
Although Portugal was a long-established maritime nation, the Portuguese navy remained relatively small throughout the Cold War. This was in part due in the early years to colonial commitments in Africa and Asia, but also, throughout the period, to the fragile state of the Portuguese economy. The navy sustained a small force of frigates and corvettes, but managed eventually to obtain three large and modern German-built frigates, for which a group of other NATO nations provided 60 per cent of the funding. The navy also operated four small submarines and a number of patrol vessels.

Spain
Spain did not join NATO until 1982, and even then it did not become a part of the integrated command structure, although from 1953 onwards it had received considerable assistance from the United States under a bilateral agreement. Some ships were supplied from surplus US stocks, but others, such as the Baleares and Numancia classes, were to US designs but built in Spanish yards. The Spanish navy also operated an aircraft carrier, with a V/STOL air wing, and a number of submarines, which were licence-built in Spanish yards to French designs.

The UK
The United Kingdom emerged from the Second World War essentially bankrupt, but still retaining a large empire and with the second largest navy in the world. The manpower needs of the civil economy, combined with the need to reduce expenditure, ensured that the navy was reduced very quickly. Despite all these factors, the navy failed to appreciate its reduction in status and, while strongly supporting the founding of NATO, it challenged the paramountcy of the US navy in areas such as the Atlantic and Mediterranean, although it eventually had to be satisfied with the Channel command.

In the early years the British navy had to combine its Cold War duties in European and Atlantic waters with a wide range of imperial and post-imperial duties. There was an understandable wish to retain larger ships, although the largest of them all, the battleships, were quickly disposed of. Cruisers were smaller and cheaper to run than battleships and were retained for somewhat longer, but even they proved large and expensive by post-war standards and the last of them were phased out in the late 1970s.

Great efforts were put into retaining a carrier capability, as carriers were of great value in both NATO and 'out-of-area' operations. Numbers and effectiveness both peaked in the early 1960s, but thereafter a steady reduction saw the final fixed-wing carrier paid off in 1978. Fixed-wing carriers were succeeded by a smaller and innovative design, the V/STOL carrier, which was originally envisaged as an ASW platform, operating helicopters for anti-submarine duties and Sea Harrier fighters for self-defence, although the Falklands War (1982) showed that they were also capable of serving as attack carriers in a limited-war setting.

The main strength of the British navy in the Cold War, however, lay in its surface escorts (destroyers and frigates), of which it built 123 new ships between 1950 and 1990. Other types like amphibious-warfare ships, MCMVs and coastal-attack craft were also built, but in much more modest numbers.

In the field of nuclear propulsion, the British followed closely on the US lead – a process which was eased by considerable US help, another tangible result of the close relationship between the two navies. Throughout the 1970s and 1980s the navy operated four SSBNs and fifteen SSNs, although, unlike the US navy, it also continued to produce and operate diesel-electric submarines.

In NATO, the UK's principal task was anti-submarine warfare in the north Atlantic, the Channel and the North Sea, which also involved air-force maritime-patrol aircraft. The British navy also made modest contributions to the Alliance's amphibious-warfare capabilities.

STANDING NAVAL FORCES

As evidence of Alliance solidarity, NATO navies contributed to three standing naval forces, which were maritime equivalents to the land-based Allied Command Europe Mobile Force (AMF). The Standing Naval Force Atlantic (STANAVFORLANT) was formed in 1967 and consisted of one destroyer or frigate each from Canada, West Germany, the Netherlands, the UK and the USA, with periodic additions from Belgium, Denmark, Norway and Portugal. This force operated as a group and came under command of SACLANT, with command delegated to CINCLANT when in European waters.

A second force, the Naval On-Call Force Mediterranean (NAVOC-FORMED), was formed in 1969 for service in the Mediterranean. As its name indicated, the ships were 'on call' and not permanently assigned, although they exercised together once per year. This force was later upgraded to standing-force status, becoming STANAVFORMED.

A third force, Standing Naval Force Channel (STANAVFORCHAN), was formed in 1973 and consisted of MCMVs from Belgium, West Germany, the Netherlands and the UK, with periodic additions from Denmark, Norway and the USA. The force came under the command of CINCHAN.

These standing forces carried out an annual programme of exercises, manoeuvres and port visits, and provided a practical demonstration of NATO's naval solidarity. Within each group, command was exercised by one of the captains, rotating on an annual basis between nations. The groups carried out NATO tasks and could be deployed at short notice to a crisis area.* They also provided continuing experience in multinational tactics and operations, command-and-control procedures, communications, data links, and replenishment at sea.

NATO'S STRENGTHS

Both NATO and the Warsaw Pact were dominated by a single navy whose resources, technical skill and sheer size were far greater than those of any of its allies. The essential difference, however, was that in NATO the United States allowed the allied navies to play a full role and to develop their fleets according to their traditions and abilities. This resulted in a great disparity in ship design and internal operating procedures, but also in a greater sense of mutual confidence and common purpose, as was particularly demonstrated by the standing naval forces.

---

* Albeit after the end of the Cold War, both STANAVFORMED and STANAVFORCHAN were deployed to the Adriatic during NATO operations after the break-up of Yugoslavia.

16

The Warsaw Pact Navies

Unlike the USA and the West, the Soviet Union and the Warsaw Pact did not depend upon the sea, since they were all part of a contiguous land mass and thus operated on what strategists define as 'interior lines'. During the Second World War the Axis powers suffered an inherent disadvantage because Germany and Italy were each separated by thousands of miles of Allied-dominated ocean from their only other important ally, Japan, and contact was confined to a few submarines and a diminishing number of merchant vessels. For the USSR in the Cold War, however, there were no overseas allies of any significance, and minor allies such as Cuba, Angola, Vietnam (post-1974) and Egypt (pre-1972) were countries whose loss in a war with NATO the Soviet General Staff could have viewed with total equanimity. There was therefore no inherent requirement for the Soviet Union to move troop reinforcements, military equipment, supplies or oil by sea and, as a result, the fleets of the two rival power blocs were intended to meet totally different requirements and developed in quite different ways.

THE SOVIET NAVY

Overview
During the Cold War the Soviet navy underwent a more fundamental change than any other navy in the world. The German, Italian and Japanese navies having been destroyed, the Soviet fleet emerged from the Second World War as a very poor third to the US and British navies in size and modernity, and, of possibly greater importance, with extremely limited experience of open-ocean ('blue-water') operations. During the Cold War, however, the Soviet navy rose to become second in size only to the US navy, while its designers produced ships, weapons and electronic systems which in most cases were at least the equal of those in the West, and in some cases

well in advance. During this process it became a highly professional and competent naval force which was at home in any part of the world's oceans.

Although it was considered a major threat to the West, however, the Soviet navy suffered from four inescapable problems. The most intractable of these was that its naval resources had, of necessity, to be split between four major fleets: the Northern, Baltic, Black Sea and Pacific fleets. (A fifth, much smaller, fleet in the Caspian Sea was of little strategic significance.) This geographical separation was so great that there was no practical way in which these fleets could provide mutual support for each other. It was at least theoretically possible for ships to transfer between the Northern and Pacific fleets via the Arctic Ocean (in summer) or via the Atlantic, Indian and Pacific oceans, but whether either route would have been feasible in wartime was improbable, and a rerun of Admiral Zinovy P. Rozhdestvensky's fatal voyage would have been a distinct possibility.*

A further problem was that each of the four major fleets could reach the open ocean only by passing through choke points which were not under Soviet control. Thus the Northern Fleet had to sail past the long Norwegian coastline and then transit through either the Greenland–Iceland, Iceland–Faroes or Faroes–UK gap to reach the Atlantic. The Baltic and Black Sea fleets had even tighter gaps to pass through: the former through the Danish Belts, the Kattegat and then the Skagerrak, and the latter through the Bosporus and the Dardanelles. In the Far East the fleet, except for units based at Petropavlovsk on the Kamchatka Peninsula, had to pass through either the Korean, Tsugaru or La Pérouse straits to reach the Pacific.

In addition, most of the Soviet navy's home ports were ice-bound for at least part of the winter, and the navy lacked the many forward bases that were available to the US navy, which could use harbour facilities around the world, except in Communist-controlled countries, while the Polaris/Poseidon-armed SSBNs were permanently forward-based in Scotland (Holy Loch), Spain (Rota) and Guam. Until late in the Cold War, this Soviet problem was exacerbated by the lack of under-way replenishment ships which could resupply task groups in distant waters with everything they needed.

Finally there was an intangible factor: the lack of recent naval combat experience. The Soviet navy had played only a very limited role in the

---

* During the Russo-Japanese War (1904–5), its Pacific Fleet having been virtually eliminated by the Japanese, the Imperial Russian Navy dispatched its Baltic Fleet, commanded by Rozhdestvensky, to the Pacific. It left its home ports in October 1904 and sailed via the North Sea and the Atlantic Ocean, around the Cape of Good Hope, and then across the Indian Ocean and the South China Sea. Near the end of a desperate voyage, on 27 May 1905 the Russians met the Japanese fleet, commanded by Admiral Togo Heihachiro, at Tsu-shima, where they were decisively defeated.

Second World War; indeed, almost one-third of it – the Pacific Fleet – had played no part at all. The rest of the navy had fought a small-unit war in motor torpedo boats, submarine-chasers (small escorts), submarines and river flotillas. They had fought hard, certainly, and the submarine service had lost no less than eighty-nine boats in action (107 in all), but the overall results had been negligible. Thus, although the Soviet navy expanded very rapidly from the 1950s onwards, built many large and innovative warships, and became a true blue-water navy, it was all based on theory. On the other hand, the larger NATO navies, and in particular the Americans, British and French, had great experience in large-ship operations, the use of carriers, the employment of naval air power, the use of amphibious forces, the need for and the practice of damage control, and maintaining fleets in distant waters. Above all, they had experience of the command, control and communications needed to tie all this together.

Four external factors spurred the major developments in the Soviet navy. First was the deployment in the 1950s of US navy carrier groups operating aircraft such as the North American AJ-2 Savage, which could carry nuclear weapons to attack targets deep inside the Russian homeland. Second was the Soviet realization during the 1962 Cuban Missile Crisis that they were unable to influence events in the Atlantic and Caribbean because they lacked blue-water surface forces. Third was the requirement to combat the threat posed by the US navy's strategic missile submarines. The fourth and final factor was the perceived need to develop amphibious forces to deploy land forces on distant shores – something it had seen the US navy do on numerous occasions and was unable to match.

The Soviet navy's operational priorities for surface warfare changed as the Cold War progressed and the threat from the USA and NATO was seen to alter. In the late 1940s the coastal navy was capable of little more than the defence of it bases, but the 1950s threat posed by bombers launched from US aircraft carriers forced the Soviet navy to become more of a blue-water navy. This US threat was supplemented by cruise-missile-armed submarines in the mid-1950s and then totally replaced by the submarines armed with Polaris SLBMs. Against all of these, however, the Soviet fleet's tasks were still defensive in nature.

In the 1960s and 1970s the Soviet navy, under the leadership of the redoubtable Admiral Gorshkov,* espoused offensive strategies. Foremost was an oceanic role in a general war, which might, according to some Soviet naval strategists, even have been an entirely naval conflict, at least in the initial stages. In addition, a peacetime role was seen in protecting pro-Soviet revolutionary movements in the Third World.

---

* Admiral of the Fleet of the Soviet Union Sergei Georgiyevich Gorshkov was commander-in-chief of the Soviet navy from January 1956 to December 1985.

Soviet naval strategy could not, however, be developed in isolation and was subject to intense criticism from the army, air force and strategic rocket force, all of which opposed plans to increase the resources allocated to the most junior of the Soviets' services. The other influence was the Western response to Soviet naval expansion, which was to plan to take the offensive in war and to fight the naval battle as close to Soviet shores as possible. It thus became noticeable that, whereas Soviet naval exercises in the 1970s and early 1980s were essentially aggressive in nature, by the middle and late 1980s they were once again defensive in character.

Soviet Naval Activity
In the immediate post-war years the only naval units of even marginal significance were three battleships: a Russian vessel dating back to tsarist times and two British ships of First World War vintage, which had been lent to the USSR during the war. One of the latter was returned to the UK in 1949, having been replaced by the ex-Italian *Giulio Cesare*, which the Soviets renamed *Novorossiysk*.* There were also some fifteen cruisers – a mixture of elderly Soviet designs, nine modern Soviet-built ships, a US ship lent during the war (and returned in 1949), and two former Axis cruisers, one ex-German, the other ex-Italian. There was also a force of some eighty destroyers, also of varying vintages and origins.

During the 1940s and 1950s these Soviet warships were rarely seen on the high seas, apart from a limited number of transfers between the Northern and Baltic fleets, which tended to be conducted with great rapidity. The only exception was a series of international visits, mainly by the impressive Sverdlov-class cruisers, which were paid to countries such as Sweden and the UK. The navy suffered a major setback in 1955 when the battleship *Novorossiysk* was sunk while at anchor in the Black Sea by a Second World War German ground mine, an event which led to the sacking of the commander-in-chief, Admiral N. M. Kuznetzov; he was replaced by Admiral Gorshkov.

In the early 1960s, however, individual Soviet units began to be seen more frequently in foreign waters, as did ever-increasing numbers of 'intelligence collectors', laden with electronic-warfare equipment. These ships, generally known by their NATO designation as 'AGIs', monitored US and NATO exercises and ship movements. The original AGIs were converted trawlers and salvage tugs, but, as the Cold War progressed and the Soviet navy became increasingly sophisticated, larger and more specialized ships were built, culminating in the 5,000 tonne Bal'zam class, built in the 1980s. In addition to such ships, conventional warships regularly carried out intelligence-collecting and surveillance tasks, particularly when Western exercises

---

* The second British battleship was retained by the Soviet navy. It was broken up at Sevastopol in 1957.

were being held. Apart from general eavesdropping on Western communications links and studying the latest weapons, such missions helped the Soviet navy to learn about US and NATO tactics, manoeuvring and ship-handling.

The Soviets also put considerable effort into espionage (human intelligence, or HUMINT, in intelligence jargon) against Western navies. This included the Kroger ring in the UK, which was principally targeted against British anti-submarine-warfare facilities, and the Walker spy ring in the USA, which gave away a vast amount of information on US submarine capabilities and deployment.

The growth and increasing ambitions of the Soviet navy were best illustrated by the size, scope and duration of its exercises. The first important out-of-area exercise was held in 1961, when two groups of ships – one moving from the Baltic to the Kola Inlet and the other in the opposite direction (a total of eight surface warships, four submarines and associated support ships) – met in the Norwegian Sea. There they conducted a short exercise before continuing to their respective destinations.

In early July 1962 transfers between the Baltic and Northern fleets again took place, coupled with the first major transfer from the Black Sea Fleet to the Northern Fleet. This was followed by a much larger exercise, extending from the Iceland–Faroes gap to the North Cape, which included surface combatants, submarines, auxiliaries and a large number of land-based naval aircraft. The activity level increased yet again in 1963, and the major 1964 exercise involved ships moving through the Iceland–Faroes gap for the first time, while units of the Mediterranean Squadron undertook a cruise to Cuba. By 1966 exercises were taking place in the Faroes–UK gap and off north-east Scotland (both long-standing preserves of the British navy) and also off the coast of Iceland.

In 1967 the naval highlight of the Arab–Israeli Six-Day War was the dramatic sinking of the Israeli destroyer *Eilat* by the Egyptian navy using Soviet SS-N-2 ('Styx') missiles launched from a Soviet-built Komar-class patrol boat. Not surprisingly, Soviet naval prestige in the Middle East was high, and the Soviets took the opportunity to enhance it yet further by port visits to Syria, Egypt, Yugoslavia and Algeria, employing ships of the Black Sea Fleet.

The following year saw the largest naval exercise to date; nicknamed *Sever* (= North) it involved a large number of surface ships, land-based aircraft, submarines and auxiliaries. The exercise covered a variety of areas, but the main activity took place in waters between Iceland and Norway. One of the naval highlights of the year, for both the Soviet and the NATO navies, was the arrival in the Mediterranean of the first Soviet helicopter carrier, *Moskva*.

Further exercises and deployments took place in 1969, but in the following year *Okean 70* proved to be the most ambitious Soviet naval exercise ever staged. This involved the Northern, Baltic and Pacific fleets and the Mediterranean Squadron in simultaneous operations, with the major emphasis in the Atlantic. A large northern force, comprising some twenty-six ships, started with anti-submarine exercises off northern Norway between 13 and 18 April, and then proceeded through the Iceland–Faroes gap to an area due west of Scotland, where it carried out an 'encounter exercise' against units from the Mediterranean Squadron. The two groups then sailed in company to join the waiting support group, where a major replenishment at sea took place. Other facets of the exercise included units of the Baltic Fleet sailing through the Skaggerak to operate off south-west Norway, and an amphibious landing exercise involving units of the recently raised Naval Infantry coming ashore on the Soviet side of the Norwegian–Soviet border.

This was a very large and ambitious exercise, from which the Soviet navy learned many major lessons, one of the most important of which was the falsity of the concept of commanding naval forces at sea from a shore headquarters. Such a concept had been propagated for two reasons: first, because it complied with the general Communist idea of highly centralized power and, second, because it also avoided the complexity and expense of flagships. Once *Okean 70* had proved this concept to be impracticable, 'flag' facilities were built into the larger ships,* although the Baltic Fleet continued to be commanded from ashore.

The exercise which took place in June 1971 rehearsed a different scenario, with a group of Soviet Northern Fleet ships sailing down into Icelandic waters, where they reversed course and then advanced towards Jan Mayen Island to act as a simulated NATO carrier task group, which was then attacked by the main 'players'. Again, a concurrent amphibious landing formed part of the exercise.

There were no major naval exercises in 1972, but in a spring 1973 exercise Soviet submarines practised countering a simulated Western task force sailing through the Iceland–UK gap to reinforce NATO's Northern flank, while a similar exercise in 1974 took place in areas to the east and north of Iceland. *Okean 75* was an extremely large maritime exercise, involving well over 200 ships and submarines together with large numbers of aircraft. The exercise was global in scale, with specific exercise areas including the Norwegian Sea, where simulated convoys were attacked; the northern and central Atlantic, particularly off the west coast of Ireland; the Baltic and Mediterranean seas; and the Indian and Pacific oceans. Overall, the exercise practised all phases of contemporary naval warfare, including the deployment and protection of SSBNs.

In 1976 an exercise started with a concentration of warships in the North

---

* 'Flag' facilities are the command, control and communications facilities and the additional working and living accommodation necessary to enable a ship to embark an admiral and his staff and to serve as the flagship of a group.

Sea, following which they transited through the Skagerrak and into the Baltic. Although not an exercise as such, great excitement was caused among Western navies when the new aircraft carrier *Kiev* left the Black Sea and sailed through the Mediterranean before heading northward in a large arc, passing through the Iceland–Faroes gap and thence to Murmansk. NATO ships followed this transit very closely, as it gave them their first opportunity to see this large ship and its V/STOL aircraft.

The following year saw two exercises in European waters, the first of which was held in the area of the North Cape and the central Norwegian Sea. The second was much larger and consisted of two elements, one involving the Northern Fleet in the Barents Sea, while in the other ships sailed from the Baltic, north around the British Isles and then into the central Atlantic. Also in 1977 the Soviet navy suffered the second of its major peacetime surface disasters when the Kashin-class destroyer *Orel* (formerly *Otvazhny*) suffered a major explosion while in the Black Sea, followed by a fire which raged for five hours before the ship sank, taking virtually the entire crew to their deaths.

In 1978 the passage of another Kiev-class carrier enabled an air–sea exercise to take place to the south of the Iceland–Faroes gap. Similar exercises followed in 1979 and 1980. The 1981 exercise involved three groups and took place in the northern part of the Barents Sea.

There were no major naval exercises in 1982, but the following year saw the most ambitious global exercise yet, with concurrent and closely related activities in all the world's oceans, involving not only warships, but also merchant and fishing vessels. In European waters, three aggressor groups assembled off southern Norway and then sailed northward to simulate an advancing NATO force; they were then intercepted and attacked by the major part of the Northern Fleet.

The major exercise in 1985 followed a similar pattern, with aggressor groups sailing northeastward off the Norwegian coast, to be attacked by a large Soviet defending task group which included *Kirov*, the lead-ship of a new class of battlecruiser,* Sovremenny-class anti-surface destroyers and Udaloy-class anti-submarine destroyers, as well as many older ships. There was also substantial air activity, which included the use of Tu-26 Backfire bombers. Although not apparent at the time, this proved to be the zenith of Soviet naval activity, and in the remaining years of the Cold War the number and scale of the exercises steadily diminished.

---

* The term 'battlecruiser' dated back to the early years of the twentieth century, when battleships optimized firepower and protection at the expense of speed, while the equally large battlecruisers had firepower equal to that of a battleship, but achieved rather greater speed at the expense of protection. The term was resurrected in the West as being the only appropriate designation for the Kirov class.

These major exercises enabled the Soviet navy to rehearse its war plans and to demonstrate its increasing capability to other navies, particularly those in NATO. There were, of course, many smaller exercises, such as those involving amphibious capabilities, which took place on the northern shores of the Kola Peninsula, on the Baltic coast and in the Black Sea. It is noteworthy, however, that the vast majority of the exercises held in European waters, and particularly those held from 1978 onwards, while tactically offensive, were actually strategically defensive in nature, involving the Northern Fleet in defending the north Norwegian Sea, the Barents Sea and the area around Jan Mayen Island.

Soviet at-sea time was considerably less than that of the US and other major Western navies. The latter maintained about one-third of their ships at sea at all times, while only about 15 per cent of the Soviet navy was at sea, reducing to 10 per cent for submarines. The Soviets did, however, partially offset this by placing strong emphasis on a high degree of readiness in port and on the ability to get to sea quickly.

OTHER WARSAW PACT NAVIES

The non-Soviet Warsaw Pact nations made only a small contribution to the Warsaw Pact naval capability; those with navies maintained them at a relatively small size, while Czechoslovakia and Hungary had no access to the sea at all. The Bulgarian, East German and Polish navies were closely directed by the Soviet navy and their roles were subordinated to the Black Sea and Baltic fleets respectively. They were supplied with Soviet ships, weapons and technology, but were seldom allowed access to the very latest developments, receiving instead modified ships with downgraded armament and sensors; in particular, they were never supplied with any naval nuclear weapons. As in other spheres, the Romanian navy had an intermittent relationship with the Soviets, but might have joined Warsaw Pact naval operations in war if Ceauşescu had deemed it advantageous to do so. Until 1961 there was also the Albanian navy, but this could have contributed nothing of significance in a war.

Albania
Albania was a close Soviet ally from 1945 onwards and was one of the founder members of the Warsaw Pact, allowing the Soviet navy to construct a greatly valued Mediterranean base at Sazan in the Gulf of Vlorës. In return, it received a number of small Soviet warships, including two Whiskey-class submarines, at favourable prices. A rapid decline in the relationship with the USSR led to a split in December 1961, when the Albanians ejected the Soviet navy from Sazan, taking the opportunity to seize two

Whiskey-class submarines in the process. Thereafter Albania depended on China for naval equipment, but its naval potential was extremely limited.

Bulgaria

The Bulgarian navy was subject to a ceiling of 7,250 tonnes and 3,500 men under the terms of the 1947 peace treaty. Its first significant military aid from the USSR was a destroyer supplied in 1947, although the vessel concerned had actually been built for the Russian navy in 1917. This was followed by several small frigates and diesel-electric submarines, but the Bulgarian navy was never a significant force in the Black Sea.

East Germany

The East German navy started as a small police marine unit in 1949, becoming the *Seestreitkräfte* (Naval Strike Force) in 1956 and the *Volksmarine* (People's Navy) in 1960. It originally undertook coastal patrol and minesweeping tasks, but in the late 1970s it assumed amphibious and ASW responsibilities as well, and a naval air division and a regiment of marines were also formed. Numerous warships were supplied by the USSR, but never included any surface ships larger than frigates, nor any submarines at all. An increasing number of warships were designed and constructed by the Peenewerft shipyard at Wolgast, some of which were supplied to the Soviet navy.

The East German navy's operational role was always subordinated to that of the Soviet Baltic Fleet, and from the late 1970s it contributed, together with the Polish and Soviet navies, to the Baltic Joint Squadron, which was intended to be the Warsaw Pact's response to NATO's three standing multinational units.

Poland

Throughout the Second World War the Polish navy had maintained a small force which operated as part of the British navy, with most of the ships and men involved returning to Poland after the war. On the formation of the Warsaw Pact in 1955 the Polish navy, small as it was, was the second largest after the Soviet navy – a position it retained until the early 1980s, when it was overtaken in size by East Germany's *Volksmarine*. Several modernization and enlargement plans were produced, but, although some successes were achieved, full implementation was always frustrated by the weakness of the Polish economy and the higher priority accorded to the army.

Throughout the Cold War, the navy operated at least one destroyer (two between 1958 and 1970), a small number of diesel-electric submarines, and a larger number of amphibious-warfare vessels, patrol craft and minesweepers. The one indigenous shipyard (the Polnocna yard at Gdańsk) constructed warships including the Polnocny-class landing ships, eighty-six of which were built: twenty-four for Poland, fifty-one for the USSR, and the remainder for various Soviet-approved export customers.

Romania

The only other Warsaw Pact nation to maintain a sea-going navy was Romania, which followed an erratic development pattern. A tonnage limit of 15,000 tonnes was imposed by the 1947 peace treaty, although the Romanians failed to approach even this comparatively low ceiling for many years. The USSR supplied some ships, and in 1951 it also returned two Romanian destroyers which had been seized by Soviet forces in 1944. The transfer of Soviet ships stopped in 1964 as Romania became more difficult to deal with, and for a while China was the principal supplier of new vessels (all small missile-armed patrol craft) or of designs which were then built in Romanian yards.

By the late 1970s the Romanian navy operated a collection of Soviet- and Chinese-supplied patrol boats and was urgently in need of modernization, but unfortunately for Romania this coincided with President Ceauçescu's grandiose dreams, resulting in an over-ambitious construction plan which played a major role in the eventual collapse of his regime. The largest single result was the 5,800 tonne *Muntenia*, a destroyer which was far larger than anything required by the Romanian navy for operational reasons, although, despite its size, the armament was weak and its sensor equipment derisory, while the ship suffered from serious stability problems. A somewhat more successful frigate design was developed, of which six were built. The Romanian navy also had a tradition of operating submarines, operating four small Soviet boats from 1957 to 1967, which were followed by a gap until 1986 when a single Soviet Kilo class diesel-electric submarine was acquired, although it proved too large for Black Sea operations.

17

Nuclear-Powered Attack Submarines

Despite the success of diesel-electric submarines during the first half of the twentieth century, it was clear that they suffered from an inherent weakness, in that there was an inescapable requirement for the submarine to surface regularly in order to recharge its batteries. During the First World War and the early days of the Second this was normally done at night, but the introduction of radar, initially aboard ships but later aboard aircraft, rendered surfaced boats increasingly vulnerable. As a result, the German navy developed the snorkel tube, which enabled the submarine to cruise at periscope depth while simultaneously recharging its batteries and clearing the foul air inside the submarine.*

This was, however, only a palliative, and in the 1930s forward thinkers in the Soviet Union† and Germany saw that what was really required was a submarine which could spend protracted periods underwater without having to approach the surface at all. In other words, they needed some form of air-independent propulsion (AIP) system. The US and British navies came to the same conclusion during the war, and both realized that nuclear propulsion would offer a very effective solution, although the potential costs were extremely high at the time, and the small amounts of plutonium then available were earmarked for bomb programmes. After the war, the Soviet navy examined a possible alternative to nuclear propulsion, the hydrogen-peroxide system developed in Germany by Dr Helmuth Walter, and developed submarines to test the system, but, having experienced its inherently

---

* The snorkel tube was actually invented by the Dutch navy in the 1930s, to enable submarines in East Indies waters to recharge their batteries without exposing themselves to the tropical heat.
† The Soviet navy carried out experiments in the late 1930s with the *Kreislauf* air-independent propulsion system, which used liquid oxygen as the source of oxygen for submerged propulsion. It was later used in a class of post-war submarines.

dangerous nature, they abandoned it and, like the Americans, turned to nuclear propulsion.

THE US NUCLEAR SUBMARINE PROGRAMME

The US nuclear-propulsion programme started just after the war, when a team of officers was sent to the Oak Ridge nuclear research plant, their leader being an obscure electrical specialist who was due to retire shortly: Captain Hyman G. Rickover. More by luck than judgement, the US navy had placed the right man in the right place at the right time: the acerbic and energetic Rickover overcame initial official indifference, and the first two nuclear-powered attack submarines (SSNs), *Nautilus* and *Seawolf*, were launched in 1954 and 1955 respectively. Their overall designs were generally similar, the main difference being that in *Nautilus* the reactor was cooled by pressurized water, while in *Seawolf* the coolant was liquid sodium. The former quickly proved its superiority, and all subsequent US nuclear-propelled submarines have had such a reactor, while *Seawolf* itself was changed to a pressurized-water system in 1959. Despite their prototype status, these first two submarines were used as operational submarines, and they were followed by four smaller boats, the Skate class (2,584 tonnes), which were commissioned in 1957–9 and remained in service until the mid-1980s.

These first six SSNs all had the traditional long, thin hull and twin propellers of the German Type XXI, but in the early 1950s the US navy examined the whole question of submarine shape and manoeuvrability, and tested the conclusions with one of the most influential submarine designs of all time, the *Albacore*. This diesel-electric boat had a 'teardrop' hull (i.e. it was shorter and fatter than the traditional design), new types of control, and a single propeller. The shape of the hull not only made the submarine much more manoeuvrable, but also gave a great increase in internal volume, resulting in a much larger battery and thus much greater submerged speed: initially 27 and later a remarkable 33 knots.

The immense success of this experimental design led to a new SSN class with an 'Albacore' hull, the Skipjack class, of which six were commissioned between 1959 and 1961. These were, however, quickly followed by the Thresher class, which were larger and had a stronger hull, enabling them to dive to greater depths, and a much improved sonar, mounted in a dome which fully occupied the bows. Eleven Thresher-class SSNs were built, followed by forty-two of the slightly different Sturgeon class, all with a primary ASW mission.

Just as this massive programme was getting under way, however, the US submarine service suffered a major blow with the loss of *Thresher* on 10 April 1963. The submarine was undergoing routine diving tests with 104 crew and twenty-five observers aboard when it experienced what it reported as a 'minor problem', but shortly afterwards it dived out of control, lost communication with the surface, and imploded as it neared the seabed. This loss led to a total re-examination of the SSN design, resulting in delays in the construction programme, but improvements were made and building restarted.* The Skipjack-class submarine *Scorpion* was later lost, also with all hands, off the Azores in May 1968. These have, however, been the only losses in the US nuclear-powered-submarine programme.

Finally came the Los Angeles-class SSNs, which were commissioned from 1976 onwards and continued in production throughout the remainder of the Cold War, until the sixty-second was commissioned in 1995. They were designed for three principal missions. The first was anti-submarine warfare, in which these boats would have patrolled off Soviet ports, in choke points and in the Soviet SSBN bastions, with the task of tracking Soviet submarines in peacetime and tension and of sinking them in war. The second role was to serve as part of an aircraft-carrier task group, particularly to detect and attack Soviet cruise-missile-launching submarines. The third role was as covert signals-intelligence (SIGINT) and electronic-intelligence (ELINT) surveillance platforms.

These boats displaced 6,260 tonnes and were equipped, like the previous Permit/Sturgeon class, with a sonar which occupied the entire bows, so that the four launch tubes had to be mounted amidships, firing outwards. The original weapon load was twenty-six torpedoes, but there were various changes. First it was decided to add SubRoc (an anti-submarine missile), then Sub-Harpoon (an anti-ship missile), and finally, from 1983 onwards, Tomahawk land-attack cruise missiles. All these missiles were carried internally, were launched from the torpedo tubes and had to be within the overall total of twenty-six,† which made the question of weapon mix for each patrol a matter of nice judgement. This problem was, however, later alleviated when it was found possible to locate twelve vertical launch tubes for Tomahawk outside the pressure hull but within the outer casing, which enabled the original torpedo load to be restored.

Differences in weapon load were, however, only an outward indication of improvements, since the Los Angeles class also improved dramatically internally during its nineteen-year production run. Analogue fire-control and sonar systems gave way to digital systems, new silencing methods were introduced, while from *San Juan* (SSN-751) onwards numerous changes were incorporated, including moving the foreplanes from the sail to the bows (to ease surfacing through ice in the Arctic), as well as a new integrated command system.

---

* With the loss of the original name-ship, the class was then officially redesignated the Permit class.
† There was also a sub-limit of eight on Tomahawks.

Not surprisingly, such highly effective weapons platforms were very expensive. Sample figures for a single Los Angeles-class submarine (in 'then-year' dollars) were $225 million in 1976, $326 million in 1979 and $844 million in 1983.

SOVIET NUCLEAR-POWERED ATTACK SUBMARINES

With the commissioning of the first US nuclear-propelled attack submarines in 1955, NATO naturally looked for the arrival of the first Soviet SSN, and the first November-class boat, *Leninsky Komsomol*, duly ran on nuclear power on 4 July 1958, some three years after its US counterpart. Despite having watched so carefully for this event, however, Western intelligence was still taken by surprise when three different types of nuclear-powered submarine all appeared within a year of each other: a ballistic-missile class (Hotel) a cruise-missile class (Echo) and an attack class (November). All were powered by the same propulsion system, consisting of two separate power trains, each with a 70 megawatt reactor and a single turbine set driving a motor-generator; there was also a creep motor on each shaft. This propulsion system was known as the 'HEN' power plant in the West (derived from the initials of the NATO reporting names, Hotel–Echo–November). As can be seen from Appendix 19, this system was somewhat unreliable in its early days, resulting in numerous accidents and a large number of deaths and injuries to the crews.

Like the early US SSNs, the November class had been designed along the lines of the German Type XXI, with a long, thin, figure-of-eight-section hull and twin propellers, but with the next class, the Victors, Soviet designers changed to a shorter, body-of-revolution design with a single propeller.* As in most navies, the naval staff was very reluctant for change, and it took some time for the design bureaux to persuade the naval leadership that this was the best way ahead. In the end, forty-nine Victor-class SSNs were built, to three slightly different designs.†

At this point the Soviet navy sought to make a major leap in design practice by replacing the high-grade steel traditionally used in hull construction with titanium, to produce a submarine capable of diving to a depth of 700 m. Designated the Alfa class, this new design also had a very high-powered and highly automated propulsion system, which gave it a very high maximum speed. A submarine of this class created consternation in Western navies when it ran under a NATO task force at a speed in excess of 40 knots and

---

* A body of revolution is one which is symmetrical about its main axis – e.g. an Indian club or a baseball bat.

† Specifications of Soviet SSNs are given in Appendix 20.

then dived deep, indicating a performance which contemporary Western ASW ships, sensors and weapons could not begin to match. The Soviet programme was very expensive, but it also compelled the West to initiate some even more expensive programmes, to deal with it, including faster and more capable surface ASW ships, ASW helicopters, faster submarines, and faster, deeper-diving torpedoes.

The Soviet navy next developed two new designs in parallel – a practice already observed in ICBM development, where a radical design was backed up by a second which was more conventional and less risky technically. In this case the more advanced design was the Sierra class, which had a titanium hull, and was both fast (35 knots) and deep-diving (700 m or more). It was also the quietest Soviet SSN yet produced, but it was also extremely expensive, and the programme was cancelled after four had been completed. The parallel design was the Akula, which had a steel hull and was considerably cheaper; sixteen were produced before production ceased after the end of the Cold War.

THE UK

As in the USA, early British design work on nuclear power plants for submarines started during the Second World War, but it was given a low priority and eventually the British purchased US propulsion technology, resulting in *Dreadnought*, which was commissioned in 1963. This was followed by five of the slightly larger Valiant class, commissioned between 1966 and 1971. One of these, *Conqueror*, established a record as the first (and so far the only) nuclear-powered submarine to have sunk an enemy ship in battle, when it dispatched the Argentine cruiser *General Belgrano* on 2 May 1982, during the Falklands War (although it had to use two Mark VIII torpedoes of Second World War vintage to do it). Subsequently, a very small number of British SSNs patrolled off the Argentine coast and not only were able to confine the Argentine navy within its national territorial waters, but also were able to give early warning of Argentine strike aircraft taking off from shore airfields and starting offensive missions towards the Falkland Islands.

After their slow start, and despite the smallness of their SSN fleet, the British introduced some innovative design features, including the pump-jet propulsor and anechoic (sound-proofing) tiles, and claimed that their SSNs were the quietest in any navy. Six Swiftsure-class SSNs were commissioned between 1973 and 1981, followed by seven of the improved Trafalgar class between 1983 and 1991.

The tasks of British SSNs included countering Soviet SSBNs in their bastions, operations in choke points (e.g. the Greenland–Iceland–UK gap) and ensuring the safe departure and return of British SSBNs from their base in the Clyde.

FRANCE

Although the first French SSN programme was started in 1964, it was then postponed so that all efforts could be devoted into getting SSBNs into service; only when that had been achieved did France turn to developing SSNs. The four Rubis-class boats were commissioned between 1983 and 1988; displacing 2,670 tonnes, these were the smallest operational SSNs to enter service in any navy, and were also reputed to be the noisiest.

CANADA

The only other Cold War country to give serious consideration to SSNs was Canada, which in the 1980s needed to replace three British Oberon-class diesel-electric submarines which had been purchased in 1965–8. What started out as a fairly simple and modest project rapidly turned into a large, sophisticated and extremely expensive undertaking, principally because the Canadians wished to establish proper control over their northern waters. The eventual requirement was for twelve SSNs, and not surprisingly France and the UK fought tooth and nail for the order. The project eventually came to naught, but only after much money had been spent without a single piece of hardware to show for it.

18

Diesel-Electric Submarines

Diesel-electric submarines, which were also known as 'conventional' submarines, played a significant role in the Cold War from the very start. When NATO became operational in the early 1950s the Soviet surface fleet was generally considered to be of minor importance, since it had achieved little of strategic significance during the Second World War and by the late 1940s most of its ships were obsolescent, if not obsolete. The Soviets were outnumbered in every category, and had no ships at all to match the West's aircraft carriers and amphibious shipping. There was, however, one area in which they were believed to pose a significant threat: that of attack by diesel-electric submarines on Allied sea lines of communication across the Atlantic. With the memories of the German U-boat attacks in the north Atlantic still fresh, this perceived Soviet threat became one of the driving influences in NATO fleet development and deployment throughout the Cold War.

Fortunately for the Allies, the revolutionary new German submarines, the ocean-going Type XXI and the coastal Type XXIII, were only just entering service as the war ended, but there was no doubt as to their excellence. Both were real submarines, whose natural habitat was below the surface and which surfaced only when forced to do so. Compared with its predecessors, the Type XXI had a stronger and much more streamlined hull, a larger battery and new control systems which enabled it to fight underwater, and its snorkel tube enabled it to recharge its batteries while remaining submerged. Its underwater speed of 17 knots made it faster than most contemporary ASW ships, especially when there was bad weather on the surface. The Type XXIII was a smaller, coastal equivalent; it too was fast and capable, although its value was limited by its ability to carry only two torpedoes.

At the war's end, the victorious Allies shared forty U-boats between them, with top priority being given to the Types XXI and XXIII; they then scuttled the rest. On receipt of these prizes, only the French and the Soviets put a few Type XXIs into service, while the Americans and British, after very careful examination and trials, used the design innovations, first to adapt their existing submarines, of which both had very large numbers, and subsequently as the basis for new designs.

US SUBMARINES

The US navy found itself in 1946 with a vast stock of very recently built and virtually identical Second World War submarines, and a wide variety of conversions was made to these between 1946 and the mid-1950s. Most were modified under the Greater Underwater Propulsive Power (the so-called 'Guppy') programme, in which they were streamlined, given much more powerful batteries, and fitted with sonars and snorkel tubes. These conversions remained in service with the US navy until the early 1970s, and many were transferred to overseas, navies, within NATO in particular, where for some (e.g. Greece and Turkey) they formed the backbone of the submarine service for the remainder of the Cold War.

Numbers of Second World War submarines were also converted for special roles. These included radar pickets, which were fitted with large radars to enable them to give mid-course guidance corrections to carrier-launched bombers and, later, to the Regulus submarine-launched cruise missile. Some were converted to troop transports to deliver covert parties to hostile shores, and others as seaplane refuellers.

One development in early US Cold War naval strategy was a plan to prevent Soviet submarines leaving their home ports in war by positioning large numbers of specially-developed 'hunter/killer' ASW submarines outside the ports. In 1951–2 three such submarines (Barracuda class) were commissioned. These were intended to be prototypes for a large class which would have been built during a future mobilization process, but the whole scheme was dropped in 1959. Meanwhile, a new class of attack submarines was built (Tang class), which incorporated the design lessons of the German Type XXI. Only six were built, followed by three of the more advanced Barbel class, before the US navy abandoned diesel-electric submarines altogether in favour of nuclear propulsion.

THE SOVIET DIESEL-ELECTRIC SUBMARINE FLEET*

In 1945 the Soviet navy operated some 285 submarines, all of Soviet design and manufacture, of which 159 were ocean-going and 126 coastal types.

---

* Specifications of Soviet diesel-electric submarines are given in Appendix 21.

These were, however, all of pre-war design and lacked modern refinements such as streamlined hulls and snorkel tubes, having been, like the submarines of other Allied navies, outdated at a stroke by the German Type XXI.

Soviet submarines were supplemented in 1945–6 by a number of ex-German submarines. Twenty Type XXIs were found incomplete when the Red Army captured Danzig, and it was assumed by Western intelligence that these were completed and pressed into Soviet service. With the knowledge available at the time, this was a reasonable conclusion, but it has since come to light that they were scrapped, still incomplete, in 1948–9. In addition, four serviceable Type XXIs and one Type XXIII (plus four Type VIIc and one Type IXC) were handed over to the Soviet navy in 1945–6 from the stock of captured U-boats administered by the British on behalf of the Allies, and all served in the Baltic Fleet until the mid-1950s. The Soviet navy also received two Italian submarines as part of the peace settlement with Italy.

Design of the first post-war submarines began in 1946, and these, based on earlier Soviet designs, entered service in the early 1950s, quickly building up in numbers. The early versions of the two larger classes, Whiskey and Zulu, were armed with deck guns but did not have snorkels. Contemporary Western intelligence assessed that these types were Soviet adaptions of the German Type XXI, but this was incorrect: they were developments of previous Soviet designs, but incorporating a few German ideas.

Western intelligence was convinced that the Soviet navy was intent on repeating the German U-boat war on the NATO sea lines of communication across the Atlantic, and the large-scale production programmes for the Whiskey and Zulu classes appeared to reinforce this theory. There was therefore some surprise when the production of both types ceased in 1957–8, and this was thought to be a prelude to production of the first Soviet SSNs, until it was discovered that a new conventional submarine was in production: the Foxtrot class.

The Foxtrot design was larger, and was in fact the first Soviet design properly to incorporate all the lessons of the Type XXI. Sixty-two were produced for the Soviet navy, and the type became the workhorse of the fleet, being found in every ocean of the world. A second, and very similar, class, the Romeo, was produced by another design bureau, but presumably the Foxtrot proved the better boat, as production of the Romeo finished with the twenty-first unit. The Romeo was, however, exported and the design and tooling were sold to China, where it was built in large numbers.

It was then expected in the West, once again, that the Soviet navy would follow the US lead and build only nuclear-powered submarines in future, but this too proved to be erroneous, and twenty Tango-class boats were built between 1971 and 1982. Displacing 3,900 tonnes, these were the largest diesel-electric submarines to be built during the Cold War and were intended to contribute to the ASW defences for the SSBN bastions. Significantly, although all other Soviet diesel-electric submarines were exported, no Tango-class submarine was ever passed to another navy.

Construction of diesel-electric submarines continued with at least twenty-four Granay-class (NATO = 'Kilo') boats built from 1979 onwards for the Soviet navy. A very similar but less sophisticated design, the Washavyanka class, was designed for the export market, particularly for Warsaw Pact navies.

The Soviet navy also experimented with unconventional, but non-nuclear, air-independent propulsion systems. Thirty Quebec-class boats were built in the 1950s which ran on a Russian-developed *'Kreislauf'* system, using liquid oxygen, while the German Walter hydrogen-peroxide system was tested in the single Project 617 submarine. Neither type proved successful, but intelligence reports of the existence of the Walter project caused some alarm in the West.

Perhaps the greatest significance of the Soviet submarine fleet was that throughout the first twenty years of the Cold War its strength, capabilities and intentions were consistently overestimated by Western intelligence. This was partially due to the imposition of an information blackout by the Soviets themselves, which led to Western naval experts taking the worst-possible view (from the Western aspect) of Soviet capabilities and production, as was their wont. These estimates were reinforced by debriefings of repatriated German prisoners of war and scientists who were abducted to the USSR in 1945 and returned in the 1950s. These men gave reports which were frequently incorrect or exaggerated, or were based on the knowledge of just one element of a large programme. Western intelligence, alarmed by other elements of the Soviet threat, extrapolated from these and all too often came up with conclusions which were widely wrong. The Soviets, of course, did nothing to contradict the Western estimates.

BRITISH SUBMARINES

In 1945 the British had the third largest submarine fleet and, as in the USA, early post-war efforts were devoted to converting Second World War boats. The hulls were streamlined, new and more powerful batteries were fitted, and new sensors were installed – all of which enabled these boats to serve until the 1960s and 1970s.

The British pursued the Walter hydrogen-peroxide design (and even used the services of Dr Walter from 1945 to 1948), mainly because they thought that the Soviets had a similar design and they required fast under-water boats with which to train their ASW forces. One ex-German Type

XVIIB was trialled, and two British-designed boats were built. The Walter system proved to be very hazardous in service, however, and (to the great relief of the crews involved) further development was dropped.*

Another British idea was to deliver 15 kT nuclear mines to the entrances to the main Soviet ports, such as Kronstadt, using specially built mini-subs, designated 'X' craft. These would have been towed to the vicinity of their target by a larger submarine, as had happened during the war in attacks such as that on the German battleship *Tirpitz*. Although four of these mini-subs were completed, the project was cancelled in 1956.

Despite developing nuclear-powered attack submarines, the British did not follow the US example by ceasing to construct diesel-electric submarines, since they considered the conventional boats to have continuing roles in the hunter/killer role (e.g. in the Greenland–Iceland–UK gap) and in clandestine operations. Accordingly, they built the eight-strong Porpoise class between 1956 and 1961, the twelve-strong Oberon class between 1957 and 1967, and, after a long gap, the four-strong Upholder class between 1983 and 1992.†

FRANCE

In 1946 France operated a small number of pre-Second World War submarines and received five ex-German U-boats in the Allied share-out, only one of which was a Type XXI. Study of the latter boat led to the Narval class, six of which were built between 1951 and 1960 and remained in service to the late 1980s. A class of four smaller boats was built at the same time, the Arethuse class; these were enlarged and much heavier-armed versions of the German Type XXIII, designed to prevent Soviet submarines attacking French convoys between North Africa and France in war. Two more classes, the Daphne class (eleven boats, 1958–69) and the Agosta class (four boats, 1972–8), completed the post-war rehabilitation of the French navy's submarine arm.

WEST GERMANY

Germany was banned from constructing U-boats after the Second World War, but when the Federal Republic entered NATO it was decided to create

---

* A measure of the boats' popularity can be gauged from the fact that *Explorer* and *Excalibur* were known to their crews as *Exploder* and *Excruciator* respectively.
† The Upholder class in fact proved to be the last British diesel-electric class, being retired after a very brief spell of front-line service following the end of the Cold War.

a new submarine service, whose mission would be to defend the Baltic and North seas in co-operation with other NATO navies. Whereas the German surface fleet was restarted using foreign ships, the submarine service used entirely German-designed and -built boats. To start with, three sunken Second World War U-boats were raised, repaired and returned to service: two Type XXIIIs in 1956 and a single Type XXI in 1958.*

All post-war U-boats for the West German navy have been relatively small, with the largest, the Type 206, displacing only 500 tonnes. Twelve boats were originally to have been constructed of the first post-war design, the Type 201, but the hull was constructed using non-magnetic steel, which suffered from severe corrosion, and a new type of steel had to be developed, resulting in the Type 205. This was succeeded by the Type 206, eighteen of which were built between 1971 and 1974, and which then served as the navy's main submarine for the rest of the Cold War.

The German submarine industry, however, remained extremely healthy, owing to orders for some seventy-three boats from overseas customers, both within NATO and from some twenty customers in South America and Asia. The main NATO customer was Norway, which purchased fifteen Type 207s, followed by six of a new design, the Type 210, for service in the fjords and the Norwegian Sea.

OTHER NATO NAVIES

Other NATO navies started their post-war submarine arms using American Second World War boats supplied under the Mutual Defense Assistance Program. Italy, which had the world's largest submarine fleet in September 1939, subsequently produced its own submarines in small numbers, as did Denmark. Greece and Turkey both opted for the German export submarine, the Type 209, with the former buying complete boats from Germany, while the latter bought a few boats direct and then undertook its own production at the navy yard at Gölcük. Spain and Portugal both bought French designs. The Netherlands produced their own, very sophisticated submarine designs, albeit in small numbers.

Thus, although the largest navy ceased to build diesel-electric submarines, the type remained very active in other navies. All Warsaw Pact members with navies operated them, as did all NATO navies except that of Belgium.

---

* The Type XXI was restored to fully functioning order, but, in the event, was used only for experiments and trials and did not actually become operational.

19

Aircraft Carriers

Throughout the Cold War the mightiest concentration of usable military power lay in the US navy's carrier task groups (CTGs). The carrier force had been the core of the US surface navy since about 1943, when carriers replaced battleships as the capital ships of the fleet, although their huge costs – especially when the air wing, purpose-built replenishment ships and escorts were added in – made them a subject of almost constant criticism. Nevertheless, the US navy 'supercarriers' were a force which no other nation could challenge, while their ability to move anywhere in the world in international waters provided a facility which the US air force – like other air forces, limited by overflying rights and the need for foreign bases – could never match.

The Soviet navy entered the Cold War without any tradition of carrier warfare at all, but gradually accumulated expertise and experience which, towards the end of the Cold War, enabled it to build some unusual and innovative carriers. The expense and complexity of carrier operations restricted the number of other operators, however. The British navy, which had the second largest carrier fleet in 1945, managed, by a huge effort, to rebuild its carrier fleet and to produce new aircraft, so that by the early 1960s it was an effective force; but thereafter it decreased rapidly, and at one time nearly disappeared completely. Other countries managed to operate small carrier forces for some years, and the advent of the V/STOL aircraft, specifically the Anglo/US Harrier, brought carrier operation within the reach of a number of new operators from the 1970s onwards.

The most important technical innovation in the early post-war years was the jet-powered aircraft, first with straight and later with swept wings, but greater performance was matched by ever-increasing demands on the carriers. The speed and weight of the new aircraft presented totally new requirements for take-off and landing, while their ever-increasing size made new demands on handling facilities, hangar and deck space, and deck lifts, their fuel consumption increased the bunkerage requirement for aviation fuel, and their load-carrying capacity demanded more armament space. The US navy's reconstructed Essex class, for example, was the typical front-line carrier of the 1950s and carried 1,135,620 litres of fuel and 736 tonnes of ordnance for its aircraft, while a 1980s carrier, the Nimitz class, carried 12,730,000 litres and 2,611 tonnes, respectively.*

To provide longer and wider flight decks and hangars, the ships simply became bigger, while aircraft handling was greatly improved by installing side (as opposed to centre-line) lifts – a US innovation. Many other inventions, however, came from line officers of the British navy, including the angled deck, the steam catapult and the deck-landing mirror, although all three innovations first went to sea with the US navy's first supercarrier, USS *Forrestal*, in 1955.

US CARRIERS

Carrier Development

At the end of the Second World War the US navy found itself with a large fleet of carriers, but these were rapidly made obsolescent by the advent of jet aircraft. The first attempt at a modern carrier was the design for the USS *United States* (CVA-58), but this was rejected by the defense secretary (largely at the prompting of the newly formed air force) and there was then a pause until the Korean War demonstrated the continuing need for carriers. This resulted in the Forrestal-class carriers, which were the largest warships built up to that time.

The last of the Second World War carriers, the Essex class, had a full-load displacement of 31,643 tonnes, whereas the Forrestals displaced 71,222 tonnes and were over 30 m longer. These proved a most successful design and, with regular modernizations, the four ships, which joined the fleet between 1955 and 1959, each gave some forty years of service. They were followed by two carriers of the Kitty Hawk class, both commissioned in 1961, which were essentially a refined version of the Forrestal and were intended to be the last to use conventional propulsion. Thus the next carrier, *Enterprise* (CVN-65), was the first to have nuclear propulsion, which made it extremely capable, but so expensive that Congress baulked at the idea of more at the same cost and insisted that the navy revert to conventional (i.e. fossil-fuel) propulsion, which it did, building two more Kitty Hawk class.

Thereafter, the navy managed to persuade Congress that it really did

---

* The ordnance load was reduced to 1,985 tonnes from the third–of–class onwards, to compensate for the new Kevlar protective lining over the ship's vital spaces..

need nuclear carriers, and the result was the Nimitz class, the first of which was commissioned in 1975 and was followed by four more before the Cold War ended. The cost of these carriers was enormous and became a matter of dispute within most administrations and within Congress. There were also criticisms from inside the navy itself as various factions fought for larger slices of the budget.

One consequence of these criticisms was that designs for smaller and cheaper carriers were repeatedly examined. In the 1960s the Medium Carrier Project was considered, which was initially a 40,000 tonne, conventionally powered carrier, but, as almost invariably happened, the design grew to 60,000 tonnes in the course of the examination. This design was dusted off and re-examined in 1973, again in 1975 and, finally, in the early 1980s, but, when the navy managed to persuade Congress of the need for nuclear propulsion, more Nimitz class were built instead.

Another 1960s project was for a 'Sea Control Ship', displacing some 12,400 tonnes and operating V/STOL (i.e. Harrier) aircraft; and the then chief of naval operations (CNO) spoke enthusiastically of obtaining eight such carriers for the price of one nuclear carrier. The next CNO dropped this in favour of the V/STOL Support Ship, which would have been somewhat larger and operated more aircraft (a mix of Harriers and helicopters), but this too was dropped.* In the end, and despite repeated examinations of the alternatives, the US navy continued to build its supercarriers.

The huge size of the US carriers since *Forrestal* has enabled them to accommodate numerous facilities apart from those directly related to the air wing. These included an integrated combat information centre and an airborne ASW classification and analysis centre, with the latter being on-line to the United States and also enabling the carrier to share its ASW information with other ships in its task group.

In the years immediately following the Second World War the US navy planned to deploy as many as six carriers to the Barents Sea and eight (including some British carriers) to the Mediterranean. Later in the Cold War the British no longer operated attack carriers, and the US planned to maintain four carriers in forward areas – one each in the Atlantic, Mediterranean, Pacific and Indian oceans – with eight others in refit, in pre-deployment training or in transit.

Less immediately obvious was that the carrier did not prowl the ocean alone, but moved in company with a number of other ships in a carrier task

---

* The Sea Control Ship design was eventually sold to the Spanish navy, which, having modified and updated it, built it as the *Príncipe de Asturias*. The V/STOL Support Ship project also lives on, as the new Wasp-class amphibious assault ships have a secondary role as Harrier/ASW helicopter carriers.

group. Typically, a later Cold War CTG comprised one, or sometimes two, aircraft carriers, two missile-armed cruisers, four frigates and two fast replenishment vessels.

US Carriers in the Nuclear-Attack Role

The US navy quickly appreciated that a significant area for future naval warfare lay with atomic bombs delivered against targets well inland, and as early as 1945 the service began to formulate plans for delivery systems. One area of development was ship- and submarine-launched cruise missiles, but the second was a new attack bomber, the North American AJ-1 Savage. As only a few could be accommodated by existing carriers, however, plans were made for a new class of carrier, the United States, displacing some 75,000 tonnes, of which four were planned.

As mentioned above, the newly created air force took exception to this plan, as it considered strategic bombing to be its business and was already heavily engaged in building up a force of strategic bombers with intercontinental capabilities. It therefore carried out the first of several successful congressional campaigns, in which it not only achieved the cancellation of the carrier programme in 1949 (and the transfer of the funds to the air force) but also succeeded in having the strategic role of naval aviation restricted. Once tempers had cooled, however, the navy reached an accommodation with the air force, whereby the latter would undertake the strategic nuclear role while the navy would concentrate its nuclear weapons on ports and on inland targets which could affect the naval battle, such as airfields.

From 1945 to the early 1960s nuclear weapons were both large and heavy, the Mark VI atomic bomb, for example, weighing some 4,500 kg. The US navy's first attempt at a nuclear bomber was to convert twelve Lockheed P2V-3C Neptune ASW patrol aircraft to carry one Mark VI atomic bomb each. These aircraft had twin piston engines, their wings did not fold, and they were not fitted with arrester hooks for carrier landings. As a result, they would have been loaded on to the carrier flight deck by crane and, with rocket assistance, would have been launched on a one-way mission against Soviet targets from as near to the Soviet coast as was feasible.*

The first nuclear-capable carrier bomber, which had caused such problems with the air force, the AJ-1 Savage, was powered by two piston engines

---

* This plan was a virtual rerun of the raid led by Lieutenant-Colonel James Doolittle against Tokyo, Nagoya and Kobe in Japan on 18 April 1942. In this raid, sixteen B-25 Mitchell bombers were loaded aboard the carrier USS *Hornet* and were successfully launched at a distance of some 1,250 km from Japan. One bomber made an emergency landing at Vladivostok, while the others flew on to China, where the crews bailed out.

199

and one turbojet, giving it a mission radius of 1,850 km carrying a single nuclear weapon, which was delivered at a speed of 720 km/h and a height of 9,150 m. It entered service in September 1949 and could be operated from both the Midway-class (eight aircraft) and Essex-class carriers (three aircraft) then in service, but only at the expense of a large number of fighters. The Savages were based at Port Lyautey in French Morocco from 1949 and at Atsugi in Japan from 1953, and served in the nuclear-strike role until 1959.

Nor was the size of the aircraft the only complication. According to the rules for the safety of nuclear weapons at the time, the plutonium cores had to be stored in the United States and were flown out in transport aircraft to an airbase near the carriers only on receipt of warning of warlike conditions. On arrival in the theatre of operations they were transferred to TBM-3 Avenger aircraft for delivery to the carriers, but, since the protective packaging was so heavy, each aircraft could carry only one core. On arrival a team of some forty specialists then assembled each bomb in turn.

From 1956 onwards the Savage was succeeded by the twin-jet, swept-wing A-3 Skywarrior, which also carried a single nuclear weapon, but with a mission radius of 3,220 km, at a height of 12,000 m. This aircraft was designed to take advantage of the newly introduced Forrestal-class super-carriers, whose air wing included twelve A-3s, although the A-3 also served in the air wings of the older carriers, such as the Midway class (nine A-3s) and the Essex class (three A-3s). Sometimes, however, the Midway-class carriers went to sea with an air wing consisting entirely of nuclear-capable bombers: eleven A-3 Skywarriors, sixty A-4D Skyhawks and twelve AD Skyraiders.

The final aircraft in the series was the A-5 Vigilante, which entered service in 1965 and was the largest aircraft ever to operate from carriers. This had a maximum range of 5,150 km and overflew the target at 15,000 m at a speed of Mach 1.5. It was the first bomber in any air force to carry an inertial navigating system, which, since it was passive, emitted no electronic radiations. Another feature of the Vigilante was its linear bomb bay, which ejected the nuclear weapon through a large hole in the tail.

With the entry into service of the Polaris missiles, however, the need for specialized nuclear-bombing aircraft disappeared and the aircraft still in service in 1961 were switched to other roles. The US navy still continued to operate numerous aircraft types which could deliver nuclear weapons, but by this time the weapons were very much smaller and lighter, enabling them to be carried by much smaller planes.

In the 1950s US carriers were fitted with relatively heavy gun and missile armaments, but these were gradually decreased until only a few close-in weapons were carried. Thereafter, carriers relied on their aircraft and escorting vessels for protection.

Carrier-Borne Fighter Aircraft

In addition to the nuclear bombers, the carrier-borne aircraft developed rapidly. The straight-wing Grumman F9F-1 Panther of 1950, for example, had an all-gun armament, a top speed of 1,110 km/h and a range of 1,600 km, while the F-4 Phantom of 1960 had swept wings, a mixed missile and gun armament, a top speed of 2,400 km/h and a range of 2,800 km. The fighter of the late 1970s was the F-14 Tomcat, which employed swing wings to combine great speed (maximum 2,500 km/h) with a reasonable landing performance and a range of 3,200 km. As with the F-4, the F-14's armament was a mix of guns and missiles. These figures show an increase in speed of 125 per cent and in range of 100 per cent over thirty years, but less easily quantifiable were the increases in manoeuvrability and in the range and capabilities of the sensors, the much more sophisticated electronic-warfare capability, and the greater safety – all of which resulted in a major increase in combat capability.

Carrier Types

US carrier tasking developed during the period of the Cold War. In the 1950s, 1960s and early 1970s carriers were divided into two types: attack carriers (which were known by their US navy designation of CVAs) and ASW carriers (CVSs).

The CVA force during this period consisted of three Midway-class and two Essex-class carriers, which had been built at the end of the Second World War, plus a steadily increasing number of supercarriers. The core force aboard a CVA usually comprised three attack squadrons (one medium, two light) and two fighter squadrons, which were supported by squadrons or detachments for specialist roles such as airborne early warning, air-to-air refuelling, electronic warfare and reconnaissance.

ASW carriers (CVSs) were found from the Essex-class carriers and a decreasing number of other Second World War carriers. They embarked specialist ASW fixed-wing aircraft and helicopters, supported by a few airborne-early-warning aircraft and, possibly, a few A-4 Skyhawks as a token fighter force.

The Essex-class carriers reached the end of their useful lives in the mid-1970s, which coincided with the arrival in service of the first jet-powered ASW aircraft, the S-3 Viking, which not only replaced the piston-engined S-2 Tracker, but also provided a far greater ASW capability with many fewer aircraft. As a result, the supercarriers were re-roled as multi-purpose carriers (CVs) and the Essex-class and Midway-class carriers were paid off.

Appendix 22 shows a typical multi-purpose-carrier air wing in 1980, which consisted of eighty-nine aircraft. The functional spread included airborne early warning, air superiority, air defence, attack, fighter-bomber, anti-submarine warfare, electronic warfare, air-to-air refuelling, search-and-rescue, and photographic reconnaissance.

The fighters represented the 'glamorous' side of the air wing, but in fact made up only some 27 per cent of the 1980s air wing. The offensive reach of the carrier was provided by attack aircraft such as the long-range Grumman A-6 Intruder and the medium-range Vought A-7 Corsair, both of which were capable of carrying nuclear weapons. Photographic reconnaissance was provided by three RF-8 Crusaders (converted fighters), while electronic warfare was the responsibility of four EA-6 Prowlers (converted A-6 bombers). Long-range radar surveillance was provided by five Grumman E-2 Hawkeyes, while ASW protection was provided by four Lockheed S-3 Vikings (long-range) and four SH-3D Seaking helicopters (close-range). The air wing was completed by two KA-6D tankers and four SH-3D search-and-rescue helicopters. This was, in effect, a greater combat capability packaged into one hull than most countries had in their entire air force.

BRITISH CARRIERS

Between 1945 and 1990 the British navy had an astonishing record for originating some of the most exceptional new concepts in carrier design, even though its own force of carriers was rapidly diminishing and at one point almost reached zero. One British idea of the late 1940s for a flexible landing deck for use by aircraft without undercarriages was a failure, but the others were very successful, enabling carrier aviation, especially in the US navy, to flourish throughout the Cold War. Three of these British innovations appeared in the late 1940s, at a time when jet-propelled aircraft were coming into service; these were much heavier, much faster, and generally more difficult to take off and land than the previous generation of piston-engined aircraft.

The first British innovation was the angled deck, which was offset to port and enabled the take-off and landing areas to be separated, thus speeding up the aircraft handling rate, increasing the deck space available, and adding considerably to the overall safety of flying operations. Next came the steam catapult, which provided much greater energy to launch the heavier aircraft then entering service. Third, came the mirror deck-landing equipment, replacing the 'batman' who had stood on the flight deck, using brightly coloured bats by day and luminous sticks by night to assist the pilot in the final stages of his approach. This mirror system was very popular with pilots because it not only was much safer, but also put them back in charge of landing their aircraft. Some time later the British navy was the first to take the fixed-wing V/STOL aircraft to sea, and it also invented the 'ski jump', which dramatically increased the V/STOL aircraft's take-off payload.

The British emerged from the Second World War with six fleet carriers, all of which had been hard worked throughout the war, and nine of the smaller light fleet carriers, with a further two fleet and six light fleet carriers in various stages of construction. Some of the light fleet carriers were sold to Commonwealth and foreign navies, and the navy then endeavoured to operate a viable force of carriers to support its role as a major sea power. As with the Americans, the situation was complicated by the advent of jet aircraft, and, while the British were not short of good ideas, they suffered the frustration of seeing most of them come to fruition aboard American carriers rather than their own. Great efforts were also devoted to developing British aircraft, but the numbers required were small and the British development programmes were very protracted by comparison with those in the USA, so that, in general, British aircraft came into service some years after their US equivalent and did not have such a good performance.

The one exception was the Blackburn Buccaneer low-level bomber, which originated in 1953 with an operational requirement for an aircraft capable of approaching the target *below* the enemy's radar beam at a speed of some 890 km/h. At the time this was an unheard-of requirement, although it became commonplace thereafter, and the Buccaneer was so successful it was ordered by the UK air force (which had rejected it some twelve years earlier).

The British carrier fleet peaked in effectiveness and efficiency in the early 1960s, when the front-line strength consisted of five fixed-wing carriers (*Ark Royal*, *Eagle*, *Hermes*, the completely rebuilt *Victorious* and the light fleet carrier *Centaur*), plus two commando carriers. The fixed-wing carriers operated Scimitar fighters, Sea Vixen night fighters, Buccaneer strike bombers, Gannet anti-submarine and airborne-early-warning aircraft, and Whirlwind anti-submarine/rescue helicopters.

An important limiting factor, however, was that, as the aircraft became larger and heavier, the numbers embarked gradually decreased. Thus in the 1960s *Victorious* carried twenty-eight fixed-wing aircraft plus eight helicopters, which reduced in the last few years of her service to twenty-three fixed-wing plus five helicopters, while *Eagle* and *Ark Royal* operated thirty-five fixed-wing (plus ten helicopters). The smaller *Hermes*, which entered service in 1959, could operate only twenty-eight fixed-wing (no helicopters), and when it was realized that it would not be able to operate the F-4K Phantom it was converted to a commando carrier.

The situation was made worse by the troubled project for a carrier intended to replace *Eagle* and *Victorious*. Designated CVA-01, the new carrier project dragged on from 1963 to 1966, and many ingenious ideas were produced to design a ship which was within the size and financial limitations – a problem made more severe by the fact that the latter were not only stringent but tended to change regularly. In 1966, however, it was finally decided that CVA-01 should be cancelled and that the navy would cease to operate fixed-wing carriers when the current ships had wasted out. This duly took place, with the last of the fixed-wing carriers, *Ark Royal*, being paid off in 1978.

The British navy is nothing if not ingenious, however, and very rapidly produced a totally new concept in order to retain a fixed-wing capability. A design was already under preparation for a helicopter-carrying cruiser displacing 12,700 tonnes, and the design was steadily amended until it had become a V/STOL carrier, capable of embarking five Sea Harriers and nine Seaking ASW helicopters. Three of these ships were ordered, joining the fleet in 1980, 1982 and 1985. The oldest carrier, *Hermes*, was converted to a helicopter carrier in 1977 and then into an interim Sea Harrier carrier in 1980. The effectiveness of the Sea Harrier-carrier concept was demonstrated during the Falklands War in 1982, but an additional benefit was shown when air-force Harriers were able to fly direct to the Falklands and then operate from the carriers there – something which would not have been possible with any other type of aircraft. The soundness of the concept was also shown by its adoption by the Indian, Italian and Spanish navies.

SOVIET CARRIERS

Unlike its US and British counterparts, the Soviet navy had no tradition of operating aircraft at sea, and its first efforts involved fitting some destroyers to carry one or two helicopters in the late 1950s. When the USSR found itself faced by US Polaris-armed SSBNs in the Mediterranean, however, it designed two dedicated helicopter carriers, the Moskva class, the first of which was commissioned in 1967. This was greeted in the West with some admiration, as not only was the purpose-built Moskva a far more efficient design than the former cruisers which had been converted to helicopter carriers in several European navies, but it also carried an impressive missile armament on the foredeck.

The Soviet navy's dynamic leader, Admiral Gorshkov, was, however, determined to catch up with the US navy in every respect, including the construction of a force of fixed-wing carriers. Intense efforts were devoted to espionage and other methods to derive as much information as possible from US and British sources, and Soviet warships and intelligence-collecting auxiliaries (AGIs) regularly deployed with NATO carrier task groups to monitor every detail of their activities.

Next to appear was the Kiev class, the first of which was commissioned in 1975. This again was unusual, in that it had a flight deck aft angled to run abreast the superstructure (which was offset to starboard), leaving the foredeck covered in guns and reloadable missile launchers. Most Western observers considered that the ships were designed to defend the SSBN bastions in the Sea of Murmansk and the Sea of Okhotsk, using helicopters to counter US and British SSNs, Yak-38 VTOL fighters against ASW aircraft such as the P-3 Orion, and missiles against surface ships. Whether they would have been effective in such a role is difficult to assess.

The final carriers to be produced by the Soviet navy were the two ships of the Kuznetsov class, the first of which entered service as the Cold War was ending. They had a displacement of 67,000 tonnes, were fitted with a large, angled flight deck, and carried a predominantly fixed-wing air group. As so often, however, the Soviet navy produced some surprises, including launching the conventional-take-off aircraft over a 'ski jump'* and a missile battery inset in the flight deck. The air wing, however, numbered only some eighteen fixed-wing aircraft and twelve helicopters, which was about one-quarter of that of a US carrier. One vessel only, *Kuznetsov*, was completed, giving the Soviet navy the world-class aircraft carrier it had hankered after for so long, but it was too late.

OTHER NAVIES

In the early years of the Cold War a number of other navies appreciated the value of sea-borne air power and established naval air arms to exploit it. Virtually all were based on the British light fleet carrier, a design prepared in 1943 for utility ships which would last until the end of the war. Fifteen were laid down and, of these, nine were completed for overseas navies, only three of which belonged to NATO, the recipients being Argentina (one), Australia (two), Brazil (one), Canada (two), France (one), India (one) and the Netherlands (one).[†] Like the British navy, most of these found great difficulty in keeping their carriers up to date, and, as a result, several countries ended their involvement with carriers: Argentina in 1985, Australia in 1982, Canada in 1970 and the Netherlands in 1968.

Meanwhile, France operated one British-built and one US-built carrier until they were replaced by two French-designed and -built carriers in the early 1960s. Italy had made several false starts into naval aviation, but eventually succeeded with a very handsome V/STOL carrier, *Giuseppe Garibaldi* (13,850 tonnes), operating AV-8B Harriers, which entered service in 1985. Spain also saw the Harrier as a means of gaining a fixed-wing capability and acquired a surplus US carrier for this purpose in 1967. This was replaced in 1968 by a Spanish-built ship, *Principe de Asturias*, which was based on the US navy's earlier Sea Control Ship design.

---

* Some authorities suggest that this may have been the result of an inability to develop a reliable steam catapult rather than the 'ski jump' having been developed on its own merits.
† The Dutch carrier was later also sold to Argentina.

ANTI-CARRIER WARFARE

The Soviet Union considered itself particularly vulnerable to the threat posed by the US navy's extremely powerful carrier task groups – a belief which originated with the AJ-1 Savage, and which was responsible for the development of the Northern Fleet over the years 1950–72. Marshal Sokolovskiy, first writing in the late 1960s, described how it was 'essential to attempt to destroy the attack carriers before they can launch their planes . . . these units are highly vulnerable during ocean crossings, during refuelling, at the moment they are preparing to launch their planes, and also when the planes are landing again on the carriers'.[1] He then went on to describe how such attack carriers were vulnerable to nuclear strikes and to attacks by torpedoes with nuclear warheads, by naval and long-range aviation using air-to-ship missiles, and from coastal missile batteries. This agreed with the perceived strategy of the Northern Fleet in the 1950s, which was to seek to prevent US carrier task groups from reaching the launch areas, using co-ordinated attacks by aircraft, surface ships and diesel–electric submarines.

In the late 1950s, with the entry into service of the A-3 Skywarrior, with its 3,220 km radius of action, the launch point was moved beyond the reach of current Soviet land-based aircraft, which meant that Soviet naval strategy was forced to swing towards attacks by nuclear-powered submarines and by specialized, long-range, anti-shipping aircraft, operated by the navy. When the US naval threat changed yet again, to Polaris missiles launched from SSBNs, the increasing range of the missiles took the launch submarines further from the northern waters, but the threat from US carrier groups remained, both in the north against Soviet SSBN bastions and in the Mediterranean and Pacific against the Soviet land mass and against fleets at sea.

Thus the Soviet navy developed an 'anti-carrier warfare' concept, which was regularly practised in major seagoing exercises. The submarine component of this concept was the specialized cruise-missile submarine, of which there were two versions: the diesel–electric Juliett class and a succession of nuclear-propelled classes (SSGNs). (The US navy had briefly deployed such specialized missile-carrying submarines, but in the land-attack role, and the Soviet navy was the only one to develop this type of submarine for anti-ship missions.)

The original Soviet anti-carrier weapon was the SS-N-3 missile, which entered service in 1963. It was very large, weighing 4,500 kg, carried a 350 kT nuclear warhead, and was launched in pairs from a surface warship, a surfaced submarine or a Tupolev Tu-95 Bear-B patrol aircraft. Its range was some 450 km, and it cruised at Mach 1.2 and a height of some 4,000 m. The SS-N-3 was tracked and guided by the launch vessel until the missile's own radar acquired the target, whereupon it began a diving attack. The system had several inherent drawbacks. First, a submarine had to surface in order to perform three functions: deploy its radar, obtain the latest target information from a co-operating aircraft (usually a Bear-D), and, finally, launch the missiles. Second, the ship or submarine radar was unable to track more than two missiles at once, and had therefore to continue with one pair of missiles until their onboard radars had locked on to the target before the next pair of missiles could be launched. Despite these disadvantages the SS-N-3 weapon system was formidable for its time and certainly posed a substantial threat to US carrier task groups. Its effectiveness was further enhanced when some of the submarines (Echo IIs and Julietts) were fitted with the Punch Bowl satellite targeting system.

The anti-ship SS-N-3 weapons system was carried by two types of submarine: the Echo II nuclear-powered submarine (twenty-nine built) carried eight missiles, while the diesel-electric-powered Juliett (sixteen built) carried four. Both designs suffered from large, blast-deflecting cut-outs in the hull sides, which generated much noise when submerged, making them easily tracked by Western submarines.

In the submarine-launched role, the SS-N-3 was complemented by the SS-N-7/SS-N-9, which was launched from Charlie I/II submarines. This was a short-range system with a range of some 40 km and cruised at a height of some 90 m at a speed of Mach 0.9, but it possessed a major advantage over SS-N-3 in that it was launched from a submerged submarine. These weapons compounded the problems facing a US carrier task group, since it now had to defend itself against two different missile threats.

The final weapon in this sequence was the SS-N-19, which entered service in 1983 aboard Oscar-class SSGNs and, like previous Soviet anti-ship missiles was also carried aboard surface warships – in this case the aircraft carrier *Kuznetsov* and the Kirov-class battlecruisers. The SS-N-19 had a turbofan engine with a rocket booster and was extremely fast, enabling it to be fired from a submerged Oscar on the basis of information received from a satellite via the Punch Bowl data link, thus avoiding the need for mid-course guidance. It could carry a nuclear 350/500 kT warhead, high explosive, or bomblets.

For many years the ship- and submarine-launched missiles required mid-course corrections to enable them to find their targets, and this was usually supplied by high-flying aircraft such as the Tupolev Tu-95 Bear-B, operated by the Soviet navy. Mid-course guidance could also be supplied by versions of the Kamov Ka-25 shipborne helicopter.

The ultimate threat to the US navy carrier task groups was that a small proportion of the Soviet Union's SS-18 land-based ICBMs were available to be targeted against US carrier task groups.

20

Surface Warships

The major element in every navy, and also the most visible to the public, the media and other navies alike, was the surface fleet, and vast amounts of money were expended on its vessels. These ships were given a variety of traditional designations – cruiser, destroyer, frigate and corvette – but these terms not only were interpreted differently by different navies, but were also applied in a contradictory manner within some navies. This has caused considerable confusion in the past, so two functional designations will be used here: fleet escort and ocean escort.

The fleet escort was designed to provide area air and anti-submarine defence for a fast task force, usually centred on an aircraft carrier. Such a task group typically consisted of one carrier, six fleet escorts (usually three for air defence and three for anti-submarine warfare) and one or more fast replenishment ships. Towards the end of the Cold War surface-action groups made a somewhat surprising comeback, centred upon an Iowa-class battleship in the case of the US navy and on a Kirov-class battlecruiser in the Soviet navy. Such high-value assets also needed an escort.

The primary mission of the ocean escort was to defend convoys against attacks by Soviet submarines. This function was of far greater importance to NATO than to the Warsaw Pact, since the former depended upon transatlantic convoys to bring men, equipment and supplies to Europe in the event of a war.

THE US NAVY

Fleet Escorts
The fleet escort was required to accompany surface task groups and to operate at fleet speeds, which meant good sea-keeping with a high cruising

speed (which can be translated as a speed in excess of 30 knots in rough weather) and long range. There were, in essence, two types: the area air-defence ship and the anti-submarine ship.

The area air-defence ship stemmed from the realization in the late 1940s that guns were no longer capable of providing effective air defence against modern high-performance jet aircraft and that missiles were therefore required. Contemporary radars and missile systems were bulky and heavy, and large magazines were needed to accommodate the number of missiles judged to be necessary. This, in conjunction with the speed and sea-keeping requirements, meant that large hulls were required, and, in order to get the systems to sea quickly, eleven Second World War cruisers were converted to the new role, entering service as missile ships between 1955 and 1964. Some had their main guns completely removed and replaced by missile launchers both fore and aft, while others retained their gun turrets forward and had the launchers on the quarterdeck. These ships served as a 'quick fix' for air defence and gave the navy valuable experience in operating missiles, but they were never intended to provide more than an interim solution and their service lives were relatively brief.

This line of development led to the *Long Island*, the first purpose-built, post-war fleet escort, which joined the fleet in 1961. Displacing 15,060 tonnes, this ship was the largest surface combatant (apart from aircraft carriers) built in the United States during the Cold War, and was the first escort ship to have nuclear propulsion. It had a huge fixed array for the air-search radar and carried a very substantial armament, including three SAM launchers for air defence and an anti-submarine-missile launcher, as well as more conventional weapons such as two 127 mm guns and twelve 533 mm torpedo tubes. Proof of its capabilities came in 1968 in the Gulf of Tong-king when, on two separate occasions, its missiles engaged and destroyed MiG fighters flying over North Vietnam at a range of some 105 km from the ship.

Long Island was very expensive, even by US standards, and the eight missile-armed, nuclear-powered fleet escorts which followed were somewhat smaller, displacing between 8,200 and 10,000 tonnes, the reduction in size being achieved by halving the number of missiles carried and deleting the flag facilities. These nuclear-powered ships were paralleled by two classes, each nine strong, of conventionally powered ships.

The capability of the air-defence systems carried by these ships developed steadily over the years, culminating in the Aegis system.* This versatile, sophisticated and very expensive radar/computer system was designed to integrate the management of a task group's weapon systems,

* In Greek mythology, the aegis was a short cloak, later a shield, which protected Zeus from harm.

with the emphasis on air operations. Among many other attributes, it could control up to eighteen missiles simultaneously on a time-share switching system.

The original plan was to install Aegis in nuclear-powered cruisers, but after a long debate it was eventually decided to install it in the same hull as the Spruance-class destroyers. Twenty-seven of these fleet escorts were built under the designation Ticonderoga-class cruisers, joining the fleet between 1983 and 1994. Two Ticonderoga-class ships were used very successfully to control US aircraft in the Gulf of Sirte during the US air strikes on Libya in 1986. One of the class, *Vincennes,* subsequently achieved considerable notoriety when, while operating in the Persian Gulf in 1988, it shot down an Iranian civil airliner with heavy loss of life, mistaking it for a combat aircraft carrying out a diving attack.

The other type of fleet escort was optimized for anti-submarine warfare. The ships were, in effect, large destroyers, their size being dictated by the 30 knot, rough-seas requirement. Originally, these ships were required to make a contribution to the fleet air-defence umbrella and they therefore carried missiles, but, as the Soviet submarine capability grew and began to threaten even fast-moving surface task forces, these escorts became increasingly oriented towards ASW. Ninety of these ships were built over a period of forty years: Mitscher class (4,404 tonnes) – four (1953–4); Farragut class (5,124 tonnes) – ten (1959–61); Forrest Sherman class (4,460 tonnes) – eighteen (1955–9); Charles F. Adams class (4,106 tonnes) – twenty-three (1960–64); and, finally, the Spruance and Kidd classes.*

The Spruance and Kidd classes, which joined the fleet between 1975 and 1983, were large, displacing 8,350 tonnes, and all thirty-five were built at the same shipyard – a volume of business which no other country could match. As was usual with US warships throughout the Cold War, they came in for considerable criticism, being described as too large for their purpose, poorly armed and with inadequate sensors. The size was, once again, a consequence of the requirement to maintain a 30 knot speed in rough seas. Adverse comments on the armament and sensors arose from comparison with contemporary Soviet ships, which had decks bristling with weapons and masts covered with antennas. The facts were, however, that US sensor systems were far more sophisticated and capable than their Soviet counterparts and required many fewer antennas, while the missile magazines, which were below decks, held a greater number of missiles. The Spruance design predated the British experience in the Falklands War and, having carried out a detailed analysis of this experience, one of the many changes decided upon

---

* The four Kidd-class ships were ordered by the shah of Iran, but, following the shah's overthrow, the new government cancelled the order and the US navy bought the ships. They were, in essence, anti-aircraft versions of the Spruance class.

by the US navy was to add armour protection to these ships, lining all vital spaces with Kevlar.

Ocean Escorts

Like other NATO navies, the US navy was seriously concerned at the threat posed by Soviet submarines to convoys crossing the north Atlantic – a problem which was exacerbated by the fact that Soviet submarines grew in both numbers and capability as the Cold War progressed, becoming quieter and carrying greater numbers of more effective weapons. The most significant feature of these submarines' design, however, was their underwater speed, which in the Alfa class, which entered service in the early 1970s, was in excess of 40 knots. During the Second World War the corvettes, frigates and destroyer-escorts used in the ASW role had a maximum speed of between 10 and 12 knots in a rough sea. Their quarry, the German U-boats, however, had a maximum submerged speed of about 6 knots, but spent most of the time at much lower speeds in order to conserve the charge in their batteries. As a result, the surface ships had an adequate margin of speed over the submarines.

The Soviet Whiskey-class diesel-electric submarines which entered service in the 1950s had a maximum submerged speed of 13 knots, but the nuclear-powered attack submarines raised this to 30 knots or more. As a result, the war-built destroyer-escorts, of which a huge number were in reserve, were simply of no use, since such small ships simply could not be designed to operate at the necessary speeds. The inevitable result was a move to much larger ASW ships, and great numbers of Second World War destroyers were either converted or, in cases where construction had been halted at the war's end, were completed so as to meet the demand for ASW ships. Some forty ships fell into this category, and most of these were subsequently given a major upgrade in the 1970s.

The first post-war design for an ASW escort was the Dealey class, of which thirteen were built between 1954 and 1957. They displaced some 1,730 tonnes and were expensive to build, even though their construction had been simplified in order to make them easy to produce in large numbers in the event of a war. Both the Dealey class and a cheaper design (the Claud Jones class) were disliked by the navy, which was forced to produce a proper ocean-escort design. This led to a series of four classes, which were originally designated destroyer-escorts, although in 1975 this was changed to frigates. All of these were much larger than previous ASW escorts, displacing between 2,730 and 3,640 tonnes, and some were built in considerable numbers: Bronstein – two; Garcia – seventeen; Knox – forty-six; Perry – fifty-one.

All were criticized. The Bronstein class was considered to be too slow; the Garcia and Knox classes had only one propeller, limiting their manoeuvrability; the steam plant in the Knox class was too complicated and difficult to maintain, and all were considered to have insufficient weapons. Nevertheless, they gave valuable service and were effective ASW platforms. One feature of the last of these classes, the Perry, was its use of major items of equipment which originated in other NATO countries: the Mark 92 fire-control system was of Dutch (Signaal) origin, while the main gun was a 76 mm weapon designed by OTO Melara in Italy.

THE SOVIET NAVY

The Soviet navy's first major post-war building programme included fourteen new Sverdlov-class cruisers, which began to enter service in 1951, causing considerable alarm in Western navies. They were fast, had a long range (9,000 nautical miles at 18 knots), and were well armed, with twelve 152 mm guns, twelve 100 mm anti-aircraft guns and ten torpedo tubes. They were considered to pose a major threat as 'surface raiders', following the pattern of German operations by ships such as *Bismarck*, *Scharnhorst*, *Gneisenau*, *Graf Spee* and *Scheer* during the Second World War; these had caused considerable problems to the British, since they had required a large number of ships and aircraft to track down each of them. In addition to this, the Soviet cruisers were handsome, well-balanced ships and *looked* powerful – a factor of some significance, since it enabled them to create a major impression during numerous visits to foreign ports in the 1950s and 1960s.

Khrushchev cut back drastically on the surface fleet in his 1956 review, but allowed the navy to build four light cruisers (Kynda class) and twenty destroyers (Kashin class), which started to enter service in 1962. Both types created further alarm in the West. The main armament of the Kynda class comprised two quadruple SS-N-3 missile launchers, giving them a 250 nautical mile anti-ship capability, with one SA-N-1 anti-aircraft-missile launcher, guns and torpedoes for self-defence. The Kashin-class destroyers were the first major warships in any navy to be powered exclusively by gas turbines, and mounted a primary armament of two quadruple SA-N-1 anti-aircraft-missile launchers. Both Kyndas and Kashins also exhibited a Soviet trend that was to increase with time, mounting a plethora of antennas and sensors whose function and capability Western experts could for many years only guess at.

This trend continued throughout the Cold War, with the Soviet navy building a series of powerful, well-armed, well-equipped cruisers and destroyers. The Russians appear, however, to have always been fascinated by sheer size, and the culmination of their naval building programme was the Kirov class, three of which were commissioned between 1980 and 1988 (a fourth was completed in 1996). With a full-load displacement of 28,000 tonnes, these were the largest surface warships to be built for any navy during the Cold War and were intended to serve as flagships for surface-warfare groups, which would consist of missile-armed cruisers. The Kirovs mounted a heavy armament, consisting of a mix of anti-surface, anti-air and anti-submarine missiles, together with guns, torpedoes and three helicopters. Apart from their size and armament, however, one of their most impressive feature was the power plant, which consisted of two nuclear reactors plus oil-fired steam boost. Again, the superstructure of these ships was covered with antennas and sensors.

The Soviet navy also built three Slava-class cruisers,* which, with a displacement of 12,500 tonnes, were among the largest surface ships of the Cold war. They were armed with sixteen SS-N-12 missiles mounted in four pairs on either side of the forward superstructure, making them look very menacing.

Soviet ship design was followed with great interest in the West, not least because Soviet designers seemed much less reluctant than their Western counterparts to make daring innovations. For all their powerful weapons, their impressive electronics and their excellent performance, however, the Soviet surface fleet never overcame the basic problem, referred to earlier, of being split into four widely separated fleets. Thus, by the time the ships had been split between the fleets and allowance had been made for ships in refit, the numbers actually available in any one area were much less impressive than the overall figures might suggest.

THE BRITISH NAVY

The British navy had for many years rested its strength on its surface fleet, and it entered the Cold War as the second most powerful navy in NATO – a position it retained, despite successive reductions, to the end of the Cold War. Early in the Cold War, the British, having been the principal victims of the German 'commerce raiders', felt particularly vulnerable to the Soviet Sverdlov-class cruisers, but a class of cruisers intended to deal with this threat was never built, and reliance was placed instead on the carrier-borne Buccaneer low-level anti-shipping bomber.

The numbers of frigates in service tell the story of the decline in British sea power. In 1960 the navy was operating sixty frigates of various types, but this had decreased to fifty-five by 1970, although that figure was held until 1981, when major cuts began. At the end of the Cold War only thirty-four were in service.

---

* A fourth was greatly delayed during construction by the ending of the Cold War, and was eventually commissioned into the Ukrainian navy in 1995 with the name *Vilna Ukraina*.

Fleet Escorts

Defence from air attack clearly had to be a major priority, although the first attempt to provide it was not a particularly happy one. Three cruisers which had been launched in 1944–5 were, after repeated delays and at very considerable expense, completed between 1959 and 1961. These ships, the Tiger class, originally had a traditional cruiser armament of four 152 mm guns, although these were of a new, fully automatic type, with water-cooling, giving a rate of fire of twenty rounds per minute per barrel.* It had, however, already been accepted that the most effective defence against modern aircraft was missiles, and little use was found for these ships. As a result, between 1965 and 1972 two were converted to ASW helicopter carriers by installing a huge hangar and flight deck aft – again at considerable expense – but even this was not really satisfactory and the ships were disposed of in 1980.

The next attempt at an air-defence ship was the County-class destroyers, of which eight were completed between 1961 and 1970. These were armed with the inelegantly named Seaslug missile, which was launched from a twin launcher at the stern, using a beam-riding guidance system which was already obsolescent when the system entered service. All eight were deleted in the early 1980s. The only other large ship to be completed, *Bristol*, was the first of a group of four to provide air defence for the new carrier CVA-01. When the carrier was cancelled only *Bristol* was completed, but it was employed mainly as a trials and training ship.

Ocean Escorts

The navy's ASW force subsisted for many years on Second World War destroyer hulls, many of which were converted into ASW ships in the early 1950s, but new-design ships began to enter service from 1957 onwards, and in considerable numbers. These new frigates included twenty-six of the Leander class, which entered service between 1963 and 1967 and proved a great success; they also achieved major export orders. These were followed by the Broadsword class (also known as the Type 22), of which fourteen were completed between 1979 and 1990, and the Duke class (Type 23), which was just entering service as the Cold War ended.

The Falklands War

Uniquely among the Cold War navies of both alliances, the British fought a major naval conflict – the 1982 Falklands War – which particularly affected the surface fleet. In that conflict two destroyers and two frigates were lost as a result of air-launched-missile or bombing attacks, and one destroyer was

---

* This rate of fire was theoretical; in practice there were many stoppages, which reduced the rate considerably.

damaged by a land-based missile. In addition, the threat posed by Argentine submarines resulted in great efforts being expended in hunting for them.

Among the many lessons of the war, three were of particular importance. The first was that air-launched anti-ship missiles represented a major threat to a fleet – a threat which had previously been underestimated. The second lesson was that airborne early warning was essential to the safety of the fleet. The third lesson was that a long period of peace had resulted in damage control being reduced from an essential feature of warship design to a low priority, where economy and the fashion of the moment prevailed. Every navy in the world learned lessons from the British navy's experience in the Falklands, as a result of which the design of surface warships and the relative priorities of numerous design features altered radically.

FRANCE

The French fleet emerged from the Second World War in a poor state. A few pre-war French cruisers and destroyers survived, and the French were given a generous allocation of ex-German and ex-Italian ships.* The Americans and British also supplied a number of modern ships.

As with the army and the air force, the navy moved rapidly to equip itself with French designs, armed with French weapons and using French equipment. This resulted in some fine ships, but the navy was dogged throughout the Cold War by the high costs of two major programmes: first, the nuclear-propelled missile submarines and, second, the *Charles De Gaulle* aircraft carrier. There was also a commitment to expenditure at the other end of the scale, since the French navy's contribution to the country's continuing colonial responsibilities was met by two series of small frigates, known as *avisos*, which were produced in relatively large numbers. Squeezed in the middle, the fleet- and ocean-escort programmes were frequently subjected to delays and deletions in an effort to balance the budget.

Fleet Escorts
The cruiser *De Grasse*, which had lain unfinished in 1945, was completed in 1956 as an anti-aircraft cruiser, while a similar ship, *Colbert*, was built after the war, joining the fleet in 1959. Both these ships originally had an all-gun armament, but in the early 1970s *Colbert* underwent a refit which included installing a twin air-defence-missile launcher aft. Seventeen fleet escorts of the closely related Surcouf (T47) and Duperre (T53) classes (3,740 tonnes) were commissioned between 1956 and 1958, these were intended to provide

---

* The Italian ships were two cruisers and four destroyers, which were allocated to France under the terms of the 1948 peace treaty with Italy.

area air defence and air control, but their all-gun armament was plainly inadequate for modern conditions. As a result, in the mid-1960s four were converted to take a single launcher for the US Tartar missile, making them much more effective, while the remainder were converted into ASW escorts.

Next came two ships in the Suffren (FLE60) class, which were commissioned in 1967 and 1970. These were much larger, displacing 6,090 tonnes, and were equipped throughout with French weapons, sensors and equipment. Meanwhile, replacing the T47 air-defence conversions became a serious problem and it was planned to build four ships of the Cassard class, which would have entered service in the mid-1980s. In the event, budget problems resulted in the programme being stretched and two ships being cancelled, with the first ship being commissioned in 1988 and the other in 1991, and the T47s had to be kept in service for much longer than had been planned. In fact, again as an economy, the two new ships were equipped with launchers taken from the T47 ships, although the missiles were newly acquired US Standard SM-1 SAMs.

Ocean Escorts

In the 1950s France accepted a tasking from NATO to produce convoy escorts, and quickly produced eighteen ASW ships with a 1,700 tonne displacement, of which ten were funded under the Mutual Defense Assistance Program. Completed between 1955 and 1960, these French-designed ships were handy and served until the late 1970s. Next came *Aconit*, a much larger ship, displacing 3,900 tonnes, which was similar in general design to the contemporary US Knox class and which, unusually for a large French warship, had only a single propeller. *Aconit*'s main limitation was the lack of a helicopter, and so the next three ocean escorts, commissioned between 1974 and 1977, were much larger ships, displacing 5,800 tonnes. Designated the Tourville class, they used the extra length to accommodate two Lynx ASW helicopters.

The need to replace the ASW versions of the T47 and T53 classes resulted in the Georges Leygues class, whose ships, with a displacement of 4,350 tonnes, were larger than those they were to replace, albeit not as large as the Tourville class. As with the contemporary Cassard-class fleet escorts, the programme was delayed and one ship was cancelled as an economy measure, with the result that seven ships joined the fleet between 1979 and 1990. These ships reflected the larger size of 1980s ASW ships and were powered by a mixed power plant of British gas turbines and French diesels.

Small Escorts

Alone among the major navies, the French produced a series of small ships, usually known as *avisos*, which were intended to combine the roles of colonial patrolling in peacetime and ASW escorts in war. Nine of the

Commandant Rivière class (2,230 tonnes) were commissioned between 1962 and 1965, followed by seventeen of the D'Estienne D'Orves class (1,250 tonnes) in 1976–84.

BATTLESHIPS AND BATTLECRUISERS

The battleship, once the very symbol of naval power, survived – just – into the Cold war, and deserves a postscript of its own. At the start of the Cold War a few battleships were still in service, although experience in the recently concluded Second World War had shown that they were extremely vulnerable to air attack. The Japanese *Yamato*, for example, the largest super-battleship ever built, displaced some 70,000 tonnes and was armed with nine 460 mm guns and numerous anti-aircraft guns; it also had heavy armoured protection. Despite all this, when it was caught in the open sea on 7 April 1945 and attacked by some 400 US navy aircraft, *Yamato* was reduced to a blazing wreck within one hour and sunk within three.

As a result of such wartime experiences, by 1950 most navies had either scrapped their battleships or placed them in reserve. Many navies considered a number of plans to utilize the battleship hulls for a variety of other purposes, such as missile ships, but, except in the United States, these all came to naught, and the leviathans were eventually scrapped.

Two French battleships survived the war: *Richelieu*, which had taken part in the fighting, and *Jean Bart*, which was not only unfinished but had also been badly damaged. Popular pressure forced the government to authorize *Jean Bart*'s completion, which was done at vast expense. The two battleships looked very impressive, but their operational value was minimal, and they required huge crews. Both saw service during the first decade of the Cold War, and *Jean Bart* took part in the 1956 Suez operation, but they were withdrawn from service in 1959–60 and were scrapped in 1968–70.

Italy possessed five battleships in 1946, of which three were assigned as war reparations. The Soviet Union, the UK and the USA received one each, with the latter two immediately selling theirs for scrap. That left two, which saw brief service as training ships and were then scrapped in 1957.

In the USSR the situation was different, since early post-war naval plans were heavily influenced by the close interest being taken in maritime affairs by Stalin, who was determined to build up a large ocean-going fleet. Initially he laid heavy emphasis on battleships. Two very elderly Soviet battleships were retained in service until the early 1950s, while a battleship borrowed from the British during the war was returned in 1949 and replaced in the Soviet fleet by an ex-Italian ship, which was commissioned as *Novorossiysk*. Various plans were made in the late 1940s for three or more battleships, but these were cancelled in 1950, and when *Novorossiysk* was sunk on 29 October

1955 by a Second World War German mine the battleship era in the Soviet navy came to an end.

The British retained four King George V-class ships after the war. These were used actively for a very short period, but all had been placed in reserve by 1951 and they were scrapped in 1957. The last British battleship, *Vanguard*, was not completed until 1946, but was paid off in 1954 and scrapped in 1960.

In the US, however, four Iowa-class battleships were kept in reserve and were brought back into service during the Korean War and then returned to reserve again. *New Jersey* was briefly reactivated for the Vietnam War. President Reagan, however, had all four thoroughly modernized and then, with Tomahawk land-attack and Harpoon anti-ship missiles added to their armament, they were recommissioned: *New Jersey* in 1982, *Iowa* in 1983, *Missouri* in 1986 and *Wisconsin* in 1988. They were employed in surface-action groups, and *New Jersey*'s awesome shore-bombardment capability was employed off Lebanon in the early 1980s. They served on until the end of the Cold War, then all were decomissioned between 1990 and 1992 and were stricken in 1995.

21

NATO's 1950s Mine-Warfare Programme

The NATO mine-warfare programme of the 1950s showed the Alliance at its best. A threat was identified, concerted action was agreed, and a small number of designs were produced quickly.

Mine warfare has been a major feature of the naval scene for well over a hundred years, but interest in the subject has alternated between spurts of enthusiasm, with an attendant allocation of funds and resources, and periods of almost total uninterest, when the mine-countermeasures community has been starved of funds, manpower and resources. The latter periods end abruptly when a major ship is sunk or severely damaged by a mine, at which point the subject suddenly receives the highest priority, accompanied by renewed enthusiasm and funding.

The late 1940s was a period of uninterest, despite the fact that mines had been a major feature of naval warfare during the Second World War, during which the Axis and Allied navies laid some 350,000 mines each.* Casualties are sometimes difficult to attribute, but a British analysis concluded that Axis mines sank 281 British warships and 296 merchant vessels, while British-laid mines sank 1,047 enemy ships and damaged 5,412. Further analyses of the Second World War showed that, important as they were, the number of sinkings achieved was not the sole criterion of success and that mines had a number of additional and significant effects. First, they diverted enemy naval and merchant vessels into areas where they could more easily be attacked by other means; second, they forced the enemy to divert considerable manpower to mine-countermeasures (MCM) tasks; and, third, enemy production capacity was diverted into manufacturing both mines and MCM equipment.

Such telling evidence was ignored in the face of post-war manpower and

---

* Details of sea mines laid in the Second World War and the damage they caused are given in Appendix 23.

financial cuts, and in the late 1940s other naval threats, particularly those posed by fast submarines and high-speed cruisers, were accorded a higher priority. As a result, minesweepers were given a very low priority for retention, although, ironically, the only elements of the defeated German and Japanese navies to serve on after the war were special minesweeping forces, which worked from 1945 until the early 1950s clearing the vast minefields which had been laid between 1939 and 1945.

There were a number of additional reasons for the lack of enthusiasm for MCM activities at this particular time. First, since the minesweepers had to go into minefields to ply their trade, their losses were inevitably heavy. Second, all existing sweeping methods were slow, and the speed of clearance could be increased only by having large numbers of sweepers, which would require considerable manpower to operate them. The problem was exacerbated by the requirement to construct the vessels using materials such as amagnetic steel, aluminium, wood or, later, glass fibre, which would be less likely to trigger a magnetic mine.

In the Korean War, however, United Nations naval forces found themselves severely hampered by the minefields laid by the weaker force, the North Korean navy. Some 4,000 mines were supplied to North Korea by the Soviet Union, 75 per cent of which were actually laid during a period of three weeks, using very primitive laying methods. There were two types of mine – a relatively modern Soviet magnetic mine and an ancient contact mine whose design dated back to the Russo-Japanese war – and both caused repeated problems, especially at the Wŏnsan landings, where four minesweepers and one fleet tug were sunk and five destroyers were damaged before the swept channel was fully cleared.

Having observed the Korean War closely, NATO planners concluded that, if war came, the Soviets would make massive use of offensive mining around the coasts of western Europe, where just a few mines could close vital ports, estuaries or choke points for days – perhaps even weeks. It was also assessed that mines would be one of the measures used to disrupt US and Canadian reinforcements reaching Europe.

This threat to NATO was made even more serious by technological developments. The traditional moored contact mine was still in use, floating at a fixed height above the bottom, held in place by a cable anchored to the seabed. Such mines were swept by one or more minesweepers towing 'mechanical sweeps' consisting of long cables which engaged the mooring cable and then cut it, whereupon the mine rose to the surface, where it was detonated by rifle or gunfire. Magnetic, acoustic and pressure mines were introduced early in the Second World War, but, after initial successes, their *modis operandi* were identified and countermeasures were developed which reduced, although they did not totally remove, their danger.

While all NATO navies faced the same type of threat, there was a significant difference in the scale, since the Soviet navy of the early 1950s was unlikely to be able to mine the US coast or harbour entrances, although there was a small threat from submarine-laid mines. European waters, on the other hand, were within easy reach. As a result, an urgent programme was started to build mine countermeasures vessels (MCMVs) for many European navies. Both the American and the British navies had been working in parallel on the mine problem since the late 1940s and came up with generally similar countermeasure designs, which were adopted, in one form or another, by most other NATO navies, with the great majority of construction being funded under the Mutual Defense Assistance Program. In addition, foreign designs which had been approved by the US navy were built in foreign yards under the Off-Shore Purchases scheme, funded by the US Military Supply Agency. Further ships were also acquired by the foreign countries concerned, using national funds. The programme involved three types of MCMV.*

OCEAN-GOING MINESWEEPERS

Ocean-going minesweepers built during the Second World War had steel hulls, since it was considered that the dangers of the new magnetic and acoustic mines were less in open waters. Nevertheless, the threat from more sensitive Soviet mines led the US navy to develop a new wooden-hulled ocean minesweeper, the Agile class, with a hull constructed of laminated timbers and in which fittings were made of bronze or stainless steel, to reduce the magnetic signature to the absolute minimum. Despite their small size (they displaced 735 tonnes) these were extremely sophisticated ships, whose cost per tonne was equalled only by contemporary submarines. Ninety-six were built between 1953 and 1960, of which sixty-two went to the US and thirty-four to other NATO navies.

COASTAL MINESWEEPERS

Two wooden-hulled coastal-minesweepers designs were developed: the US Bluebird and the British Ton classes. The Bluebird class was an enlarged version of a wartime design, with improved sweeping capabilities and better sea-keeping – particularly stability. One hundred and twenty-eight were built in the USA (twenty for the United States and the remainder for overseas), and many more were built abroad.

---

* Details of the MCM programme and specifications of the ships involved are given in Appendix 24.

The British Ton was somewhat larger than the Agile, although it generated a less powerful sweeping current to counter magnetic mines. A total of 205 were built, of which twenty were built in Canada as the Bay class (ten for Canada, six for France, four for Turkey), thirty-four were built in France (all for France), thirty-two were built in the Netherlands (all for the Dutch navy), four were built in Portugal (all for Portugal), and the remaining 115 for the British navy.

INSHORE MINESWEEPERS

There were also two designs for inshore minesweeper. Fourteen of the US Cove class were built – two for the United States and the rest for other NATO countries – but the British Ham class was built in considerably larger numbers. One hundred and eight were built in the UK, of which fifteen went to France and the remainder to the British navy, while another twenty were built in Italy (all for Italy) and sixteen in Belgium. Sixteen more were built in the Netherlands to a Dutch design which was generally similar to the Ham class. The British also built a further eleven minehunters of the Ley class, which was adapted from the Ham class.

AN IGNORED LESSON

This MCM programme showed just what NATO was capable of, when all the member nations put their minds to it. As shown in Appendix 24, the 1950s MCM programme resulted in the production of 703 vessels and totally transformed the Alliance's capabilities. Furthermore, by restricting the origins of the designs to two sources (the USA and the UK) a large degree of commonality was assured, which was further strengthened because the recipient navies naturally found themselves using common equipment and procedures. In the following decades there were many more areas where such a common approach would have resulted in more equipment, produced more quickly and at less cost, but sadly it was not to be.

22

Amphibious Warfare

The end of the Second World War found the US and British navies with huge fleets of amphibious-warfare ships and a wealth of expertise in their use, arising from landing operations in North Africa, in Sicily, mainland Italy, Normandy and the south of France in Europe, and in the US island-hopping campaign in the Pacific. Although the Soviet navy had conducted over 100 amphibious landings, those were almost always as a flanking move in support of a land operation, typically involving 3,000 troops, which was minuscule in comparison with the scale of their Western allies' operations, and without the benefit of specialized shipping.

In the late 1940s there was little perceived requirement for amphibious landings, and it was thought at high levels in the Pentagon that the atomic bomb had outdated such massive concentrations of ships. The Inch'ŏn landings in Korea (September 1950) and the Anglo-French landings at Suez (6 November 1956) brought the subject back into focus, but with a marked change in emphasis. Second World War amphibious tactics had centred on large fleets of flat-bottomed landing vessels running on to a beach to deliver their loads of men, tanks, vehicles and equipment. Such vessels were relatively cheap, easy to build (most were constructed by non-specialist shipyards), could be produced in vast numbers, and were usually able to take their loads direct from the port of loading to the target beach without any need for cross-loading.

Unfortunately, they were also very slow – even the US navy's post-war tank landing ships (LSTs) were not capable of more than 15 knots – while the landing beaches had to be carefully selected to meet stringent criteria for slope and composition. In addition, there was a firm commitment in the US navy to a 20 knot speed for task groups, which no LST design could ever meet. As a result, there was a steady move away from such ships to dock landing ships (LSDs), which carried small landing craft internally, to be launched offshore and used for the final run-in to the beach. A second type of ship was the helicopter carrier, which not only enabled troops and equipment to be delivered ashore, but had the great advantage of missing out the very dangerous beach-line altogether and delivering the troops to a point of the commander's choosing, which could be anything from 500 m to 50 km inland.

Above all, the advantage of amphibious troops, as was repeatedly demonstrated during the Cold War, was that they could move around the globe in international waters, 'hover' just over the horizon from a trouble spot, and then land within a few hours of being given the order to deploy.

THE US MARINE CORPS

Throughout the Cold War, the US Marine Corps (USMC) was in a class of its own as regards size, complexity, equipment and capability. In 1987, for example, it numbered 199,600 men and women and fielded three mobile divisions, equipped with their own armour and artillery, and with their own logistic support. It should be noted that a USMC division is far larger than a division in any other armed force in the world, and consists of some 18,000 Marines, including attached navy personnel, but excluding the support personnel who would normally deploy with the division.

Until the late 1980s each of these Marine divisions was composed of three regiments, each of three battalions. Combat support troops included an artillery regiment (each of three artillery battalions), a tank battalion, a reconnaissance battalion, a light-armoured assault battalion and an engineer battalion. Support units included a service battalion, a shore-party battalion, a service battalion, a medical battalion and a motor-transport battalion.

Each division had an associated Marine Air Wing, which operated some 315 aircraft, including fighters, attack aircraft and helicopters. There were also some sixty amphibious-warfare ships dedicated to moving and landing Marines. Even just one USMC division and its associated air wing represented a greater concentration of power than the totality of the armed forces possessed by most nations.

USMC doctrine was to tailor forces to the requirement, and the basic building block for this was the Marine Amphibious Unit (MAU), which combined an infantry battalion, an aviation squadron and a service/support unit. Two to five MAUs could be combined into a Marine Amphibious Brigade (MAB).

The Reagan administration made strenuous efforts to strengthen the Marine Corps. Not only did the president and his supporters advocate a strong corps, but they actually made the money available to achieve it, increasing USMC funding from $5 billion in 1975 to $7.5 billion in 1985 (at 1985 dollars). This included replacing or upgrading virtually every weapon system in service, replacing old M60 tanks by the new M1, for example, and funding a series of new ships, including the Wasp-class assault ships, which could each carry 1,900 troops. On top of all this, the elderly Iowa-class battleships were returned to service, with their nine 406 mm guns and Tomahawk missile launchers intended primarily for shore bombardment. Curiously, however, in the midst of all this modernization one item remained unchanged: the CH-46 helicopter, which had entered service in the early 1960s and was fated to remain the workhorse of the Marine Corps well beyond the end of the Cold War.

One of the major achievements of the USMC in the Cold War was the plan to reinforce Norway. In this, the majority of the combat equipment required by a full Marine Amphibious Brigade was pre-positioned in Norway, housed in specially built caves in the Trondheim area. (In order to comply with Norwegian sensitivities about stationing non-Norwegian troops in the country during peacetime, the stocks were maintained by the Norwegian authorities.) The task of the MAB, reinforced by up to two more USMC brigades, a Canadian brigade and the Netherlands–UK Amphibious Group, was to reinforce the Norwegian armed forces in repelling any Soviet invasion.

THE SOVIET NAVAL INFANTRY

The Soviet Naval Infantry fought during the Second World War, but was then transferred from the navy to the coastal-defence forces before being disbanded in the mid-1950s. On 14 July 1958, however, the president of Lebanon requested urgent aid from France, the UK and the USA to counter a threat by the USSR to deploy Soviet 'volunteers' to support pro-Nasser rebels. The US Sixth Fleet was able to land three Marine battalions the very next day, and the threat from the Soviet 'volunteers' immediately disappeared. The Marine battalions withdrew on 21 August after what had been a classic exhibition of the value of sea power and amphibious capability.

The Soviet leadership, never slow to learn from such experiences, responded by re-establishing the Naval Infantry, which rapidly became a *corps d'élite*. The force expanded, peaking in size and effectiveness around 1988, when it was some 18,000 strong. It fielded:

- one division (7,000 men) of three infantry regiments, one tank regiment and one artillery regiment;
- three independent brigades (3,000 men), each of three infantry battalions, one tank battalion, one artillery battalion and one rocket-launcher battalion;

- four *spetsnaz* (special forces) brigades, each of three underwater battalions and one parachute battalion.

The Naval Infantry was transported by a growing number of amphibious-warfare ships. Largest were two Ivan Rogov-class dock landing ships, displacing 13,100 tonnes, which carried one Naval Infantry battalion and forty tracked or larger numbers of wheeled vehicles, plus helicopters and surface-effect ships. Fourteen Alligator LSTs were similar in many respects to the British Sir Galahad-class logistics landing ships (LSLs); with a large cargo capacity and bow and stern doors, these were intended for follow-up operations rather than the assault wave. Principal assault vessels were the thirty-seven Ropucha LSTs, which were built in Poland. Smallest were forty-five Polnocny-class small tank landing ships (LCTs), also built in Poland, which displaced some 1,000 tonnes and had a payload of six battle tanks.

The Naval Infantry seized on the surface-effect ship (SES) as an effective way of transporting marines ashore, and developed a number of types including the Pomornik, which could carry three battle tanks, and the Aist, which carried two. Under development at the end of the Cold War was the Orlan-class wing-in-ground-effect (WIG) vessel,* designed to transport up to 150 troops at speeds of up to 300 knots. Both the SES and the WIG vessels were very fast compared with normal amphibious shipping, and were designed for short 'hooks' in support of a ground advance, or for lightning attacks on crucial targets in the Baltic and Black seas, both types of operation having precedents in the Soviet experience in the Second World War. These craft were another example of the flexibility of thought in the Soviet forces, which produced some novel solutions to the problems facing them.

OTHER AMPHIBIOUS UNITS

The British Royal Marines generally numbered around 7,000–8,000 and formed one self-supporting commando brigade, plus the Special Boat Squadron (special forces). The amphibious shipping available to the Royal Marines varied, but at its peak it included two commando carriers (former aircraft carriers converted to handle helicopters, and to accommodate marines and their equipment), two dock ships, and six LSLs.

Other nations involved in the Cold War also produced marine units. In the Warsaw Pact, the Polish army fielded one amphibious assault brigade,

---

* WIG craft fly at a height of between 5 and 15 m, taking advantage of the increased aerodynamic lift that occurs when a wing operating near the ground experiences a reduction in induced drag.

while the East Germans had an army amphibious regiment; both had sufficient landing craft to transport these on short-range operations.

Among the NATO nations, the main amphibious forces, apart from those of the USA and the UK, were provided by the Netherlands (two commando groups), Portugal (three battalion groups) and Spain (11,500 men organized into one marine regiment and five marine garrison regiments); Turkey had one brigade.

PART IV

THE LAND BATTLE ON THE CENTRAL FRONT

23

NATO's Central Region Ground Forces

Nowhere was the Cold War more intense, nowhere was it more likely to have broken out, and, provided it remained non-nuclear, nowhere was it more likely to have been decided than in Europe – NATO's Central Region. In compliance with their wartime agreements, the Allies divided Europe into two, split by a line which was christened the 'Iron Curtain' by Winston Churchill, although where it ran north–south through Germany it later became known, rather more prosaically, as the 'Inner German Border' (IGB). Belgium, Denmark, Luxembourg, the Netherlands and the major part of Germany were in the Western camp, while Czechoslovakia, the remainder of Germany, Hungary and Poland lay in the East. Sweden and Switzerland were long-standing neutrals, while Austria, after a ten-year Allied occupation, became neutral in 1955.

On the Western side the dispositions on the Central Front were principally the outcome of wartime agreements between the UK and the USA, with a last-minute amendment to accommodate the French. Thus the British forces were in the north, with contingents from Belgium, Canada, the Netherlands and Norway all within the British zone. US forces were in the south, but with an enclave at Bremerhaven to ensure their supplies. The French were given a smaller zone in the south-west. Generally speaking, the victors occupied former *Wehrmacht* barracks and *Luftwaffe* airfields in accordance with where units came to a halt in 1945.

By the early 1950s some of the occupation forces had departed and those that remained did so under the terms of newly concluded treaties with the Federal Republic of Germany. In addition, the formation of the new German armed forces (*Bundeswehr*), and in particular of the army (*Bundesheer*), resulted in some reshuffling, the situation then remaining substantially unchanged for the remainder of the Cold War.

THE NATIONAL ARMIES

The great majority of nations depended upon conscription to man their armies, but Canada, the UK and the USA changed during the Cold War to all-regular armies. Among those that depended upon conscription, however, not only were there considerable differences between the systems, but, in addition, the terms decreased in severity and the length of service grew shorter as time passed. By the late 1980s, for example, Danish conscripts served for nine months, those in Belgium and France for twelve months, and the Germans for fifteen months, while the Dutch served for a nominal twenty-four months, although the final few months were spent on 'short leave'. These reductions in service inevitably reduced efficiency, especially as equipment became more sophisticated and needed greater skills for its operation.

Belgium

In the 1960s Belgium was supposed to provide two corps in West Germany, each of three divisions, giving a total of nine brigades. By 1970, however, the reality was that it fielded only one corps, composed of two divisions, each of two brigades, and then in 1977 there was a further retrenchment, which involved moving one brigade from each of those divisions back into Belgium. A yet further reorganization in the early 1980s resulted in the forces in West Germany being reduced to the corps headquarters plus one division of two brigades and an independent reconnaissance brigade. The second division, consisting of two brigades, was relocated in Belgium.

Canada

In proportion to its population and resources, during the Second World War Canada made a very large contribution to the Allied efforts; it then continued to maintain a force in western Europe throughout the Cold War. For many years the 4th Canadian Mechanized Brigade Group (4CMBG) was located in the north, forming an essential element of NATO's NORTHAG (Northern Army Group) reserves, but in the 1970s it was moved south to Lahr, where it became a CENTAG (Central Army Group) reserve. The Canadians struggled manfully to maintain this as a viable force, and its troops were extremely professional, but 4CMBG's combat equipment was always less than that of a normal brigade, both in quantity and, sometimes, in quality.

Denmark

In the original NATO force goals Denmark was committed to field two full-strength divisions, but this was never achieved, partly because of financial difficulties, but also because of a high level of domestic opposition to heavy defence spending. As a result, there were military manpower cuts in 1973, 1985 and 1987. The main element of the field force was the Jutland Division of three mechanized brigades and one regimental combat group, which was located in peacetime in Denmark, but which deployed to Schleswig-Holstein in war; this deployment, however, would have taken place only some one to three weeks after mobilization, which was needed to round the division out to wartime strength. The second Danish division, which was even more dependent on reserves, defended the whole of the Jutland peninsula, although, as described below, it would have been assisted in this task by the UK Mobile Force.

West Germany

Following its admission to NATO, the FRG rapidly built up its forces, particularly the army (*Bundesheer*). The initial organization – *Heerstruktur I* – was tailored to meet NATO requirements and consisted of five divisions, which were completed by 1957 and manned principally by conscripts on a twelve-month engagement. This was subsequently changed in 1958 to *Heerstruktur II*, to comply with NATO's new 'tripwire' strategy (MC 14/2), and concurrently the army reached its target of twelve divisions. In the aftermath of the 1961 Berlin crisis, conscription was extended to eighteen months. The 1967 NATO change to 'flexible response' (MC 14/3) resulted in *Heerstruktur III*, which included strengthening the panzer (armoured) divisions, increasing the 'teeth-to-tail' ratio, and creating a territorial army. Finally, *Heerstruktur IV*, introduced in 1981, strengthened the brigades in the regular army and restructured and strengthened the territorial army.

The *Bundesheer* produced three corps, whose composition varied according to their combat role, plus one division:

- 1 (GE) Corps was part of NORTHAG, being positioned between the Dutch and British corps, and consisted of three panzer (armoured) divisions and one panzer grenadier (armoured infantry) division – a total of twelve brigades.
- 2 (GE) Corps was in the south, facing the Czechoslovak border and essentially defending the hilly country of Bavaria. Its composition reflected the complexity of its role: one panzer, one panzer grenadier, one mountain and one airborne division – a total of twelve brigades.
- 3 (GE) Corps was the northernmost corps in CENTAG, and on deployment would have been located between the Belgian and US corps. It consisted of two panzer divisions and one panzer grenadier division – a total of nine brigades.
- The twelfth division was committed to NATO's LANDJUT (Land Forces Jutland) and was located in Schleswig-Holstein.

An efficient conscription system maintained this force at a high degree of readiness. Combat units (i.e. brigades and below) normally required only an additional 5 per cent to bring them up to war strength, while divisional support units needed 25 per cent and corps support units 50 per cent.

Luxembourg

In the early days of NATO tiny Luxembourg produced a regimental combat team of three battalions, but this commitment slowly decreased until by 1988 there was just one light-infantry battalion, whose war role was with the Allied Command Europe Mobile Force (Land) (AMF(L)).

The Netherlands

The Dutch provided 1 (NL) Corps, which was responsible for NORTHAG's left flank, where it was located between LANDJUT and 1 (GE) Corps. One of the major problems for 1 (NL) Corps was that only the 41st Armoured Brigade, a reconnaissance battalion and some support units were stationed in the FRG in peacetime; the remaining units were in the Netherlands, and, from the time the Dutch government gave the order, would have required ninety-six hours to reach their combat positions.

The Dutch conscription system was known as 'Direct Intake into Reserve', and each regular unit had a reserve 'shadow' unit. Conscripts served for two years in a regular unit, of which the last six months, sometimes longer, were spent on 'short leave', which meant that they were liable to rapid recall, following which they were transferred as a group to their 'shadow unit', where they served for a further eighteen months. Efficient as this system was, it still took time to implement.

The UK

The main British contribution was 1 (BR) Corps, which was part of NORTHAG. During the Cold War few countries reorganized their army as frequently as the British; on some occasions the reorganization was due to changing national, political or economic circumstances, although on others the reasons baffled friend and foe alike.

In the 1950s 1 (BR) Corps consisted of three armoured divisions and one infantry division, but in the 1960s this was reduced to three all-arms divisions. Then, in 1976, it underwent a fundamental reorganization, in which the brigade level of command was eliminated and command over units was then exercised by four divisional headquarters. By 1982, however, these changes, which had been achieved at considerable expense, were seen to be fundamentally flawed and were totally reversed (at further expense), this time to three, much stronger, armoured divisions, two of them with three armoured brigades and one with two armoured brigades and an infantry brigade. (The infantry brigade was stationed in the UK in peacetime.)

To implement the 1976 changes a fourth divisional headquarters (HQ 3 Division) was taken over to Germany, while to implement the 1982 changes a different divisional headquarters (HQ 2 Division) was returned to the UK. In the UK this divisional headquarters retained its war role in Germany, being committed to the new task of rear-area security of 1 (BR) Corps, for which it fielded three motorized infantry brigades, one of which was regular and the other two from the Territorial Army.

As a quite separate commitment, the British provided the United Kingdom Mobile Force (UKMF), which consisted of the 1st (UK) Infantry Brigade (four motorized infantry battalions, one armoured reconnaissance battalion, one artillery battalion and an armoured squadron) and an air-force component of three fighter squadrons. In addition, since by NATO rules communications and logistics were a national responsibility, the force required a large logistics tail, bringing the UKMF total to well in excess of 15,000 men. This force was stationed in peacetime in the UK, and in war would have had to mobilize (approximately one-third was from the Territorial Army) and then move either to Jutland, where it came under command of the Danish Commander LANDJUT, or to northern Italy.

The USA

The United States made a major contribution to NATO land forces on the Central Front, with the US army undergoing a number of reorganizations during the years of the Cold War. In the military excitement of the 1950s, the post-Second World War army in Europe was converted into the 'Pentomic Army', equipped with battlefield nuclear weapons and organized on the basis of a 'rule of five' – i.e. five battalions to a brigade, fire brigades to a division, and so on. In the 1960s the Vietnam War, not surprisingly, took priority in all US military thinking and Europe was something of a backwater, regaining its precedence only in the early 1970s. Conscription ended in 1973, although legislation for the 'draft' remained for use in an emergency, but US manpower in Europe actually increased over the years, from 197,000 in 1975 to over 227,000 in 1988, of whom 204,700 were army personnel stationed in the FRG.

US ground forces were commanded by the Seventh (US) Army and organized into two corps, 5 (US) Corps in the north of the former US zone and 7 (US) Corps in the south, both of which came under CENTAG in wartime. Most US units were stationed in the FRG in peacetime; however, some elements were 'dual-based', which meant the manpower was stationed in the USA in peacetime but in war would make use of a full duplicate set of equipment located in Germany.* Each corps also included an armoured cavalry regiment, which was permanently based in the FRG. In addition to these divisions, there were seven artillery brigades, four independent artillery groups and nine surface-to-surface-missile battalions (three with Pershing II, six with Lance), as well as numerous engineer, aviation, communications and logistics units permanently in Germany, with many more in the USA, earmarked for the Central Front in war.

The US goal was to have ten full divisions in western Europe within twenty-one days of a deployment order. This would have enabled them to field two full-strength corps in CENTAG, one full-strength corps (3 (US) Corps) in the north as CINCENT's reserve, and one division (2 (US) Armoured Division) as part of NORTHAG.

France

In 1945 the French army occupied a zone in south-west Germany abutting on the French border, where it remained throughout the Cold War, first as an occupying power, then under a bilateral treaty with the Federal Republic on the admission of the latter to NATO, and finally under a new bilateral treaty following France's withdrawal from the NATO integrated command structure. From that time, however, France's forces in the FRG were no longer assigned to NATO, and their precise role in war was never totally clear, although, as described elsewhere in this book, while the French relationship with NATO underwent a number of changes, the relationship was always closer than was depicted in the media.

The major field formation was always the First French Army (FFA), but its internal organization underwent a number of reorganizations over the years. Once French nuclear weapons became operational, the ground forces were organized to serve as a 'trigger' for French nuclear intervention, but they were subsequently reorganized to enable them to play a more positive role in the land battle. The most significant factor on the ground was that, if NATO defences in West Germany failed to halt an attack, there was little likelihood that victorious Soviet forces would halt on the Franco-German border; it thus made sound sense for French ground forces not only to defend the border, but also to bolster NATO defences to the east of that border. For this reason detailed plans were made for French counter-attacks, particularly in the NORTHAG area.

By the 1980s the FFA consisted of three corps:

- 1 (FR) Corps – three armoured and two light armoured divisions, of which one armoured division was stationed in the FRG;

---

* This equipment was known as 'POMCUS' – Pre-positioned Materiel Configured to Unit Sets.

est Berliners watch a US transport aircraft bringing essential supplies to Tempelhof
Airfield during the Berlin Airlift. The Soviet blockade of Berlin lasted from
22 June 1948 to 12 May 1949, and the Western Allies' united and steadfast
response to it was a prelude to the Cold War

General of the Army Dwight D. Eisenhower was recalled from retirement whe he was appointed NATO's fi Supreme Allied Commander Europe (SACEUR) on 19 December 1950. He served the Alliance until 1952, whe he returned to the United States to run for president

NATO's first secretary-gener was the British Lord Ismay. He made major contribution to the Alliance, helping to se up its structure and procedures, and overseeing the accession of Greece and Turkey in 1952 and of the Federal Republic of German in 1955. He retired from NATO in 1957

President John F. Kennedy's significant and emotional visit to West Berlin in June 1963 symbolized United States commitment to NATO and to West Berlin. Here he returns from a visit to a Western checkpoint, with West Berlin's governing mayor, Willy Brandt, second from his right

Much of NATO's work took place in conference rooms, where the members made plans for the future, discussed common problems, and resolved the differences which arose from time to time. Here the North Atlantic Council meets in The Hague, the Netherlands, on 30 May 1979

Some of the East–West confrontations took place in full view of the international media, which added to the danger of the situation. These Soviet T-55 tanks are taki up position facing Checkpoint Charlie in Berlin, in October 1961

US tanks face the East at Checkpoint Charlie, also in October 1961.
Such incidents appeared to be part of a ritual; however, they were very tense,
and one false or unintentional move by either side could have seen rapid escalatio
to a conflict which neither side wanted

Confrontation in the skies as US navy Phantom fighters intercept a patrolling Soviet 'Badger' bomber. Such meetings took place daily throughout the Cold War; the rules were well understood, but occasionally they were broken and aircraft were shot down as a result

The Cold War was fought on many fronts, one of the most intense being the battle for people's hearts and minds. A seemingly endless stream of documents appeared, of which these two are typical: the US *Soviet Military Power* and Moscow's response, *Whence the Threat to Peace?*

Public knowledge of Warsaw Pact capabilities was usually derived from carefully managed 'photo opportunities', which were designed to give the impression of awe-inspiring might. A typical example was this huge fleet of tanks, which was assembled after a major exercise

Marshal V. G. Kulikov (*centre, seated*) endorses the record of a meeting of Warsaw Pact defence ministers in December 1984. In all Warsaw Pact countries the defence ministers were army generals and, unlike NATO, the Pact was not headed by a civilian secretary-general

he Soviet Typhoon-class missile submarine was originally intended to lie under the
rctic ice cap for up to twelve months at a time, emerging only to launch its twenty
long-range missiles in a 'second strike'

This huge Soviet bomb is thought to be the type used in the world's largest known nuclear explosion. This involved a 58 MT weapon (equivalent to 58 million tons of TNT), and took place in an airburst at 3,700 m above the Novaya Zemlya test site on 30 October 1961

A Valiant V-bomber drops an inert version of the Blue Danube, the first British atomic weapon. Blue Danube entered service in November 1953 and, despite its large size, had a yield of only 20 kT – approximately the same as that of the bomb dropped on Nagasaki in 1945

A US Minuteman III intercontinental ballistic missile climbs away from the Vandenberg test site in California. This three-stage, solid-fuelled missile carried two or three MIRVs over a range of some 13,000 km. The yield of each warhead could be set to either 172 kT or 335 kT prior to launch

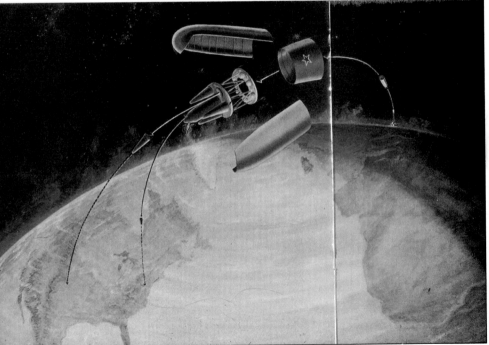

A US artist's depiction of a Soviet MIRVed missile in space. The shroud and bustle have broken away and the control computer aboard the bus has already deployed three MIRVs, with two more ready to leave. Each MIRV will head for a different target

The first of the battlefield nuclear weapons was the 280 mm 'atomic cannon', which served in the US army in Europe in the 1950s. Later battlefield weapons were much smaller and considerably more mobile

The W19 atomic shell was designed specifically for the 280 mm cannon. It had a yield of approximately 15 kT and a range of about 30,000 m

he US carrier *John F. Kennedy* launches an air strike off the Norwegian coast during NATO's Exercise Strong Express in 1972. NATO exercises took place at frequent intervals, and not only practised real plans but also demonstrated a willingness to carry them out if forced to do so

The US carrier *Kitty Hawk*, with its air wing on deck. Such US 'supercarriers' operated an air wing that was more powerful and sophisticated than most national air forces, and they played a unique role in the Cold War, providing mobile airbases that could patrol in international waters

The British navy was the second most powerful in NATO, its main strength lying in a large number of very capable anti-submarine frigates. The design of this Type-22 frigate, HMS *Cumberland*, made use of British experience in the Falklands War, which taught all Cold War navies some very valuable lessons

A Kresta II-class cruiser, one of a long series of daring and innovative ship designs built by the Soviet navy. During the Cold War the Soviet navy was transformed from a minor coastal force into an impressive 'blue-water' fleet, exercising naval power in all the world's oceans

A NATO naval force assembled in Malta's Grand Harbour in 1960.
Among the navies represented are those of France, Italy, Turkey, the UK
and the USA. NATO navies used common procedures as a matter of routine,
which enabled them to work together easily and with only minimal preparation

A Boeing E-3 Sentry of NATO's Airborne Early Warning Force. Based at
Geilenkirchen in West Germany and with the aircraft registered in Luxembourg,
this force was completely multinational, demonstrating how well member nations
could work together when the will was there

The Soviet army met many of its low-level air-defence requirements with the
ZSU-23-4. This weapon married an existing chassis and weapon to a new radar,
resulting in a highly effective system which was viewed with great respect by the
NATO pilots who might have had to fly against it

The US army also took an existing chassis, weapon and radar to produce the
Sergeant York air-defence system, but the outcome was unsatisfactory
and the system was discontinued before it could enter service

In the 1950s the French and Germans held a competition to produce a common tank design. The French entry was the AMX-30, seen here, which was lighter but less well armed and with thinner armour than the German entry. When the AMX-30 was not declared the winner, the French left the project and produced the tank for their own army

The German entry for the 1950s competition, the Leopard, was heavier than the French AMX-30 and armed with the British 105 mm gun – at that time the most powerful tank gun in the world. Once the French withdrew, the Germans produced the Leopard for the *Bundesheer* and exported it to many other armies

The Cold War ends in November 1989. A demonstrator hammers at the Berlin Wall striving to demolish the hated symbol of the separation of the two Germanies. Meanwhile, East German guards look on passively, symbolizing the Communist failure to bind the nations of eastern Europe together

- 2 (FR) Corps – two armoured divisions and one infantry division, with the majority located in the FRG;
- 3 (FR) Corps – two armoured divisions and one infantry division, all stationed in north-east France.

In addition, the *Force Action Rapide* (FAR) consisted of four divisions (one light armour, one marine, one airborne, one alpine) and the Foreign Legion Operational Group. These were designed to conduct intervention operations outside Europe in peacetime, but would have been available for national defence in time of war.

DEFENDING THE CENTRAL REGION

NATO ground forces in central Europe believed themselves to be facing an aggressive-minded enemy, which, if it attacked, would do so in a series of rapid drives, led by tanks and highly mobile infantry in armoured personnel carriers, with the aim of eliminating NATO forces as rapidly as possible. NATO also believed that the Warsaw Pact would attack along six main axes:

- along the Baltic coast and north into Jutland;
- towards Hamburg and then along the North Sea coast;
- across the North German Plain, using the flat, rolling countryside with its abundance of roads, through the 1 (BR) Corps position and towards the Ruhr;
- through the Fulda Gap in the direction of Mannheim;
- from Zwickau through the so-called 'Hof Corridor' towards Nuremberg and Stuttgart;
- from Czechoslovakia, with two pincer movements meeting west of Munich.

The defence of the Central Region against these threats was not an easy task. Western Germany stretched approximately 700 km from north to south and was some 300–400 km wide, which meant that, from a military point of view, it was seriously lacking in depth. The original strategy for the defence of the Central Region was based on a thin 'crust' of conventional forces, penetration of which would have resulted in the virtually automatic use of nuclear weapons.[1] This was subsequently changed in December 1967 to the strategy of 'flexible response', which required a credible conventional defence, sufficiently strong to contain any attack as far forward (i.e. as near to the IGB) as possible. Both these strategies were, however, within the overall concept of 'forward defence', which, not surprisingly, was insisted upon by the West Germans and required that Warsaw Pact forces be held as far to the east as possible, even though this was not necessarily ideal from the operational point of view.

The task of defending central Europe fell to NATO's Allied Forces Central Europe (AFCENT), which was originally located in France and commanded by a French general, but in 1967 it moved to Brunssum in the Netherlands, at which time a German general took command. The command was divided into two – Northern Army Group (NORTHAG) and Central Army Group (CENTAG) – commanded by a British and a US general respectively. The headquarters of AFCENT, NORTHAG and CENTAG were fully integrated NATO organizations, but below them were a number of corps, each of which was almost totally national in organization. This provided a certain degree of strength, but also caused NATO a number of difficulties, not least because nations retained the right to organize, equip and train their troops according to their national requirements, standards and traditions; nations were also, to a large degree, able to decide on their readiness and mobilization plans. As a result, there was no such thing as a standard NATO division in size, organization or tactics, and when more than one nation used the same equipment it was frequently as much by chance as by design.

There was a major anomaly in that, while Denmark and Schleswig-Holstein were the vital northern flank to the Central Region battle and overlooked the exits from the Baltic (also an area of vital interest to the Central Front), they came under CINCNORTH (in Norway) rather than under CINCENT. Two major threats faced Denmark, both of which emanated from areas of vital interest to the Central Region: a Soviet/East German overland thrust through Schleswig-Holstein, and an amphibious attack by East German, Polish and Soviet marines along the Baltic coastline.

NORTHAG

NORTHAG headquarters was at Rheindahlen, just outside Mönchengladbach, Germany, and was a fully integrated NATO headquarters, commanded by a British four-star general. It was responsible for the defence of the Federal Republic from the southern border of Schleswig-Holstein in the north, to a line running approximately from Kassel to Bonn. Its area of responsibility thus included the North Sea coast with its vital ports of Bremerhaven and (in depth) Antwerp and Rotterdam, the North German Plain leading to the Ruhr, and the Harz mountains in the south.

The army group comprised four corps and a reserve division:

- 1 (NL) Corps was on NORTHAG's left, and in the 1980s consisted of three armoured and six armoured infantry brigades, of which the 41st Armoured Brigade and a reconnaissance battalion were the only units stationed in the FRG in peacetime. There were also three divisional head-quarters (1, 4 and 5 Divisions), but there were no permanent divisions, the corps commander allocating the divisional commander between two and five brigades, according to the tactical situation.*

- 1 (GE) Corps consisted of three panzer divisions (1, 3 and 7) and one panzer grenadier (11) division, each division comprising three brigades. Each brigade was made up of four panzer or panzer grenadier battalions, of which three were fully active, while the fourth was at cadre strength only, requiring reservists to bring it up to strength on mobilization, which would have required ninety-six hours. 1 (GE) Corps's position was to the right of 1 (NL) Corps, where it shared the responsibility for the North German Plain with 1 (BR) Corps. Alone among the national contributors to the central region, the Germans were split, 1 (GE) Corps in NORTHAG being located at a considerable distance from 2 and 3 (GE) Corps in CENTAG.

- 1 (BR) Corps held the southern part of the plain, sitting astride the main east–west Hanover–Essen autobahn route, which would inevitably have been one of the Warsaw Pact's main axes of advance. The corps consisted of 1 and 4 Armoured Divisions, each with three armoured brigades. 3 Armoured Division, however, consisted of two Germany-based brigades – one armoured brigade, with two armoured battalions and one mechanized infantry battalion, and one brigade which was termed 'armoured' but in fact consisted of one armoured and two mechanized infantry battalions – while a third brigade (the 19th Infantry Brigade) was stationed in the UK in peacetime. 2 Infantry Division (three motorized infantry brigades) was also stationed in the UK in peacetime. British plans involved the move of some 60,000 troops across the Channel to bring 1 (BR) Corps and its support elements to full strength of some 120,000.

- 1 (BE) Corps was responsible for the high ground on the southern edge of the NORTHAG sector, which had the reputation of being 'difficult tank country', although whether the Warsaw Pact shared that opinion was a different matter. The Belgian corps consisted of one division (16 Mechanized) of two brigades (one armoured, one mechanized), plus the *Groupement Reconnaissance* (equivalent to a brigade) in Germany. The second division (1 Mechanized), with two brigades (both mechanized), was stationed in Belgium.

- 2 (US) Armoured Division was tasked as NORTHAG reserve and would have deployed initially on the left, in the rear of 1 (NL) Corps. The division consisted of three brigades, of which one was located in West

---

* This idea was adopted by the British army (at considerable expense) in the late 1970s and discarded (at further expense) after six years.

Germany in peacetime, while the remainder of the division was in the United States, but with duplicate equipment stockpiled in Germany.

- There were also contingency plans to deploy an additional US-based corps to the NORTHAG area, where it would have served as the CINCENT reserve. This was 3 (US) Corps, for which two divisions-worth of equipment were stored in Belgium and the Netherlands.

CENTAG

CENTAG headquarters was located at Heidelberg under the command of a US army four-star general, with four corps forward:

- 3 (GE) Corps was the left (northernmost) corps in CENTAG, located between NORTHAG's right-flank corps (1 (BE) Corps) and 5 (US) Corps. It consisted of two panzer divisions and one panzer grenadier division – a total of nine brigades.
- 5 (US) Corps, immediately south of 3 (GE) Corps, was composed of 3 Armoured Division and 8 Mechanized Infantry Division, together with the 11th Armoured Cavalry Regiment, whose specific task lay in the Fulda Gap.
- 7 (US) Corps deployed to the right of 5 (US) Corps and was composed of one armoured and one mechanized infantry division (of which one brigade was in the FRG, the remainder in the USA), plus an armoured cavalry regiment.
- 2 (GE) Corps was in the far south, facing the Czechoslovak border and essentially defending the hilly country of Bavaria, although it inevitably also had to look over its right shoulder at the Austrian border, in case the Warsaw Pact failed to respect that country's neutrality. 2 (GE) Corps was large, and its composition reflected the complexity of its role: four divisions – one panzer, one panzer grenadier, one mountain and one airborne – giving a total of twelve brigades.

Rear Areas

Since it was NATO policy that each nation was responsible for its own logistic support, each corps, plus 2 (US) Armoured Division in NORTHAG, had its own rear area, in which its logistic units were located. These required both control and protection, not least because the Warsaw Pact was known to give priority to attacking such facilities. Security of these rear areas was therefore of considerable concern to the corps commanders, although nations allocated differing priorities to the task.

Responsibility for the NATO Rear Combat Zone lay with the *Bundeswehr*'s Northern Territorial Command for NORTHAG and the Southern Territorial Command for CENTAG. These territorial commands were subdivided into a series of geographical areas, but they also included

240

ten home-defence brigades, which were equipped with older types of tanks and artillery. There were also fifteen home-defence regiments, each with three motorized battalions, which had mainly security tasks.

A particular and sometimes controversial element of the Central Region's ground forces was the paratroop units. Such units had been formed and used for the first time in the Second World War, and in all armies they immediately became a *corps d'élite*: they developed an extremely aggressive mode of fighting, and their special selection processes were coupled with very high standards of training and fitness. They also developed, not unintentionally, a mystique about their operations, which endured throughout the Cold War.

While the high reputation resulting from their performance in combat was fully deserved, other factors gradually came to the fore. Their capital costs were high, since they required a large, specially equipped air fleet to take them into battle, and they needed a great deal of specially designed lightweight equipment. Their operating costs were also high, as they required frequent exercises to maintain their standards, particularly in parachuting. On top of all these, one of the lessons of the Second World War was that parachute operations tended to be costly in lives, since, virtually by definition, units were placed in positions of great danger and this, coupled with their aggressive tactics, resulted in unusually high casualty rates.

The USA
The largest and most capable of NATO's airborne forces was 82 (US) Airborne Division, whose main combat element was three airborne brigades, each of three parachute battalions. There were also three artillery battalions, a divisional anti-tank battalion and an aviation battalion. 82 Airborne Division was based at Fort Bragg in North Carolina, where one battalion was always at eighteen hours' notice to deploy, with one company at two hours' notice and the remainder of the brigade at twenty-four hours' notice.

Some equipment was specially developed for the airborne role, such as the Sheridan light tank, but 82 Airborne Division had nothing like the range of specialist weapons and equipment developed for Soviet airborne forces. Its anti-tank defences, for example, depended upon the TOW crew-served system, and the Dragon and LAW (light anti-tank weapon), while air-defence weapons were Vulcans and Stingers, all of which were standard army weapons.

On the other hand, the division's air-transport assets were unrivalled. In the 1980s USAF air-transport assets comprised 97 Lockheed C-5 Galaxies,

250 Lockheed C-141 Starlifters and 544 Lockheed C-130 Hercules. Not all of these would have been allocated to lifting 82 Airborne Division, but there was sufficient to deploy a brigade very rapidly, with the remainder of the division following close behind. Indeed, the C-141s regularly demonstrated their ability to take off from the USA with a full load of paratroops, fly across the Atlantic, and then drop them straight on to a tactical drop zone in West Germany. Once committed to such an operation the troops would have been able to sustain themselves for three days, but would have then needed air resupply.

Other NATO Countries
Most other NATO armies maintained a parachuting capability: the Germans and French both operated a complete division of three brigades, while Belgium, Canada, Greece, Italy, Portugal, Spain, Turkey and the UK each maintained between one and three battalions. All these forces had peacetime commitments to national defence, particularly in rapid-reaction operations, and not all the battalions were necessarily in the parachuting role at all times, but all were capable of parachute operations and would have been available to NATO in war.

The French airborne forces included the most experienced paratroop units in any army, most of the units having fought in Indo-China from 1949 to 1954 and in Algeria from 1955 to 1962. Thereafter they moved to France, but continued to take part in numerous operations, particularly in Africa. From the 1970s onwards 11 (FR) Parachute Division comprised two brigades of three battalions each, with a seventh battalion under divisional control in a 'special forces' role. They were capable of 'rapid deployment' in Africa and Asia, but in a general war would have fought in Europe, albeit under French rather than NATO command. Like most other airborne units, however, their deployment ability would have been limited by the availability of suitable aircraft.

The British had built up a sizeable parachute force during the Second World War, eventually fielding two divisions, but one division was cut immediately the war ended. The force was further reduced to two brigades in 1947–8, the 16th (BR) Parachute Brigade being all-regular (three battalions) and the 44th Parachute Brigade being found by the Territorial Army (six battalions). The parachute force continued to exist up to the end of the Cold War and frequently took part in limited war and peacekeeping operations, including Northern Ireland and the 1982 Falklands War. By 1990 three regular and two Territorial Army battalions remained, but limitations of equipment, particularly in the number of transport aircraft, meant that in general war not more than one battalion-group operation could have been undertaken at a time.

The provision of air transport for parachute operations was almost always a problem; the Belgians, for example, frequently looked to the US to provide suitable transport aircraft. In a war on the Central Front, air operations by large and slow transport aircraft, flying at low level, would have been especially hazardous both on the original fly-in and in subsequent resupply operations, unless major efforts were devoted to the suppression of enemy air defences. Thus, even though most NATO paratroops units would have been declared to SACEUR in a war in Europe, there was a lack of clarity over just how they might have been used. Indeed, the occasions on which a battalion-sized or larger force might have been used in the airborne role in a battle in the Central Region remain difficult to identify.

MOBILIZATION

NATO's defences depended upon a complicated series of preparations for war, ranging from essentially covert tasks, such as the activation of war headquarters and communications systems, to overt measures such as the deployment of troops, aircraft and ships to their war locations, culminating finally in the commencement of hostilities. The Alliance would, therefore have had to persuade fifteen member nations (sixteen, once Spain had joined) not only to transfer assigned units to NATO operational command, but also to mobilize the reserves necessary in all countries to bring front-line units up to full wartime strength. The former could have been done with little public knowledge, but the latter would have been only too obvious.

All national armies depended to a significant degree on the mobilization of reservists to bring both combat and logistic units up to wartime strengths. This mobilization process was a national responsibility, with marked differences between nations, resulting mainly from different traditions and legal systems. For all, however, it was an extremely complex operation.

To take just one European member as an example, in the 1980s the four-division-strong 1 (BR) Corps required substantial reinforcements to bring it up to war strength. First, there were four infantry brigades in the UK which had to be sent to Germany: 19th Infantry Brigade, which reinforced the Germany-based 3 Armoured Division, and the three brigades of 2 Infantry Division (two of them from the Territorial Army) which were responsible for rear-area security. Second, there were also the headquarters and support units of 2 Infantry Division, as well as two signals brigades to provide the rear-area communications systems and an engineer brigade for airfield repair. In addition to these, 1 (BR) Corps needed a vast number of individual reservists (former regulars with a reserve liability) to bring the regular units up to strength and to serve as battle-casualty replacements.

It should be noted that the UK would concurrently have been mobilizing other elements of its wartime forces. Most important of these was the

United Kingdom Mobile Force, consisting of 1st (UK) Infantry Brigade, air-force elements and a large logistic 'tail', all of which was entirely UK-based. This required many reservists and Territorial Army troops to bring it to its war establishment before it moved to its most likely destination, Denmark. Mobilization was also required for the forces committed to tasks within the UK, principally for 'home defence' (i.e. the security of the UK base).

The numbers available to meet these requirements varied over the years, but in 1987 the UK had some 160,000 reservists, while the Territorial Army comprised some 85,000 men and women, most of whom were in formed units. The procedures involved in the mobilization and reinforcement of 1 (BR) Corps were given two full-scale rehearsals, the first in Exercise Crusader in 1980, the second in Exercise Lionheart in 1984. These involved moving some 15,000 troops in forty ships, and a further 15,000 by air (5,000 in air-force aircraft, 10,000 in civil aircraft); forty-nine trains were needed, as well as some 15,000 vehicles. All this involved a vast amount of road movement and large numbers of troops passing through civil and military airports, harbours and railway stations.

In a time of international tension, the calling-up of the individuals, the mobilization of the Territorial Army (both of which required parliamentary authority), and moving them all (plus, in the case of formed units, their vehicles and equipment) to Germany and Denmark would have been an even more massive operation, and could never have been hidden from the British public, the media or the Warsaw Pact.

There were numerous choke points which would have been vulnerable to hostile action, either from direct attack by Warsaw Pact forces or from sabotage and other interference by Warsaw Pact agents or anti-war protestors. Such vulnerable points included a relatively small number of ports and airports in south-east England, and in Germany and the Low Countries.

Crossing the Channel was a problem which did not affect other European countries, but their mobilization would have been as massive in scale and equally impossible to hide. The German *Bundesheer*, for example, required to mobilize approximately 1 million reservists for the regular army and a further 450,000 for the territorial army, all within the space of ninety-six hours.

The United States not only had a far wider water gap to cross, but was also committed to transporting much greater numbers to reinforce both the Central Front and the northern and southern flanks. This commitment included six divisions (some 90,000 troops), most of whom would have flown to Germany, where they would have picked up pre-positioned weapons and equipment (POMCUS), and approximately sixty air squadrons, for which the aircraft would have self-deployed, with the manpower moving by air transport. All these were scheduled to arrive over a ten-day period, with regular units arriving first, followed by army and air-force reserve units, then the Air National Guard and finally the National Guard (army). Also moving to Europe, but in this case by sea, would have been three Marine Amphibious Brigades.

The US mobilization system was based on flexibility. The president had the authority to mobilize up to 200,000 reservists for a maximum of ninety days (as was done in the 1961 Berlin crisis), or, if he declared a state of national emergency, up to 1 million reservists for twenty-four months. Congress could then have confirmed the national emergency and authorized the calling-up of all reserves. All reservists were obliged to report to their mobilization centres within forty-eight hours of receiving notification, but the majority would have needed some form of training before their onward move to Europe.

It was also planned that the draft would have been restarted to generate trained men after a gap of several months, although this would inevitably have caused short-term dislocation and required a number of trained and experienced officers and NCOs to set it in motion. The National Guard and Air National Guard would also have been mobilized and deployed as formed units, and it was estimated that all National Guard divisions scheduled to move to Europe would have arrived in less than thirty days after the mobilization order had been issued.

The massive planned move to Europe would have required a large force of aircraft and ships, for which an 'Airlift Emergency' would have been called. This would have enabled 171 commercial aircraft to have been available within twenty-four hours and a further 268 within forty-eight hours. The problem with the ships earmarked to transport heavy equipment was that they could have taken anything up to four weeks to reach the embarkation ports, and in most cases would also have needed to offload, before they could take on the Department of Defense passengers or cargoes. US mobilization and deployment plans were regularly practised in a series of exercises: air exercises were designated 'Reforger' (Reinforce Germany), while sea exercises were designated 'Ocean Safari'.

Movement

The situation within Germany and the Low Countries would have been without precedent. First, mobilization within those countries would have been taking place on a massive scale, with some 2 million men and women travelling to their reporting depots. Second, 60,000 British and some 300,000 US troops would have been moving into Germany, landing at a variety of service and civil airfields and ports. In the Low Countries four British infantry brigades (plus signals brigades and an engineer brigade), with virtually all their equipment and vehicles, would have been disembarking to follow the Belgian and Dutch brigades en route to their wartime positions in Germany. Within West Germany these new arrivals would have joined hundreds of thousands of troops resident in the country (and their vehicles, tanks and guns) as they too deployed to their wartime positions.

There would also, without a doubt, have been a serious problem with refugees fleeing in a westerly direction, which could well have caused serious delays to the reinforcement forces endeavouring to move eastward and could also have interfered with plans to demolish bridges. The problem was (and remains) completely unquantifiable, but it seems reasonable to assume that it would have been on a massive scale. The most immediate fear of the civil population would have been of becoming involved in the fighting, especially as they would have assumed that nuclear and possibly chemical weapons would be used. On top of that, however, would have been German folk memories of the atrocities committed by Soviet troops following their conquest of eastern Germany in 1945.

The only possible precedents were the flow of refugees during the 1940 German invasion of France and the Low Countries, and the 1944–5 flight of ethnic Germans in front of the Soviet advance into Germany. The refugees of those days were, however, virtually all on foot (or, in the case of a proportion of the Germans along the Baltic coast, travelled by sea), while those in any war in Europe in the 1980s would have been predominantly in vehicles – at least until they had exhausted the fuel stocks along their routes.

Control of refugees was a national responsibility, which, as far as the Central Front was concerned, meant Belgium, the FRG and the Netherlands, but whether these countries would have been able to cope and to keep the routes clear for troops moving in the opposite direction is a matter for conjecture. There was also a NATO Refugee Agency, whose task was to provide a consultation forum and to co-ordinate actions in war, but it was certainly not an executive agency and could, at best, only have provided cross-border co-ordination.

LOGISTICS

Although NATO laid down guidelines, logistical support was a national responsibility, one major consequence of which was that national lines of communication (LOC) stretched rearwards from the operational corps to the home country. For the Danes, the West Germans and the French this presented few problems, but for the others it was a major headache. The Belgian and Dutch LOC were several hundred kilometres long, but at least they were all overland, whereas the British not only had much greater distances to cover, but also had to cross the English Channel from ports in south-east England to ports on the Belgian, Dutch and German coast.

Worst of all was the position of the United States. Not only had it to cross the Atlantic, but also, following the expulsion of NATO facilities from France, its maritime LOC terminated in ports on the German and Dutch North Sea coast (principally Bremerhaven) and thereafter its supplies had to be transported by road and rail down the length of Germany – along routes which ran parallel to the IGB and within easy reach of any Warsaw Pact thrust.

There were many logistical problems, but one merits mention: that of war stocks, and in particular of ammunition. The level of war stocks was not as glamorous and vote-catching a subject as the number or quality of tanks or artillery pieces, but in the event of an actual attack those weapons would have become useless without an adequate and timely supply of ammunition. Throughout the Cold War, artillery, tanks and small arms became capable of ever higher rates of fire. Indeed, the appetite of weapons such as the Multiple Rocket-Launcher System was so voracious that the cost and capacity of the resupply system became a major constraint in both their purchase and their use.

The NATO requirement was that nations should hold ammunition stocks based on the calculated requirement for thirty days of use, but there was always some doubt about the validity of the figure. Indeed, one of the major lessons of post-Second World War conflicts such as the Korean, Middle East, Vietnam, Falklands and Gulf wars was that ammunition expenditure was greatly in excess of peacetime predictions. For example, the British noted after the Falklands War that one of the lessons learned was that '*rates of usage*, particularly of ammunition, missiles and anti-submarine weapons, were higher than anticipated'.[2] Many insiders consider this to have been a serious understatement, not least because, on the day the Argentine garrison surrendered, the British artillery had less than one day's ammunition stocks in the theatre. During the Gulf War, the British land forces (essentially one armoured division of just two armoured brigades) required 104,000 tonnes of ammunition for initial stocks, while the total cargo which would have been required had fighting continued would have been 19,000 tonnes per week.[3]

The difficulty for NATO was that, with higher than expected ammunition expenditure, forward munitions depots would quickly have been stripped bare and national stocks would have been depleted to replenish them. But, owing to ever-reducing peacetime orders, many munitions factories had been closed and their plant sold off, and those that remained would have taken time to crank up production to meet the short-term requirements. Indeed, even if they had succeeded in doing so, their output could well then have choked the resupply system.

One solution adopted in the 1980s was a programme to build ammunition depots. These would have eased transportation problems in war, but, since they were difficult to disguise, they were vulnerable to sabotage and to air attack. A further difficulty was that, in order to be of any value, such depots needed to be relatively close to the projected deployment areas, which meant that in a surprise Warsaw Pact attack they might well have been overrun before the forward troops had deployed in sufficient strength to protect them.

MALDEPLOYMENT

As the Cold War progressed, it became clear that many formations and units in the Central Region were badly deployed in peacetime. In overall terms, the southern part of the FRG was hilly and heavily wooded, making it better country for defence than the north, which was much more open, less heavily wooded and in most places 'good tank country'. Thus, in an ideal world, the US and West German forces, with their mass of armour and long-range anti-tank systems, should have been in the north. This would also have eased the US logistics problem. It would, however, have meant that the Belgians, British and Dutch, with further German support, would have been in the south. Not only would that have run in the face of history, but the exchange would have been extremely costly. In addition, the Belgians, the Dutch and in particular the British would have incurred severe logistic penalties, which they were much less able than the US to cope with.

Even within each nation's forces, however, there were serious examples of bad deployment, where units required to deploy very rapidly to the front line in a crisis were located several hundred kilometres away in peacetime. This applied not only on a national scale, e.g. with the distance between Belgian and Dutch peacetime barracks in their home country and their deployment positions near the IGB, but also within national deployments in the FRG. Such problems were examined from time to time, but, though there were a few minor adjustments, a major reshuffle was always prevented by the huge costs that would be involved. Thus maldeployment simply came to be accepted as a fact of life.

CONCLUSION

It is clear that, in the 'worst-case' scenario of a sudden and unexpected Warsaw Pact attack, Central Region forces would have required substantial augmentation to bring them up to combat strength. In the first place, even the forward units in some armies would have needed individual reinforcements, which would have been found either by redeployment of regular soldiers (e.g. by closing down the training organization) or from reservists.

The increasing practice of locating major elements of the forward divisions and brigades in their home countries meant that, even if they were regular, they would take some time to arrive and would require valuable and scarce movement facilities, while reserve units would take even longer, having to mobilize and possibly also needing to carry out some training before deploying.

Despite all these difficulties, the NATO ground forces appeared impressive to the Soviets and they never once faced a major challenge.

24

Warsaw Pact Deployment on the Central Front

As with that of the Americans, British and French, the long-term Soviet deployment on the Central Front was, in the main, a direct result of where the Red Army stopped in 1945, although there were some minor adjustments during the forty years of the Cold War. The forces permanently stationed in East Germany were designated Group of Soviet Forces Germany (GSFG),* with their headquarters at Zossen-Wünstorf, 30 km south of Berlin, and comprised five armies, most of which were approximately equivalent to a NATO corps in size.

The Soviet army believed that the basic form of military strategy was the offensive, and all its (and the Warsaw Pact's) planning, organizations and exercises were devoted to this end. The 1945 organizations lasted for only a short time, and from 1947 infantry regiments began to be mechanized, using BTR-40P wheeled trucks. This process gathered pace in the 1950s, until 1957, when a major re-equipment programme began to bear fruit and new-style tank and motor-rifle divisions were introduced, which were smaller, easier to control and much harder hitting than their predecessors. These were organized into two types of army: a 'tank army', in which tank divisions normally predominated, and a 'combined-arms army', in which motor-rifle divisions predominated, the number and type of divisions depending upon the army's combat mission.

The history of GSFG included some major equipment milestones, which marked a significant increase in tactical capability. The first of these was the fielding of T-62 tanks and BTR-60 eight-wheeled armoured personnel carriers in the early 1960s, while in the early 1970s the Mi-24 (NATO = 'Hind') helicopter gave a totally new capability to the Soviet air force's Frontal

---

* GSFG was redesignated Western Group of Forces on 1 July 1989, at the very end of the Cold War, but as the term GSFG was used for the greater part of the Cold War, it will continue to be used here.

Aviation command. The changeover in artillery from wheeled to tracked self-propelled guns, which came in the late 1970s, was also of major significance, although it was made considerably later than in NATO. The final stage was marked by the fielding of the new T-80 tank, which joined the front line facing NATO in the mid-1980s.

THE WESTERN TVD

In war the Warsaw Pact forces in central Europe would have come under the Western *Teatr Voyennykh Destiviy* (Theatre of Military Operations (TVD)), which would have been subdivided into fronts, each composed of a number of armies, and an air army. The commander-in-chief Western TVD controlled all Soviet and Warsaw Pact forces in Czechoslovakia, East Germany, Hungary and Poland, as well as the second-echelon armies which would have been generated by the western military districts in the USSR.

SOVIET ARMIES IN GERMANY

In 1945 East Germany was occupied by six armies: the 1st, 2nd, 3rd and 4th Guards Tank Armies; the 3rd Shock Army; and the 8th Guards Army.* Of these, the 4th Guards Tank Army was gradually withdrawn to the USSR in the 1950s, followed by the 3rd Guards Tank Army in 1960–61. This appears to have overstretched the headquarters that remained, since, in the aftermath of the 1961 Berlin crisis, a new headquarters unit, the 20th Guards Tank Army, was formed. The other army was Frontal Aviation's 16th Air Army, which remained in East Germany from 1945 to the end of the Cold War.

From the 1960s onwards, GSFG comprised the following.

- The 2nd Guards Tank Army, the northernmost formation, occupied an area near the Baltic south of Rostock, with its peacetime headquarters at Fürstenberg–Havel, 60 km north of Berlin. Despite its title of 'Tank Army', it actually consisted of just one tank division, plus two motor-rifle divisions.
- The 3rd Shock Army was located in the centre and, in view of its intended role of thrusting across the North German Plain, it consisted of four tank divisions and a single motor-rifle division, making it, at least on paper, the most formidable fighting formation in any army. The title 'Shock' was conferred in 1945, but the name changed to 3rd Mechanized Army in

---

* 'Guards' and 'Shock' were honorifics awarded for exceptionally distinguished service during the Second World War.

1947, before reverting to 3rd Shock Army in 1957–8. The headquarters was at Magdeburg, conveniently close to the IGB and just off the E8 autobahn, which would have been the main axis of the army's advance into West Germany in the event of war.

- The 8th Guards Army was located in the south and, as its intended role would take it through primarily infantry country, it consisted of one tank division and three motor-rifle divisions. Its headquarters was at Nohra, 10 km south-west of Weimar.
- The 20th Guards Army was located just west of Berlin, effectively in the rear of the 3rd Shock Army. It consisted of three motor-rifle divisions, and did not have an integral tank division. Its headquarters was at Eberswalde-Finow, some 40 km north-east of Berlin.
- The 1st Guards Tank Army was virtually identical to the 3rd Shock Army, with four tank divisions and one motor-rifle division. Its headquarters was at Dresden, in the south-east corner of the GDR.

GSFG also included considerably more supporting units (artillery, engineers, aviation, communications and logistic services) than other similar organizations in the Soviet armed forces. Thus, for example, GSFG was supported by 34 Guards Artillery Division, which was three times the size of a normal artillery division.

The offensive nature of GSFG's wartime missions was underlined by a further six reinforced bridging regiments and six amphibious river-crossing battalions, whose wartime mission was to ensure that the many rivers in West Germany and Denmark were crossed quickly. There were also two assault-engineer regiments, specially trained in urban clearance tasks, whose wartime missions would have been in cities such as Braunschweig and Hanover and in the Ruhr. Two aviation regiments were equipped with Hind attack helicopters, which established such a fearsome reputation in Afghanistan. There were also eight *spetsnaz* battalions for employment in NATO's rear areas, and one integral airborne regiment, although GSFG had priority call on one or more of the airborne divisions back in the USSR, which were normally under centralized Ministry of Defence control.

The peacetime strength of GSFG amounted to some 380,000 men, with 7,000 tanks, 3,000 infantry fighting vehicles, 300 helicopters and a vast amount of artillery. All were manned at Category-A levels, which was usually well in excess of 90 per cent of their wartime figure.

OTHER SOVIET FORCES ON THE CENTRAL FRONT

Situated in Poland was the Soviet Northern Group of Forces (NGF), with its headquarters at Legnica. In peacetime its troops consisted of two motor-rifle divisions and an air army. In war its position astride the lines of communication from the homeland would have been absolutely vital to the success of the offensive, and it would have been reinforced by units from the USSR.

The third element, in addition to GSFG and NGF, was the Central Group of Forces (CGF), which was formed in 1968, in the wake of the Soviet invasion of Czechoslovakia. The headquarters was located at Milovice, Czechoslovakia, some 30 km north-west of Hradec Králové, and after a rapid build-up in 1968–71 the CGF was composed of two tank and three motor-rifle divisions.

NON-SOVIET WARSAW PACT ARMIES

Czechoslovakia

Czechoslovakia had two armies: the 1st (Czech) Army (comprising one tank and three motor-rifle divisions), with its headquarters at Příbram, and the 4th (Czech) Army (two tank, two motor-rifle divisions) at Písek. Each of these Czech armies had a larger than normal engineer component, with one engineer brigade, one bridging brigade and one construction brigade in each army, with more under central control. Total strength of the Czechoslovak army (1984) was 148,000, of which approximately 100,000 were conscripts.

East Germany

The German Democratic Republic's *Nationale Volksarmee* (NVA) was considered to be both the most efficient and the most loyal of the satellite armies, and fielded two armies: the 3rd (NVA) Army, with its headquarters at Leipzig, and the 5th (NVA) Army at Neubrandenburg. Both consisted of one tank and two motor-rifle divisions, all of which were maintained at Category A (90–100 per cent strength) in peacetime and were backed by a very efficient mobilization system. The total peacetime strength of the NVA was some 120,000 (1984), of which 71,500 were conscripts.

Poland

Poland provided three armies, which in peacetime were based in each of the three military districts, and virtually all of which were scheduled to come under direct Soviet command in war:

- Silesian Military District – one army of three tank and two motor-rifle divisions;
- Pomeranian Military District – one army of two tank and two motor-rifle divisions;
- Warsaw Military District – one army of three motor-rifle divisions but no tank divisions.

253

The 6th Airborne Brigade was stationed in the Pomeranian Military District, and the 7th Sea Landing Brigade was stationed on the Baltic coast, from where it would have taken part in amphibious operations against Denmark in war. The Polish army did not have the specialist engineer brigades found in the Czech and East German armies. The total strength of the Polish army in 1984 was 210,000, of which 153,000 were conscripts.

Unlike their opponents in NATO, where commonality ceased at corps level, the non-Soviet Warsaw Pact forces were all organized on Soviet lines and used mainly Soviet equipment, some of which, such as tanks, was manufactured locally under licence. The equipment was not, however, exclusively Soviet, and Czechoslovakia, for example, produced armoured personnel carriers and self-propelled guns to its own designs, some of which were also used by Poland.

WARSAW PACT PARACHUTE FORCES

Soviet Airborne Forces
Throughout the Cold War the Soviets maintained by far the largest airborne forces in the world, and, as in most armies, these enjoyed an elite status, with special equipment and special uniforms (including a sky-blue beret). Their importance was further emphasized by the fact that they were not part of the normal army chain of command, but were subordinated direct to the Ministry of Defence. There were seven airborne divisions,* all of which were maintained at Category A in peacetime, each consisting of three airborne regiments, an artillery regiment and an air-defence battalion, together with communications, engineers and logistic units – a total of some 8,500 men. In war they would have been tasked directly by the Ministry of Defence for a major strategic mission or allocated to lower headquarters for specific operations, possibly on a scale of one airborne division to each major front, or probably more than one in the case of the Western TVD.

Soviet airborne forces were equipped with a large range of lightweight equipment, which was specially designed for the airborne role. Such airborne items ranged from self-propelled guns and tracked personnel carriers to lightweight folding saws, and airborne troops were always the first to receive new standard weapons, such as 5.56 mm rifles.

Soviet airborne units were particularly intended for *desantnyy* missions – a Russian term denoting operations in enemy rear areas, carried out in co-ordination with the forward elements of the ground troops, and with the aim of maintaining the high momentum and continuity of the offensive. Such

---

* An eighth division was responsible in peacetime for training.

missions would almost certainly have included the traditional airborne task of seizing vital ground or crossings in advance of major thrusts by ground troops, possibly as the opening move in a war in western Europe. Probable missions would have included seizing bridgeheads across major rivers, such as the Elbe, Weser and Rhine; capturing forward airfields; and attacking nuclear-supply points, communications centres and major logistics concentrations. This was confirmed by Marshal Sokolovskiy:

> In the last war, airborne troops were used chiefly for support of ground troops in defeating enemy groupings, while now they must also perform independently such missions as [the] capture and retention or destruction of nuclear missile, air force and naval bases, and other important objectives deep within the theatres of military operations.[1]

The airborne troops had a flexible organization, being designed to conduct operations in divisional, regimental or battalion strengths, depending upon the requirement. The normal tactic was for pathfinders to form the first wave of the assault, arriving in the battle area by parachute, with the aim of securing the drop zone (DZ) and marking it for the main assault force, which arrived after a minimal interval and dropped together with its heavy equipment. In most larger operations securing an airfield or creating an airstrip would have been a high priority, to enable later troops and heavy equipment to be air-landed rather than air-dropped. Soviet airborne troops' tactics were always very aggressive, and as soon as sufficient men were available they began a rapid expansion to link the DZs to each other, coupled with raids and assaults on any enemy units encountered.

The fixed-wing aircraft were provided by *Voyenno-Transportnaya Aviatsiya* (Military Transport Aviation (VTA)), which comprised some 1,700 aircraft, providing sufficient lift for the assault elements of two airborne divisions simultaneously. From the mid-1970s onwards three basic aircraft were used, the smallest being the four-turboprop Antonov An-12 (NATO = 'Cub'), which carried eighty paratroops or an equivalent load of equipment and was equivalent to the USAF's Lockheed C-130 Hercules. The second and larger aircraft was the Ilyushin Il-76 (NATO = 'Candid'), powered by four turbojets, which carried 150 paratroops. Largest of all was the Antonov An-22 (NATO = 'Cock'), which was capable of air-dropping either men or equipment, although it seems unlikely that this would have been done in any but the most benign environment, the aircraft depending instead upon the early capture of an airfield. The VTA was reinforced by further transport aircraft from the Soviet state airline, Aeroflot, which were intended to be used virtually straight away for air-landing operations, although they required lengthy preparations before undertaking parachute drops.

The VTA took part in all major exercises, but also obtained valuable operational experience in conducting the airlifts to Prague in 1968, to Egypt and Syria during the 1973 Middle East War, to Ethiopia in 1978 and in the invasion of Afghanistan in 1979.

Soviet airborne doctrine was that objectives should be a maximum of 400 km from the front line for a divisional operation and a maximum of 100 km for a battalion operation. Relief by ground troops was intended to take place between two and seven days after the landing, although experience by all armies in the Second World War suggested that such a meeting seldom went according to plan.

Unless there was a reasonable expectation of total surprise, an airborne assault would be preceded by intense air and artillery operations to destroy enemy air defences along the line of the proposed route. Following that, the transports would fly across friendly territory at medium height before descending to low level to cross the front line for the approach to the assault area. The aircraft formed into a stream for the actual drop, which took place at a height of between 400 m and 1,000 m and a speed of 330 km/h, with intervals between the waves. Divisional operations used between four and six DZs, each approximately 4 km long and 3 km wide.

Other Warsaw Pact Airborne Forces
The other Warsaw Pact countries all maintained a parachuting capability: East Germany, Poland and Romania each had a brigade-size force; Bulgaria and Czechoslovakia a regiment; while Hungary had one battalion. All were organized along Soviet lines and used Soviet equipment, methods and tactics.

CONCLUSION

According to NATO's 1984 assessment,[2] the Central Region (and the southern part of the Northern Region) was faced by some ninety-five divisions from the Soviet, East German, Polish and Czechoslovak armies. Of those, some sixty-one divisions (16,620 tanks and 10,270 artillery pieces and heavy mortars) were either deployed in the forward areas or held at a high state of readiness and could have attacked within a few days of mobilization. There were also seven airborne and two air-mobile divisions, based in the USSR, which could have been allocated specific missions within the Central Region, and a division-sized amphibious force in the Baltic. They were armed with some of the finest equipment in the world, and the three forward Soviet armies were positioned much closer to the IGB than were their opponents, adding to the Alliance's fear of a 'bolt from the blue'. But they never attacked.

25

Main Battle Tanks

During the Cold War the confrontation between NATO and Warsaw Pact tanks came to exemplify the land battle in a way that had no parallel at sea or in the air. Indeed, the tank became the dominant symbol by which armies not only were judged by others but also judged themselves; and when the Chieftain tank was described as the 'virility symbol' of the British army,* the comment could equally well have been applied to other tanks and other armies.

THE REQUIREMENT

The main battle tank, like any piece of military equipment, was designed to meet a specification laid down in a general-staff requirement. The various armies had generally similar requirements, although, since the design of any weapons system must inevitably involve compromises, they tended to make different judgements on the relative priorities.

The requirement started with the tank's offensive capabilities, which were that it had to be able to destroy the following:

- Tanks in daylight at an ever-increasing range. In the 1960s this was 2,000 m, but by the late 1970s it had increased to 3,000 m, and up to 5,000 m if possible, which had to be achievable with at least two different types of ammunition.
- Light armoured vehicles (e.g. armoured cars and armoured personnel carriers) at ranges out to 5,000 m, and troops in the open at all ranges between 75 m and 2,000 m.†

---

* In the 1960s, by the then British secretary of state for defence, Denis Healey.
† The minimum-range requirement arose from experiences of massed attacks by Chinese infantry in the Korean War and was met by canister shot, consisting of several hundred steel slugs.

257

- Field defences by direct fire using a high-explosive round (and also to fire smoke and illuminating rounds).
- Aircraft, particularly helicopters and drones, flying at low altitude (150 m) and low speed (maximum 300 km/h).

In order to perform these tasks the tank needed to be immune to enemy anti-tank weapons, using a combination of armour protection and the ability to present a small target by using ground, smoke and agility. Apart from protection against enemy anti-tank weapons, the crew also needed protection against nuclear, biological and chemical (NBC) weapons. The tank needed to have good cross-country mobility, coupled with long range to enable it to work over wide fronts and at great depths.

There was a host of other requirements, as well. For example, all nations required to move their tanks by train, which meant that the vehicle had to fit on to a standard flat wagon, and that its height and width must fit inside the relevant railways' standard loading gauge.* Similarly, weight was restricted by national road and bridge load-bearing capacities, as well as by the capability of tank-transporter vehicles. The designer's task was to endeavour to meet as many of these requirements as possible, and, where they conflicted with each other, to achieve a compromise acceptable to the general staff.

TANK DEVELOPMENT 1949–1989

The story of the development of the tank is typical of that of many weapons systems during the years of the Cold War as NATO and the Warsaw Pact vied with each other in a seemingly endless competition, which cost their countries vast sums of money and kept some of their finest scientific brains and key defence industries fully employed.†

All tanks are, in essence, compromises between mobility, firepower and protection, and the major armies came to differing conclusions about the balance, based primarily upon their experiences in the Second World War, but with some changes resulting from later conflicts such as the Korean and the Arab–Israeli wars. Thus the Soviet army, with its strategy of attack, was wedded to the concept of a fast, highly manoeuvrable tank with good firepower, which had also to be available in large numbers; protection and casualties were relatively low priorities in an army awash with manpower. The British, shaken by the way their tanks and in particular their guns had been outclassed by German tanks throughout most of the Second World War,

---

* For example, NATO's STANAG 2805E laid down that, for unrestricted travel by train in continental Europe, a tank must not exceed 3.050 m in width.
† Specifications of NATO and Warsaw Pact main battle tanks are given in Appendix 25.

vowed never to be outgunned again. Accordingly, they gave firepower the top priority, followed closely by protection, and with mobility a poor third; as a result, throughout the Cold War, British main battle tanks were almost invariably the heaviest in service. The Americans fell somewhere in between, their thrusting tactics requiring speed and manoeuvrability, with firepower second and protection third. All NATO countries, however, were convinced that the answer lay in defeating the sheer quantity of Soviet tanks by superior Western quality and sophistication.

Defeating the Opponent's Tanks
There were four types of weapon for use against other tanks:

- Very-high-velocity solid projectiles fired by other tanks. These depended upon their kinetic energy to punch their way through the armour. and included the armour-piercing discarding sabot (APDS) and the armour-piercing fin-stabilized discarding sabot (APFSDS).*
- High-explosive anti-tank (HEAT) projectiles, fired by enemy tanks or infantry. These used chemical energy to burn a hole through armour. Since the effect of these rounds did not depend on the velocity of the projectile, this type of warhead was used both in tank guns and in anti-tank guided missiles.
- High-explosive plastic (HEP)† projectiles, fired by tanks. In these the round blistered on to the face of the armour plate and then exploded, dislodging a scab on the inner face which ricocheted around the inside of the tank.
- Anti-tank mines, which attacked the belly of the tank.
- Top-attack minelets, delivered by aircraft or artillery shells, which used small HEAT charges to attack the top of the tank.

Two of the key criteria in the use of tank guns to fight other tanks were, first, their 'first-round kill probability' and, second, the achievement of ever greater range. These depended on a host of factors, each of which was repeatedly addressed during the course of the Cold War. The most effective rounds were those using kinetic energy to penetrate the enemy armour. The kinetic energy of a moving body is the product of the body's mass multiplied by the square of its velocity, all divided by two:

i.e.
$$\text{kinetic energy} = \frac{\text{mass} \times \text{velocity}^2}{2}$$

Both variables in this equation were tackled with enthusiasm.

---

* The use of a projectile with a smaller calibre than that of the barrel enabled higher velocities to be obtained. The sabot was a segmented jacket which held the projectile in place as it travelled up the jacket but then fell away immediately after leaving the muzzle.
† Also known as high-explosive squash head (HESH) in the British army.

The rounds' mass was increased by fabricating the rounds of ever denser material: first steel, then tungsten carbide and finally depleted uranium. Even greater attention was paid to increasing the velocity, since, as the equation above shows, the effect of this was squared. The original round was the armour-piercing discarding sabot, which was spin-stabilized, being 'spun up' by the rifling in the gun barrel; the mass could be increased by making the round longer, but beyond a length-to-diameter ratio of about 7:1 the round became inherently unstable. A length-to-diameter ratio of about 12:1 could, however, be obtained by making the round fin-stabilized, with almost negligible rotation. This resulted in a smooth-bore barrel, which was initially examined and rejected by the US army in the early 1950s, but which was adopted by the Soviets and the West Germans in the 1970s, even though it meant that none of the existing spin-stabilized range of ammunition could be fired and an entirely new range had to be produced.

The construction of the barrel and the methods by which it was produced were also critically re-examined, and new and more exotic production processes were developed to produce ever truer barrels. The question of increasing the accuracy of assessments of range to the target also exercised the tank designers, since, in a direct-fire engagement, the more precisely the range is known, the more likely it is that the first round will hit. In the early 1950s most tanks used an optical rangefinder, but the accuracy of such a device depends upon the length of its 'base' (i.e. the distance between the two lenses), which was limited by the width of the turret. A delicate optical device was also at an obvious disadvantage in a vehicle which travelled over rough terrain and which could expect to be hit by incoming rounds.

The British produced a simple system in which a machine-gun, mounted coaxially with the main gun and firing rounds which were ballistically matched to the APDS rounds, was used to find the range. This was accurate and cheap, but the intended target knew from the machine-gun hits that it was under attack and there was always a brief pause between the British tank gunner seeing the hit and firing the main gun. Finally came lasers, which were not only absolutely precise and gave an immediate read-out to the gunner, but were also difficult for the enemy tank to detect, although laser-warning devices started to be fitted in the 1980s.

As time went by, research revealed increasingly exotic factors which could affect the probability of a first-round hit. These included ambient weather conditions, since crosswinds could blow the round off course, while rain, temperature and humidity could also cause minor deviations. As a result, tanks were fitted with environmental sensors so that these factors could be included in the fire-control equation. Also, because the tank would be firing from a hastily chosen fire position, it was unlikely to be level, and so the angles relative to true vertical and true horizontal had to be calculated and allowed for.*

It was also discovered that, despite the ever more sophisticated methods of manufacture, barrels had become so long that they bent under their own weight. The amount of what was known as 'droop' was infinitesimal, but it was just enough to affect the gun's accuracy. Thus a reflector was fitted in a protective housing above the muzzle and a laser in the turret detected the amount by which the barrel was off true. This too then became part of the fire-control calculations.

By this time the quantity of information being fed to the gunner was so large that he needed assistance from a fire-control computer. The complexity of the computer increased rapidly as its value was more fully appreciated – not least because it could perform a number of tasks automatically, thus easing the load on the tank gunner. One effect of the introduction of computers – usually known as 'integrated fire-control systems' (IFCS) – was to cause a rapid escalation in tank costs.

Defending One's Own Tanks

The tank also had to be defended against enemy anti-tank weapons. In the 1940s and 1950s tank hulls and turrets were fabricated from cast homogenous steel, with the thickest armour in the forward quadrant, while protection against HEAT and HEP projectiles was obtained in some designs by spaced armour. As the kinetic-energy weapons became more powerful, tank designers responded by sloping the armour, thus effectively increasing the distance to be penetrated by the incoming round, as well as increasing the possibility that the round would ricochet off the plate. In the 1970s the British introduced 'Chobham' armour, which was created by mixing layers of conventional armour plate and ceramic materials, which effectively overcame the menace of the HEAT round.† Then, in the 1980s, explosive reactive armour (ERA) appeared, in which the most vulnerable areas of the tank were covered with specially tailored explosive blocks, which were detonated when hit by an APDS/APFSDS projectile, thus diverting it away from the tank. The blocks were individually bolted to the armour plate and could be easily replaced. The Soviets also developed a special lining for the interior of their tanks, which was designed to prevent small metal fragments from ricocheting around the crew compartment.

These defences were all intended to defeat direct-fire weapons, but the anti-tank mine meant that the underneath of the tank had to be protected,

---

* The technical term is 'trunnion tilt', the trunnion being the bearings upon which the barrel is mounted.
† The principal British armoured-vehicle research centre was located at Chobham in Berkshire.

as well. Such mines also attacked the tracks, damage to which could prevent the tank from moving, thus scoring a 'mobility kill'.

Finally, the tops of the tank hull and turret were for many years more lightly armoured than the rest of the tank, because they were relatively safe from attack. In the 1980s, however, these areas also became targets for attack by a new weapon, the bomblet with a HEAT warhead, which was delivered in large numbers either by artillery shells or in canisters dropped by aircraft.

Tank Propulsion

At the start of the Cold War, Soviet tanks were all diesel-powered, while all Western tanks were powered by petrol engines. A petrol engine provided greater power for a given weight than a diesel, but fuel consumption was very high, resulting in a short range and a large load on the logistics system; the British Centurion Mk 3, for example, which served in the Korean War, had a range of just 161 km and had to tow a single-wheeled trailer to increase this. Also, petrol was inherently dangerous, with the US M4 Sherman being especially notorious for 'brewing up' when hit.

One of NATO's earliest attempts at standardization was to insist that military engines should all be capable of 'multi-fuel operation', so that they could use petrol of varying grades and also diesel, with only minor adjustments required on changing over. This was tried and proved an expensive failure, and tank engines rapidly changed to diesels or turbo-charged diesels, which not only offered much greater range but also were markedly less flammable. In the 1980s, however, the US M1 Abrams entered service powered by a gas turbine, which offered exceptional power output for it size.

The ever-increasing power output from these engines tended to offset the growing weight, as is shown by the power-to-weight ratio, which is a fairly reliable means of assessing tank mobility. This increased from 10 kW/tonne for the British Chieftain in the 1970s to 19 kW/tonne for the US M1 and 20 kW/tonne for the German Leopard 2 in the 1980s.

SOVIET TANKS

Throughout the Cold War it was the Soviet tank force which held the initiative, with the West reacting to this. Soviet designers were innovative, while the Soviet General Staff appeared to be much less conservative about the design and employment of tanks than many of their counterparts in the West. There was also a fundamental difference in approach between the Soviet/Warsaw Pact and NATO armies, since the former were building tanks in very large numbers for an attack, whereas the latter built much fewer tanks for defence.

At the start of the Cold War, the Soviet armoured forces had tremendous prestige, having played a major role in the defeat of Nazi Germany. The main Soviet tank, the T-34, had come as a very unpleasant surprise to the Germans, having good armoured protection and being very robust, not too heavy (32 tonnes) and totally devoid of any frills. It was originally armed with a 76.2 mm gun, but was later upgunned with an 85 mm weapon, and in the early days of the Cold War this T-34/85 was considered to be a major threat to NATO's Central Front.

The T-34/85 was complemented by the JS-3 (JS = Josef Stalin) heavy tank, which caused particular concern to Western armies in the early years of NATO, since it was armed with a 122 mm gun – by far the heaviest and most powerful weapon in any tank of that era, and able to defeat any NATO tank. In addition, the cast hull and turret were excellently shaped and made of armour up to 230 mm thick, which would have resisted any existing NATO tank gun. The JS-3 weighed 46 tonnes, had a maximum speed of 40 km/h, and, for its time, was a very formidable threat, and Western countries produced a number of tanks specifically to counter it. The JS-3 was produced in moderate numbers and was succeeded by the T-10, essentially an improved JS-3, but with even better armour, a newer and more powerful version of the 122 mm gun, and a new engine giving greater speed. The T-10 was in production from 1957 to the early 1960s, when it was phased out in favour of the T-62 medium tank, but, with the JS-3, it remained in service with reserve units for many years.

Meanwhile the major development effort was concentrated on the first post-war Soviet medium tank, the T-54, which entered service in 1954 and served with all the armies of the Warsaw Pact. Over 95,000 T-54s and an improved version, the T-55, were produced in the USSR, Czechoslovakia, Poland and China – a production run which lasted some thirty years, setting a record which is unlikely to be surpassed. The hull was well sloped, with thick armour, and the low, squat, hemispherical turret was designed to prevent penetration by anti-tank rounds, causing considerable discussion in the West. The T-54/55's 100 mm gun was powerful for its time, and with their good cross-country performance and low profile these tanks were ideal for the Warsaw Pact requirements.

Next to appear was the T-62, which entered service in 1962 and was of generally similar shape and layout to the T-54/55, but slightly larger. It introduced the yet more powerful 115 mm gun (at a time when the West was standardizing on 105 mm), which was also the first smooth-bore tank gun to enter service, enabling it to fire fin-stabilized rounds with considerably greater muzzle velocity. The T-62 was, however, only a qualified success: among its serious shortcomings were a poor suspension, a tendency to shed its tracks, vibration, and an automatic cartridge-case ejection system which could severely injure its crews. These problems led to a much modified version, with a revised suspension, the T-72.

There then followed the T-64, a totally new design throughout, with a new 125 mm smooth-bore gun and a twenty-two-round automatic loader, which enabled the crew to be reduced to three men. The T-64B introduced a revised 125 mm gun, which was capable not only of firing normal rounds, but also of launching a radio-guided anti-tank missile with a range of up to 4,000 m. There was a new-style angular turret, which, together with the glacis (i.e. front) plate was fabricated from composite steel/fibreglass armour. The running gear, which gave good cross-country performance, was based on that of the JS-3, but, surprisingly in an army renowned for its simple, powerful and reliable engines, the power unit in the T-64 proved to be very unreliable. With horizontally opposed pistons, this was of similar layout to the British Chieftain tank engine, which also proved very troublesome. This led to the T-80, which was essentially an improved T-64 with a completely new gas-turbine power pack.

The T-72, which was produced in parallel with the T-64, had a different hull and suspension from the T-64, but mounted the same 125 mm smooth-bore gun/missile launcher as in the T-64B. Later versions also included a laser rangefinder.

All these Soviet tanks were built in vast numbers and, as happened in other armies, they were constantly being upgraded and rebuilt. As new models appeared the older models were simply passed along the chain to lower-category units, thence to reserve units, and finally to storage depots, making it almost impossible to say that a Soviet tank had actually gone out of service.

Since their tanks were built to attack, and because much of western Europe's terrain is criss-crossed by small rivers, the Soviets gave their tanks a river-crossing capability. This involved making the entire tank watertight and fitting a breathing tube to the turret hatch. Thus, if bridges were unavailable, Warsaw Pact tanks were able to wade across rivers up to 4.5 m deep, although the breathing tube was so narrow that there was no question of the crew using it for an escape, and river-crossing exercises were viewed with considerable trepidation by Warsaw Pact tank crews.

The Soviet army was consistently able to produce tanks which were at least 10 tonnes lighter than their Western counterparts. These tanks were built for a specific purpose – attacking in large numbers – and they suited that purpose well. Soviet designers were consistently innovative, producing new types of round and gun, and fielding devices such as automatic loaders at a time when Western designers were well short of perfecting them.

A major advantage for the Warsaw Pact was that its forces used only Soviet-designed tanks, which resulted in a great degree of standardization.*

---

* It should not be assumed, however, that logistical problems did not exist. Warsaw Pact tanks, for example, used four different calibres of ammunition: T-34 – 85 mm; T-54 and T-55 – 100 mm, T-62 – 115 mm; T-64, T-72 and T-80 – 125 mm.

Although Soviet tanks were never used in anger against Western tanks in Europe, they did meet in wars in the Middle East and Asia. Generally speaking, in a one-on-one engagement the Western tanks proved superior in such wars – although not by a very wide margin. In the event of a conventional Warsaw Pact attack in western Europe the vastly greater numbers could well have been difficult to counter, especially as they would then have been operated by crews with much better training than those in the Middle East.

NATO TANKS

At one level NATO did manage to achieve a degree of standardization on tanks. Standardization agreements (known as STANAGS) were agreed through NATO channels and were published on many matters concerning tanks, a common main-gun calibre and the types of ammunition to be used, so that rounds could be freely exchanged between different armies. There were also a series of NATO Standard Tank Targets, based on the known criteria of Soviet tanks, which were the baseline against which all NATO guns were tested. These STANAGS were reasonably successful, although the agreements were not absolutely binding and countries were able to abandon them without penalty, apart from the logistic disadvantage of being unable to use standard NATO items.

At the highest level, however – that of tank design – NATO standardization was much less successful. Four NATO nations – France, Germany, the UK and the USA* – designed tanks, and there were numerous attempts to achieve commonality through collaborative projects, but, without exception, these came to naught. The first was between France and Germany in 1956, when the plan was for the two countries to agree on the general specifications for a tank, following which they would each design and build prototypes. These would then be evaluated, and the resulting winner would be placed in production in both countries. The Germans had a domestic competition between two consortia, the winner of which was pitted against the sole French entrant, but the two countries could not agree on the outcome. As a result, the French placed their entrant in production as the AMX-30, while the Germans produced theirs as the Leopard 1. In a further divergence from standardization, while the West Germans armed their tank with the British 105 mm L7 gun– at that time the de facto NATO standard – the French armed the AMX-30 with

---

* Italy also had a design capability, but no tanks were sold to NATO armies. Other countries had a capability to construct tanks under licence, but did not undertake design work.

their own 105 mm design, whose rounds could not be used in the L7 barrel.*

Then, in 1963, the USA and West Germany agreed on a joint programme for a common tank to replace the American M60 and German Leopard 1 in the 1970s. The designers were given carte blanche to produce a totally new and revolutionary main battle tank (MBT), and this they certainly did. Known as the MBT-70, it included numerous innovative ideas, the most striking of which was a 152 mm gun/missile launcher, launching the Shillelagh missile, firing conventional ammunition with combustible cartridge cases, and served by a fully automated loader. The suspension was capable of 'squatting' to achieve a low profile in a static position, and could also be extended to ensure good cross-country mobility. There was a very powerful engine, capable of accepting numerous different fuels in line with NATO's 'multi-fuel' policy. In addition, the automatic loader enabled the crew to be reduced to three, all of whom were housed in the turret, with the driver in an independently rotating capsule which ensured that he always faced forward. Sensors included a laser rangefinder and an environmental-control/life-support system, while reliability standards were supposedly the highest ever achieved in a tank.

A prototype was running in 1967, but by 1969 costs were escalating out of control. Estimated unit cost of a production MBT-70 was $1 million per tank at a time when the then current production tank, the M-60A1, cost $220,000 (both at 1970 prices). A design was prepared for an 'austere' version, designated XM-803, but the US Congress stopped the entire programme in January 1970, and it was accepted in both the USA and West Germany that virtually all the money spent on the MBT-70 programme had been wasted.

Similar British–German and Franco-German collaborative projects were equally unsuccessful, although they were both cancelled before the expenditure had reached MBT-70 proportions.

US Tanks

In the late 1940s the US army was equipped with two principal types of tank. The most numerous was the M4 Sherman medium tank, armed with a 75 mm gun and weighing 32 tonnes, which had proved a great success in the war, despite an unfortunate tendency to 'brew up' (i.e. to catch fire when hit). The second was the newer M26 Pershing, which had a much more powerful 90 mm gun, although, at 42 tonnes, it also weighed considerably more. Tank development was progressing at a relatively slow pace with the aim of introducing a new tank to replace these two in the mid-1950s when in 1950

---

* Italy joined the project in 1958, but did not attempt to enter the design competition. It eventually selected the West German Leopard.

the Korean War broke out, leading to a demand from the field army for newer and better tanks, to be delivered as quickly as possible.

This led to several 'crash' programmes, in the first of which a turret designed for the proposed mid-1950s tank was mounted on the existing M26 Pershing hull to produce the M47. The second design was based on a number of features of an experimental heavy tank and resulted in the M48. However, the US army paid a severe penalty for attempting to rush these two designs through the design and development stages, and the initial production versions of both the M47 and the M48 were unfit for combat use. Neither saw service in the Korean War, for which they had been designed, and it took several years to put everything right.

In the mid-1950s most Western tanks were armed with 90 mm guns, but Soviet tank armour was increasing in effectiveness, so the major armies started to seek even more powerful weapons. The US army produced an experimental 90 mm gun with a smooth bore, which enabled it to fire fin-stabilized projectiles, but in a competition with US-designed 105 mm and 120 mm guns and the British-designed L7 105 mm gun the latter won and was adopted, albeit with a US breech-block. At the same time it was decided to replace petrol engines with diesels, not least because the range of early M48s was a meagre 112 km. All of these enhancements, coupled with a totally new turret, were then incorporated into an improved M48, which was originally designated M48A2; but it was then decided that it was so different that it warranted a new designation, and as the M60 it served for many years as the army's standard medium tank.

In the late 1950s development started of a 152 mm gun/launcher which was to be mounted in both the new air-portable light tank, the M551 Sheridan, and the planned MBT-70, which was under development with West Germany. Hopes for the new gun/launcher were very high, and, in view of the Soviet tank threat and possible delays in the MBT-70 pro-gramme, it was decided as an interim measure to mount the weapon in a totally new turret on the M60 chassis, the new version being designated M60A2. The project was approved in 1964 and a prototype was running in September 1965, leading to an order for 300 in 1967. What had appeared to be a neat interim design, however, turned into yet another major problem, with difficulties being encountered not only with the gun/launcher, but also with the Shillelagh missile, the 152 mm conventional round, and the mating of the new turret to the existing chassis. Production started in 1969, but was quickly suspended due to the unreliability of the first off the line, and service acceptance was not achieved until 1971, although even then the first opera-tional unit was not formed until 1974. Thus it had taken ten years to get an 'interim' model using a majority of existing components into service. The M60A2 actually remained in service for under ten years, in what was a sin-gularly poor programme and a very bad bargain for the US taxpayer.

With the collapse of both the US–German collaborative MBT-70 programme and the 'austere', US-only, XM-803 programme, the US army found itself in the early 1970s in the embarrassing position of being without a viable future tank. However, in 1973 contracts containing an outline specification were placed with two US companies, who then developed and built prototypes which ran competitive trials in 1976.* Later that year it was announced that the Chrysler tank had won and would be put into production as the M1 Abrams. Although the tank was a purely American design, it was constructed from the British-developed 'Chobham' armour, while the main gun was a British L7 rifled 105 mm in the first version (M1 and Improved M1) and the German smooth-bore 120 mm in the M1A1. One of the major new features of the M1 was the use of a gas-turbine power unit, which provides high power, but at the cost of high fuel consumption. The tank eventually entered service in 1982.

British Tanks

The British had suffered from a succession of somewhat indifferent tank designs during the Second World War, but at the start of the Cold War the British prime production tank was the Centurion, which proved to be a great success. It was heavier than its contemporaries, the US M48 and the Soviet T-54, but the British were determined to have a well-armed and well-armoured tank following their experiences of being been consistently outgunned by German tanks, particularly the Panther and the Tiger. The Centurion's main gun was progressively improved: the early tanks were armed with a 76 mm gun, but this was replaced first by an 83 mm gun and later by the L7 105 mm gun, which was so good that it was adopted by virtually every other army in NATO, except the French.

In the late 1940s the British also developed a heavy tank to meet the NATO requirement to defeat the Soviet JS-3. The Soviet tank's armour was so thick that a very powerful gun was required to defeat it, and the British selected a US 120 mm gun, which, with its associated ammunition, was so large and heavy that the Conqueror tank, in which it was mounted, weighed 65 tonnes. The Conqueror earned a reputation of being slow and suffering from relatively poor mobility, although its top speed was only marginally less than that of the Centurion and its power-to-weight ratio (10 kW/tonne) was identical. Only 180 were built, and all were deployed in West Germany between 1955 and 1968 as tank destroyers.

In the 1950s the British started a project for their next tank, to replace both the Centurion and the Conqueror. This again followed their invariable

---

* A version of the West German Leopard 2 was developed specifically to meet the US staff requirement. Designated Leopard 2(AV) (AV = Austere Version), this was tested by the US army but was rejected in favour of the Chrysler version of the M1.

Cold War priorities of firepower and protection, although one of their earliest decisions in this project caused considerable surprise among their NATO allies. The very powerful British L7 105 mm tank gun and its ammunition had become the virtual NATO standard in the 1950s, being installed in US M48s and M60s, British Centurions and West German Leopard 1s, but the British themselves then became the first to leave the standard by insisting on a new 120 mm gun for this new tank. Initially, the new tank – named Chieftain – was beset by problems, particularly with the engine, transmission and suspension, but these were eventually resolved, particularly when an order from the shah of Iran for 700 tanks produced both money and an even greater sense of urgency to find a cure. The original staff requirement had been issued in 1958 and a prototype was running in 1959, but the Chieftain did not enter full service with the British army until 1967.

The search for a successor to the Chieftain began with a joint future-tank project with West Germany, but when this broke down in 1977 the British were forced to continue on their own in a project known as MBT-80. However, the contract to sell Chieftain tanks to Iran had led to a much improved version, known as Shir 2, of which several prototypes had been completed when the new Khomeini government suddenly cancelled the order. The British then decided to produce a modified version of Shir 2 to meet their own requirement for a Chieftain replacement. This tank, which had a new hull and power pack, but the same L11 120 mm gun as the Chieftain, was eventually placed in production as the Challenger, entering service in 1983.

German Tanks

The West German tank industry produced just two tank designs during the Cold War – Leopard 1 and Leopard 2 – both of which were outstandingly successful. The Leopard 1 was originally produced as part of the 1950s Franco-German project, but, when this fell apart, the German entry was placed in full production in 1963 for the German army. Some 4,561 Leopard 1s were produced in Germany between 1965 and 1979, with another 920 in Italy.

The Leopard 1 was conventional in design, being armed with a British L7 105 mm gun, powered by a multi-fuel engine, and with a crew of four. The design incorporated the lessons learned by the German army on the Russian front in the Second World War and was well armoured but also highly mobile. The Leopard 1 became the virtual NATO standard tank of the 1970s, equipping the Belgian, Canadian, Danish, Dutch, West German, Italian and Norwegian armies.*

---

* It was also exported to a number of non-NATO countries, including Australia.

The Leopard 2 was started as a low-key insurance against the failure of the US–German MBT-70 programme, which turned out to have been a wise precaution. When the collaborative project was cancelled in January 1970, the *Bundesheer* placed orders for seventeen prototypes of the German design, which were completed in 1974. Production started in 1979, with 2,125 being produced for Germany, 445 for the Netherlands, and others for the Swiss and Swedish armies. One of the significant features of the Leopard 2 was the Rheinmetall smooth-bore 120 mm gun, which fired fin-stabilized ammunition and was able to penetrate the NATO standard heavy-tank target at a range of 2,200 m.

French Tanks
In the early post-war years the French worked hard to re-establish their military industries, one of the most important being tank design and production. Like the UK and the USA, the French produced a heavy-tank design in the late 1940s, intended to counter the JS-3. This 50 tonne tank was armed with a 120 mm gun, but did not go into production because large numbers of US M47s were made available under the US Mutual Defense Assistance Program. France then joined with Germany in a collaborative programme to develop a new medium tank, but, when they failed to agree with the Germans on a winner, the French placed their entry, the AMX-30, in full production in 1967. The AMX-30 was less heavily armoured and thus 3 tonnes lighter than Leopard 1. Also, whereas other NATO armies at that time were standardizing on the British 105 mm L7, the AMX-30 was armed with a French 105 mm gun. This had a rifled barrel, and its only anti-tank round was a unique HEAT projectile in which the charge was mounted on ball-bearings; this meant that, while the projectile body spun to maintain stability in flight, the charge remained stationary (or spun at a very slow rate), which, according to the French army, considerably enhanced its effect. All other NATO tanks carried at least two, if not three, types of anti-tank round, such as HEAT, HESH/HEP and APDS projectiles. The only other NATO country to buy the AMX-30 was Greece.*

Several efforts to produce a replacement for the AMX-30, including a joint project with Germany, failed. In the end a new version, the AMX-30B2, was placed in production in 1981, and 693 of the original model were upgraded to the new standard. As the Cold War ended, a totally new French tank, the Leclerc, was about to enter production.

Collaboration
The NATO countries' experiences with tanks typified much that was good about the Alliance, as well as some of its failures. There was a considerable

---

* The AMX-30 was also bought by Spain, but well before that country joined NATO.

exchange of information about the Soviet armoured threat and about each other's plans for countering it. There was also a large degree of agreement on standards – particularly on weapon calibre, ammunition types, fuel and so on.

There were also some substantial efforts – the term 'heroic' might not be an overstatement – to achieve collaboration. The Franco–German attempt in the 1950s and the German–US attempt in the 1960s both resulted in prototypes, but there were also several others, including one between West Germany and the UK in the 1970s, and another between France and Germany in the early 1980s, which came to naught even before the proto-type stage had been reached. Part of the reason was that, for the countries concerned, the tank was so pivotal to the army's prestige and to its self-image that, no matter how good the intentions at the start of a collaborative project, national considerations frequently reigned supreme. Another reason was that countries considered it vital to their national interests to maintain their own national research-and-development capabilities, as well as tank, gun and ammunition production bases. There were also the poten-tial export markets to be considered. There was, however, one advantage in all this, in that, once the major tank producers had paid the research-and-development costs and had fought out their political battles with each other, the smaller NATO nations were then able to move in and place their tank, gun and ammunition orders at very advantageous prices.

Lessons from the Tank Programmes
The national programmes outlined above were hugely expensive, but there were other aspects which added significantly to the defence budgets. There were, for example, many projects which were either purely experimental or which were intended for production but never got beyond the prototype stage. For example, the US army's experimental T92 was developed in the late 1950s. It included many new features, such as a 90 mm smooth-bore gun and a very low silhouette, but was cancelled in 1960 on the grounds that its hull and turret were so different from preceding tanks that production lines would have required complete retooling, which would have been more expensive than simply improving the M48 to produce the M60. The total costs of this abortive programme, including the development of the gun and the construction of eleven prototypes, was $25 million (at 1960 prices).

The NATO armies were faced with a major dilemma. First, information about Soviet equipment was sparse and, in general, the details of a new Soviet tank were learned only after it had entered service in East Germany with the GSFG. But, as has been made clear above, new-tank programmes were lengthy – a minimum of ten years for a completely new tank and gun – and there were many pitfalls. On those occasions that armies tried to short-cut the lengthy procurement system in order to get a new tank or a new gun into service quickly, they almost invariably landed in trouble, as did the US army with the M47 and M48 in the early 1950s. Even worse was the later experience with the M60A2, when the apparently simple 'interim' arrangement of marrying the 152 mm gun/launcher to a new turret on an existing chassis went seriously awry.

New programmes were, if anything, even worse. Design work on the replacement for the M60 started in 1965 with the German–US MBT-70 collaborative programme. After that programme had collapsed, however, and with numerous bureaucratic adventures (particularly with the US Congress) en route, the first M1s did not reach operational units until 1982 – seventeen years later. In the UK, consideration of a Centurion replacement began in 1951 and the first production Chieftains started to enter service in 1967, just one year fewer than the US M60 replacement, and without the complication of an ill-fated collaborative programme, although the new tank was not really satisfactory until well into the 1970s.

The fielding of a new type of tank was by no means the end of the story, however. Not only did design problems have to be sorted out, but in-service tanks were constantly being modified to incorporate such features as a new gun, additional armour or updated electronics. If the type was still in production, such improvements were incorporated into new builds, but they were also retrofitted into existing tanks, frequently at maintenance depots, in an effort to keep the design up to date. The British army, for example, fielded no less than thirteen major versions of the Centurion and ten of the Chieftain, while versions of the US M48 reached M48A5. One of the significant features of such retrofits was that they usually appeared in defence budgets under headings such as 'maintenance', while only new production vehicles appeared under the named tank programme, making it virtually impossible to ascertain the total 'cradle-to-grave' costs of a long-serving tank such as the M48, M60, Chieftain or Leopard 1.

ASSESSMENT

Design
The NATO and Warsaw Pact tanks of 1990 were immediately recognizable as lineal descendants of the tanks of 1949. All had a single main gun mounted in a rotating turret atop the hull, and the chassis was generally similar, with the driver at the front and the engine at the rear. There had, however, been some diversions on the way. The US developed the 152 mm combined gun and missile launcher, which served in the M551 Sheridan and the M60A2 but was then abandoned, whereas the Soviets perfected a similar system using a 125 mm barrel. The British experimented with liquid propellant for the tank round, which would have both simplified and reduced

the stowage inside the tank and greatly improved safety, but this failed owing to difficulties in measuring the precise amounts needed. In the Soviet T-64 and T-72 the use of an automatic loader enabled the crew to be reduced to three men – a radical reduction which most Western armies considered at one time or another, but which was always rejected, even though it would have helped to ease their manpower shortages.

The Swedes aroused considerable interest in many armies with their S-tank, which had no turret, the gun (a modified version of the British 105 mm L7) being fixed instead in the glacis plate. The gun was trained in line by rotating the vehicle on its tracks and elevated by using the adjustable suspension system. The British were sufficiently interested to lease a company's worth of S-tanks for a year of trials and exercises in West Germany, and they also built a prototype of a similar vehicle. But the British project was dropped in favour of the traditional rotating turret, while the Swedes, having praised the virtues of the S-tank for many years, replaced it with the German Leopard 2, which had a conventional rotating turret.

One problem designers were always wrestling with was that of the overall height of the vehicle. Taking three typical 1960s tanks as an example, the Soviet T-62 was lowest at 2.4 m and the US M60A1 the highest at 3.26 m, with the British Chieftain in between at 2.9 m. There were two limiting factors: the height of the sitting driver dictated the height of the hull, while the height of the standing loader dictated the height between the floor and the turret roof. Various solutions were found. The French and Soviet armies placed a maximum height limit on selection for tank crews, while the British introduced a semi-reclining position for the driver. The main problem, however, was that of the loader, who had to stand to perform his job, and the only effective solution was to get rid of the task altogether by installing an automatic loader. It was for this reason, rather than economy of manpower, that Soviet tanks from the T-72 onwards were fitted with autoloaders.

Some unusual solutions were tried, although few ever progressed beyond range testing. The West Germans, for example, tested a tank with two 105 mm guns, in an effort to increase the firing rate, but that proved a dead end. In a different approach in the quest for ever greater tank-killing power, the British used one Centurion chassis to test a 183 mm gun in a boiler-plate turret and another for trials with a 180 mm gun in an open mount with a concentric recoil system and an automatic rotary loader. Neither progressed beyond the prototype stage.

During the period of the Cold War, tanks certainly increased in capability, with bigger guns, thicker armour, more powerful engines and ever more sophisticated command-and-control systems, but one major consequence was that the weight grew inexorably. In the British army, for example, the initial version of the Centurion, which entered service in the mid-1940s, weighed 49 tonnes, while the final version, the Mk 13, weighed 52 tonnes.

The successor, the Chieftain (1960s) weighed 55 tonnes, and the next tank, the Challenger (1980s), a massive 62 tonnes. Even the Soviets, who believed very strongly in keeping tank weights down, suffered from similar problems: their T-34/85 (1940s) weighed 32 tonnes, while the T-54 (1950s) came in at 36 tonnes, the T-62 (1960s) at 37 tonnes and the T-72 at 43.5 tonnes.

Costs

The true cost of a tank is difficult to discover, not least because the various nations involved use differing criteria to arrive at a final figure. With these provisos in mind, a careful analysis of the unit costs of US tanks at 1972 prices arrived at the following figures:[1]

M47	$207,300
M48	$203,400
M60	$185,200
MBT70	$1,058,200
M1	$570,000

Prices steadily escalated, and the hull, turret, gun and most components cost more as the Cold War progressed; the British Challenger 1, for example, cost £3 million at 1985 prices. Most components increased in cost, but by far the greatest cost escalation was in the electronic devices, such as fire-control systems, sensors, engine controls and radios.

26

Infantry

Of all the arms in the ground forces, the infantry – arguably the most important element on the tactical battlefield – underwent the greatest change during the Cold War. Up to the early 1950s (and later in the smaller armies) the infantry was fundamentally unchanged from the Second World War, being organized into battalions of between 500 and 800 men and divided into three to five rifle companies. The main feature of all infantry battalions, however, was that the great majority of men moved on foot, as the infantry had done since time immemorial, dictating a sustained speed of advance of approximately 5 km/h, which had a major impact on the speed at which battles could be fought.

Efforts were made during the Second World War to make the infantry more mobile. Some battalions were given sufficient trucks to enable all the men to move on wheels, but, since the trucks were simply load-carriers with seats, they provided no protection and the men had to dismount in order to fight or if under threat from artillery or air attack. The trucks also had very limited cross-country capability. Attempts were made on the Allied side to introduce armoured protection, mainly by converting tanks, but the resulting vehicles entered service in relatively small numbers. The Germans produced a half-track vehicle specifically as a troop carrier, but the metal sideplates were thin and there was no overhead cover, so the protection was only marginally greater than that provided by trucks, although mobility was greater. Nevertheless, the basic problem for army commanders was that, if tanks achieved a break-through, their speed of advance far outstripped that of the plodding infantry.

PERSONNEL CARRIERS OR COMBAT VEHICLES?

As so often, the US army led the way to the next major development, the armoured personnel carrier (APC), which initially consisted of an armoured box mounted on tracks, carrying an infantry squad of twelve men. A far-seeing operational requirement was issued in September 1945, and the outcome, the M75 APC, entered service in 1951, setting a trend which has continued to this day.

Subsequent development followed two main strands. The first was for a so-called 'battle taxi' whose prime role was to move the infantry about the battlefield, giving them protection and speed of movement, and delivering them to a point near the objective from which they could then advance on foot into the assault. For such a requirement the infantry inside the vehicle needed only to be able to see out in order to orientate themselves and to be able to disembark rapidly.

The other school of thought maintained that what was required was an infantry combat vehicle, which not only carried a heavy weapon in the turret but also provided the infantry with the means of fighting from inside the vehicle. In such a vehicle, it was claimed, the infantry could actually fight from their vehicle, keeping the enemy's heads down by the sheer volume of small-arms fire and disembarking only when actually on top of the objective.

The other main area of difference was over tracks and wheels. Tracks conferred exceptional cross-country mobility but were noisy, expensive, required considerable maintenance, and tended to damage road surfaces – a major consideration in peacetime. Wheels, on the other hand, were cheaper, more reliable, quieter, easier to replace if damaged, and, when on roads, not only did less damage, but also enabled the vehicle to move much faster. On the other hand, wheels were more vulnerable to damage, and did not provide such a good cross-country capability.

The USA
The first of the 'battle taxis', the US army's trend-setting M75 APC, entered service in 1952. It carried a driver, a commander and a squad of ten men. It was of all-steel construction and was high, making it difficult to conceal, and it was not amphibious; it also had a petrol engine. Nevertheless, it was an impressive start. The M75 was followed by the M59, which entered service from 1954 onwards. This too was of all-steel construction, but was cheaper than the M75 to produce and was amphibious in calm conditions.

Still not satisfied, the US army persevered and its efforts in this particular development chain culminated in the M113 APC, which became the archetypical APC between 1960 and 1985. The original US army requirement was to provide a lightweight armoured personnel carrier for armour and infantry units; it had to be capable of amphibious and air-drop operation, have superior cross-country mobility, and be adaptable for multiple functions by means of kits and/or modification of its superstructure. The designers succeeded in meeting all of these objectives, and the M113 proved to be one of the most successful military designs of all time, with over 80,000 being produced for service in at least fifty armies in a production run which lasted from 1960 to the early 1990s.

The M113 had a body fabricated from welded aluminium, which protected the crew (commander, driver and eleven infantrymen) from shell splinters and small-arms fire. It was powered by a diesel engine, giving a maximum speed of 64 km/h and a range of 320 km (later increased to 485 km). The infantrymen sat on two benches facing inwards, and exited through a downward-opening rear ramp. The basic vehicle was armed with a pintle-mounted 12.7 mm machine-gun, although many users mounted heavier weapons, of which the largest to enter service was a turret-mounted 76 mm gun in an Australian version. The M113 was fully amphibious with little preparation, being propelled in the water by its tracks. Apart from the normal infantry versions a large range of specialized versions were produced, including bulldozers, flame-throwers, mortar carriers, radar vehicles, anti-aircraft gun/missile carriers, command posts, anti-tank weapons carriers, and transport for engineers, communications and recovery operations.

The M113 was very successful, but one of the reasons for its longevity was the difficulty experienced in finding a successor. By the early 1960s the US army had decided on a requirement for a mechanized-infantry combat vehicle (MICV), the first attempt at which was a vehicle designated MICV-65, of which five prototypes were produced, but it was considered too large and development ceased. In 1967 the Armored Infantry Fighting Vehicle (AIFV) appeared, which was in essence an M113 adapted to meet the MICV requirement, but this too was deemed unsatisfactory and development ceased, although the design was later produced in large numbers for the Belgian and Dutch armies.

In 1972 the XM723 programme started, which was intended to lead to a vehicle which would serve in both armoured and infantry units, carrying a crew of three plus eight dismounting infantry. After many vicissitudes, repeated reviews (most of them antagonistic), much criticism and many redesigns, this programme resulted in the M2 Bradley Infantry Fighting Vehicle (IFV) and the initial production vehicles were eventually handed over in 1981, with the first unit forming in March 1983. Forty-one M2s were issued to each infantry battalion, where they replaced M113s, although many M113s continued to serve in other roles.

The M2 was constructed of welded aluminium with spaced, laminated armour on the front and sides, and was armed with a turret-mounted 25 mm chain-gun, a coaxial 7.62 mm machine-gun and a twin TOW anti-tank missile launcher. The vehicle crew consisted of commander, driver and gunner, and seven infantrymen were carried, of which six were provided with firing ports and periscopes. Thus, after a protracted and very expensive development process, the US army finally obtained a MICV which was only marginally better than the German Marder (see below), which had preceded it into service by some fifteen years.

The USSR

The Soviet army initially followed a policy of transporting infantrymen in motor-rifle units in motor-rifle divisions in wheeled APCs, starting in the 1940s with the 6 × 6-wheeled BTR-152,* a very ordinary design, which used a truck chassis with a new steel superstructure to carry seventeen infantrymen. This was replaced in the 1960s by the BTR-60, an 8 × 8-wheeled, open-topped, boat-shaped vehicle, which carried a crew of two and twelve infantrymen. The original open top meant that the men could disembark quickly over the sides, but they had no protection from overhead artillery bursts, nor could the vehicle be made NBC-proof; this was rectified in later versions, which had a covered-in roof with hatches. The vehicle was fully amphibious and was powered in the water by water jets. The original pintle-mounted 7.62 mm or 12.7 mm machine-gun was later replaced by a turret-mounted 14.5 mm machine-gun, and firing ports were provided for some of the infantrymen. This was an efficient design and quite unlike anything then in service, making it another example of the radical thinking of which Soviet designers were capable. The BTR-60 was later complemented by the improved BTR-70.

Motor-rifle units in tank divisions were mounted in tracked APCs, the earliest version being the BTR-50, which entered service in the mid-1950s. This was based on a light-tank design, but, like the wheeled BTR-60, it had a large, open troop compartment, from which the men jumped to the ground. This was replaced in the 1960s by a design even more outstanding than the BTR-60: the BMP-1. This was a very low, fully tracked vehicle constructed of welded steel plate and carrying a crew of three and an eight-man infantry squad. The BMP-1 weighed 13.5 tonnes fully loaded and was armed with a new 73 mm low-pressure gun, with an AT-3 (NATO = 'Sagger') anti-tank guided missile mounted above it. The BMP-1 had full NBC protection and was fully amphibious, and excellent ballistic design gave protection against small-arms fire up to 12.7 mm calibre. A later version, the BMP-2, appeared in 1982; this was essentially a modernized BMP-1, but armed with a 30 mm cannon and an AT-5 (NATO = 'Spandrel') anti-tank missile system.

The BTR-60/70 and BMP-1/2 again showed that the Soviet General Staff and designers were capable of daring and innovative thought, producing designs which, on their appearance, caused some alarm in the West. Pictures were the only evidence that most Western defence experts had of

---

* '6 × 6' indicates that it was a six-wheeled vehicle with all six wheels powered. A 4 × 2 vehicle has four wheels with only two powered (as in a standard civil automobile).

these APCs until examples were captured in the Middle Eastern wars, but there was also a very lively debate in Soviet military journals on their employment in combat, with officers of all ranks joining in the frequently heated discussions.

West Germany

In the late 1950s the *Bundesheer* started to consider the design of its first Cold War infantry fighting vehicle, and, not surprisingly, it began by analysing the experiences of the Second World War *Wehrmacht* on the Eastern Front. These studies convinced the Germans that they needed a vehicle from which the infantry could fire their weapons, enabling them to fight their way on to the objective, thus protecting the infantry during the final – and very vulnerable – assault phase. The result was the Marder, the first prototypes of which ran in 1961, although there was then a very careful, albeit somewhat prolonged, series of trials before it entered service in 1971.

The Marder had a steel body, the front of which gave complete protection from 20 mm rounds. It was operated by a crew of three: commander, gunner and driver. The dismounting infantry numbered only six, sitting on outward-facing benches, four of whom were provided with firing ports. Armament comprised a 20 mm cannon and a coaxial 7.62 mm machine-gun in a two-man turret, with a separate remotely controlled machine-gun at the rear of the vehicle. All vehicles were later also fitted with a Milan anti-tank guided-missile launcher. The result was an extremely capable vehicle, highly mobile, with considerable firepower and good protection from small-arms fire and NBC, but with a weight of 28 tonnes, which made it by far the heaviest MICV to enter service. Marder equipped the infantry battalions in both tank and panzer grenadier divisions, and with periodic updates it served the *Bundesheer* from 1971 until well beyond the end of the Cold War.

Other Countries

All NATO and Warsaw Pact countries had little option but to follow the lead set by the US and Soviet armies, and to mount their infantry in vehicles. Most simply adopted US or Soviet carriers, but there were a number of exceptions.

Some armies adopted wheeled APCs. The Czechs and Poles, while following the Soviet lead in adopting a wheeled APC for motor-rifle troops, did not adopt the Soviet BTR-60 but instead jointly developed the OT-64 8 × 8-wheeled APC, which entered service in 1964. This carried a crew of two (driver and commander) and two sections (eighteen infantrymen) – by far the largest number of men carried by an APC. It was very successful, but was eventually replaced by the BMP-1.

The Dutch also developed an 8 × 8-wheeled APC, the YP-408, a large vehicle which was based on a DAF truck and accommodated a crew of two and ten infantrymen. It served in the Dutch army from 1964 until being replaced by the US-designed tracked AIFV from 1977 onwards. The British also used a wheeled APC, the 6 × 6-wheeled Saracen, in the 1960s, but it was employed mainly by the support troops in reconnaissance units and only rarely by infantry battalions.

The French army used wheeled APCs for roles outside Europe, but for European warfare it used tracked APCs, all of French design. The first was the AMX VCI, which entered service in 1957 and was based on the AMX-13 light tank. It had a troop compartment accommodating ten infantrymen, with eight facing outwards and two to the rear, all of them with firing ports. The VCI was replaced from 1973 onwards by the AMX-10P, an all-aluminium vehicle, armed with a 20 mm cannon on an external mount. It carried eight infantrymen, but these did not have the ability to fight from inside the vehicle.

From 1963 onwards the British also used a tracked APC, the FV432, which was generally similar in design to the M113, but constructed of steel. In the 1970s, however, when the British army started to consider a replacement for the FV432, there was an intense internal debate over the future requirement, which centred upon whether a new vehicle should be a MICV, as exemplified by the German Marder, or simply a better APC. Various prototypes were designed and tested, including a very large MICV, but in the end the Mechanized Combat Vehicle-80 (MCV-80) was selected, mounting a 30 mm Rarden cannon, and carrying eight infantrymen (one of whom was also the vehicle commander), although they did not have firing ports and therefore could not use their weapons from inside the vehicle. The title, MCV-80, was intended to demonstrate that the vehicle would enter service in 1980, but, as so often happened when such dates were included in a weapon title (e.g. the German/US MBT-70 tank), this proved to be overoptimistic and the vehicle did not enter service until 1987.

THE INFANTRY REVOLUTION

Fielding APCs and MICVs represented a true revolution in the infantry, since the men were all mounted, together with their weapons, equipment and supplies, while the tracks gave them a mobility virtually identical with that of tanks; in addition, since every vehicle was fitted with a radio (and the radio was no longer limited in size by the need for it to be carried on a man's back), commanders were able to achieve an unprecedented degree of control. Further, the vehicles were able to carry heavy machine-guns or cannon in turrets, as well as lighter machine-guns and anti-tank guided weapons, greatly increasing the firepower available.

Later it was also realized that, by creating a slight overpressure inside, these vehicles could provide collective protection against chemical and biological weapons. APCs/MICVs also proved remarkably adaptable, forming the basis for many specialist vehicles for use as command posts, ambulances, communications stations, recovery and repair vehicles, and minelayers. As a result they were produced in considerable numbers

There were, of course, some penalties. Each APC required a driver and a commander, which meant that every section was robbed of two men on the ground – a significant number of men when a battalion was equipped with some sixty or more APCs. In addition, the battalion's logistic requirements increased dramatically, principally for fuel and spares, while the maintenance requirement also increased.

The change in capability can be gauged by a brief examination of the infantry battalion in the British army, whose experiences were typical of the changes in all armies. In the 1950s a British infantry battalion consisted of some 700 men, for the majority of whom the normal means of movement was on foot. There were three rifle companies, in which the vast majority of men were armed with a 7.70 mm bolt-action rifle, although each rifle platoon also had three 7.70 mm light machine-guns and three 51 mm mortars. The heavy-weapons company operated six 7.70 mm Vickers heavy machine-guns, six 120 mm WOMBAT recoilless anti-tank guns and six 76.2 mm mortars. Mobility was limited to approximately twenty Jeeps or Land Rovers, mainly for commanders and communicators, and twenty three-tonne trucks, whose primary purpose was logistic resupply.

In the late 1980s a British mechanized battalion was still approximately the same size – 725 men – but now every one of these had his own allotted place in a vehicle. All men carried an automatic weapon, the riflemen carrying the British standard 5.56 mm rifle. The battalion operated 157 vehicles, comprising 90 MCV-80 Warrior IFVs, 19 tracked reconnaissance vehicles, 16 Land Rovers, and 4 one-tonne, 17 four-tonne and 11 eight-tonne trucks. Heavy weapons included eight 81 mm mortars, twelve Milan anti-tank guided-missile launchers, and a large quantity of 30 mm Rarden cannon and 7.62 mm machine-guns mounted on the Warriors. Logistic resupply had, however, become a severe problem, especially for fuel, ammunition and spares, while the maintenance requirement was met a by a platoon of twenty-eight men. All IFVs had at least one radio, as did most Land Rovers. The greatest change, however, was in the infantry's mobility, since it had become fully capable of moving cross-country in company with tanks or of moving at high speed along roads.

27

Artillery

FIELD ARTILLERY

The Guns

While the tank became the public and political symbol of an army's military prowess, overshadowing other battlefield weapons systems, within armies the importance of the artillery arm remained undiminished and, despite the advent of missiles and rockets, the gun remained the weapon of choice in the tactical battle.* Provided targets were within range, guns were capable of producing extremely accurate and very destructive fire at virtually any spot selected by battlefield commanders. Further, artillery command-and-control systems enabled the guns to switch targets quickly and to increase the weight of fire by bringing additional batteries into action as required.

Artillery was of great importance in the Second World War, and this continued in the many smaller wars between 1945 and 1990, when the tactical value of artillery was demonstrated repeatedly, although never more convincingly than at the Battle of Dien Bien Phu during the First Indo-China War. During that prolonged siege, which lasted from December 1953 to May 1954, Viet Minh artillery occupied the hills overlooking the French base and from there they totally dominated the battlefield, closed the airfield, cut off supplies, and eventually bludgeoned the garrison into defeat.

In the early 1950s there were only a small number of self-propelled guns, all in open mounts on converted tank chassis, which supported armoured divisions in some armies (e.g. the British and US). The great majority of

---

* Specifications of the principal artillery pieces are given in Appendix 26. To the purist, there is a difference between a gun and a howitzer: the gun can be elevated between zero and 45 degrees and the latter up to about 70–80 degrees. Most self-propelled weapons (SPs) are therefore strictly speaking howitzers, but, for ease of reference, this book uses the generic term 'SP gun'.

guns were wheeled pieces, towed either by a specially designed artillery tractor or, in some cases, by an ordinary general-purpose truck. At a US army conference held in Washington in January 1952 it was decided that the speed of modern warfare was increasing to such an extent, particularly with the infantry planning to be mounted entirely in armoured personnel carriers, that wheeled guns would no longer be able to keep up with the speed of movement. Also, the threat of nuclear weapons made it necessary to place the crews inside closed gun-houses (turrets) for protection. Furthermore, tracked vehicles were more capable of moving into temporary fire positions, getting into and out of action quickly, since there was no need to separate the gun from its tractor and set it on a base-plate. Then, after firing, they could move out rapidly – the so-called 'shoot-and-scoot' tactic – before enemy artillery could determine the source of the rounds and fire a counter-battery mission.

The US army initiative resulted in three outstanding designs – the M107 (175 mm), M109 (155 mm), and M110 (203 mm) – although the M109 was the only one to provide a gun-house to shelter the crew. These weapons came to dominate the NATO artillery arms, seeing service in virtually every NATO army except that of France. US army deployment, which was typical of other NATO armies was fifty-four M109 155 mm and twelve M110 203 mm in each armoured and mechanized infantry division, and twelve M107 175 mm in each corps.

The great majority of other NATO nations simply followed the US lead on artillery tactics and adopted US weapons, and only a few other guns were developed. The British produced the 105 mm Abbot tracked SP gun in the 1960s, but within NATO this served only with the British army, since it was by then clear that the future lay with the larger 155 mm calibre. The British did, however, collaborate with Germany and Italy in the successful 155 mm Field Howitzer 1970 (FH70) programme, producing a towed gun which was destined for use in 'out-of-area' roles by the UK and by territorial defence units in the FRG and Italy. The success of the FH70 led to a follow-on collaborative project with Germany, the ambitious SP70, a 155 mm self-propelled, tracked weapon, using the same ordnance as the FH70. Unfortunately it proved to be too ambitious, and after a great deal of expenditure it was eventually cancelled and the two countries went their separate ways.

The only other NATO nation to retain a significant domestic artillery industry was France, which produced a series of towed and self-propelled artillery pieces. The French retained towed guns for use by their front-line mechanized infantry divisions, even producing the new TR 155 mm towed gun in the 1970s, at a time when all other European armies had long since converted to self-propelled pieces.

Soviet artillery had established an awesome reputation during the Second World War, but for the next two decades it experienced a conservatism unusual in the Soviet armed forces, which not only adhered to towed artillery, but also invariably deployed it in rows of six guns in uncamouflaged fire positions. Well-established Second World War guns therefore remained in service throughout the 1950s, and their replacements in the 1960s were also towed. It was only in the 1970s that self-propelled guns came into service, in which existing tracked chassis were matched to modified versions of existing guns, producing systems of 122 mm, 152 mm and 203 mm calibre. Although long overdue, these proved to be of excellent quality, with the usual Soviet combination of practical design, simplicity and long range, and caused considerable alarm in the West.

Czechoslovakia made a notable contribution to artillery design with its DANA system, which entered service in 1981. This featured a 152 mm gun in a split turret mounted on a modified 8×8-wheeled truck chassis. Although the wheels reduced its cross-country capability in comparison with a tracked vehicle, its performance was more than adequate for service in central Europe with its excellent road systems, and any tactical disadvantages were offset by its high road speed, long road range, considerably reduced capital cost, and ease of maintenance.

Calibres

In the 1950s NATO armies were equipped with guns of a wide variety of calibres, and in one of its early efforts at standardization NATO decided on the 105 mm round. France, the UK and the USA all produced self-propelled guns of this calibre in the 1950s and 1960s, but the shells had limited carrying capacity, lethality and range compared to those of 155 mm (as shown in Table 27.1), and 155 mm subsequently became the NATO standard for field artillery.

Table 27.1 NATO Standard High-Explosive Ammunition

Calibre (mm)	Country of origin	Weight of projectile (kg)	Range (m)
105	USA	18.1	11,500
155	USA	42.9	14,600
175	USA	66.8	32,700
203	USA	92.5	16,800

The varieties of payload also increased considerably during the Cold War. US army 155 mm rounds, for example, could carry high explosives (HE); chemical agents; direct-fire anti-tank; flares; smoke; anti-tank minelets; anti-personnel minelets; and self-forming, top attack, anti-tank munitions.

Warsaw Pact countries produced similar payloads, and also developed a communications jammer housed in a 152 mm shell.

Great efforts were also made to extend the range. One method was by lengthening the barrel; virtually doubling the length of the 203 mm barrel in the US M110, for example, increased the range of the M106 HE projectile from 16,800 m to 21,300 m. Shell design was also progressively refined, with techniques such as base bleed and rocket assistance both being used to enhance the range. Somewhat to the frustration of Western designers, however, Soviet designers always seemed to be able to obtain greater range than their Western counterparts: for example, the Soviet 152 mm gun fired a 43.5 kg shell to 24,000 m, while the US 155 mm fired a 42.9 kg shell to 14,600 m.

Nothing is ever achieved without penalty, however, and the consequence of increasing the calibre was that individual rounds were heavier, meaning that fewer could be carried on the gun, while the increase in firing rate meant that more rounds were required from the logistics system, and the increase in range placed new requirements on the target-acquisition process.

There was a major difference between the maximum or 'burst' fire rate, which could be kept up for only a short time, and the sustained fire rate; the respective rates for the M109, for example, were three rounds and one round per minute. The M109 carried twenty-eight rounds, which, even at the sustained rate, could be used within half an hour and, while no gun would fire even at the sustained rate for a very long period, all armies' ammunition consumption rates rose to a dramatic degree. The US army responded by developing the tracked Field Artillery Ammunition Support Vehicle (FAASV), which could carry either 118 rounds of 155 mm ammunition or 75 rounds of 175 mm. Despite such advances, the demands of the guns for more ammunition, coupled with rapid movement to pre-empt counter-attack by enemy guns, made artillery resupply a major problem.

As with tankmen, gunners pursued the goal of first-round accuracy. Accuracy on target depended upon knowing the precise location of the guns, and manual methods of surveying gun positions gave way to much faster and more accurate electronic systems. In addition, movements became so frequent and time in any one position so brief that the traditional method of ascertaining meteorological conditions by visual and manual methods was no longer adequate and fully automated systems were introduced.

The introduction of SP guns with the crew housed in a turret meant that visual methods of control on the gun position were superseded by radio. Ever-expanding artillery communication systems also enabled artillery commanders to exercise much greater co-ordination and control of their units, and to respond much more rapidly to requests for fire support. Many national artillery arms were also quick to latch on to the potential of computerized fire-control systems.

Counter-Battery fire

Every military system inevitably preys on its own, and, as artillery became more effective, so too did the duel between artillery systems (known as 'counter-battery' fire) intensify. In the early 1950s there were two, fairly primitive, methods of locating enemy artillery. One used analysis of craters to estimate the direction and range of the gun. The other, called 'sound ranging', used sensitive microphones placed along a line (the 'sound base') and connected by radio; the sound of gunfire was detected by operators, who used the time of detection at the different microphones to compute the point of origin.

In the 1970s, however, the scale and efficiency of Soviet artillery systems, coupled with the ever shorter time spent in any one position, forced NATO to develop more accurate, more rapid and less manpower-intensive systems, such as the US army's Firefinder, which consisted of two radars: one to detect mortars, the other to detect guns and missile launchers. On detecting a projectile, the radars tracked it briefly and then used the trajectory to compute the point of origin, presenting the precise location of the launch site to the operator before the incoming projectile had hit the ground. The operator then passed the co-ordinates of the enemy position to the fire-direction centre, for it to be included in the counter-battery fire plan.

AIR DEFENCE

From about 1943 to the end of the Second World War the Allied armies operated in an environment of air supremacy, leading to the virtual neglect of air defences for armies in the field during the early years of the Cold War. There was therefore a continued dependence upon Second World War gun-based systems well into the 1950s in the West, and it was only when the Soviets began to field missile-based systems that Western development was given any real sense of urgency. As in other areas, however, the Germans had left a rich legacy of guided-missile projects, and these were used as the starting point for new air-defence systems.

US Air Defence

The Hawk missile entered service with the US army in 1959 and was also purchased by a NATO consortium (Belgium, France, Germany, Italy and the Netherlands), which laid out a complex network of static Hawk sites covering most of western Europe. These were subsequently upgraded to Improved Hawk (I-Hawk) by all except Belgium. Both Hawk and I-Hawk were effective, with a maximum range of 40 km, and not only were capable of intercepting aircraft, but also demonstrated a capability of attacking missiles and battlefield rockets such as NATO's Honest John. The British meanwhile produced a mobile air-defence missile, the Thunderbird, which was deployed in Germany from 1959 to 1976.

At the lowest end of the scale – within infantry battalions – miniaturization led to a spate of missiles which were light in weight and easy to control and which could be carried in a container which doubled as the launch-tube. Typical of these were the US Redeye and its successor the Stinger, and the British Blowpipe. Guidance methods varied, with Redeye/Stinger using an infra-red seeker to home on an aircraft's exhaust, while Blowpipe was steered by the operator, enabling it to attack an aircraft head-on. It was originally envisaged that such weapons would be distributed on a wide scale, giving a broad coverage of the AFCENT area, but NATO pilots were not very enthusiastic about flying over their own troops armed with such weapons, especially if the operators were 'trigger-happy' as a result of recent enemy air attacks. So, identification friend-or-foe (IFF) systems were fitted and missile operators were brought under centralized control to ensure that they did not blaze away regardless.

At the divisional level there were a large number of missile systems, although all took much longer to develop and cost very much more than planned. The US army rushed the Chapparal system into service in 1966, by mounting four Sidewinder missiles, normally used by aircraft, on an existing tracked chassis and adding a simple radar. Chapparal was to have been replaced by Roland, a Franco-German programme which started in 1963 and eventually entered service with the French and German armies in 1977 – fourteen years later. It was then adopted by the US army for service in late 1977, but there was a four-year delay before it actually entered service, and even then the promised large orders were cut back to just twenty-seven. Meanwhile, Chapparal, the interim system, remained in service until the 1990s. The British developed the mobile Rapier, which went into service in 1967 as a fairly simple optically guided system, towed by a light truck, but was then developed into a much more sophisticated weapon mounted on a tracked vehicle.

At the corps level the US Patriot system also suffered from a long-drawn-out development, which started with intensive studies in 1961. By 1965 the system had been designated SAM-D and was intended to defeat saturation air attacks by large numbers of aircraft at all heights and by short-range missiles, both of them in an intense ECM environment. Full development did not start until 1967 and was protracted, to say the least, as the first unit did not form until 1984. Nevertheless, it proved to be an exceptionally good system, using a combination of command and semi-active homing guidance to control a missile travelling at speeds of Mach 2–3 and with a maximum range in the region of 65–70 km.

Soviet Air Defence

In contrast with the NATO nations, the Soviet Union gave high priority to air defence from the start of the Cold War, and in particular to missiles, and proceeded to follow a coherent development plan throughout. In the ground forces, area coverage was provided by SAM brigades, whose operations were co-ordinated with those of the tactical air army, while at division and regimental level SAMs and anti-aircraft guns provided point defence. These were tied together by an efficient target-acquisition and early-warning system, whose tasks were to provide the air-defence units with target data and other units with warning of incoming attacks. All units were encouraged to use shoulder-launched short-range missiles, machine-guns and rifles against hostile aircraft.

The first missile, the SA-1 (NATO = 'Guild'), which was also the world's first air-defence missile to be deployed on a significant scale, entered service in 1954 and was intended for homeland defence, while the first mobile missile system for the field army, the SA-2 ('Guideline'), entered service in 1957. The SA-2 missile was mounted on a wheeled transporter–erector, launched vertically, and guided by radar, and its capabilities were amply demonstrated on 1 May 1960 when an SA-2 missile hit the US spy plane piloted by Gary Powers, thus not only provoking the 'U-2 Incident' but also effectively ending the USA's ability to overfly the USSR with U-2s. The missile was widely exported and was constantly updated, particularly as a result of operational experience by its export customers, including North Vietnam, Egypt and Syria.

Next came the SA-4 ('Ganef') system, which entered full service in 1967 and consisted of two missiles mounted on a tracked carrier. This highly mobile system was designed to accompany advancing forces, each army having a brigade of twenty-seven launchers, which moved in two echelons, one some 10 km behind the front line, the other 15 km further back. The amphibious tracked carrier was specifically designed for the SA-4 system, but was subsequently used for many other systems. The SA-4 remained in service until the early 1990s but, as far as is known, was never used operationally, although a brigade was deployed to Egypt in 1971–2 and another brigade was deployed to Kabul Airport in 1979.

The series of army air-defence missile systems continued with the SA-6 ('Gainful'), which, like the SA-4, was powered by a ramjet. It entered service in 1970 and complemented the SA-4 in the forward areas, the first echelon being some 5 km behind the forward troops and the second echelon 10 km further back still. The system was designed to combat low-level fighter-bombers and was widely used in the Soviet army; it was also exported to Egypt and Syria. The initial version of the SA-6, with one radar for three launchers, was used to great effect in the 1973 Arab–Israeli war, where it initially caused great problems for the Israeli air force, due, at least in part, to surprise. After suffering losses, however, the Israelis discovered three weaknesses: the missile could be defeated by a combination of chaff and manoeuvre; the engagement radar was vulnerable to attack; and the system could be saturated.

The SA-6 was due to be replaced by the SA-11 ('Gadfly'), but problems with the new system's missile led to a stop-gap system being fielded, which was designated SA-6B by NATO, and which combined the proven SA-6 missile with the SA-11 trailer, launcher and radar; it served in limited numbers from 1979 to the mid-1980s.

The Soviets had, however, already developed another new divisional-level system, the SA-8 ('Gecko'), in which each 6 × 6-wheeled, amphibious launch vehicle also had its own engagement radar. After prolonged problems with the missile, this entered service in 1980.

The development of these Soviet missile systems followed a constant path. The early missiles were designed to counter the medium- and high-level threats that prevailed in the 1950s and 1960s, while the SA-6, SA-8 and SA-11 also countered the low-level threat that started to become important from the 1970s onwards. These systems were deployed at divisional level and above, while at regimental level there were SA-9 ('Gaskin') vehicle-mounted missiles and air-defence guns (e.g. the ZSU-23–4 – see below) and at battalion level there was a plethora of shoulder-launched missiles (e.g. the SA-7 'Grail'). There was at least one SA-7 launcher in each tank and motor-rifle platoon, while each regiment had a platoon of four quadruple SA-9 launchers and a platoon of four ZSU-23–4 guns. The missile's infra-red seeker was reported to be fairly susceptible to deception, and the West developed a multitude of countermeasures, including baffles over helicopter engine exhausts, flares with varying heat intensities, and infra-red decoy pods.

One of the notable achievements of the Soviet system was that it managed to develop a series of missiles and associated radars which could be deployed both on land and at sea, only the launchers being different. Another strength was that most of them were very simple to use.

Those missiles that were used operationally in conflicts outside the USSR usually achieved some success in the early days of the conflict, followed by diminishing returns as pilots learned how to cope with them. In a war in central Europe, however, these systems would have been operated by much more skilled operators and would have been at much greater density; they would undoubtedly have caused NATO pilots considerable difficulty.*

The Soviets claimed that their goal was to produce an air-defence 'umbrella' over their forces, and in this they substantially succeeded.

---

* The experience of the Coalition air forces in the Gulf War is relevant: they found Iraqi air defences very powerful, especially at very low levels.

Low-Level Air-Defence Guns – a Case History

Nowhere was the difference in approach between the Western and Soviet approaches to weapons procurement shown more clearly than in the development by each side of a self-propelled, tracked, low-level gun system to provide air defence for rapidly moving armoured units.

First to be fielded was the Soviet ZSU-23-4,* which Soviet designers based on a standard tracked chassis, virtually identical to that already in wide-scale use for the SA-6 missile system. To this was added a simple turret with 360-degree traverse, in which was mounted an already proven quadruple 23 mm cannon system, each barrel being capable of firing short bursts at an effective rate of 1,000 rounds per minute. The one new item was the 'Gun Dish' radar, which performed all the necessary functions of search, detection, automatic tracking, and range and angle calculation. The result was a devastating and totally autonomous weapon system, which achieved great success in various Middle East wars. During the 1973 war, for example, thirty of the eighty Israeli aircraft lost in low-level missions fell victim to the ZSU-23-4. The weapon was not without its problems: barrels had a short life and were prone to overheating, the radar was ineffective below about 60 m, and there were some safety problems. Nevertheless, it was regarded with considerable respect by NATO aircrew and was considered to be a major threat to low-flying aircraft – particularly ground-attack types such as the US A-10, the British Harrier and all types of helicopter.

The US army developed a system known as the Sergeant York, which was similar in concept to the ZSU-23-4, using the chassis of the M48A5 tank, two standard L70 40 mm cannon, and a radar system developed from that installed in the F-16 fighter; the only totally new item was the turret. Development started in 1973, but, despite taking so many elements 'off the shelf', the project lasted for ten years and was dogged by difficulties, particularly in integrating the various systems, and costs escalated out of control. One of the consequences of the time taken was that by the early 1980s the threat had moved on, with the introduction into Soviet service of stand-off weapons for fighter-bombers and helicopters. The concept of the Sergeant York was to attack the aerial platform (i.e. the fighter-bomber or helicopter) rather than the stand-off missile, and in the end the gun system, with an effective range of 3,000 m, was perceived to be of limited value. This, coupled with the severity of the technical problems, resulted in its cancellation in 1985 after fifty production vehicles had been delivered.

Having cancelled the Sergeant York, the US army turned to SHORAD (Short-Range Air Defense), based on the French Roland missile; this entered service in very limited numbers. Next came the Air-Defence/Anti-

---

* ZSU = *Zenitnaia Samokhodnaia Ustanovka* (self-propelled, anti-aircraft gun); '23' denotes the calibre in millimetres; '4' indicates the number of barrels.

Tank System (ADATS), which was also cancelled. Thus by the end of the Cold War, and after some twenty years of development and very considerable expenditure, the US army still did not have an adequate short-range air-defence system.

TARGET ACQUISITION

Targets had to be identified, their nature and co-ordinates passed to the artillery command system, fire brought to bear, and the results assessed. The increasing range of artillery, however, made this a severe problem: the US M107 175 mm gun, for example, had a maximum range of 32.7 km, while the Lance artillery rocket reached out to 120 km. This meant that, whereas looking into enemy territory to a depth of 10–15 km had once been sufficient, it now became necessary to see up to 100 km or more. Also, the rapidity of movement across the modern battlefield meant that it became increasingly important to acquire targets such as concentrations of tanks in real time, if advantage was to be taken.

Front-line troops could acquire targets using optical methods, but were limited to the line of sight, which under central-European conditions could vary between 1 km and 5 km. Air reconnaissance by manned fighters was important but for many years depended upon the aircraft returning to base for films to be developed and for the prints to be passed to artillery HQs, which, however slick the processes became, involved an in-built delay. There were also other methods, such as monitoring enemy communications and using breaches of security, decryption or traffic analysis to obtain information on such factors as nodal points or artillery nets.

A solution which became increasingly widespread was the use of unmanned aerial vehicles (UAVs), which were directed either by an on-board computer programme (drones) or by a pilot on the ground sending directions via a radio link (remotely piloted vehicles (RPVs)). Such UAVs relied on their very small size, quiet engines and 'stealthy' construction to escape detection. Wide-scale use of such devices originated in the 1960s, when they were introduced into the Vietnam War and Israel. At first such devices simply brought back photographs of the targets they had been sent to look at, but later they became capable of transmitting photographs or TV pictures in real time, enabling them to be used to detect targets and also to send back spotting information, so that artillery staffs could assess the results of the fire mission and, if necessary, re-engage.

PART V

AIR WARFARE

28

NATO Air Forces

With the exception of strategic aircraft and some other elements which remained national preserves, the vast majority of NATO's operational air assets were organized into Allied Tactical Air Forces (ATAFs). Within these air forces there was a high degree of standardization and interoperability, although there was never a truly standard aircraft used by all the air forces, even though some aircraft almost achieved that status. The F-86 Sabre was widely used in the 1950s, for example, as was the F-4 Phantom in the 1970s and the F-16 in the 1980s, but never by all, and true standardization at this level remained a dream. Standardization was, however, achieved in such important areas as fuel, refuelling (both on the ground and air-to-air) and weapons attachments, but many problems remained: there was no standard machine-gun, for example.* Of equal, if not greater, importance was standardization in procedures, and here progress was much more marked, so that a German squadron could fly into and operate from a British base or a US squadron into an Italian base with equal ease on the operating side (although there could be some logistic difficulties).

This air-force standardization was strengthened by a process known as 'Tactical Evaluations' (Tacevals), in which a NATO team would arrive at an airbase and put the headquarters, squadrons, aircrews and support elements through a series of unannounced tests to ensure that they were up to the commonly agreed NATO tactical standards. This was a sternly applied and much respected system which, unfortunately, had no equivalent in the ground forces.

---

* Before condemning NATO for a lack of equipment standardization, it should be pointed out that many nations failed to achieve internal standardization. To give just two examples in the US forces: the navy and the Marine Corps used one type of ejector seat, the air force another, while in air-to-air refuelling the navy and the Marine Corps used probe-and-drogue and the air force the 'flying-boom' method.

One of the most dramatic examples of NATO air forces' ability to operate together was the NATO Airborne Early Warning Force (NAEWF) at Geilenkirchen. This force operated a fleet of Boeing E-3 AWACS aircraft and was totally multinational, operating entirely to NATO standards and procedures. The original charter laid down that, while the crews operating the AEW equipment and sensors in an aircraft were to be multinational, for 'safety reasons' the flight-deck crew (i.e. pilot, second pilot and flight engineer) all had to be from the same nation. In a telling indication of its multinationality, however, the NAEWF personnel themselves demanded that this rule be dropped, as being both unnecessary and divisive.

At a somewhat higher level, there was a constant struggle between land and air commanders. The land commanders wished to exert direct control over the deployment and tasking of their allocated air assets, whereas air commanders believed in what they regarded as the 'essential unity of air power' and required an exclusively air-force chain of command, with the land forces submitting tasking requests which would then be met, at their discretion, by the air forces, who would decide on the relative priorities.

In some ways the air-command structure was very flexible. A NATO air commander covered every area in the Central Region, and any air assets deployed to that area came under his command. Additional squadrons could therefore be flown in as required, without the need to deploy additional large headquarters, as was the case for ground forces.

CENTRAL REGION ORGANIZATION

When NATO was first established there were two headquarters within the Central Region: AFCENT and an air headquarters, designated AIRCENT. The latter was, however, disbanded when NATO headquarters was compelled to leave France in 1967, and when HQ AFCENT reopened at Brunssum in the Netherlands it subsumed both land and air functions, although it incorporated an air cell to provide co-ordination between the two Central Region tactical air forces. For the air forces this was a retrograde step, since, in their view, it removed the focal point for air matters and, despite the existence of the air cell, allowed disparities in doctrine and procedures to arise between the two ATAFs.

These air-force reservations, coupled with the introduction of the strategy of flexible response, led to one of NATO's many reviews, which resulted in the establishment of a new body – Headquarters Allied Air Forces Central Europe (HQ AAFCE). When the Military Committee agreed to this in mid-1973, it stipulated that AAFCE was to be an international headquarters commanded by a USAF officer, who would be responsible to CINCENT, and that it would be collocated with HQ AFCENT in both peace and war.

It was also agreed that the two ATAF commanders would be collocated with their respective army groups in both peace and war, but would be operationally responsible to Commander AAFCE.

HQ AAFCE was formally established in June 1974, but in an 'interim' headquarters at Ramstein in southern Germany, and not, as ordained by the Military Committee, with HQ AFCENT at Brunssum. One of the early improvements was the establishment of the Central Region Air Operations Centre (CRAOC) alongside AAFCE, with Allied Air Tactical Operations Centres (ATOCs) interposed in the air command chain between ATAFs and the airbases. Thus AAFCE and the ATAFs were responsible for overall planning and co-ordination, while the CRAOC and ATOCs were responsible for tactical planning and the execution of the resulting plans by bases, wings and squadrons.

The air situation over the Central Region involved six elements:

- Second Allied Tactical Air Force (2ATAF) comprised elements from the Belgian, British, Dutch, German and US air forces. Its peacetime headquarters was in Mönchengladbach in northern Germany, where it was collocated with NORTHAG headquarters. 2ATAF was commanded by a British four-star officer.

- Fourth Allied Tactical Air Force (4ATAF) was composed of elements of the Canadian, German and US air forces, with its headquarters in Ramstein in southern Germany. It was commanded by a US four-star officer.

- 2ATAF and 4ATAF were part of AFCENT and were in support of NORTHAG and CENTAG, respectively. As noted above, however, in order to achieve the air-force requirement for the 'unity of air power', a separate Headquarters Allied Air Forces Central Europe (HQ AAFCE) was established at Ramstein in southern Germany. Its commander was a US four-star officer.

- As with the ground forces, the Central Region air forces had a strong interest in events over the Baltic and the Jutland peninsula, but this was the province of Commander Air Baltic Approaches (COMAIRBALT-AP), who was responsible to Commander-in-Chief Northern Europe (CINCNORTH). COMAIRBALTAP air assets included the Danish air force, German air-force units stationed in Schleswig-Holstein, German naval air units committed to action in the Baltic, and British air-force units when deployed with the United Kingdom Mobile Force.

- Immediately in the rear of the Central Region was France, whose air forces were under national command. Despite the existence of a separate national command chain, however, there was considerable co-operation between France and the NATO air commands in peacetime, which would have been even closer in war.

- Also in the rear was the United Kingdom, which was the base for many US and UK aircraft committed to supporting the Central Region. The air defence of the British Isles (less Irish airspace, which was outside NATO) was originally an exclusively British national responsibility, but in April 1975 this area became NATO's UK Air Defence Region. Its commander was Commander-in-Chief UK Air Forces (CINCUKAIR), a British officer, with his headquarters at High Wycombe, to the west of London. The forces at his disposal were, however, exclusively provided by the British air force.

THE AIR FORCES

Belgium
The Belgian air force was totally committed to 2ATAF, to which it contributed fighters and ground-attack aircraft. Belgium was one of the NATO partners involved in the purchase of the Lockheed F-104 Starfighter, and was then one of the few NATO air forces to purchase French aircraft, acquiring 106 Dassault Mirage 5s in the late 1960s. Subsequently, it was one of the major partners in the F-16 programme. In the 1980s it fielded some 144 combat aircraft, a mixture of F-16 Fighting Falcons and Mirages.

Canada
In addition to its land contribution to the Central Region, Canada also provided an air group, which consisted of three fighter squadrons. In the 1960s the aircraft were CF-104 Starfighters (the Canadian version of the USAF's F-104 Starfighters); these were later replaced by the CF-116 (the Canadian-produced version of the F-5 Freedom Fighter) and finally by the CF-18 (the Canadian-produced F-18 Hornet).

Denmark
In war, virtually all Danish air assets would have been assigned to COMAIR-BALTAP. In the 1980s the Danish air force comprised four squadrons of F-16 Fighting Falcons (sixty aircraft) for air defence and ground attack. There were also two squadrons of the Swedish F35 Draken (thirty-four aircraft – the survivors of forty-six purchased in 1968–9), which were used for reconnaissance and ground attack. There were also small transport and air–sea rescue elements.

West Germany
Front-line equipment of the *Luftwaffe* went through four major stages. The first three generations were US aircraft – F-86 Sabres in the 1950s and 1960s, F-104 Starfighters in the 1960s and 1970s, and F-4 Phantoms in the

1970s – but these were followed by the Anglo-German-Italian Tornado in the 1980s. Front-line strength amounted to some 630 fixed-wing aircraft, which were split between 4ATAF in southern Germany, 2ATAF in northern Germany and COMAIRBALTAP in Schleswig-Holstein. One of the *Luftwaffe*'s main concerns was that its bases could be vulnerable to pre-emptive strikes by the Warsaw Pact, and its airfields were therefore sited as far to the west as was practicable.

The transport force was centred on some ninety C-160 Transall aircraft, which were built in a collaborative programme with France. Because the weather over West Germany was frequently poor and the skies were crowded with military and civil flights, all except the most basic flying training was conducted in the United States.

Luxembourg

The small Grand Duchy had no air force of its own, but was selected as the official country of registration for NAEWF. The aircraft were eighteen Boeing E-3A Sentries and three second-hand Boeing 707s used for crew training and transports, which were purchased between 1983 and 1985. Even though the aircraft were registered in Luxembourg, they were actually based in West Germany, at Geilenkirchen, and they also used forward operating bases in Greece, Italy, Norway and Turkey.

The Netherlands

Like those of Belgium, all Dutch operational aircraft, which in the late 1980s amounted to some 225 aircraft, were committed to 2ATAF. In the 1960s the Dutch acquired a large number of F-104 Starfighters, which were replaced in the 1980s by 213 F-16s. There was also a small transport force. All Dutch airbases were on national territory.

The UK

The majority of British air assets assigned to the defence of the Central Region was Royal Air Force (Germany) (RAF(G)), which, in war, became part of 2ATAF. Throughout the Cold War, RAF(G)'s tasks were long-range interdiction, air superiority, ground attack and reconnaissance. In the 1950s and 1960s its principal strength lay in its large number of Canberra squadrons, which carried nuclear weapons as part of SACEUR's deterrent force, and Hunter fighters, both of them British-built. In the 1970s and the early 1980s these were replaced by Buccaneer long-range strike aircraft and Phantom fighters, and from the mid-1980s by Tornados. RAF(G) was also the only land-based air force to deploy the Harrier V/STOL aircraft. Unlike in most other forces, the British army's transport helicopter support was provided by the air force, for which RAF(G) operated CH-47 Chinook and Puma helicopters.

By the 1980s RAF(G) comprised fourteen operational squadrons. There were six interdictor/strike squadrons (Tornado); one squadron (Tornado) which specialized in the suppression of enemy air defences (SEAD); two (Phantom) for air defence; one (Tornado) for reconnaissance; two (Harrier) for close-air support and two (one Chinook, one Puma) for helicopter support.

In war, additional UK-based RAF aircraft would have been available to the Central Region, including strike, airborne-early-warning and fighter aircraft, and two Harrier V/STOL squadrons were earmarked for Denmark.

Among the aircraft operated from the UK was the airborne-early-warning force, which for many years was provided by Shackleton aircraft. Powered by four piston engines, and essentially slightly updated versions of a Second World War bomber, these were totally inadequate for modern conditions. It was originally planned to replace them by a force of Nimrod AEW aircraft, but after lengthy development the Nimrod was abandoned, and Boeing E-3 Sentry AWACS aircraft were entering service as the Cold War ended.

The USA

United States air assets in Germany were commanded by the Seventeenth Air Force, with its headquarters at Sembach in southern Germany, its missions including air superiority, conventional and nuclear strike, suppression of enemy air defences, reconnaissance and electronic warfare. In the 1980s it comprised some 350 combat aircraft in four squadrons of F-15 air-superiority fighters;* three squadrons for SEAD (an equal mix of F-4s and F-16s); five squadrons in the tactical-fighter role (F-16s); two squadrons in the EW role (one with EF-111s,† one with EC-130s) and two reconnaissance squadrons (RF-4s).

In war, the Seventeenth Air Force would have received massive reinforcement from the continental USA and would also have received support from US aircraft based in the UK – mainly F-111s and A-10s, but again including many reinforcements from the USA. All of these came under the command of the Third Air Force at Mildenhall, England.

France

In accordance with national policy, the French air force made a very determined effort to use only French aircraft, unless there was no domestic alternative. This was successfully achieved, although some Boeing C-135FR

---

* One of these squadrons was based in the Netherlands and was under the operational control of the Dutch air force.
† Based in southern England.

tanker aircraft and E-3 Sentry AEW aircraft were purchased from the USA,* while others were developed in collaboration with European partners.†

The major part of French air strength was concentrated in the *Force Aérienne Tactique* (FATac), whose missions included destruction of enemy aircraft at their bases, offensive action in support of ground forces, and gathering intelligence. To achieve these tasks it consisted in 1984 of 322 front-line aircraft in five strike squadrons (Jaguar and Mirage III), ten ground-attack squadrons (Mirage III/Mirage 5 and Jaguar) and three reconnaissance squadrons (Mirage III/Mirage F1).

The air-defence command (*Commandement 'Air' des Forces de Défense Aérienne*) had twelve interceptor squadrons equipped with approximately 220 Mirage III and Mirage F1 fighters. These were tasked using data obtained from the French radar chain (STRIDA), which was linked into the NATO Air Defence Ground Environment (NADGE).

---

* The four E-3As did not arrive until after the end of the Cold War.
† Such collaborative projects included the SEPECAT Jaguar strike aircraft with the UK, and the Alphajet trainer and Transall transport with the FRG.

29

NATO Fighter and Attack Aircraft

As was to be expected in an alliance based on democracy and commercial opportunities, there was open competition in the very lucrative aircraft market, especially for fighters. Challenging the overwhelming industrial might of the United States was always a daunting experience, however, and was frequently both frustrating and very expensive too.

Quite by chance, the start of the Cold War coincided with the advent of the jet age, and competition between the Warsaw Pact and NATO spurred a frantic pace of advance in aircraft technology, as each side sought to achieve an advantage over the other. In the late 1940s all Western air forces were equipped with predominantly propeller-driven combat aircraft, but everyone understood very clearly that these had been outdated at a stroke by the invention of the turbojet engine. Among the Western powers, only two – the United States and the United Kingdom – had viable aircraft design and production facilities, but even for them the first priority was to dispose of their massive stocks of obsolescent and obsolete aircraft, to help pay for the state-of-the-art jet aircraft they needed for their own air forces. For both the US and the UK (as well as for the Soviets on the other side of the Iron Curtain) their existing wartime aircraft industries were a valuable starting point, although the wealth of research data they had captured from the Germans in 1945 was to prove of inestimable value.

FIGHTER AND ATTACK-AIRCRAFT DEVELOPMENT

The USA

The United States' first operational turbojet fighter was the straight-wing F-80 Shooting Star, deliveries of which started in 1945, just too late to see service in the Second World War. It had a maximum speed of about 950 km/h – little better than the last of the propeller-driven fighters – and survived long enough to become heavily involved in the early days of the Korean War. It was, however, quickly succeeded by the F-84 Thunderjet, also with a straight wing, but with a much higher performance. Some 3,600 of these were built, many of which were exported to NATO countries in the early 1950s.

Design of the first swept-wing interceptor, the F-86 Sabre, began in 1945, with the first prototype flying in 1946 and service deliveries starting in 1948 – a rate of progress that would have been inconceivable thirty years later. The F-86 was the most successful fighter of its day and, with a maximum speed of just over 1,000 km/h and armed with a mixture of guns and rockets, it proved superior to the Soviet MiG-15, which it met in combat in the skies over Korea. The F-86 also became widely used in NATO, being produced in Canada and Italy as well as the United States. Even the UK, which was suffering a delay in production of British-designed fighter aircraft, was forced to operate a number in the early 1950s. Also widely used at this time was the F-84F, which had been created by fitting swept wings to the F-84 Thunderjet, in place of the earlier straight wings; some 2,713 were built, again, many of them for NATO countries.

Meanwhile, intense efforts were being made to exceed the speed of sound, which was eventually achieved in October 1947. Thereafter numerous fighters were able to exceed Mach 1 in a dive, but in 1949 a programme was started to develop the first operational fighter capable of exceeding the speed of sound in level flight.

During the late 1940s the pace of these and many other development programmes both in the USA and the UK was as rapid as peacetime conditions allowed, but when the Korean War broke out, and in particular when the MiG-15 was encountered, all military programmes, especially those involving new technology, were greatly accelerated. The F-100 Supersabre programme was one of those affected; the first flight took place in May 1953, and production aircraft, which had a maximum speed of 1,390 km/h, began to reach squadrons in October of that year. Unfortunately, as happened in many of the programmes rushed through in the early 1950s, the aircraft hit snags and had to be grounded in November 1954 to enable major modifications to be carried out. By the time production ended, however, 2,294 had been produced and the type had been sold to several NATO air forces. It started to leave service in the mid-1960s, but remained with the US air force long enough to take part in the Vietnam War.

In the early 1950s there was rising concern in the USA that the Soviets were developing long-range bombers which would be capable of reaching the continental United States. This led to a requirement for a high-performance interceptor, and the resulting F-102 Delta Dagger became the only delta-winged fighter to operate with the USAF and the first to be designed as a 'weapon system', where the aircraft became relatively less important than the avionics that controlled it. Work started in 1952 and the first prototype flew in October 1953, when it exhibited very disappointing flying characteristics, leading to a total redesign. The revised design proved satisfactory and was placed in production, with 875 single-seat fighters and 63 two-seat trainers being delivered within twenty-one months.

The F-102 design was modernized to produce its replacement, the F-106 Delta Dart, which entered service in 1959, but only after further and lengthy development problems. Once these were solved the F-106 served as the continental USA's only manned interceptor, the last squadron standing down in 1991, exactly thirty years after production had ceased.

The McDonnell F-4 Phantom fighter was designed for the US navy and Marine Corps as a carrier-borne aircraft, but went on to become one of the most successful of all Cold War Western land-based fighters. The naval version first flew in 1958 and entered service in 1961; then, following its adoption by the USAF, the first land-based version flew in 1963. The F-4 was an outstanding design, with a maximum speed at altitude of 2,400 km/h (Mach 2.27) and a ceiling of approximately 20,000 m, outperforming not only other US fighters in the 1960s, but also the Soviet fighters it met over North Vietnam. At one stage production was running at a remarkable seventy-five aircraft per month, and the F-4 was used by numerous NATO air forces: 2,612 were delivered to the USAF, 263 to West Germany, 170 to the UK, 12 to Spain, and 8 each to Greece and Turkey (who both subsequently received a large number of surplus F-4s from West Germany).

During the course of the Cold War there were periodic revulsions against the seemingly inexorable increase in the complexity and cost of fighter aircraft. One outcome of such a feeling was the Northrop F-5 Freedom Fighter, which was designed as a simpler and cheaper, but nevertheless high-performance, alternative. It was funded by the company and first flew in 1959, but it attracted only a relatively few orders from the US air force. Despite this, the type sold well overseas, including to several NATO air forces.

The General Dynamics F-111 started life as the TFX (Tactical Fighter, Experimental) programme in an effort to produce a long-range, high-performance attack aircraft which would meet the needs of the US navy, Marine Corps and air force, and which would also, it was hoped, obtain large overseas orders. The key design feature of the F-111 was its swing wing, and the programme started in 1960, with the first flight in 1964 and initial service delivery in 1967. From the start, however, the programme was beset by problems, which ranged from excessive aerodynamic drag, through ever-escalating weight and cost, to inter-service rivalry. The problems were eventually overcome, and the F-111 fighter and the FB-111 strategic-bomber version became very successful and capable aircraft, although they were only ever purchased by the air force. The FB-111 was also due to have been ordered by the British air force in place of the abandoned TSR-2 (see below), but this order was cancelled and the only overseas order was for twenty-four from Australia.

Another 1960s aircraft, the A-7 Corsair II light attack aircraft, was designed for carrier operations with the US navy and Marine Corps, but then, like the F-4 Phantom, it was adopted by the air force as well. The first flight was in 1965, and the Corsair II showed a realization that supersonic performance was not necessary for a tactical fighter. The type also served with other NATO air forces, Greece purchasing sixty-five and Portugal twenty.

The Fairchild A-10 Thunderbolt was designed to meet a USAF requirement (known as 'AX') for a highly capable but low-cost ground-attack aircraft, which would provide a very heavy 'punch' enabling it to destroy large numbers of Warsaw Pact tanks. This necessitated an extremely strong airframe and armoured protection for the pilot, to enable both to survive at low altitude above the European battlefield. The aircraft was also required to operate from and be maintained at forward bases with limited facilities. Having won the AX competitive fly-off, the A-10 was placed in production and entered service in 1977, with a total of 707 being produced, all for the USAF; there were no export orders. Main armament was a seven-barrelled 30 mm gun, plus 7,247 kg of ordnance on eleven pylons.

The F-15 Eagle air-superiority fighter was the successor to the F-4 Phantom, with the first flight in 1972 and service delivery in 1974, following which the type served as the main USAF fighter for the remainder of the Cold War and beyond. With a maximum speed of 2,655 km/h (Mach 2.5), it climbed to 15,240 m in 2.5 minutes and, while it was an outstanding interceptor fighter, it was also adapted to the attack mission. The aircraft and its back-up systems were, however, so expensive that no NATO orders were forthcoming.

Yet another attempt was made to reduce the costs of fighter aircraft in the late 1960s, this time with considerable success, as the outcome was the General Dynamics F-16 Fighting Falcon. This started life as the YF-16 lightweight fighter for the US air force, but it was then developed by the company and proved so sound a design that it quickly evolved, first into a 'no-frills' interceptor, and subsequently into a very effective multi-role fighter. It was ordered for the US air force in 1975, with 2,795 being delivered; others, as described below, were ordered by other NATO countries. The F-16 was armed with a 20 mm Vulcan cannon and carried 5,420 kg of ordnance if the aircraft was to be manoeuvred at its maximum of 9g, but an even greater load was possible if restrictions on manoeuvrability were imposed.

Canada

In 1944 Canada became one of the earliest countries to start work on turbo-jets, and in March 1947 detailed design began on a large, long-range, twin-turbojet interceptor. Designated CF-100, the first prototype flew in 1950 and some 670 aircraft were then built for the Canadian air force, with deliveries starting in 1952. The CF-100 had a maximum speed of 1,060 km/h and a range of some 4,000 km, making it an exceptional aircraft for its time.

Experience with the CF-100 encouraged the Canadian air force and industry to develop an even more ambitious design, the CF-105 Arrow, which, like the CF-100, was a very large, twin-engined, twin-seat interceptor, but this time with delta wings. The first of five prototypes flew in 1958 and immediately demonstrated a very high performance; the production model would have had a maximum speed of 2,100 km/h and a ceiling of 18,300 m, which, with its advanced avionics, placed it ahead of any contemporary Western aircraft in its field.

By early 1959 the programme was going well, with $C300 million already spent and an estimated $C200 million required for completion; anticipated unit cost was $C3.7 million per aircraft. Then, in late February 1959, the Canadian government announced the immediate cancellation of the programme; all aircraft, jigs and tools were immediately destroyed, and some 14,000 workers were laid off. The reason for this sudden change of course, which was a devastating blow to the Canadian aircraft industry, was given as the disappearance of the need for manned interceptors in the missile era.

Such an explanation seemed somewhat hollow (to say the least) when, just two years later, the Canadian air force placed an order for sixty-six US-designed McDonnell F-101 Voodoo twin-seat interceptors, which were built in Canada as the CF-101. Since that time, apart from some Canadian-designed light transports, virtually all aircraft built in Canada have been licence-built US designs.

The UK

At the start of the Cold War the UK was second only to the USA as an aviation power, and considerable resources were lavished on the aircraft industry's survival. The British actually developed a turbojet engine before the USA, and the Gloster Meteor twin-jet fighter entered service in 1944, followed by the de Havilland Vampire single-jet fighter in 1946, both of which were exported to several NATO air arms in the late 1940s and early 1950s.

The Meteor and Vampire then provided the backbone of the British air force's fighter force for a decade, while a series of swept-wing designs was developed, culminating in the Hawker Hunter, which entered service, after lengthy delays, in 1957. Once its problems had been resolved it proved to be an effective and popular interceptor and ground-attack aircraft, and a total of 1,525 were manufactured in the UK and a further 381 in Belgium (192) and the Netherlands (189). Thirty Hunters were exported direct to Denmark, and many more to non-NATO countries.

In the 1950s the British judged the major air threat to the UK to be from high-flying Soviet bombers armed with atomic weapons, for which the answer was an extremely fast-climbing, short-range interceptor. Several different prototypes were built and tested, but the English Electric Lightning was selected; this could reach 12,000 m in under 2.5 minutes, and had a ceiling of 18,000 m. It was originally armed with both air-to-air missiles and cannon, but the latter were deleted in later marks. The Lightning entered service with the British air force in 1961 and was deployed in both the UK and Germany, but, although popular with its pilots, it was not bought by any other NATO nation.

In March 1957 the British Air Staff produced an operational requirement for a new aircraft to replace the Canberra, which was in service in large numbers as the air force's standard light bomber. The aircraft, designated TSR-2 (TSR = tactical strike/reconnaissance), was to be an all-weather, autonomous aircraft, capable of operating at high subsonic speed at very low level, the number required being 138. Numerous initial bids were received, including one, which was rejected out of hand, from Blackburn Ltd for a land-based version of the Buccaneer carrier-based bomber, then under development for the British navy. In 1960 a development contract was awarded to the newly formed British Aircraft Corporation. In 1962 the total programme cost was estimated at £220 million, but this had risen to £272 million in October 1964 and to an extraordinary £750 million in April 1965, when the recently elected Labour government cancelled the entire project. A further echo of the Canadian CF-105 debacle was that all jigs and tools were destroyed, although, as a result of subterfuge, one aircraft survived.

A provisional order was then placed for the American F-111, but this too was cancelled, in January 1968. The yawning gap in air-force capabilities was then filled in two ways. To meet the tactical-fighter requirement, orders were placed for the F-4 Phantom. For the long-range-interdiction, Canberra-replacement role, the Buccaneer (which had been so summarily rejected twelve years previously) was selected as the 'interim' solution, while the long-term requirement would be met by a totally new Multi-Role Combat Aircraft (MRCA), which eventually became the Tornado. The TSR-2 was, however, to be the last major British national project, and the MRCA was planned from the outset as a multinational collaborative programme.

France

The French aviation industry made a quite remarkable recovery following the Second World War, and after a decade during which the air force had to depend on US and British aircraft the French air force has been equipped with French or French-led collaborative designs. French designs included the very successful Mystère and Mirage fighters, while collaborative programmes included the Jaguar with the British and the Transall transport and the Alphajet trainer with West Germany.

INTERNATIONAL CO-OPERATION

Some NATO countries had no history of aircraft design and production, and did not wish to establish such a capability during the Cold War; they were therefore content to place orders with the USA or other European countries for existing designs. Such countries included Denmark, Norway and Portugal, and also West Germany until it had re-established its own aircraft industry. For those that wished either to maintain an existing domestic capability or to set up a new one, however, the design, development and production of advanced fighter aircraft became prohibitively expensive on a domestic basis, leaving two possible choices: one was to produce a foreign design under licence; the other was to collaborate with one or more other countries to design and develop a new aircraft.

Production under Licence

One of the earliest co-production deals concerned the British Hawker Hunter fighter, 445 of which were manufactured in Belgium and the Netherlands for their respective air forces in the late 1950s.

The next major licence-production project concerned the Lockheed F-104 Starfighter, which first flew in 1954 and which, despite having been bought in small numbers by the USAF and regarded by it as too dangerous, went on to become very important to NATO. The F-104 was designed to maximize performance, and, with a top speed of 2,330 km/h and a ceiling of 17,680 m (27,400 m in a 'zoom'), it certainly achieved that. Unfortunately, it did so by having a long body and two tiny, very thin wings, resulting in an aircraft which, by the standards of the day, was hard to fly and 'hot' (i.e. fast) on landing. Despite this, a NATO production programme was set up, which involved factories in Belgium, Canada, Germany, Italy and the Netherlands. Between them these factories produced no less than 1,445 aircraft for service with NATO air forces: Belgium 101, Canada 200, Denmark 40, Germany 749, Greece 45, Italy 125, the Netherlands 120, Norway 19 and Turkey 46. In its early years the difficult handling and a number of accidents gave the F-104 a bad reputation, and what appeared to be excessive losses became a matter of major public concern, especially in the *Luftwaffe*. In its later years, however, the F-104 had an accident rate no worse than any other type.

The Northrop F-5 Freedom Fighter was built under licence in Canada as the CF-5 for the Canadian forces (240 built) and as the NF-5 for the Dutch air force (102 built). The types entered service with Canada in 1968 and in the Netherlands in 1969.

Apart from being purchased in large numbers by the USAF, the General Dynamics F-16 was also selected by a consortium of European air arms in what was termed the 'sale of the century', which led to additional production lines being established in Belgium and the Netherlands. Deliveries were Belgium 128, Denmark 70, the Netherlands 100 and Norway 42. The USAF and these four European air forces subsequently co-operated in the F-16 Operational Capabilities Upgrade (OCU) programme in the 1980s, which resulted in much improved avionics, electronics and weapons fits.

Multinational Collaboration
The second path was multinational collaboration in design and development, as well as in production, sometimes under the auspices of NATO, but sometimes as a government-to-government deal in which NATO had little or no involvement. One of the early attempts at a common solution to a NATO problem was the competition announced in December 1953 for a light attack aircraft, in which all continental European air forces had expressed an interest. There were three entries from France and one from Italy, but when the latter was judged the winner the French withdrew from the entire project. In the event, all but two air forces withdrew, and the Italian entry, the Fiat G91, was ordered only by the Italian (174) and German (438) air forces, with manufacture taking place in both countries.

The Jaguar was an Anglo-French project to produce a dual-role tactical-support aircraft and advanced trainer, although, in the event, only a few two-seat aircraft were produced and the majority were strike aircraft. The first flight was in 1968, and each country purchased 200 aircraft.

One of the most successful military collaborative programmes was the Panavia Tornado (originally known as the Multi-Role Combat Aircraft (MRCA)), which was produced by a consortium comprising British Aircraft Corporation (42.5 per cent), Messerschmitt-Bolkow-Blohm (42.5 per cent) and Aeritalia (15 percent).* The engine was also a collaborative effort between Rolls-Royce (UK; 40 per cent), MTU (Germany; 40 per cent) and Fiat (20 per cent). The project began in 1968, the first prototype flew in 1974, and the aircraft entered service in 1982. The basic swing-wing multi-role aircraft (the Tornado IDS – i.e. interdictor/strike) was designed to conduct attack, interdiction and reconnaissance missions, but there were also two specialized versions: one for electronic combat and reconnaissance

---

* These firms were the forerunners of the contemporary British Aerospace (BAe), Daimler-Benz Aerospace and Alenia, respectively. Belgium, Canada and the Netherlands also took part in the initial feasibility study. The first two did not join the consortium set up in March 1969, while the Dutch did, but then withdrew in July 1969.

(ECR), the other an air-defence (i.e. fighter) version (ADV). Production totalled 929 – 697 IDS, 35 ECR and 195 ADV – all of which went to the air forces, except for 112 of the IDS version which went to the German navy. Collaboration in design and production was mirrored in other fields, with the aircrew being trained at a trinational unit in the UK, while logistics support was controlled by the NATO MRCA Maintenance Agency (NAMMA). Although the programme was not without its complications, overall it was a major success, proving that European nations could co-operate on a very advanced technical project. The aircraft demonstrated its combat capabilities in the Gulf War, showing an unrivalled ability to carry a huge range of underwing stores and to fly at high speed at very low levels.

The Two-Way Street

Although the US imported or manufactured under licence a wide range of aircraft components and engines, there were only two major examples of European aircraft being adopted by the US armed forces – both of them British. The English Electric Canberra, which first flew in 1949, was a very successful twin-engined light bomber which was produced in large numbers for the British air force. It was also adopted by the USAF as the B-57, becoming the first foreign aircraft to be procured in large numbers since 1918: 403 were manufactured under licence by the Martin company.

The other example was the British Aerospace Harrier V/STOL fighter, which used a turbojet with rotating nozzles to achieve vertical/short take-off and landing. The original prototype (designated P.1127) first flew in 1960, and a trinational (German, UK, US) air-force squadron was established to ascertain the potential of this revolutionary concept. In the event neither the German nor the US air forces placed an order, but a completely redesigned aircraft was then adopted by the British air force, with a prototype flying in 1967 and service entry as the Harrier GR.Mk 1 in 1969. The US Marine Corps became interested in the type in 1968, and this was followed by an initial order for twelve. The type was then manufactured under licence as the AV-8A by McDonnell Douglas in the United States. Later McDonnell Douglas became the leading partner in development of the AV-8B, which was procured in large numbers by the US Marine Corps and in smaller numbers by the British air force and the Italian and Spanish navies.

The US armed forces have placed other, but much smaller, orders for non-US aircraft. The largest of these orders concerned the series of light, rugged, short take-off and landing (STOL) aircraft produced by de Havilland of Canada, including 959 single-engined L-20 Beavers, 202 of the larger, single-engined U-1 Otter and 10 of the twin-engined Twin Otter. The US army also bought 159 of the twin-engined, thirty-two-passenger CV-2 Caribou, but these had to handed over to the USAF in 1967 when the latter took responsibility for large fixed-wing aircraft. The US army also helped to pay for development of the larger UC-8 Buffalo, but, because of the deal with the USAF, no orders were forthcoming. Later de Havilland STOL types were bought by the US armed forces, but only in very small numbers: three DHC-7 'Dash Seven' by the US army, and two DHC-8 'Dash Eight' by the USAF. Other US purchases from NATO partners included twenty-eight British Short C-23s for the US army and National Guard, and ten Italian Alenia G.222 twin-engined C-27A transports for the USAF.

CONCLUSION

Aircraft development proceeded at a frantic pace throughout the Cold War, as Western air forces sought to retain what was thought to be a technological lead over the Warsaw Pact. As a result, many new fighter and light-bomber designs appeared, although by no means all of them entered service.

There were two significant changes during the period. The first of these was that, whereas in the 1940s and 1950s the aircraft and its engines had been the most glamorous and expensive part of the package, from the 1960s onwards the airframe simply became a carrier for a complex package of avionics and electronics. The cost of the latter represented by far the largest proportion of the overall package.

A further factor was that in the 1940s and 1950s the time from concept to service entry was very short, even though the designs were pushing contemporary technology to its limits. The F-86 Sabre, for example, took just three years from conception to realization. That compares well with the seven years it took to get the F-111 into service, and over ten years for the F-15. On the other hand, the F-86 was in front-line service with the US air force for less than ten years, while the F-111 and F-15 had served for twenty-three and fourteen years respectively by the time the Cold War ended, and had many years to go after that.

30

Warsaw Pact Air Forces

The Soviet aircraft industry produced some remarkable aircraft during the Cold War, and its products were watched with special intensity by Western intelligence agencies and media. The early development of such aircraft was always shrouded in mystery, and first vague reports were usually followed by very blurred and heavily retouched photographs. The first firm indications of the shape and performance then came either when the type entered service with 16th Air Army in East Germany or when it appeared at one of the rare Soviet air displays. In the 1980s, however, the US government took to publishing blurred photographs taken from satellites, showing new proto-types on the flight line at testing centres such as Ramenskoye.

The early revelations were always accompanied by speculative articles in the Western technical and defence press, usually overestimating the type's performance and its significance to the West. The first reliable assessment of a new type's performance came only when it was exported or used in a war somewhere in Asia, Africa or the Middle East, where it could be compared against Western aircraft. Not infrequently this resulted in a reversal of the earlier assessment, with the aircraft's performance and capability then being undervalued, although this was often because the aircraft was being flown by less highly skilled pilots and with a less effective ground-control system than would have been available in a war on the Central Front.* A further factor was that export aircraft were frequently equipped to a lower standard, especially in radar and electronic countermeasures, than were Soviet air-force versions.

---

* Western pilots flew many Soviet aircraft following the end of the Cold War. In general, their comments were that reliability and serviceability were poorer than had been thought in the West, but performance and capability were much better. The German *Luftwaffe*, for example, initially decided to sell the MiG-29s it inherited from the East German air force, but once it had taken full measure of their capabilities (and had solved the maintenance problems) it decided to retain them.

In contrast to the numerous manufacturers on the NATO side, tactical aircraft flown by the Soviet and other Warsaw Pact air forces were the products of just two design bureaux, both in the Soviet Union.* The better known – at least in the early days of the Cold War – was the Mikoyan and Gurevich (MiG) bureau, whose name first achieved international prominence when the MiG-15 fighter burst on the scene in the Korean War. The first major jet-powered attack aircraft of significance to NATO, however, was the MiG-17 (NATO = 'Fresco') which entered service in the mid-1950s and carried a 500 kg bombload over a combat radius of some 700 km. Next came the MiG-21 (NATO = 'Fishbed'), although the original versions were air-superiority fighters. The later MiG-21bis had a ground-attack capability, enabling it to deliver a 2,000 kg payload over a radius of some 700 km. Whereas the MiG-17 and the MiG-21 were air-superiority fighters with a secondary ground-attack capability, however, the swing-wing MiG-27 (NATO = 'Flogger') was designed specifically for the ground-attack mission, being capable of carrying a 4,000 kg load over a 540 km radius on a 'lo-lo-lo' (low level out, low level over the target, low level back) mission profile.

The second design bureau, named Sukhoi, produced some excellent aircraft. The Sukhoi Su-7 (NATO = 'Fitter') entered service in the late 1960s and was capable of delivering a 2,500 kg load, but over a radius of only 350 km, although when the aircraft was fitted with swing wings and redesignated Su-17M (NATO = 'Fitter C') this was increased to some 685 km with a 2,000 kg payload. The next to appear was a totally new design, the Sukhoi Su-24 (NATO = 'Fencer'), which entered service in 1974 and was one of the finest attack aircraft of its era, being capable of delivering an 8,000 kg ordnance load to any target in the Central Region, including most of Spain and all but a very small part of the United Kingdom.

A totally different design was the Sukhoi Su-25 (NATO = 'Frogfoot'), with high speed and agility providing protection, although the pilot also sat in a titanium-protected cockpit. The Su-25 carried a 4,000 kg load of bombs and rockets, and entered service in time to be committed to the war in Afghanistan in 1981. It would undoubtedly have given a good account of itself in an attack on the Central Front.

The Soviet air force's Frontal Aviation command and most other Warsaw Pact air forces also used the Mil Mi-24 (NATO = 'Hind') series of attack helicopters, which again showed the difference between Soviet and Western approaches to equipment development. In the West the tendency was to develop totally new equipment, but the Soviets took the engines, drive system and main rotor of the well-tried Mil Mi-8 transport helicopter and

---

* Not all Warsaw Pact aircraft were of Soviet design. All Pact air forces used the Czech L-29 Delfin trainer, for example.

married them to a new fuselage. A new tail rotor and stub wings of the type used on the Mil Mi-6 completed what was to become an extremely effective combat helicopter, which established a fearsome reputation in Afghanistan.

Apart from the aircraft themselves, the Soviets also developed a wide range of aircraft weapons. Further, the all-weather capability improved dramatically too, as did the offensive and defensive ECM capabilities.

Dramatic improvements were also made to the Warsaw Pact air defences – the ability to resist NATO offensive air operations. The SAM systems in the non-Soviet Warsaw Pact countries and the western military districts of the Soviet Union grew rapidly in both numbers and sophistication over the years, as did the air-defence fighters.

THE SOVIET AIR FORCE

Like most organizations on both sides in the Cold War, the Soviet air force changed its internal organization over time. For the greater part of the Cold War, however, it consisted of five operational commands: Frontal Aviation, Long-Range Aviation, Air Transport, Fighter Aviation and Naval Aviation. The most significant of these to the Central European battlefield was Frontal Aviation (*Frontovaya Aviatsiya*), which, in the latter half of the Cold War, was equipped with some 5,000 aircraft, of which approximately 4,000 were in eastern Europe facing NATO. Frontal Aviation's specific roles were:

- attacking targets to about 400 km into hostile territory;
- low-altitude interdiction;
- counter-air operations in order to achieve air superiority;
- air cover over ground troops and for airborne operations;
- air reconnaissance by visual, photographic and electronic means;
- tactical airlifting of troops and cargo.

Soviet doctrine ensured that there was the closest possible co-operation between ground and air forces, with air-force representation at frontal and divisional level. Air strikes were considered to be an extension of the artillery fire plan, with priority being placed on command posts, tactical nuclear-delivery systems, communications systems, and neutralization of enemy artillery systems. A particular priority was to undertake pre-emptive strikes against enemy nuclear-delivery systems when it appeared probable that they were about to launch a nuclear strike of their own. In the counter-air battle, enemy airfields would have been the highest-priority targets. At all levels commanders of Frontal Aviation and air-defence forces were collocated to ensure that the two systems were always in co-operation and not in conflict.

Frontal Aviation was organized into tactical air armies of varying sizes, depending upon their strategic importance. The majority were deployed in eastern Europe, with each of the western military districts having its own air army, as did each of the four groups of Soviet forces in the Warsaw Pact countries. By far the most powerful, however, was the 16th Tactical Air Army, which was stationed in East Germany as part of GSFG.

A tactical air army was normally composed of a fighter division and a fighter-bomber division (each subdivided into regiments and squadrons, each of four flights of four aircraft), an independent reconnaissance regiment and a helicopter regiment. The 16th Tactical Air Army was, however, much larger, and in the mid-1980s it comprised one fighter division, two fighter-bomber divisions and two mixed fighter/fighter-bomber divisions, all of three regiments each, plus five helicopter assault regiments, three reconnaissance regiments and two aviation transport regiments. In the late 1980s these totalled some 900 fixed-wing aircraft and 400 helicopters.

Large Soviet air assets were also stationed in other Warsaw Pact countries in peacetime. Soviet elements in Czechoslovakia before 1968 were small, but following the invasion they grew rapidly and in the 1980s comprised a fighter regiment, an interdiction regiment and a ground-attack regiment, plus five helicopter regiments.

Soviet air units in Hungary were part of the Southern Group of Forces and consisted of three fighter regiments, a ground-attack regiment and two helicopter regiments.

Soviet air-force elements stationed in Poland were allocated to the Northern Group of Forces and had a particularly important task in protecting the Soviet lines of communication and providing air cover for Soviet troops moving forward into East Germany. The forces included one fighter division (three regiments), an independent attack regiment, a reconnaissance regiment and two helicopter regiments. In addition, there were two regiments of Su-24 interdictors, part of the 24th Tactical Air Army, whose missions were long-range attacks on targets in western Europe.

OTHER WARSAW PACT AIR FORCES

Czechoslovakia
The Czechoslovak air force was usually the first of the non-Soviet air forces to receive the most modern Soviet equipment. The 10th Tactical Air Army consisted of two air divisions equipped with fighters and fighter-bombers, one reconnaissance regiment (three squadrons), five helicopter regiments (three squadrons) and a transport regiment. The 7th Air Army was responsible for air defence and consisted of three missile divisions, each of two regiments, plus two fighter divisions, each of three fighter regiments (eighteen squadrons).

Hungary

Hungary maintained an air force that was somewhat different to others in the Warsaw Pact, as it was not independent but was an integral part of the army. The air-defence element consisted of three fighter and three SAM regiments, while the limited tactical element consisted of two ground-attack regiments (reduced to one in 1980) and one reconnaissance regiment. The air force also operated one regiment of helicopters.

East Germany

The East German air force was wholly committed to operations as tasked by the Soviet 16th Tactical Air Army in support of the combined Soviet and East German ground forces. It comprised two air divisions, one with two fighter/ground-attack regiments, the other with three, each regiment having three ten-aircraft squadrons. There were also two reconnaissance squadrons, a transport regiment and three helicopter regiments. Air-defence elements comprised seven SAM regiments. All equipment came from the Soviet Union, except that all trainer aircraft were of Czech origin.

Poland

Poland maintained the largest Warsaw Pact air force outside the Soviet Union, comprising three fighter-bomber divisions (eighteen squadrons), two reconnaissance regiments (six squadrons), two transport regiments and three helicopter regiments. For many years the National Air Defence Force was a separate service and co-operated extremely closely with the Soviet air force in the air defence of the Soviet lines of communication between the USSR and the forward elements in East Germany. In the late 1980s, however, the Air Defence Force was integrated into the air force, while remaining organized into three air-defence corps (one to each Polish military district), each of one air-defence division (three fighter regiments) and one SAM division. All front-line aircraft were of Soviet design, but Polish and Czech trainers and some Polish helicopters were also used.

PART VI

THE MAJOR ISSUES

31

The Mechanics of Going to War

One of the greatest problems facing NATO was that, as a defensive alliance, it could only *react* to Warsaw Pact aggression or threat of aggression. Of necessity, it required time to implement the many measures required to bring its forces and individual member nations on to a war footing. Thus there was a heavy dependence upon accurate and timely strategic warning which would indicate that Warsaw Pact offensive operations were imminent, and upon which firm decisions could be made to set the mobilization process in train.

Such strategic warning depended upon intelligence staffs receiving clues, which could have come from satellites, electronic intelligence (ELINT), airborne sensors, political analysis, covert or overt human intelligence (HUMINT) sources, or the ever-inquisitive media. Receipt of such warning signals was, however, insufficient in itself, and adequate strategic warning also required correct interpretation (i.e. translating information into intelligence) and, once that had been made, a determination to take action.

The outbreak of the Yom Kippur War on 6 October 1973 was one of several lessons to NATO about what could go wrong. Before the invasion that began the war, many strategic surveillance systems had been focused on the Middle East, and military, political and media interest in the area were intense. Despite all of these, the Egyptians, Jordanians and Syrians managed not only to co-ordinate their plans but also to conduct preliminary moves, involving large numbers of men and a great deal of equipment, without causing undue alarm in either Israel or the United States. When the attack came, at 1400 hours on 6 October, it achieved both strategic and tactical surprise, and was a brilliant military success, with Egyptian troops pouring across the Suez Canal to eliminate the Israeli strongpoints. The Egyptians then withstood a succession of armoured counter-attacks, during which they achieved a further tactical surprise by employing a combination of artillery, heavy anti-tank guided weapons and RPG-7 hand-held anti-tank weapons, which, in combination, completely halted these counter-attacks until the Israelis had devised methods of dealing with this new threat.

That the Israelis then managed to turn the tables on the Arab forces is not of great relevance here; the inescapable fact was that the Egyptians had achieved a masterly surprise, and, if that could be achieved in the Middle East, it was clear that it might also happen in central Europe. What was more, the Arabs had used essentially Soviet methods, as expounded publicly by Marshal Sokolovskiy, which can be summarized as being intended to mislead the enemy commanders by developing attacks in the least expected direction, concealing moves to prepare for the offensive, and deceiving the enemy with regard to the time, place and strength of the attack.[1] These tactics were not original, however, but were originally postulated by the Chinese strategist Sun Tzu, who wrote in about 500 BC that 'all warfare is based on deception . . . offer the enemy a bait to lure him; feign disorder and strike him . . . attack when he is unprepared; sally out when he does not expect you'.[2]

Before the Yom Kippur War, NATO planners had assumed that they would receive adequate warning of a lengthy Warsaw Pact process of mobilization. The lessons of Yom Kippur, however, coupled with the increasing strength and readiness of Warsaw Pact forces, meant that a surprise attack using in-place forces appeared to be a distinct possibility.

THE NATO ALERT BOOK

The essential requirement for NATO was that, should an attack have appeared imminent, the Alliance had to bring its military forces and member nations to a state of war in an orderly manner, at similar speeds, and in time for their armed forces to occupy the planned deployment positions from which they would repel the invaders. This would have been achieved by means of the NATO Alert System, which was codified in the 'Alert Book'.[3]

The Alert Book set out a number of 'readiness states', each broken down into a number of discrete 'measures', each of which was carefully described. These measures could be 'called' either individually or in groups, and, under normal circumstances, the calling of a higher readiness state meant that any outstanding measures from the previous, lower, state would automatically be implemented. As always in NATO, however, nations retained certain rights, and many measures were subject to national caveats. These procedures were routinely tested, particularly during exercises known as 'FALLEX' and 'CIMEX', and were progressively refined during the years of the Cold War.*

---

* FALLEX = Fall [i.e. Autumn] Exercise; CIMEX = Civil/Military Exercise. Both were normally suffixed by the year – e.g. FALLEX84.

Military Vigilance (MV)

The lowest alert state was Military Vigilance, which was designed to be called in a period of low-level but increasing tension. It was intended to be applied by major NATO commanders (MNCs) to assigned forces without prior reference to the North Atlantic Council or to governments, although these would of course have been informed that it had been called. It consisted of a number of precautionary military measures which were estimated to have neither economic nor political effects, and which could be maintained for a protracted period without serious effects on individuals or units. Measures to be called could have included some or all of: manning war headquarters with skeleton staffs, activating reserved communications circuits,* rechecking mobilization plans, covert reconnaissance of planned emergency dispersal sites, and conducting readiness exercises. These were all aimed at making it easier for NATO's military forces to move rapidly into the first of the formal alert states, Simple Alert.

The Formal Alert System

The Formal Alert System consisted of a set of three progressive states, which were designed to provide increasing readiness in a period of rising tension, to ensure an orderly transition from peace to war, and to ensure the survival of NATO forces. Each state contained a series of measures:

- *Simple Alert* placed 'assigned' forces (i.e. those firmly promised to NATO in time of war) at combat readiness, and advised nations to place 'earmarked' forces (i.e. those promised subject to provisos) at maximum readiness for war. Under normal circumstances, Simple Alert could be called by MNCs only after they had obtained approval from governments through their permanent representatives to the North Atlantic Council. In the case of a sudden emergency, however, such as intelligence of an imminent attack by the Warsaw Pact, the MNC could call Simple Alert on his own authority, provided previous authority to do so had been given by the governments concerned.
- *Reinforced Alert* brought all NATO forces to the highest possible degree of readiness, and was normally the signal for operational command of 'earmarked' forces to be transferred to the MNC. Reinforced Alert would normally be called by the North Atlantic Council, but, in urgent cases, could be called by the MNC in consultation with the governments immediately affected.
- *General Alert* meant that hostilities had either commenced or were

---

* Reserved circuits were those which had been identified for NATO use and pre-booked with national telecommunications authorities (e.g. *Deutsches Bundespost* (the German Federal Telecommunications Authority)) for activation in a crisis.

321

immediately imminent, although (at least in theory) it could have been called in a period of tension. General Alert was also the signal for MNCs to implement their emergency deployment plans if these had not already been implemented under a previous measure.

Within these three alert states there was a host of measures, which were placed, by agreement between the MNCs and individual governments, in one of four categories:

- Category 1. MNCs could order a Category-1 measure with or without the related alert stage having been called.
- Category 2. Governments agreed to MNCs implementing such measures once the appropriate alert stage had been called with their approval.
- Category 3. Governments reserved the decision to execute the measure, either wholly or in part, even though the related alert stage had been called.
- Category 4. Such measures did not apply to the government concerned.

In the 'tripwire' era, the alert states automatically included the whole of NATO, but with the advent of flexible response the system was amended so that an MNC could call General Alert either throughout his command or only in specified areas.

Counter-Surprise

The alert system was designed to cope with discernible increases in tension, but there was clearly a danger of a situation where the Warsaw Pact attacked with such suddenness that the Formal Alert System could not have been implemented in time. To cope with this a 'Counter-Surprise' system was devised, which enabled MNCs to take 'crash' action if their forces were actually under attack or where an attack was clearly imminent within hours.

There were a number of possible scenarios. One was where Warsaw Pact forces were on a large-scale exercise close to the Inner German Border and then suddenly started to advance towards a NATO country. Another was where military forces were taking part in 'internal action' against a member of the Pact and then swung to invade NATO territory. The latter could have arisen in 1968 when, following the invasion of Czechoslovakia, a number of Soviet and East German divisions suddenly swung westward and advanced to within a few kilometres of the Czechoslovak–West German border.

Counter-Surprise consisted of two states: State Orange, based on a possible attack within hours, and State Scarlet, which would have been called when under actual attack or with an attack expected in less than an hour. In the early days, even when either of these states had been called, the MNC still had to wait for Reinforced Alert to be called before he obtained operational command of his assigned forces, but from 1964 such command was transferred automatically on the calling of either state.

Issues

The alert system highlighted a number of significant issues and was the subject of repeated negotiations between NATO commanders and national governments. From the national point of view, no government wished to give up its authority to take steps to protect its own national interests. To protect this authority, few forces were under NATO's operational command in peacetime, being either firmly promised in time of war ('assigned' forces) or promised with provisos ('earmarked' forces). On the other hand, NATO commanders wanted to assume operational command of forces, particularly the assigned forces, as early as possible during the transition-to-war process. The transfer of authority (known colloquially as 'chopping') was originally specified for Reinforced Alert but was later reduced to Simple Alert, although certain nations still placed caveats on this.

Such caveats – and there were many scattered through the Alert Book – meant that when a particular measure was called it excluded a specified country, whose explicit agreement to the measure had to be obtained. Such caveats were sometimes based on national political requirements, but some were also based on practical considerations. A particular problem, for example, concerned Berlin, whose defence was a tripartite responsibility – involving only France, the UK and the USA – and did not directly involve NATO. Thus the UK, for example, placed caveats on the transfer of command of certain of its Germany-based forces, since these might have been required to implement one or other of the various contingency plans under tripartite command rather than under NATO command.*

The measures were extremely comprehensive. Within the assigned forces they involved many hundreds of actions involved in preparing for war, such as (to take but a few examples) outloading stores and munitions, the recall of people from leave and courses, the general examination of plans, preparations for the control and reception of refugees, and so on. Within national defence ministries plans were also re-examined, reservists were recalled, civil transport was requisitioned in accordance with previously prepared plans, and many other actions were set in train.

The measures went far wider than defence ministries, however, and involved action by most civil ministries as well. Transport ministries had to implement actions at airports, at ports and on the railway systems, and had to requisition transport and position it according to defence-ministry requirements. Health ministries had to take precautionary measures at hospitals and to clear ward space for wartime casualties among both military forces and the general population. Interior ministries were required to activate civil-defence plans, to place the police, gendarmerie and fire units on standby, to take over the direction of national media, and, in some countries,

---

* These contingency plans are fully described in Chapter 32.

to prepare and, if necessary, to implement evacuation plans. In addition, since the administration of NATO forces remained a national responsibility, there were national plans (e.g. for US and British troops in West Germany) for such matters as closing down schools for forces' children and repatriating civilian staff and forces' families.

THE WARSAW PACT

The Soviet air force and the strategic rocket force were virtually fully manned at all times, and the vast majority of units were in their wartime locations. The Soviet navy, while ships in commission were well manned, still required reservists to bring crews up to war establishment and to activate ships in the reserve fleet. A major factor, however, was that in normal times the navy maintained only about 10 per cent of its active vessels at sea, which meant that a substantial number of ships and submarines would have had to leave port during a very short period to reach their wartime stations.

The combat formations and units of the land forces – by far the largest element of the Soviet military machine – were placed in three categories in peacetime: Category-A units were manned at between 75 and 110 per cent of their war establishment; Category-B at 50–70 per cent; and Category-C at 10–33 per cent. All units in the Western Group of Forces (i.e. in East Germany, Czechoslovakia and Poland) were in Category A and were usually manned up to 100 per cent, while those in the western USSR were at slightly lower levels. Category-B units would have been available for deployment in thirty days, and Category-C units in sixty days. In very general terms the categories also reflected the equipment, with Category-A units having the latest and best equipment and Category-C the oldest and least effective, with Category-B lying somewhere in between.

Officially, in the Soviet Union mobilization had to be ordered by the Presidium of the USSR Supreme Soviet, which instructed reservists to report for duty and ceased the discharge of serving conscripts until further notice. Mobilization would have been effected through the local military headquarters, which were also responsible for the local drafts and thus experienced in assembling and dispatching manpower. Similar systems were employed in the other Warsaw Pact countries by their respective governments.

A SURPRISE ATTACK

Throughout the Cold War NATO claimed that it was possible for the Warsaw Pact to carry out a surprise attack, in the course of which NATO's in-place forces could have been overwhelmed before their reinforcements could have reached them. Certainly the later moves during the 1968 invasion of Czechoslovakia, when the Soviet and East German divisions suddenly closed up to the border with West Germany, showed that such a move was at least possible.

Such an attack would have fitted in with Soviet military thinking, since the Category-A forces facing NATO could have attacked from a 'standing start' with the aim of throwing NATO off balance and gaining time until, first, the Category-A units in the western USSR arrived to take over, followed by the Category-B units, which would have taken longer to mobilize.

Both sides, but particularly the West, had very complicated mobilization and deployment plans, which involved a lengthy series of interlocking and mutually dependent events. Many of the elements of these plans were tested in peacetime, but the realism of the tests was constrained by peacetime actualities: before an exercise, for example, merchant ships and civil aircraft had to be ordered months in advance, to enable owners to programme their availability; in the real thing, they would have been required at very short notice, without argument, and commercial compensation would have been a matter for later negotiations. Further, the sheer scale and complexity of the totality of the plans was impossible to test.

There can be no doubt that the military staffs in NATO and in national capitals would have been pressing hard for the politicians to make the decisions necessary to start the mobilization process. Nor can there be much doubt that most politicians in most countries in any situation short of an all-out Warsaw Pact attack would have been urging caution, counselling patience, questioning the validity of the intelligence assessments, indicating the escalatory nature of mobilization, seeking other ways of resolving the crisis, and, in all probability, declining at least some of the military requests.

Such decision-making processes were, of course, practised in peacetime exercises, but there were two factors which caused possible disputes to be played down. The first was that an exercise, by definition, was not the 'real thing' and thus arguments and pressures which could have arisen in reality were either glossed over or ignored altogether. Second, there was strong pressure to keep an exercise moving forward in accordance with a planning timetable, in order that all phases of the war could be practised before the unalterable end-of-exercise time was reached. This in itself prevented any major problem being allowed to delay matters for too long.

Had the reality ever arisen, however, dissension in the North Atlantic Council, particularly over calling Simple Alert and Reinforced Alert and in setting national mobilizations in train, was highly likely and could have proved very difficult to resolve. The military would then have pressed even harder for action, arguing that their plans would disintegrate into chaos if held back for too long, and pointing out the disasters that would occur if the

Warsaw Pact attacked before all NATO's troops were deployed. Such differences of opinion within the Alliance would have been exploited for all they were worth by the Soviets and their supporters in the West.

The August 1914 Precedent

The lesson of August 1914 was very relevant to NATO and the Warsaw Pact in the Cold War. In the hothouse climate of Europe in 1910–14, most countries were tied into one of the major alliances; the rest were neutral. The general staff of the likely belligerents, all of whom, except for Great Britain, had conscript armies, had prepared the most detailed mobilization and deployment plans (and Britain, too, needed to mobilize certain categories of reservists if war was imminent). Such mobilization could be either total or partial in order to meet a specific threat from a particular country or group of countries.

Under such plans, the announcement of national mobilization would set in train a series of events. This began with individuals being required to report within a designated time to specified depots, where they would be kitted out; then, as soon as the units were formed, they were automatically moved to a designated location, which was part of the national war plan. Such movement was almost entirely by railway, plus, in the case of France, sea transport from North Africa to the metropolitan country, and, in the case of the UK, ferries across the Channel. These plans necessitated manually prepared and controlled timetables of extraordinary complexity, which were carefully intermeshed with each other; as a result, the whole mobilization process became very rigid and inflexible.

For the general staffs, there were two major dangers. The first was that a potential enemy could, quite literally, steal a march by completing its mobilization process first. Thus mobilization itself became an act of war. The second was that, in every country, the mobilization plans could not start without a political decision, except for some very minor preliminary moves. As a result, when the time came in July/August 1914, the generals had to demand the mobilization order early and often, until it was actually given.

The deed which sparked the First World War mobilizations was a totally unexpected event – the murder in Sarajevo of Archduke Franz Ferdinand and his wife on 28 June 1914. This generated an ever-deepening crisis until Austria-Hungary declared war on Serbia on 28 July, whereupon Imperial Russia ordered mobilization against Austria-Hungary, but not against Germany, with whom at that time it had no immediate quarrel. Germany, however, demanded that Russia should demobilize; when the latter refused, Germany, fearing attack, declared war and started full mobilization on 1 August. France, knowing that this made a German attack inevitable, ordered mobilization on the same day. Germany, in accordance with the Schlieffen Plan (as modified by Helmuth von Moltke, the younger), thereupon declared war on France and invaded neutral Belgium on 4 August, the latter act provoking an ultimatum from Great Britain. When the Germans rejected this, Great Britain declared war on Germany and also mobilized.

In hindsight, the whole business possessed a dreadful inevitability, as the political and military leaders, like lemmings leaping over a Norwegian cliff, rushed helter-skelter to war. For those taking part, however, it was a nightmare period as each general staff sought to ensure that its nation was not caught off-balance.

During the Cold War, NATO's plans too were extraordinarily detailed and interdependent, and there was a strong possibility that their complexity and inflexibility were such that a situation analogous to that of August 1914 might have arisen. Thus a modern equivalent of the 'tyranny of the railway timetables' could have forced leaders on both sides of the Iron Curtain into a war which few of them, like most of the leaders in 1914, really wanted. If the result in 1914 was dire, however, the consequences of such a mobilization race during the Cold War would have been unimaginably worse.

32

Berlin: Front-Line City of the Cold War

Throughout the Cold War there was no other place or group of people that epitomized the issues at stake as clearly as Berlin and the Berliners; indeed, on more than one occasion, events in and around Berlin dragged Europe – and the world – to the brink of war. The city's curious status stemmed in part from its role as the traditional capital first of Prussia and then of united Germany (from 1871), but mainly from its political and emotional significance as the capital city of, first, Kaiser Wilhelm II's Imperial Germany and subsequently of Hitler's Third Reich. Thus the very name 'Berlin' struck a chill into the hearts of its enemies, and reaching and controlling it became the symbolic military goal of all four Allies during the Second World War.

THE LEGAL POSITION

In international law, the four occupying powers derived their rights and status in Berlin from the unconditional surrender of Germany in May 1945. This was formalized by a declaration issued on 5 June 1945, under which, in the absence of any German central government or authority, the Four Powers assumed supreme authority over the country.[1]

The post-war status of Germany was first considered by the American–British–Soviet European Advisory Commission (EAC),* which began its meetings in London in early 1944. This group quickly decided that Germany would be divided into three zones of occupation, giving the USSR an area stretching to within 100 km of the Rhine and including some 36 per cent of the population and 33 per cent of the country's industrial resources.

---

* The EAC was formed by order of the Conference of Allied Foreign Ministers (Moscow, November 1943) and consisted of representatives from the UK, the USSR, the USA and (from November 1944) France.

Berlin was deep inside this proposed Soviet zone, but was designated a 'special area' which would be occupied by and come under the joint administration of the three Allied powers.* This was subsequently documented in the London Protocol of 12 September 1944, although the Yalta Conference of Heads of State (4–11 February 1945) later amended this to include a French Zone of Occupation and a French sector in Berlin. Significantly, the EAC was unable to agree on the methods of access to the Western garrisons in Berlin from their occupation zones, thus creating a problem which was to endure for some forty-five years.

When the Red Army took Berlin on 2 May 1945 it found a devastated city, which had been heavily bombed by both the British and the US air forces, and then subjected to relentless Soviet artillery shelling during the final battle. Some 3 million inhabitants had survived. At an inter-Allied meeting in Berlin on 29 June the details of the Western move into the city were agreed with the Russians, and the British and the Americans were allocated the use (but not the control) of one main highway and one railway line each, plus two air corridors. They used these routes to move their occupation forces to Berlin, starting on 1 July, and were followed later by the French.

Initially 'the four occupying powers', acting through the Allied Kommandantura, administered the city as a self-contained entity, quite separate from the four zones of occupation (i.e. the American, British, French and Soviet zones), and for administrative purposes the city was sub-divided into four sectors, each controlled by one of these powers. Despite these arrangements having been agreed relatively amicably, the problem of access for the three Western garrisons raised itself immediately, since it was obvious that regular contact was required with the Western occupation zones, but they were physically separated from these by a wide stretch of Soviet-controlled territory.†

Air access was negotiated and agreed in a written document, signed on 30 November 1945, which guaranteed the use of three corridors, each 32 km wide. A further agreement established a quadripartite Berlin Air Safety Centre (BASC), which managed an air-control zone 32 km in radius and was also responsible for regulating traffic in the corridors from Berlin to the boundaries of adjacent control zones. BASC operated continuously from 12 December 1945 to 31 December 1990, providing a twenty-four-hour service, and was the one Allied body from which the Soviets never withdrew. All flight plans – giving full details of the planned route, height, arrival and departure times, and speed – had to be filed at the BASC and agreed before

---

* 'Berlin' was defined as 'Greater Berlin' as delineated in the German Law of 27 April 1920.
† The shortest distance was 177 km, between Helmstedt and West Berlin, for the British, and much further for the Americans and French.

an aircraft could enter the air-control zone. At the time this agreement was signed, the practical height limit for contemporary transport aircraft was some 3,050 m, and, while this was not written into the agreement, this became accepted 'by custom and practice', together with a minimum of 914 m.*

Unfortunately, no equivalent formal agreement was ever achieved for the use of the overland access routes by road, rail and canal. All three were originally used in 1945–6 and were then maintained by custom and practice, although they were subject to frequent interference by the Soviet and (later) East German authorities.

POST-WAR DEVELOPMENTS

When the planning for setting up the Federal Republic of Germany began in 1949, the German drafters of the proposed Federal Constitution (Basic Law) included a statement in Article 23 in which 'Greater Berlin' was listed as the twelfth *Land* of the Federal Republic.† The three Western Allies' military governors, however, prevented this in a letter dated 12 May 1949, denying authority for Berlin to be declared a *Land* and also stipulating that, while Berlin might send a small number of representatives to the Bundestag (Federal parliament) and the Bundesrat (Senate), they had to be non-voting.‡ The Allied Kommandantura later also stated that Federal legislation had to be voted into Berlin law by the Magistrat (the Berlin City Assembly) before it could become valid in Berlin.

The Federal Republic of Germany duly came into being on 21 September 1949 (though still formally occupied by the Western Allies), and the Soviets responded on 7 October by declaring that the Soviet Occupation Zone had been redesignated the German Democratic Republic (GDR), with its capital in Berlin. This was followed by announcements on 10 October that the Soviet Military Administration had been redesignated the Control Commission, and on 12 November that the Soviet military governor had transferred his functions to the East Berlin Magistrat.

---

* A problem arose somewhat later when the US and the British wished to operate helicopters in Berlin. Helicopters had been in their infancy in 1945 so they were not mentioned in the 1945, agreement, as a result of which the Russians refused to allow them to be flown into or out of the city. Thus they had to be dismantled and moved into the city either in a transport aircraft or by road.

† A West German *Land* is a constituent state of the Federal Republic, with its own parliament, government and local administration. It is approximately equivalent to a US state.

‡ The Berlin City Assembly sent eight representatives to the Bundestag and four to the Bundesrat.

The position of West Berlin was further redefined in 1952, when the 'Relations Convention' was under discussion. On 26 May 1952 the three Western Allies informed the Federal chancellor that, while they formally maintained their position that West Berlin should remain excluded from the Federal Republic, they would nevertheless permit the Federal Republic to provide economic assistance to West Berlin, where the currency would be the West German Deutschmark (DM). Thus, by the late 1950s, and with little change for the remainder of the Cold War, the position in West Berlin was that:

- The Federal government represented West Berlin overseas.
- Berlin was represented in both the Bundesrat and the Bundestag, and both of these bodies met from time to time in West Berlin.
- The Federal president had an official residence in West Berlin.
- The Federal government maintained some fifty governmental offices in West Berlin, but not the Ministry of Defence, which was specifically excluded from West Berlin.
- Federal German Law had been adopted almost in its entirety in West Berlin, and the superior Federal courts had jurisdiction in appeals, except for the Federal Constitutional Court, which had no jurisdiction in Berlin.
- The Federal government subsidized the West Berlin economy, balanced the budget, and maintained strategic stockpiles in the city.*
- The Western Allies and the Federal authorities maintained an amicable difference of view on the status of the city. Thus the Federal Constitutional Court laid down that Berlin was a *Land* of the Federal Republic, but accepted that Federal German responsibility was temporarily limited by the Allied occupation rights. The Allies, however, never varied from their view that the city was not a *Land* and were always careful to maintain its status as an occupied city under Four Power authority, because this was the basis for defending West Berlin, for upholding Western rights there and for access.

Within Berlin, the top policy body was the Four Power Allied Control Council, attended by the four commandants, which met regularly until 20 March 1948. On that day the three Western commandants met their Soviet colleague for what promised to be a routine meeting, but, to their astonishment, as soon as the proceedings opened, Marshal Sokolovskiy, the Soviet representative, launched into a prepared statement containing a long list of charges against the Western Allies, reading them at a tremendous pace. As soon as he had finished he stormed out, and for the remainder of the Allied stay in Berlin the three Western commandants continued to meet in the Allied Kommandantura, but with the Soviet seat remaining empty.

---

* These are estimated to have been six months' supply of coal and gas and one year's supply of food.

On 1 April 1948 Red Army units stopped the regular British, French and US trains to Berlin just inside the Soviet zone. All three were shunted into a siding, where they were left engineless for some fourteen hours, after which they were pulled back into their respective Western zones. Citing the introduction of the new Deutschmark as the reason for their action,* the Soviets increased the harassment until a total land blockade was imposed on 22 June 1948. The Western Allies decided that West Berlin must be maintained as a bastion of Western freedom, but, although it was a fundamental assumption in their responses that the Soviets would not go to war over the issue, great care was nevertheless taken not to push the Soviet leadership into a corner from which either open conflict or humiliation would be the only route out.

Soviet measures included blocking all road, rail and canal routes from the Western zones to Berlin – the Western commandants suddenly realized they had neglected to obtain written agreements for these from the Soviets – and the cessation of all direct deliveries of food, coal and electrical power from the Soviet zone. Air was left as the only means of supplying the city, and, to the surprise of the Soviets, the Western Allies organized the 'Berlin Airlift', which proceeded to deliver sufficient food and coal to maintain the Western garrisons and the population of West Berlin through the winter of 1948 and into the spring of 1949. The blockade lasted for 318 days, during which the Allies flew in some 2,360,000 tonnes of supplies in a total of 277,728 flights, at a cost of seventy-five American, British and German lives. The land blockade was quietly lifted on 12 May 1949, although the Allied air-resupply operation continued until the situation had stabilized at the end of September.

The Berlin Airlift was an enormous and extremely complicated operation, and when the Soviets eventually relaxed their blockade it appeared that they had lost. However, a pattern had been established which was followed throughout the years during which Berlin was divided: if there was a written agreement, the Soviets stuck to it.

The airlift also had two other, perhaps less publicized, results. First, it broke down the barriers which had existed since May 1945 between the Western troops and the German population, removing the psychological barriers between victors and defeated, and creating a mutual respect and considerable sympathy for each other. Second, it showed the French that they could not act on their own over Berlin or occupied West Germany, and from 1948 onwards they were much more co-operative.

The relationship between East Berlin and the GDR was, however, somewhat different, and in the late 1950s the eastern sector was progressively

---

* Before this the currency throughout Berlin had been the Allied Military Mark, which was printed by the Soviet authorities in East Berlin.

integrated into the GDR – a process clearly directed by the USSR. Despite this, the Western Allies were always convinced that there was a strong feeling of contempt for their East German allies among the Soviet forces, which had no parallel in the relationship between the Western Allies and the population of the Federal Republic.

WESTERN PLANS

The Western powers knew that their garrisons in West Berlin were militarily extremely vulnerable. They were some 180 km from the Inner German Border and totally surrounded by Soviet and GDR ground and air forces. Each of the three Western powers maintained a nominal brigade in the city: in 1986, for example, there were 4,300 US troops, 3,000 British and 2,700 French. It would, however, be wrong to visualize these as brigades in the normal sense, since they were tailored to their role. The combat elements of the British Berlin Infantry Brigade, for example, consisted of a company of eighteen tanks,* three lorry-borne infantry battalions (with just six armoured personnel carriers each), a company of engineers and (from 1977) a platoon of helicopters. A 'normal' infantry brigade based in Western Germany, however, had a battalion of tanks, three infantry battalions mounted in armoured personnel carriers, a battalion of helicopters, a battalion of artillery and a company of engineers.

The Berlin brigades did, however, have a strong representation of combat-support elements, including an intelligence company, a signal company, a military-police company and administrative assets such as a transport company. It was also widely reported that the large antennas on a hill named the Babelsburg, all of which pointed into East Germany, were for SIGINT purposes.

Command
The chain of command for the Western garrisons was complex, since it reflected both national and allied requirements, and covered political and civil matters as well as military. In addition, it differed between peace and war. Within Berlin the four Allied commandants worked together as the Allied Kommandantura, although after the walkout by the Soviet commandant in 1948 it was left to the three Western commandants to correlate their plans and responses to Soviet pressures, with the chairmanship revolving between the three on a monthly basis. The chairman had specific duties, which included making the co-ordinated response to Soviet or East German

---

* Originally Comets, later Centurions, and finally Chieftains.

initiatives, as well as co-ordinating action during the early stages of a military confrontation. It was, however, appreciated that in war the three Western Allies would have to work even more closely together, and so it was agreed from early during the occupation of the city that in a crisis and conflict the US commandant would become the single commander.

In January 1951 the Allied Staff Berlin was established, with the tasks of preparing tripartite plans for the defence of West Berlin, setting up the command posts and communications necessary to control such plans, and establishing 'Force B'. This was a new section of the West Berlin Police, organized and equipped as light infantry, with one battalion in each of the three Western sectors. The force eventually numbered some 1,850 men, but it was disbanded in the early 1960s.

In 1961, however, the Allied commandants proposed that the arrangement for the single commander should become more formal. In particular, they wanted it to be implemented earlier in a crisis, especially in a situation where communications between Berlin and the zones in West Germany had either broken down or were (much more likely) blocked by the Soviets.

The three Western commandants had civil as well as military responsibilities, and to help with the political side they were supported by a senior diplomat, who served as 'deputy commandant and minister'. Each of the Western commandants reported politically to the appropriate ambassador in Bonn, and militarily direct to their defence ministry in their national capital, but keeping their national commander-in-chief in the Federal Republic (i.e. CINCFFA for France, CINCBAOR for the UK, and CINCEUR for the USA) informed. Overall co-ordination was the responsibility of the Washington Ambassadors Group in Washington DC, chaired by the US secretary of state and comprising the British, the French and (informally) the West German ambassadors.

Military Command and Live Oak

Any military help for the Western garrisons would have had to come from the three national contingents in West Germany, but, since Berlin was an Allied responsibility, NATO was not involved in the military command chain for the city during peacetime and the early stages of a crisis. The overall military commander of Berlin was therefore Commander-in-Chief US Forces Europe (CINCEUR),* whose peacetime planning function with regard to Berlin was exercised through a tripartite headquarters.

This headquarters, known as Live Oak, was formed on 4 April 1959 and

---

* The same man served as a NATO commander (SACEUR) served by NATO staffs, as a US national commander (CINCEUR) served by an exclusively US staff, and as a tripartite (French–UK–US) commander for Berlin, in which he was served by a tripartite staff with its own headquarters. Such 'double [or triple] hatting' was quite usual in NATO.

was originally situated in the US forces' HQ European Command (HQ EUCOM) barracks at Saint-Germain-en-Laye, some 32 km south-west of Paris. The British detached a major-general from commanding a division to become the first chief-of-staff – a step which underlined the extreme importance attached to the task – and he began the process of preparing reinforcement and defence plans, assisted by three teams of officers, one each from France, the UK and the USA, with each team comprising one officer (at colonel level) from the navy, army and air force. By mid-1960, however, draft plans were ready and the HQ was allowed to run down in numbers and prestige, until the 1961 construction of the Berlin Wall brought it back into the limelight, where it stayed for the rest of the Cold War.

The HQ moved from HQ EUCOM to SHAPE at Fontainebleau in October 1960, to be closer to the main operational headquarters; then it moved to Belgium, where it took up residence in a separate building within the SHAPE compound at Mons.* It continued to be headed by a British major-general (Chief-of-Staff Live Oak), with a small staff from the US, France and the UK, who were responsible for keeping the contingency plans up to date and for conducting the regular exercises. Live Oak was not, however, a command headquarters, and in war it was planned to form a small headquarters run by a senior US officer on SACEUR's staff and under the personal command of SACEUR.

Maritime operations associated with a Berlin crisis were co-ordinated by a naval headquarters designated Deep Sea, collocated with SACLANT at Norfolk, Virginia. Air operations were controlled by another headquarters, designated Jack Pine, which was located at Headquarters USAF Europe (USAFE) at Ramstein in southern Germany.

It was natural that the West Germans should have taken an intense interest in everything to do with Berlin, and in particular with the Western sector. As a result, a *Bundeswehr* liaison team was located with Headquarters Live Oak, and the West German authorities were aware of the contingency plans. They did not, however, take part in any of the operations or exercises, and right up to the end no *Bundeswehr* personnel were allowed into West Berlin in uniform.

A constant preoccupation among the Western commandants was the need to react promptly and firmly to any action which might imperil the status or well-being of the Western garrisons in Berlin. The most serious threats came from actions by the Soviets, which ranged over the years from relatively short delays to road traffic, trains or canal barges (usually blamed on 'difficulties over paperwork'), through temporary closure of the routes, to total blockade, although the ultimate threat – a direct attack – never

---

* Despite being placed within a NATO compound, Live Oak was never a NATO unit and access to its building was restricted to British, French and US people with business there.

materialized. There were also less direct threats, particularly from uprisings by the discontented population of East Germany, either within East Berlin or in East Germany as a whole. Such uprisings were considered to be particularly worrying, since they would attract intense media attention and could unintentionally threaten the Western garrisons, while lacking an identifiable leadership to negotiate with, as happened in 1953, and as nearly happened again in 1989.

The more likely threat, however, was of action by the Soviets to restrict access to Berlin, and the Western commandants identified a requirement to discover Soviet intentions and, where necessary, to deliver a warning that the Western powers were determined to resist. Throughout, however, there was a firm desire to keep the situation under control and to avoid provoking the Soviets into further action.

During the build-up to the closure of the land routes in March 1948, General Lucius Clay, the first US commandant in Berlin, proposed that each of the Western Allies should bring a division to Helmstedt and that the force should then advance to Berlin. By July he had recast his proposal so that the force consisted of a more realistic 200 trucks, escorted by a US contingent consisting of a constabulary regiment, some infantry and an engineer battalion, while the British were to provide an infantry battalion and the French a detachment of anti-tank troops.

The plans were slowly refined over the years, and by the early 1960s there were four phases of reaction. In Phase 1, reconnaissances (known colloquially as 'probes') were carried out to determine the seriousness of Soviet intentions. If these failed to achieve the desired result, Phase 2 consisted of a pause on the ground while political action took place, either at the United Nations or between the three Western Allies and the Soviet leadership. If this failed and access was still being denied, then Phase 3 was implemented, which involved stronger military action. If that too failed, then Phase 4, nuclear action, was considered.

Contingency Plans
The military staff tried to picture every possible contingency which might arise, and then prepared a plan to deal with it.* In 1962, for example,

---

* Contingency planning frequently gives rise to misunderstandings among those not familiar with the way the military operate. Headquarters exist in peacetime to plan and train for war, so that, should war break out, they are familiar with their roles, their missions and the units under their command. A certain amount of their time is spent in peacetime administration, but the bulk is devoted to planning. The existence of a plan does not mean that an HQ wishes to carry it out, or even that it is considered likely that it will have to, but simply that there is a remote possibility. Thus, if an HQ has a contingency plan for a nuclear attack, that does not mean that it wants to carry it out, but simply that it *might* have to and so the plan considers what factors might be involved in doing so.

the military plans, known as 'BerCons' (Berlin contingency plans), included:[2]

- BerCon Alpha 1 – large-scale fighter escorts for transport aircraft using the Berlin air corridors;
- BerCon Alpha 2– conventional battle for air superiority over Berlin;
- BerCon Bravo – five low-yield, airburst nuclear weapons against selected targets, to demonstrate Western resolve to resort to more powerful nuclear weapons if necessary;
- BerCon Charlie 1 – an attack by a reinforced division along the Helmstedt–Berlin autobahn;
- BerCon Charlie 2 – an attack by two divisions (i.e. a weak corps) in the Kassel area;
- BerCon Charlie 3 – an attack by three divisions (i.e. a normal corps) from Helmstedt along the axis of the Mittellandkanal as far as the river Elbe;
- BerCon Charlie 4 – an attack by three divisions towards Berlin, launched from the Thüringerwald area in the US zone.

There were also plans for a tripartite battalion group, which comprised a British infantry battalion, a US tank company, a French armoured-car platoon, a US engineer platoon (including an armoured bridgelayer), and a leading platoon made up of equal numbers of infantrymen from the three nations. Such a force was designated Trade Wind if mounted from West Germany or Lucky Strike if mounted from West Berlin.

The contingency plans developed by Live Oak from 1959 onwards included possibilities physically far removed from Berlin and even from Germany. There were, for example, a number of naval plans (known as MarCons – i.e. maritime contingency plans) consisting of a series of naval measures, varying from distant blockades of the type that had been so successful off Cuba to close-in blockades off Soviet ports such as Vladivostok.

Naval operations in support of Berlin were occasionally very positive. In May 1959 there was a feeling of crisis over Berlin. There had been a number of incidents on the autobahn and more trouble over the 3,050 m aircraft ceiling, and a Four Power foreign ministers' conference was held in Geneva, opening on 11 May. One of the measures taken by the Western Allies was for the US Sixth Fleet in the Mediterranean to ensure that at least one carrier task group was at sea throughout May, with each carrier maintaining at least six aircraft at immediate-launch status. Again in 1961, during the crisis caused by the erection of the Berlin Wall, the Sixth Fleet was placed on the alert, and on this occasion was reinforced by extra long-range ASW aircraft, while a further ASW carrier group was deployed to the Norwegian Sea.[3]

All such plans included arrangements for informing the Soviets that these actions were directly related to Berlin, which was usually achieved through the Washington Ambassadors Group, consisting of the US secretary of state and the French and UK ambassadors (with the informal presence of the West German ambassador).

Air Reconnaissances

The Berlin Airlift demonstrated that the air corridors were essential to the survival of the Western garrisons, and a number of contingency plans were devoted to ensuring that such access continued. One plan, devised by Live Oak in the early 1960s, involved flying a civil airliner of the type normally used on the Berlin run down one of the air corridors if there was any threat to close it. It was, of course, appreciated that this was not a reasonable mission for a civil aircrew, so, in the British case, the Royal Air Force negotiated a contract with state-owned British European Airways (BEA), which involved six military crews being trained to fly the then current Viscount turboprop airliner. The plan was that, during a crisis, one of these aircraft would be taken over by the British air-force aircrew at Hanover Airport and flown without passengers to Berlin (Tempelhof) and back.

This contingency plan was actually put into operation for the first time on 16 February 1962, at the request of General Lauris Norstad (CINCEUR), although all did not go as smoothly as had been intended.[4] First, despite the planning and training, when the time came BEA officials refused to hand over one of their aircraft to the air force. This was in part because they did not believe the threat to be sufficiently serious, but also because they were concerned at the commercial consequences of one of their aircraft being shot down or otherwise forced to land by the Soviets, who would then discover that a civil airliner was being flown by a military crew. The matter was so complicated and feelings ran so high that it had to be resolved by a meeting between the company chairman, Lord Douglas, and the secretary of state for air, where Douglas, albeit with considerable reluctance, eventually agreed to make the aircraft available. It was duly taken over, and the flight plan for the *northern* corridor was cleared with the Soviet representative at the Berlin Air Safety Centre, whereupon the crew flew the aircraft down the *central* corridor. Not surprisingly, such an error caused considerable embarrassment, although, despite the tensions at the time, the Soviets failed to take any advantage. There were, however, serious repercussions in London, where it was eventually established that there had been a misunderstanding between the relevant authorities in Berlin and Hanover. The US forces developed a similar arrangement with Pan American Airlines, as did the French forces with Air France.

Land Reconnaissances

In any crisis on land, the initial aim of the Western Allies was to establish the seriousness of the Soviet threat. This was achieved by using a tripartite force known as a 'probe'. The codewords changed over the years, but in the 1960s this operation was known as Operation Free Style if the probe force was mounted from the West German end of the autobahn and as Back Stroke if it was mounted from the Berlin end. Such probes were always preceded by a very precise warning to the Soviets, and there were three levels:

- If it was planned to accept any Soviet physical obstruction of the autobahn and to turn back without further discussion, the probe force would consist of fifty-six men in fifteen vehicles.
- If it was planned to accept any physical obstruction placed by the Soviets but only to turn back on being forced to do so (i.e. following protests and a confrontation), the probe force would consist of seventy-seven men in eighteen 'soft' vehicles (i.e. trucks) and two armoured personnel carriers.
- If it was planned to take positive action to remove any physical obstructions, but only to use force in self-defence, then the force would consist of 120 men, mounted in twenty-two 'soft' vehicles, two armoured cars and two armoured personnel carriers.

INCIDENTS

In total there were many hundreds of incidents involving the Western garrisons during the years they were in Berlin, ranging from the trivial to the extremely serious, with causes varying from incompetence, overenthusiasm or accident to sophisticated planning and co-ordination. In November 1950 tension in Berlin led to the Western Allies reinforcing their garrisons, which included reinforcements from the US 6th Infantry Regiment, together with a British tank squadron equipped with thirty Comet tanks. Then in May 1951 land travel between East and West Berlin was cut, and telephone systems were severed.

The period 1950–51 also included the 'barge war' between the British (who controlled three important canal locks in Berlin) and the Soviets. This started with the Soviets interfering with barge traffic between the Western occupied zones and West Berlin; the British responded firmly to this at their locks, where they stopped all East German traffic. This was resolved by an agreement signed on 4 May 1951, although the Soviets and the GDR later built a new stretch of canal, which removed the need for them to use the British-controlled locks.

May 1952 saw intermittent interference with Western military traffic on the British autobahn route; this was aimed at the military police patrols rather than at the traffic itself. Also in 1952 the USSR responded to the recent agreements between the Western Allies and the FRG by instructing the GDR to declare a 5 km 'security zone' along the inter-zonal border and the Baltic coast. East German civilians residing in the zone were ruthlessly evicted and resettled elsewhere.

The East Berlin uprising broke out on 16 June 1953, when building workers in the Stalinalee protested against a 10 per cent increase in production norms without any increase in pay, although when crowds gathered the next day the nature of the protest quickly changed from economic to political. The GDR's *Volkspolizei* (National Police) were overwhelmed, and the Soviet army had to be called in to restore order. On 18 June the Western commandants sent a 'strong protest' to the Soviet commander, but there was little else they could do and it was all soon over. Thirty-five people were killed and 378 injured in the actual fighting, with an unknown further number executed or imprisoned by the GDR authorities afterwards.

Knowing of the shortage of food in the GDR, on 10 July 1953 President Eisenhower offered to supply $15 million worth of foodstuffs for the people. The offer was resisted by both the GDR and the Soviet governments, but the USA went ahead and set up supply depots in West Berlin, and some 3 million people from East Berlin and elsewhere in the GDR managed to collect at least one food parcel each.

The USSR handed over responsibility for borders and for civil traffic on the autobahns to the GDR on 21 January 1956; Soviet military-manned checkpoints were, however, retained for military traffic. The Western Allies protested, particularly when the GDR raised civil vehicle charges on the autobahns by between 100 and 1,000 per cent, and the increases were later reduced, but not eliminated.

On 27 November 1956 two US congressmen and the wife of one of them were visiting East Berlin when they were arrested and detained by the *Volkspolizei*. Not surprisingly, this caused immediate and strong US reactions, and the group was quickly released.

On 10 November 1958 Khrushchev made a speech in Moscow in the course of which he proposed that West Berlin should become a 'Free City', adding that if he failed to receive agreement within six months he would transfer all Soviet powers over West Berlin to the GDR. He then sent identical notes confirming this to the British, French and US governments on 27 November. This led to a new 'Berlin crisis', and there was some low-level harassment – for example, a US convoy was halted for two days at the Soviet checkpoint at Helmstedt (2–4 February 1959), and aircraft were also harassed in the corridors. The situation was further complicated in February 1959, when new passes for the Western missions to the Soviet commander-in-chief were issued in the name of the GDR. The Western Allies immediately protested, since the missions were accredited to the Soviet commander-in-chief in person, and demanded that the previous passes be reinstated, which they were. Finally, in this particular episode, Khrushchev's six-month deadline arrived on 27 May 1959, but the Western

Allies allowed it to pass without any response and the Soviets took no further action.

In the late 1950s the question of the 3,050 m ceiling in the air corridors became a major issue, as piston-engined airliners were being replaced by new types, powered by turboprops, which had an economical cruising altitude considerably in excess of that figure; the Viscount aircraft used by BEA, for example, normally flew at 4,250 m. In an effort to force the issue, on 27 March 1959 a US air-force C-130 Hercules transport flew towards Berlin at an altitude of 7,600 m along the southern corridor, where, to nobody's surprise, it was buzzed by three Soviet fighters. Similarly, a US C-135 jet transport flying at 3,600 m on 3 April and another C-130 at 6,000 m on 15 April were both buzzed. These incidents led to bitter arguments over the 3,050 m maximum, which the Soviets said had become accepted by 'custom and practice'. Eventually this maximum was accepted by President Eisenhower in person, who declared that it was not an issue worth going to war over.

Meanwhile, escape to West Berlin and West Germany was relatively easy, and the loss of people from the GDR was becoming such a serious problem that it was beginning to threaten the future of the state itself. Table 32.1 shows the annual losses (mostly into West Berlin) since the end of the Berlin Airlift.

The Communist state's problems were exacerbated when, in late 1959, the GDR started to collectivize the remainder of its privately owned farms; this proved to be an even more unpopular move than usual, but was never-

Table 32.1 Numbers of People Escaping from the GDR

Year	Number
1949	129,245
1950	197,788
1951	165,648
1952	182,393
1953	331,390
1954	184,198
1955	252,270
1956	279,189
1957	261,622
1958	204,092
1959	143,917
1960	199,188
1961 (to 30 June)	103,159
Total	2,634,099

341

theless ruthlessly implemented. It was completed by mid-1960, resulting in at least 15,000 farmers fleeing to the West and, coupled with the inefficiencies always associated with collective farming, leading to yet another food crisis in the GDR that year. As a result, escapes to the West increased dramatically, reaching 30,000 in July 1961 and 20,000 in the first twelve days of August, with no less than 4,000 on 12 August alone.

It was widely realized, even in the West, that the GDR would have to do something to halt this outflow of people, but when it came the action caused considerable surprise and dismay. At 0230 hours precisely on 13 August 1961 East German troops and workmen began to build the 'Berlin Wall', which was not only to separate the two parts of the city for the next twenty-eight years, but was also to become the very symbol of the Cold War. The *S-bahn* (overground railway) and *U-bahn* (underground railway) were closed, but, significantly, no move was made to interfere with the military rights of access to West Berlin. Initially, thirteen crossing points were left open between West and East Berlin, although these were later reduced: first to twelve and later to seven.

The Western commandants protested, but soon West Berlin was ringed by more than 160 km of wall. US vice-president Lyndon Johnson visited the city to boost morale, the US sent a 1,500-strong battlegroup along the southern autobahn, while the British dispatched reinforcements on a slightly smaller scale, including eighteen armoured personnel carriers and eighteen reconnaissance vehicles. On 22 October the East German *Volkspolizei* attempted to prevent the US deputy commandant from going into East Berlin and, although that particular incident was resolved, the situation escalated during the next few days and US tanks were deployed to the main East–West crossing point, Checkpoint Charlie. The Soviets countered by deploying their own tanks, and the two groups of tanks confronted each other (with, as always, the world's press looking on) at a range of 100 m for two days. In December President Kennedy called up 300,000 US reservists, while on 13 December 1961 the Operation Free Style force in West Germany was put on forty-eight-hours notice to deploy to the border, although it was not in fact used.

The escapes continued, albeit on a very much reduced scale. As each method was discovered, the GDR took steps to prevent a recurrence, whereupon the next escapers tried an even more ingenious technique. The Berlin Wall eventually included 290 watchtowers, 136 bunkers, 105 km of trenches, 257 km of dog runs and 122 km of fencing with warning devices, all of which required a garrison of no less than 14,000 East German troops.[5]

In March 1962 the Soviets tried a new tactic in the three air corridors by attempting to reserve so much time for their own flights that there was no capacity left for use by Western aircraft. Even more seriously, they also jammed the air-safety radio frequencies and, on one night, dropped chaff in the corridors to jam the radars. After high-level protests these practices ceased.

There were also incidents on the ground. On 12 March 1962 East German guards shot at a car from the British mission and the British driver was wounded and taken to an East German hospital, where he was operated on. Eventually the Soviet commander-in-chief, Marshal Ivan Konev, apologized, and the soldier was returned to West Berlin. On 20 March 1962 a car from the US mission was shot at, also by East German troops, although nobody was wounded on this occasion, and the occupants were released after being detained for several hours.

In 1963 the Canadian entertainer Hughie Green, who was due to record a TV show in Berlin, decided to fly to the city in his personal aircraft, a twin-engined Cessna 310. His agreed route took him along the southern corridor from Stuttgart to Gatow, but as soon as he was in the corridor he was buzzed by a succession of Soviet jet fighters. These flew very close to his aircraft, rocked their wings, and lowered their undercarriages ordering him to land, and eventually fired warning shots on six separate occasions. Green, a very experienced Second World War pilot, maintained his course and eventually landed safely in Berlin.

Two incidents in 1964 were potentially very serious. The first took place on 10 March, when a US RB-66* electronic-surveillance aircraft was shot down over East Germany. This was followed on 28 June by the shooting down of a US North American T-39 aircraft,† which had strayed just outside the southern corridor. Both types of aircraft were employed on electronic monitoring missions, but the events were eventually resolved by diplomatic action.

In 1965 the Soviets took exception to sessions of the Bundestag being held in Berlin, and staged manoeuvres by both Soviet and East German troops to show their displeasure. The autobahns were closed to traffic, and Soviet air-force fighters created sonic booms over West Berlin, aimed at the Kongresshalle where the sessions were taking place.

Similar problems recurred in 1969, when the FRG decided to hold a session of the Bundesversammlung in Berlin.‡ Again the Soviets closed the autobahns for several days, deploying a division of troops along the British autobahn, but when the British ran a low-level probe the Soviets allowed it

---

* The Douglas RB-66 was a highly specialized photographic- and electronic-surveillance version of the B-66 twin-jet bomber. It carried a crew of three.
† The T-39 was an air-force version of the North American Sabreliner executive aircraft. It was powered by two turbojets and carried a crew of two. Military transport versions carried up to nine passengers, but the type was also used as a radar trainer and may also have been used for electronic surveillance.
‡ The Bundesversammlung was a special body which was convened only to elect a new president.

to pass and the crisis was over. The West Germans persisted, and Dr Gustav Heinemann was duly elected president on 5 March, although no further presidential elections were held in West Berlin while the Cold War lasted. There was further interference with traffic along the autobahn during 1971, as well as attempts to close the air corridors, which were countered by flying probes under the control of the Jack Pine air headquarters.

One of the final serious incidents occurred on 24 March 1985, when Major Arthur Nicholson, a member of the US mission, was shot dead by a Soviet soldier while attemping to discover details of the then new Soviet T-80 tank at the Ludwigslust training range near Berlin. The incident took place at a time when global US–USSR relations were particularly good, and the case was dealt with quietly and caused very little public friction.

THE BERLIN ACCORD

In 1971 the Federal German government prompted the four wartime Allies into seeking to achieve an agreement on the status of Berlin, and this resulted in a series of meetings culminating in the 'Berlin Accord' of early September 1971. So tortuous were the negotiations that the document avoided actually specifying what was meant by Berlin, referring only to 'the area in question', although, since the Soviets refused to discuss East Berlin, the accord actually dealt only with West Berlin. Despite this, both sides gained something. All renounced the use of force in trying to solve Berlin's problems, while the Western powers acknowledged that Berlin was not only not part of the FRG, but remained under Four Power occupation; they also agreed that Federal bodies would not meet there.* In return, the Soviets dropped their assertion that West Berlin lay within the GDR and agreed that the West German government could represent West Berliners internationally. A number of minor problems were also dealt with, and the accord, having been signed by the Four Powers, was then turned over to both German states for implementation, which, not by chance, gave East Germany equal status with West Germany, which had long been a Soviet goal.

THE END

After the Berlin Accord had been signed, life in the city and the corridors followed a much more even path until January 1989, when twenty people,

---

* This covered formal meetings of the Bundesversammlung, the Bundesrat and the Bundestag, although committees could continue to meet in West Berlin.

frustrated in their desire to emigrate to the West, occupied the West German mission in East Berlin. These left after obtaining a promise that their applications would be processed by the GDR authorities, but in August another and much larger group occupied the building. Again they were persuaded to leave, and the would-be emigrants turned their attention to escape routes through Hungary and Czechoslovakia.

On 7 October, when the Soviet leader, Mikhail Gorbachev, attended the GDR's fortieth-anniversary celebrations in East Berlin, there were a number of freedom demonstrations in major cities in East Germany. Unrest in the GDR gathered strength, causing the Western commandants to feel considerable concern, especially in the late summer and autumn of 1989, as the activities of dissident East Germans were something over which they had no control, and they reviewed their plans.

Erich Honecker, the long-time Communist Party leader, was removed from office on 18 October and was replaced by Egon Krenz, who on 24 October also became state president and military commander-in-chief. The problems persisted, however, with some 150,000 demonstrators marching in Leipzig on 23 October, but, significantly, without any interference by the East German security forces. Two days later the demonstrations spread to Dresden, Erfurt, Gera and Rostock, and Krenz spoke on the telephone to West German chancellor Helmut Kohl about possible relaxations in the cross-border controls.

The political temperature in the GDR steadily rose, Krenz visited Moscow and Warsaw, and on 4 November a crowd of some 1 million demonstrated in East Berlin. The Western commandants in West Berlin were concerned at the situation and opened their emergency operations centres, although there was little they could do other than dispatch patrols to monitor what was happening on the other side of the Wall.

The focus of attention switched rapidly between the GDR, the FRG, and Moscow, but it was fitting that the crucial event took place in Berlin. On 9 November the Communist Party leader in East Berlin gave a radio and television interview in which he gave the impression that any GDR citizen could now go to the border and obtain an exit visa, thus avoiding the lengthy bureaucratic procedures which had caused so much frustration in the past. A huge crowd immediately formed and headed for the checkpoints at the Wall, where the bemused guards, lacking clear orders, opened the gates, allowing the East Berliners to flood into the West. Some 3 million were estimated to have visited the FRG and West Berlin over that weekend, and there were long delays on the Helmstedt–Berlin autobahn as it was flooded with the East Germans' infamous slow-moving Trabant cars.

The momentum of change then increased rapidly, and it was soon agreed that reunification would take place. The threat to the Western garrisons in

West Berlin was over, and the formal ending of the Live Oak mission came on 2 October 1990.

LIFE IN BERLIN

Life in Berlin between 1945 and 1989 could never have been described as 'normal', but this is not a social history and only a couple of features can be mentioned to illustrate the extraordinary *modus vivendi* which was reached there, despite all the stresses of the Cold War.

First, one of the curious features of life in Berlin was that the members of all four garrisons were always allowed into each other's sectors. This was of little consequence between the Americans, British and French, but it also meant that members of these three Western garrisons regularly visited East Berlin in uniform, either for sightseeing or to attend events such as the opera. They also went shopping in the East – an activity that was made more attractive by obtaining East German marks at seven times the normal exchange rate. The Soviet armed forces enjoyed similar rights in West Berlin, although these were exercised much less frequently, with small parties of troops being closely supervised by political 'minders' to prevent any contacts with Westerners or defection.

Another curious feature was that for many years the Federal German government met a significant part of the costs of the three Western garrisons through the 'Berlin Occupation Costs Budget', usually simply known as the 'Berlin Budget'. Towards the end this amounted to DM1,300 million a year, which was distributed as follows: USA – DM600 million; UK – DM400 million; France – DM300 million. Under this arrangement the Western garrisons met their own salaries and financial allowances, as well as the costs of 'warlike equipment' such as weapons and ammunition, but the Berlin Budget funded infrastructure costs, ranging from vehicles and radio equipment to typewriters and paper. As some 90 per cent of the Berlin Budget was spent in West Berlin and the Federal Republic, however, it was essentially recycled within the German economy.[6]

FORTY-FOUR YEARS IN THE FRONT LINE

The tensions caused by the very existence of West Berlin – a bastion of Western democracy and capitalism deep inside a Communist state – were very real, and it was considered, not unrealistically, that if conflict was ever to break out between the Soviet Union and NATO it would be over (or in some way related to) Berlin. The city enjoyed a unique status throughout the Cold War, not least because it was the one place where the French never for one moment left the Western Allies' forum but continued to play a full part in all planning, discussions, command arrangements and reactions to crises. Nor were there any arguments about the French troops serving as an integral part of the probes, where, depending on the situation, they could find themselves under US or British command.

The soldiers and airmen on both sides in Berlin, on the corridors and in West Germany did their level best to keep matters under control. Naturally, they responded to the orders from their superiors, but they also did all they could to ensure that the 'other side' was never left without room for manoeuvre, so that problems could be resolved without serious loss of face. Thus, when Western soldiers sometimes unintentionally strayed into East Berlin or the GDR (e.g. by falling asleep on a train), they would be detained, their parent force would be informed, and then the chastened individuals would be quietly returned after a two- or three-day interval.* In a much more serious incident on 5 April 1948 a Soviet fighter aircraft collided with a BEA Viking transport aircraft which was coming in to land at the British military airfield at Gatow. Fourteen people, including the Soviet pilot, were killed. The British and Americans were preparing to provide fighter escorts for all transport flights, when Marshal Sokolovskiy informed the British commandant that no interference had been intended. Thus it was presumed that the incident was either a genuine accident (the airspace over Berlin tended to be crowded) or was the result of a miscalculation by the Russian pilot, and the proposed countermeasures were cancelled.

Perhaps the tensest period was in October 1961, when the US and Soviet tanks faced each other at Checkpoint Charlie. One false move by a junior officer or a soldier on either side could have resulted in an extremely rapid escalation of the situation, but it never happened. Again, this speaks very highly for the troops of both sides.

Where individuals broke the recognized rules, however, action could be swift and direct, and there were numerous instances of Western officers or soldiers being shot, although, so far as is known, there were never any cases of Soviet or East German soldiers being shot by Western troops.

The vulnerability of West Berlin was palpable. The Western garrisons totalled some 10,000 troops, but these were predominantly infantry. There was a small number of tanks, but only the US had artillery – a token force consisting of just one battery of six 155 mm guns. There were airfields in

---

* One senior Western officer went to sleep in his staff car on the autobahn between Helmstedt and Berlin. He awoke to discover that he was deep in the GDR, his driver having taken a wrong turning, and that his car had been stopped by a Soviet patrol. An English-speaking Russian officer was sent for, who, with only the slightest hint of a smile, politely enquired whether the Western officer was trying to defect. On being assured that this was not the case, he personally escorted the chastened Westerner back to the autobahn and sent him on his way to Berlin with a salute.

West Berlin, but modern fighters or bombers were never stationed there; they would have been far too vulnerable, and would have been eliminated within minutes in a pre-emptive strike, if conflict had broken out. Thus the Western garrisons were unable to conduct aggressive action, and their weapons and equipment were demonstrably intended only for defensive purposes.

The officers and troops of the three Western garrisons were accompanied by their wives and families, and there were plans to evacuate these dependants in time of crisis, although it was highly unlikely that there would have been an opportunity to do so. In war, all that could have been done was to concentrate the three Western garrisons quickly, probably centred on the Olympic complex in the British zone, and struggle to survive until the outcome of the war had been decided elsewhere.

The Western outpost in Berlin was surrounded and greatly outnumbered by the Group of Soviet Forces Germany (GSFG), supported by the large East German army (NVA). As was discovered after the end of the Cold War, the plan had been for the Soviets to ignore West Berlin, leaving its fate to the NVA, which had detailed plans to take West Berlin by storm.

The low-level contingency plans for Berlin designed to ascertain Soviet intentions – the land and air probes – proved their worth on several occasions, if only because the Soviets chose to let them do so. The larger plans, however, which involved forces of battlegroup, brigade and divisional strength, were of dubious utility. They were predicated on the force following the authorized route (i.e. the autobahn), which would have meant that the battlegroup would have been spread out over a distance of several miles, but with a frontage only one or possibly two vehicles wide. Despite the inclusion of engineer equipment such as bridgelayers in the convoys, all that the Soviets would have needed to do to bring the whole force to a standstill would have been to put a barrier across the autobahn or demolish one of several bridges, leaving the force commander with an agonizing choice of what to do next: go on and run the risk of starting a major war, or turn back in a massive and humiliating retreat. It was perhaps as well that nobody was ever confronted by that dilemma.

33

Battlefield Nuclear Weapons

Tactical-nuclear-weapon development originated not with a statement of operational requirement from the military, but with US scientists in the late 1940s, who realized that it had become technically feasible to develop nuclear warheads which could fit into both small missiles and artillery shells. The first fruit of this was a massive 280 mm cannon, which was fielded by the US artillery in 1952 – the same year that NATO set itself a goal of ninety-six divisions. By 1954, however, it had become clear that this NATO goal was unattainable, and it was proposed that fielding tactical-nuclear-weapons systems would offer a method of substituting artillery for infantry and tanks. This was seized upon by the military in general, not least because at that time the Soviet Union did not possess any tactical nuclear weapons, thus giving NATO an absolute superiority. The proposal was also particularly popular with the artillery arms of the NATO armies, who saw themselves promoted to become the major arm on a nuclear battlefield. The Soviet army was not far behind, however, and it too began fielding tactical nuclear missiles in the late 1950s.

Once the first tactical nuclear weapons – both guns and missiles – were in service they increased rapidly in both type and quantity, although their roles differed significantly between the Warsaw Pact and NATO. For the Soviet army, battlefield nuclear weapons were simply an extension of the Warsaw Pact's offensive doctrine and were primarily intended to eliminate NATO's tactical nuclear forces. NATO, on the other hand, saw these weapons as a new type of defensive weapon, whose power very conveniently made up for a lack of manpower. So long as NATO possessed a monopoly in such weapons this theory had a certain validity, but once the Soviet Union possessed them too the theory was seriously weakened, although the fielding of such weapons continued unabated until almost the end of the Cold War. The situation was further complicated by the French, who, as will be seen, had a fundamentally different rationale for the use of such weapons.

349

GUNS

There were two types of battlefield nuclear weapon: guns/howitzers and missiles.* First in the field in 1952 was the US army's massive 280 mm atomic cannon (officially the 'Gun, Heavy, Motorized, 280 mm, M65), although this was regarded as something of a military curiosity, even at the time. The original projectile was the W19, with a yield of 15 kT, but this was later replaced by the W23, with a variable 10–15 kT yield. These projectiles had a range of 30,300 m, but each gun required a crew of several hundred and some twenty vehicles, and a deployed gun detachment was reputed to resemble a small village. Despite its disadvantages, the system remained in service for eleven years.

Advancing technology then enabled the USA not only to develop smaller-calibre atomic projectiles, but also to make the guns dual-capable, so that they could fire conventional high-explosive rounds as well. The most widely used of these weapons were the M109 and M110. The first of these to enter service, in 1961, was the M110 203 mm cannon, firing the W33 atomic round, which had a maximum yield of 12 kT; in 1963 this was followed by the M109 155 mm howitzer, firing the W48 round with a yield of 0.1 kT. Both of these weapons were always used for airbursts.

Both the M109 and the M110 were mounted on tracked chassis, which gave them a high degree of battlefield mobility. Both proved to be excellent systems, and their barrels, chassis and rounds were developed throughout their long periods of service, particularly to enhance the range, which in the case of the M109 increased from 18,100 m (M109A1) to 30,000 m (M109A3). These weapons were widely exported, although only NATO countries (West Germany, Greece, Italy, the Netherlands, Turkey and the UK) received the nuclear rounds. As of 1983, 1,000 W33 and 3,000 W48 rounds were held in western Europe, but the United States alone possessed the 203 mm W79 enhanced-radiation (ER) round with a yield of 10 kT (W79-0) and 1–2 kT (W79-1), although this was never deployed to units.

The artillery has always been of great importance in Soviet military doctrine, and it must have seemed natural for the USSR to follow the Western lead and develop atomic rounds. The first of these to appear were fielded in the late 1960s, when a 0.2 kT atomic round for the S-23 180 mm towed cannon was introduced. The next nuclear artillery piece was the 2S3 152 mm M-1973, which fired a 2 kT round over a range of 24,000 m, followed by the 2S7 203 mm gun in 1975. As far as is known, the Soviet Union never supplied nuclear shells to any of its Warsaw Pact allies.

---

* Specifications of the main types of battlefield nuclear weapon are given in Appendix 27.

MISSILES

In the late 1940s both the USA and the USSR not only owned and tested samples of the German A-4 (V-2), but also had teams of German scientists from Peenemünde to help them with further developments. Although this eventually led to missiles with intercontinental ranges, the original missiles were for battlefield use, and a series of such missiles was developed throughout the Cold War.

US Missiles

Between 1945 and 1950 the US army built a number of virtual copies of the A-4 under the name Hermes, one model of which carried a 454 kg high-explosive warhead over a range of 242 km. Although the German army had operated the A-4, it had employed it as a strategic rather than a tactical weapon, but when, in the early 1950s, atomic warheads became sufficiently small to enable them to be mounted on missiles, the US army saw them as battlefield weapons. These US missiles can be considered in three groups, according to their range.

The first long-range army missile (and the third missile system to enter service) was developed by the original V-1 team, headed by Werner von Braun. The Redstone entered service in 1958, and was essentially an enlarged and much improved V-1 with a range of 400 km, though its payload of either a 1 MT or a 2 MT atomic weapon gave a totally new dimension of firepower to a battlefield commander. The liquid-fuelled Redstone needed many men and vehicles, one particular requirement being a special plant capable of producing 20 tonnes of liquid oxygen per day.

Next was the Pershing, which entered service in 1962 and rapidly replaced the Redstone. This was a two-stage, solid-fuelled missile, which was launched vertically from a ground-mounted base-plate, with four tracked vehicles forming a fire unit. This was subsequently replaced by the Pershing IA system, which used the same missile but with wheeled trucks, including a trailer-mounted launch platform, making the whole system airportable. The Pershing I/IA missile delivered 60 kT, 200 kT or 400 kT warheads over a 740 km range with an accuracy of 400 m. Pershing I and IA all served in West Germany, with the US army and the German *Luftwaffe*.

Development of the Pershing II system, a modification of the Pershing IA, began in 1976, with the intention of producing a system with greater accuracy and reliability, but with the same range as the Pershing IA. A requirement for much greater range was added during the development process, which involved the new system in a major political controversy, since the new 1,800 km range enabled it to reach targets in the western USSR. Despite this, 120 Pershing IIs were eventually fielded (by the US army only) in 1983 as part of NATO's twin-track strategy. The warhead was a W-85 nuclear weapon, with a yield, selectable according to the desired terminal effects, of between 5 and 50 kT, and a CEP of 45 m. A proposed earth-penetrator warhead was cancelled in 1982.* All Pershing systems were directly affected by the terms of the 1987 INF Treaty, which banned missiles with ranges between 500 and 5,600 km, and by May 1991 all Pershings had been withdrawn and destroyed.

The first of the medium-range missiles to enter service (and also the first US army missile) was the Corporal, which was fielded in 1953, having been rushed into service as a result of the Korean War. In essence a modified meteorological rocket, Corporal carried a 60 kT atomic weapon over a range of 138 km and a fire unit was carried on a series of wheeled trucks, with the missile being launched vertically from a base-plate. It saw service only with the US and British armies, from 1953 to 1967, and, principally because of its liquid fuel, it was extremely cumbersome and manpower-intensive, requiring fifteen vehicles and 250 men per launcher. A far more serious tactical limitation, however, was that it took seven hours from entering a location to launch the weapon.

The second medium-range weapon was Sergeant, which was much smaller and lighter than the Corporal. Its use of solid fuel enabled very considerable economies to be made, since a fire unit required just three semi-trailers and a standard truck, while the missile was ready to fire in thirty minutes after arriving in a location. Sergeant carried a 60 kT warhead over a maximum range of 140 km, and entered service in 1961.

The shorter-range systems began with Honest John, a small (7.6 m long) and light (2,141 kg) free-flight rocket, which was fired from a ramp fixed either on the back of a six-wheeled truck or on a ground-mounted tripod. Honest John was widely used throughout NATO from 1954 onwards, but was replaced by Lance in the 1970s, except for Greece and Turkey, who kept it in service well into the 1980s. Highly mobile, Honest John had a range of 6–38 km.

The Lance system, which replaced both Honest John and Sergeant in most NATO armies, was smaller, lighter, more mobile, more reliable and had a much greater maximum range, of 125 km. It carried either a variable 1–100 kT fission warhead or a 1 kT ER warhead, which was procured only by the US army and was never in fact deployed. Lance was designed for use against depth targets.

At one time thought was also given to two very short-range missile systems to be controlled by a battlegroup commander. Known as the Weapon System Battlegroup Lightweight M28 and Heavyweight M29,

---

* This would have enabled the warhead to penetrate a considerable depth into most soil types before detonating, giving the resultant sub-surface explosion a considerable capability against underground bunkers.

these had a range of 2,000 m and 4,000 m respectively. The lightweight system was more widely known as the Davy Crocket and was a 120 mm recoilless weapon, consisting of a launch tube which sat on a tripod mounted either on the ground or on a light vehicle such as a Jeep. In both cases the crew was totally unprotected. The projectile was very small, being 64.8 cm long and 28 cm in diameter, and contained a 0.25 kT warhead, which could be fired to a maximum range of 2,000 m. It did not take long, however, for it to be realized that it was singularly ill-advised for the crew to be caught in the open just 2,000 m from a nuclear explosion (indeed, the front-line 'friendly' troops would have been even closer), and, to the great relief of the troops involved, the system left service in 1971. The British army had shown initial interest in this system, but wisely decided not to purchase it.

Soviet Missiles

Like those of the USA, the Soviet Union's first post-war missile was a development of the German A-4; this led to the SS-1A (NATO = 'Scunner') with a range of 300 km and a 750 kg high-explosive warhead. The first nuclear battlefield missile to enter service (in 1957) was the Scud-A, which was mounted on a converted JS-3 heavy-tank chassis and carried a 50 kT warhead over a range of some 150 km. This was later supplemented by the Scud-B system, which carried a 70 kT warhead over a range of 300 km. Although Scuds were supplied to many other countries, nuclear warheads were only ever issued to the Soviet army and the system served throughout the Cold War, as plans to replace it with the SS-23 were cancelled as part of the INF Treaty.

The SS-12 ('Scaleboard') was a road-mobile, solid-fuelled ballistic missile, which was first fielded in 1962, followed by a modified version, the SS-12B (initially designated SS-22), in 1979. The missile had a maximum range of 900 km and a CEP of 30 m, carrying either a high-explosive or a 500 kT nuclear warhead, and system reaction time was estimated at sixty minutes. The SS-12B was withdrawn under the terms of the INF Treaty, and all missiles were destroyed.

One of the significant features of both the SS-1 and the SS-12 was that later versions were transported by 8 × 8-wheel TELs. These were highly mobile for off-road driving, were air-conditioned, accommodated the full crew and all necessary equipment, and even had an automatic tyre-pressure-regulation system. All these features enabled the missile detachment to move into a new location, set up the missile quickly, launch, and then move to a resupply point – the so-called 'shoot-and-scoot' tactic.

All Warsaw Pact exercises made use of battlefield nuclear weapons in support of attacks. A typical scenario, as shown in Map 3 (page 360), used some 233 weapons in the first strike, followed by 294 in the second strike. As used in these exercises, the intended purpose was to eliminate NATO forward troops – Area B, for example, coincided with the North German Plain. Following such a strike, the Warsaw Pact tank and motor-rifle units would have been able to advance rapidly into NATO rear areas.

Other NATO Countries

The UK made one attempt at a battlefield missile system in the late 1950s. Known as Blue Water, it was intended to replace the American Corporal, but, despite working very satisfactorily, it was cancelled in 1962.

The other west-European project, the French Pluton, was much more successful. The French operated a number of Honest John battalions in the early 1960s, but when France left the NATO integrated command structure in 1966 the units were deactivated and the missiles were returned to the USA.

There was then a gap until the French developed the Pluton system, which first flew in 1969 and entered service in 1974. The entire system – including nuclear warhead, missile, launcher, chassis and electronics – was of French design. The missile was mounted in a large, open-fronted box atop an AMX-30 tank chassis and required a crew of four. The missile could carry either a 10 kT warhead for use against targets in the forward areas or a 25 kT warhead for use against rear-area installations such as tank, vehicle or troop concentrations; headquarters; railways; or bridges. As with all missiles, CEP varied with range, and was 400 m at the maximum range of 120 km. Unlike many other systems, Pluton was purely nuclear and had no high-explosive or chemical capabilities.

Pluton was deployed only on French territory in peacetime, in five missile regiments, each with seven operational launchers. A total of seventy missiles was deployed, giving one on each launcher, plus one reload. A second-generation French system, Hades, was developed in the 1980s. Some thirty missiles were actually produced, but were then put into storage and were never fielded.

TARGET ACQUISITION

One problem affected the battlefield nuclear weapons of both sides: that of accurate and timely target acquisition.* Static targets – a railway station, say, or a bridge, an airfield or a major crossroads – could be selected off a map. Targets of military opportunity, however – such as a concentration of tanks, a headquarters or a logistics unit – were much more difficult, especially as both sides tended to make the great majority of such units move at frequent

---

* The problem affected all weapons, including aircraft, conventional artillery, mortars, and so on, but was most acute for nuclear weapons.

intervals. The problem was fourfold: first, to have a means of acquiring a target; second, to transmit the target-acquisition information to an intelligence-gathering centre; third, a command system had to allocate destruction of the target as a nuclear task; and, finally, a control system had to find a weapon within range and task it.

The most difficult of these was the acquisition process, which became progressively more difficult with distance from the front line. Increasing resources were allocated to this as the Cold War progressed, including ground radar, aircraft reconnaissance, drones, stay-behind parties, remote sensors and the airborne warning and control system (AWACS), to name but a few.

SAFETY

A large number of battlefield nuclear weapons were deployed from the 1950s onwards, being fielded by the Soviet army on one side and by the majority of NATO armies on the other. On both sides the actual warheads were under very strict control. On the Soviet side nuclear warheads were the responsibility of special KGB detachments, who held the warheads and issued them only on orders received down an entirely separate chain of command.

The US system involved devices known as Permissive Action Links (PALs), which required a coded password to be inserted, either mechanically or electronically, in order to unlock the arming circuits. Such devices became increasingly sophisticated over the years – for example, the numerical combination increased from four to twelve digits, with the later codes being used not only for release but also to specify such factors as the permitted yield in a variable-yield warhead. Such PALs were operated by US army custodial detachments, which served with every US and NATO unit possessing such weapons.[1]

THE BATTLEFIELD-NUCLEAR-WEAPONS ISSUES

The US attitude to battlefield nuclear weapons went through several variations. During the Eisenhower administration, Secretary of State John Foster Dulles stated that 'The present policies will gradually involve the use of atomic weapons as conventional weapons for tactical purposes',[2] and the field army was restructured into what was known as the 'Pentomic' organization. Under President Kennedy, however, the emphasis changed to 'flexible response', with the major emphasis on conventional forces, and it remained that way for the remainder of the Cold War.

In its Fiscal Year 1975 report to Congress, the US Department of Defense stated that:

> as a practical matter, the initiation of a nuclear engagement would involve many uncertainties. Acceptable boundaries on such a conflict would be extremely difficult to establish. A nuclear engagement in the theater could well produce much higher military and civilian casualties and more widespread collateral damage than its non-nuclear counterpart . . . What is more, it is not clear under what conditions the United States and its allies would possess a comparative military advantage in a tactical nuclear exchange . . . We must recognize in our planning that the decision to initiate the use of nuclear weapons – however small, clean, and precisely used they might be – would be the most agonizing that could face any national leader.[3]

However, such doubts appear to have disappeared by the time the 1982 report was written, for this stated that:

> Our theater nuclear programs are designed to provide a wide range of options to respond appropriately to any level of potential attack. A credible TNF [theatre nuclear forces] capability will strengthen and enhance the links between conventional and strategic forces and is designed to convey to a potential aggressor the capability of the United States and its allies to respond across the full spectrum of potential conflict . . .[4]

The 1983 the US Joint Chiefs-of-Staff made a significant addition to the possible uses of theatre nuclear forces when they stated that:

> TNF are designed for use in conjunction with conventional forces to deter conventional, theater nuclear, and chemical attack . . . TNF may be used in the event of enemy first use of nuclear weapons, or in the event of significant failure of the conventional defense. They could also have utility in retaliation against the enemy's initiation of widespread chemical warfare if US chemical retaliation is ineffective or not available . . .[5]

Two British examples are relevant. Sir Solly Zuckerman, the government's chief scientific adviser, wrote that:

> these . . . conclusions are borne out by the results of war-games played by experienced commanders under proper conditions. The average pay-off for the defenders has turned out to be about one minor unit [about 250 men] per strike, and for the offensive somewhere between one and two strikes [are needed to obtain the same results] against the better entrenched defenders. A fairly consistent picture is that of between 200 and 250 nuclear strikes of average yield about 20 kT exploded in the space of a few days in an area 50 miles by 50 miles.[6]

If this was extrapolated to cover the entire Central Front, and deep interdiction strikes were added, the number of weapons, their total yield and their effect became almost incalculable, as another British study showed. This is examined in more detail in Chapter 35, but suffice it here to say that this postulated the use by *each* side of 500 tactical nuclear weapons in the northern part of the Central Front and 250 in the south, with an average yield of 30 kT each, plus a further 250 interdiction strikes (i.e. against bridges, railway yards, and so on) averaging 300 kT each.

The effects of the use of weapons in such numbers would have been catastrophic. Within the zone where such weapons had been used, towns and villages would have been devastated, all but the strongest buildings would have been destroyed, roads and bridges would have become impassable, forests would have been razed, enormous fires would have been raging, and civilian casualties would have been vast. In addition to all this, since NATO was defending, many of the attacking Warsaw Pact forces it was targeting would have been on NATO – particularly West German – territory, while the depth attacks would have stretched well into East Germany.

On the NATO side, nuclear artillery units were allocated to army group, corps and even divisional level, but 'nuclear release' (i.e. the authority to start using them) was retained at the very highest level. All the weapons were US-owned and controlled by a PAL, and it would have been impossible for NATO to use them without the authority of the president of the USA, while it seems improbable that he would have given such authorization without consulting NATO. At the very least, the president would have had to consult the West German chancellor, since not only would the great majority of the weapons have been launched from West German territory but they would in many cases have landed on targets on either West or East German soil. Further, West Germany would have been a very likely target for many of the retaliatory Soviet strikes.

This very issue was highlighted by the French Pluton system, which was declared to be part of the French *pre-stratégique* force, intended to deliver a 'final nuclear warning' to an aggressor. The announced French intention was that in wartime most, if not all, Pluton regiments would join the French Second Army Corps in south-west Germany, where German territory is about 300 km wide. As Pluton's maximum range was 120 km, this meant that even if the Plutons were sited well forward the missiles would have been launched against targets on West German territory – a concept over which the Federal government expressed some concern. As a result, at the end of a visit to West Germany in 1987, President Mitterrand gave an assurance that France would never deploy Pluton in this way, which raised the question of just how it could be used.

34

Conventional War in Europe

There were many possible scenarios for Soviet aggression in central Europe, but the worst case for NATO was a sudden attack launched by the in-place Warsaw Pact forces, which would have been reinforced covertly to the greatest extent Soviet commanders deemed feasible without being spotted by the West. The British assessed that the maximum that could have been used in an attack on the Central Front under such conditions was fifty-two divisions, of which twenty-three (nineteen Soviet and four Polish) would have faced NORTHAG and twenty-three (eleven Soviet, four Polish and eight Czech) would have faced CENTAG, with three East German divisions attacking Schleswig-Holstein. A further three East German divisions would have surrounded and attacked West Berlin, before moving on to further tasks.

A different scenario might have involved a Warsaw Pact attack to seize a specific and significant area in as short a time as possible, possibly using a major exercise in eastern Europe as the initial cover for such an operation. NATO experts believed that the Alliance would have detected such an exercise and called Simple Alert and Reinforced Alert, and a British study assumed that (with D-day being the day of the Soviet attack) Simple Alert would have been called on D-3 and Reinforced Alert on D-1, but this seems excessively optimistic. Even if it was correct, however, the Warsaw Pact would have started to attack well before NATO mobilization was complete, and the prospects of reinforcements such as from the UK to West Germany or Denmark reaching their deployment positions in time would have been very slim.

Some pretext for the attack would have been concocted, and the military moves would have been accompanied by messages to Western governments and to non-NATO nations that this was a limited attack with restricted aims. If the Warsaw Pact forces had achieved these limited aims and then halted, they would have placed NATO in a major dilemma, even supposing that members of the Alliance had been unanimous in their reactions to the initial attack. NATO's first aim would have been to contain and halt the Soviet attack, while exerting heavy diplomatic pressure in an effort to force the Soviets to withdraw. The most serious possibility for NATO would have been to counter-attack immediately using tactical nuclear weapons, but it is highly questionable whether this would have been feasible, since public opinion in many Western countries could have been opposed to such a move. In particular, the West Germans would have been in a major dilemma, since it would have been they who had lost territory, but it would have been Germans who would bear the brunt of the casualties from a retaliation. If, eventually, the Soviets had withdrawn to their side of the Inner German Border under some face-saving pretext, they would have lost little, apart from a few hundred casualties. A second option would have been to sit tight and challenge NATO to oust them.

THE WARSAW PACT ATTACK PLANS

In the mass of documents released since the end of the Cold War, no evidence has been found of any Warsaw Pact defensive plans, except for a few formulated in the final three years, after President Gorbachev had insisted that the General Staff prepare them. Instead, all plans concentrated on a series of massive attacks, which were aimed at securing Soviet control of the entire west-European land mass. According to Soviet and East German planning documents, the major plan for the Central Front aimed at reaching the German–French border in between thirteen and fifteen days, and then of overrunning France so that the leading troops arrived at the Atlantic coast and the Franco-Spanish border by the thirty-fifth day. The attack would have been conducted by five, possibly six, 'fronts' (see Map 3, to which the numbers/letters refer):[1]

- Jutland Front (2). This front was to advance northward through Schleswig-Holstein, across the Kiel Canal, and then on up through Jutland (2A). The Danish island of Bornholm would also have been captured. This would have opened the Belts (thus enabling the Soviet Baltic Fleet (1) to sail into the North Sea), closed the Baltic to NATO naval forces, and obtained valuable forward airfields for use in the land battles on the Central Front and in the naval battles in the North Sea. The advance along the Baltic coast would have been aided by amphibious assault forces from East Germany, Poland and the USSR, and possibly also by paratroops.
- Coastal Front (2B). The Coastal Front would have initially followed behind the Jutland Front attack and then broken away to swing south of

The Soviet Attack Plan

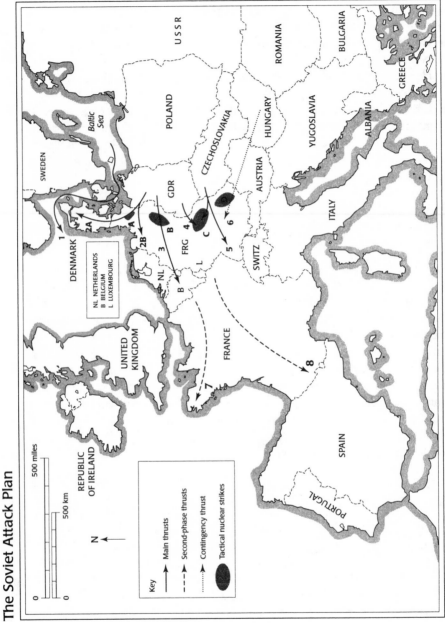

Key
→ Main thrusts
⇢ Second-phase thrusts
⋯ Contingency thrust
● Tactical nuclear strikes

NL NETHERLANDS
B BELGIUM
L LUXEMBOURG

N ←

0   500 km
0   500 miles

Note: Adapted from *Militärische Planungen des Warschauer Paktes in Zentraleuropa: Eine Studie*, Federal Ministry of Defence, Bonn, February 1992.

Hamburg and along the northern edge of the North German Plain, with its right flank following the line of the North Sea coast. This would have secured the ports of Bremerhaven, Wilhelmshaven, Emden and Rotterdam (closing them to NATO maritime traffic), and secured the right flank of the main attack.

- Central Front (3). The main axis of this attack would have been across the North German Plain along the line Braunschweig–Hanover–Bielefeld–Hamm, then on through the northern edge of the Ruhr and thence to Aachen, Maastricht and Liege to the French Channel coast.
- Luxembourg Front (4). This advance would have begun in Thüringia and passed through the Fulda Gap, crossing the Rhine north of Frankfurt and then moving on towards the French cities of Reims, Metz and Paris.
- Bavarian Front (5). This attack would have originated in Czechoslovakia and swept through Bavaria and onward through Baden-Württemburg, over the Rhine and then into France.
- Austrian Front (6). Plans existed for a sixth front, which would have been mounted from Hungary, advancing through eastern Austria and on past Munich, with its left flank passing through Swiss territory to the south of the Bodensee (Lake Constance). This appears to have been a contingency plan, depending on whether or not the forces were required for operations in Italy, Greece and Yugoslavia.

Once west of the Rhine, two major thrusts would have been made towards the Atlantic coast (7) and the Spanish border (8).

The Forces Involved

The forces involved in these massive attacks would have totalled sixty divisions, of which some thirty-eight would have been Soviet, including a Naval Infantry brigade. Other Warsaw Pact forces were, however, an integral part of the plan. The East Germans would have contributed eight divisions to the Jutland, Coastal, Central and Luxembourg fronts, with a further three divisions being responsible for attacking and taking over West Berlin.*

The Polish army would have contributed six divisions to the Jutland and Coastal Fronts, plus an amphibious assault brigade to take part in the landings along the Baltic coast. Czech forces would have contributed four divisions to the Bavarian Front, and, had it been activated, some Hungarian divisions would have been allocated to the Austrian Front. Coming up fast from the east would have been second- and third-echelon Soviet forces from Belorussia and the Ukraine, having first been brought up to war strength by mobilization.

---

* These would almost certainly have overrun West Berlin very rapidly, and then, having handed over mopping-up operations to a reserve formation, moved westward to reinforce one of the northern fronts.

It appears that the non-Soviet forces would not have been used in the advance into France. The East Germans, once their main operational missions had been accomplished, were required to impose military control on West Germany, with the immediate priority being to ensure that the territory could be used as an advanced operational and logistic base for continuing Soviet operations further West. The East Germans would presumably have been helped in this by the Czechs and Poles, since the task would have been enormous, involving, among many things, the imposition of military government, securing NATO prisoners of war, restoring of essential services, controlling refugees, and isolating nuclear-contaminated areas.

In these plans it was intended to use nuclear weapons as an integral part of the attacks, even if NATO did not use them first, and many targets had already been selected. The main attacks on the Central Front would have been allocated 205 Scud rockets at army level and 380 short-range missiles at divisional level, with 255 nuclear bombs carried by aircraft; of these, the first-echelon armies could each have expected some twenty Scuds, fifty-five short-range missiles and ten air-delivered bombs. Yields would have varied between 3 kT and 100 kT, and the weapons would have been targeted on NATO nuclear-weapons and nuclear-support facilities, airbases, headquarters and communications centres, troop concentrations and naval bases.

35

If Nuclear War had Come

In considering the Cold War, it is inevitable to speculate what might have happened if, events having worked out differently, war had broken out, leading to a nuclear exchange. Such an assessment is beset by difficulties, one of the most important being that only two atomic bombs have ever been dropped in anger. There were many subsequent tests, but these were, almost without exception, conducted in clinical conditions, and were concerned with small numbers of representative objects, such as houses, tanks, aircraft and ships. In particular, there is no precedent from which to judge how populations or the military might have reacted. When the A-bombs were dropped on Hiroshima and Nagasaki, the unsuspecting populations had no idea what had caused the disasters that had befallen them, and their subsequent behaviour gave little guidance as to how the survivors of a massive nuclear attack might have behaved; equally well-researched studies have reached conclusions varying from total discipline to total anarchy.*

THE US STRATEGY FOR NUCLEAR WAR

The original US nuclear-war plans were prepared at a time when bombers predominated, atomic bombs were in very short supply, and there was a lack of co-ordination of plans. The 1947 plan concentrated on destroying the war-making capability of the Soviet Union through attacks on government,

---

* In the early 1960s the author attended two separate study periods in Malaya on the conduct of nuclear war in the jungle. In the first, the basic assumption made by the team running the study was that nuclear weapons would have swept away vast swathes of jungle, making movement by both vehicles and men relatively easy. In the second, the opening assumption by a different team was that the nuclear weapons had created an impenetrable obstacle, making movement impossible.

political and administrative centres, urban–industrial areas and fuel-supply facilities. It was to have been achieved by dropping 133 atomic bombs on seventy Soviet cities in thirty days, including eight on Moscow and seven on Leningrad.[1] This plan was ambitious, to say the least, primarily because the USA possessed a total of only thirteen atomic bombs in 1947 and fifty in 1948.[2]

In May 1949 a new plan, named Trojan, required 150 atomic bombs, with a first-phase attack against thirty cities during a period of fourteen days. Then, also in 1949, came another plan, named Dropshot, in which a war in 1957 would be centred on a thirty-day programme in which 300 atomic bombs and 20,000 tonnes of conventional bombs would be dropped on about 200 targets, with the atomic bombs being used against a mix of military, industrial and civil targets, including Moscow and Leningrad.[3]

All these plans included substantial quantities of conventional bombs and were essentially continuations of Second World War strategies. Interestingly, even as early as 1949, planners were earmarking command centres for exemption from early strikes ('withholds' in nuclear parlance), so that the Soviet leadership could continue to exercise control.

Up to about 1956 the US authorities based their plans on intelligence which was far from complete and, as a result, they deliberately over-estimated their opponent's strengths. In 1956, however, the Lockheed U-2 spy plane started to overfly the USSR, and this, coupled with more effective ELINT and SIGINT, meant that a more accurate picture was obtained.

By the early 1950s the production rate of atomic bombs had increased to the point where US field commanders – both air-force and navy – began to make plans for their use, each of them planning to use them in support of *his* battle. There was nothing in this situation to prevent several commanders from selecting the same target; indeed, a US Senate committee was told that in the Far East 155 targets had been listed by two commanders and 44 by three, while in Europe 121 airfields had been targeted by two commanders and 31 by three.[4]

A first attempt at some form of co-ordination was made in a series of conferences held in the early 1950s, which achieved partial success. The situation came to a head, however, when the navy's Polaris SLBMs and the air force's Atlas ICBMs became operational in the early 1960s, and a Joint Strategic Target Planning Staff (JSTPS) was established, with an air-force lieutenant-general at its head but with a naval officer as his deputy. The first outcome of the JSTPS' work was the Comprehensive Strategic Target List (CSTL), which identified 2,021 nuclear targets in the USSR, China and their satellites, including 121 ICBM sites, 140 air-defence bases, 200 bomber bases, 218 military and political command centres, 124 other military targets, and 131 urban centres.[5] This CSTL duly became an integral part of the first Single Integrated Operational Plan (SIOP), which was produced in December 1960.

There were no alternatives in this SIOP-60, which consisted of one massive nuclear attack, and it was one of the earliest targets for reform when President Kennedy took power in January 1961. US planners were now, however, aided by virtually complete satellite coverage of the USSR, giving them information on the potential enemy never previously available (and which, among other things, made it clear that the supposed 'missile gap' did not exist). This resulted in SIOP-63, which consisted of five categories of counter-force option: Soviet missile sites; bomber and submarine bases; other military targets; command-and-control centres; and urban–industrial targets. This received serious criticism from three separate quarters. First, from within the USA, because of what appeared to be a first-strike strategy; second, from the USSR, which denied the possibility of controlled counter-force warfare; and, third, from NATO allies, who were very alarmed by the total absence of any urban targets (the so-called 'no cities' strategy).

President Kennedy's secretary of state for defense, Robert McNamara, then developed the concept of Assured Destruction, which he described in public first as 'one-quarter to one-third of [the Soviet Union's] population and about two-thirds of its industrial capacity' and later as 'one-fifth to one-fourth of its population and one-half to two-thirds of its industrial capacity'. Whatever was said in public, however, within the US armed forces SIOP-63 was not withdrawn, and thus there appears to have been a marked divergence between the public and the internal rhetoric.

Proponents of this policy of Mutually Assured Destruction (MAD) argued that the one way to make nuclear war impossible was to make it clear that any nuclear attack would be answered by a total attack on an enemy's population, together with its industrial and agricultural base. While such a concept might have been valid in the early days of the nuclear confrontation, it rapidly lost its credibility when it became clear that, even after such a strike, the USSR would still have sufficient weapons to make a response-in-kind on US cities.

The strategy of 'flexible response,' introduced in 1967, required facing an opponent with a credible reaction which would to inflict losses outweighing any potential gain. The deterrent power of such a strategy depended on the capacity of the proposed response to inflict unacceptable losses on the opponent, while its credibility depended upon its ability to minimize the risks of higher-order losses on the responder's own country in subsequent rounds. This posed something of a dilemma, in that the deterrent power of the response was enhanced by escalation to a higher level, while credibility tended in the other direction, since a lower-level response carried no inherent escalatory risks. The plans implement this strategy were promulgated in a revised version of the SIOP which became effective on 1 January 1976.

It became customary for all incoming presidents to initiate a review of the strategic nuclear-war plans, and that carried out by President Jimmy Carter in 1977–9, was expected to result in major changes. In the event, however, it led only to a refinement of the previous plan, together with the introduction of rather more political sophistication. Thus, for example, targets were selected in the Far East, not so much for their immediate relevance to the superpower conflict, but because their destruction would make the USSR more vulnerable to attack by the People's Republic of China.

A further review was conducted when the Reagan administration came to power in 1981. This resulted in a new version of the SIOP, which included some 40,000 potential targets, divided into Soviet nuclear forces; conventional military forces; military and political leadership command posts and communications systems; and economic and industrial targets, both war-supporting and those which would contribute to post-war economic recovery. The plan allocated these targets to a number of discrete packages, of differing size and characteristics, to provide the National Command Authority (the president and his immediate advisers) with an almost limitless range of options.

The new plan also included particular categories of target for other plans, for possible implementation on receipt of an unequivocal warning of a Soviet attack. These included a pre-emptive strike, launch-on-warning and launch-under-attack. The plan also included a number of 'withholds', but stipulated that a reserve of weapons must be retained for possible use against those 'withholds' if the developing scenario so dictated.

The real calculations of strategic nuclear war – known as 'dynamic' assessments – were extremely detailed and were far more complex than the static measurements. One such 'dynamic' calculation in the period following the Soviets' fielding of the SS-18 resulted in an assessment that, under certain conditions, a Soviet counter-force first strike would appear to be a possibility. In this assessment it was calculated that the USSR, which normally had only about 10 per cent of its SSBN force at sea, would gradually, and covertly, increase that number, and, if the US command decided to ride out the attack, the Soviets would then destroy approximately 45 per cent of the US strategic forces. As a result, the ensuing US counter-military retaliatory strike on the Soviets (who would be on full alert) would leave the Soviets with 75 per cent of what had been left *after* their first strike. This meant that the USSR would retain not only a reserve capable of carrying out either an urban–industrial strike on US cities or an attack on US 'other military targets', but also a reserve for use against another opponent (the so-called '*n*th-country reserve') – an outcome which would have been distinctly favourable to the Soviets. If the USA managed to launch all its ICBMs under attack, however, the damage ratio more or less reversed: 40 per cent damage to remaining Soviet forces versus 25 per cent damage to US strategic forces.

Thus, argued the US planners, a credible US launch-on-warning/launch-under-attack capability was a mandatory element of an effective deterrent. These results posed a problem encountered in numerous US war games: that neither side could enhance stability by pursuing its own best interests of a secure deterrent potential, but, conversely, neither side could unilaterally lower its deterrent. For the US to do the latter gambled on a US judgement of how the Soviets treated 'uncertainty' and what their perceptions of relative advantage might have been.

This whole area highlighted the decision to launch as one of the major problems associated with missiles. Launching bombers for possible nuclear missions was relatively easy, since crews were under firm instructions that they had to receive a positive (and encoded) order from the ground to continue before reaching specified waypoints, otherwise a return to base was mandatory. Missiles, on the other hand, received only one order – to take off; there was then no turning back.* Thus the decision to launch the missile was much harder to make.

THE OTHER SIDE OF THE HILL

As outlined above, the plans made by nuclear planners on both sides during the Cold War were primarily concerned with the dispatch of missiles and bombers. But what really mattered was what happened at the far end.

During the Cold War it was not particularly difficult to discover the effects of nuclear weapons on individuals, and official books such as *The Effects of Nuclear Weapons*[6] were available on the open market. Numerous unclassified assessments of the effects of nuclear war were prepared by official bodies, such as the US Department of Defense and the US Office of Technology. Similar assessments were also prepared by private bodies, such as research departments and magazines, but all faced similar problems. First, truly detailed studies inevitably required considerable time and great computing power. Second, all study findings were extremely sensitive to the initial assumptions on questions such as the military attack plan, the choice of airbursts or groundbursts, and the assessment of civil-defence measures. Third, there was the inescapable fact that all studies were looking at a situation which included an almost endless series of imponderables for which no previous human experience provided a reasonable guide.

In the British Public Record Office, however, there is a series of once

---

* From the mid-1970s onwards it was possible to retarget Minuteman missiles in flight, but it was not possible to terminate the flight.

highly classified studies carried out between 1960 and 1962 by a body known as JIGSAW',* a group of high-level experts which reported direct to the British Chiefs-of-Staff Committee and prepared a variety of reports on the possible outcomes of nuclear wars.[7] Since JIGSAW was working at such a high level, it can safely be assumed that its researches were thorough, that it obtained the most reliable expert inputs, and that the settings it considered were based on existing plans. The JIGSAW assessments can therefore be taken as being as authoritative as those of any other body, in the USA or the USSR.

A STRATEGIC ATTACK ON NORTH AMERICA

JIGSAW conducted a study of an attack on the United States and Canada which examined various aspects of an attack on cities. The first study assumed a Soviet attack on the 283 cities with a population exceeding 50,000 (1970 figures), each being hit by a single nuclear weapon, targeted on the geographical centre of the city. These attacks would have destroyed 30 per cent of the buildings and killed or rendered ineffective the total population of those cities, amounting to 81 million people. The study then looked at what would have happened to the remaining 149 million people in the other, smaller, urban areas and the countryside. It found that:

– Using 1 MT weapons, thirty-one million [people] would have been within the area of significant fallout, of whom some five million would have received a radiation dose of 200 roentgens or more, thus becoming casualties, while six million would have received between 50 and 200 roentgens, thus becoming ineffective.
– Using 8 MT weapons, the numbers within the area of significant fallout would have risen to seventy-nine million, of which twenty-one million would have received more than 200 roentgens, and seventeen million between 50 and 200 roentgens.[†]

Next JIGSAW examined the effects of different scales of attack, from attacking the sixty-three cities with a population exceeding 300,000 to attacking all 600 cities with a population of 25,000-plus. It also compared the effects of attacks using all 1 MT weapons or all 8 MT weapons. The outcome is shown in Table 35.1. This shows that, for all levels of attack, the number of people rendered ineffective in the cities by blast and radiation was always greater than the number of those outside the cities rendered ineffective by fallout alone. It should, however, be noted that, as the weight

---

* JIGSAW was the (doubtless carefully chosen) acronym for the *J*oint *I*nter-Service *G*roup for the *S*tudy of *A*ll-out *W*arfare.
† Note that JIGSAW gave radiation doses in roentgens and that, for the purposes of this book, the roentgen and the rad are synonymous – see the note on page 75.

Table 35.1 JIGSAW Assessments of the Effects of a Soviet Attack on North America

| Scale of Soviet attack | | People in cities rendered ineffective by attacks on target cities | | People outside the cities rendered ineffective by fallout | | | |
| | | | | 1 MT weapons | | 8 MT weapons | |
Cities attacked	Number of warhead deliveries	Number of people (millions)	% of national population	Number of people (millions)	% of national population	Number of people (millions)	% of national population
All over 300,000	63	57	25	3	1	10	4
All over 200,000	90	64	28	4	2	14	6
All over 100,000	150	72	31	6	3	22	9
All over 50,000	283	81	35	11	5	38	17
All over 40,000	400	86	37	15	7	52	23
All over 25,000	600	98	43	27	12	79	34

of the attack increased, the number of rural fallout victims rose much more sharply than did the number of victims in the cities.

When JIGSAW examined a strategic attack on the mainland UK (population 53 million) it had to modify its approach, since, compared to the USA and the USSR, the area was much smaller, and the 113 cities with a population of over 50,000 were much closer to each other. In fact, according to JIGSAW's calculations, deliveries of 1 MT weapons on all these 113 cities would have resulted in the deaths of more than 90 per cent of the total population.

JIGSAW therefore examined an attack using twenty-five weapons: six on Greater London and one each on nineteen other cities. This would have rendered 33 million people in the target cities ineffective. For the remainder in smaller towns and rural areas:

– Using 1 MT weapons, five million people would have been within the area of significant fallout, of whom some three million would have received a radiation dose of 200 roentgens or more, thus becoming casualties, while two million would have received between 50 and 200 roentgens and thus become ineffective.

— Using 8 MT weapons, the numbers within the area of significant fallout rose to sixteen million, of which ten million would have received more than 200 roentgens, and six million between 50 and 200 roentgens.

It is impossible to escape the conclusion that, had the Soviet Union decided on a heavy attack on the UK, the country would have been devastated by the use of a comparatively small proportion of the Soviet nuclear arsenal.

A STRATEGIC ATTACK ON THE USSR

The papers on JIGSAW's assessment of a strategic attack on the USSR as a whole remain closed, but one study is in the public domain; this uses a slightly different approach to examine '*the effects of a strategic nuclear attack on Soviet ground forces located in the Western USSR*'. The attack was confined to the Baltic and Belorussian military districts, principally because these contained the bulk of the forces threatening the NATO Central Front.* The area concerned covered 400,000 km², which is 2 per cent of the Soviet land

---

* The second reason given in the paper is that the JIGSAW staff were advised by the director of military intelligence that 'there was a lack of precise information on the location of Soviet forces in other areas of the USSR'. This is a most surprising admission at that stage of the Cold War.

mass, and included 6 per cent of the population. The paper assumed that the remainder of the USSR was being attacked with equal severity, and that heavy (but possibly less severe) attacks would also be delivered on the satellite countries.

The paper is based on the NATO doctrine of the time, according to which the targets of a nuclear strike on the USSR would be the political and military command structures and civil targets such as communications hubs (e.g. railways). In essence, this meant targeting cities, and JIGSAW considered three scales of attack:

– Attack A. A single 1 MT attack on each city with a population exceeding 50,000, of which there were twenty in the area under consideration (364 in the USSR as a whole).
– Attack B. An attack designed to kill about eighty per cent of the Soviet population, which would require 250 deliveries, averaging 3 MT on the area under study (4,000 deliveries on the whole USSR).
– Attack C. An attack designed to kill about sixty-five per cent of the Soviet population in the selected area, which would require 120 deliveries, averaging 3 MT (2,000 deliveries on the whole USSR).

It was assumed that a period of escalating political tension had led to a period of warning, in which the military forces had deployed to their 'survival locations', where they had dug in and covered their vehicles.

Attack A

This attack would involve one 1 MT weapon being dropped on each of the twenty cities with a population of over 50,000. The cities would have been devastated, with heavy casualties. The area of high contamination (a cumulative dose of 1,000 roentgens measured one hour after the explosion) from each burst would have covered some 310 km^2 and extended to a distance of some 48 km downwind from ground zero. For the lower-contamination criterion (450 roentgens after forty-eight hours) the area covered would have been some 26,000 km^2.

The outcome of such an attack would have been the devastation of every city, with very heavy casualties, leaving the survivors totally involved in the struggle for their own survival and in dealing with those casualties for whom treatment might offer a glimmer of hope. Communications within the cities would have been disrupted – and almost certainly destroyed in the area round ground zero. The normal system of supplies would have completely broken down, and the competition for the remaining stocks of food, fuel and medical treatment would have been both intense and frantic.

Because Soviet cities were widely spaced, however, the situation outside the cities would not have been so serious. Much of the rural population would have survived, and some travel would have been possible. The troops

371

who had dispersed from the cities had a very strong possibility of survival, their chances being improved by distance from the city, by taking cover and maintaining movement discipline, and by adopting positions upwind (i.e. to the west) of the potential targets.

Attack B

The second attack to be considered was one designed to kill about 80 per cent of the Soviet population, which would have required about 4,000 deliveries on the whole USSR, averaging 3 MT each, of which 250 would have been on the area under study. JIGSAW estimated that this would result in contamination of 1,000 roentgens after one hour over 350,000 km^2, which was 85 per cent of the area under study, while a lower level of 450 roentgens after forty-eight hours would have covered the entire area. Even for those who, through taking precautions or through chance, survived the blast effects, the prospects of survival were very bleak, since they would have had to move very rapidly to an area of insignificant fallout to continue to survive – a journey which would have been difficult, if not impossible. The transport system would have been virtually destroyed, and the areas of insignificant radiation would have been difficult to identify and, even if they were identified, might well have been on the other side of a region of high contamination. The lack of supplies and the probable breakdown of public order would have added yet further to the dismal prospects.

Attack C

This attack, intended to kill about 65 per cent of the Soviet population, would have required about half the weight of strikes involved in Attack B: i.e. 2,000 3 MT deliveries on the whole of the USSR, with 120 in the area under study. In this case, a contamination level of 1,000 roentgens after one hour would have covered about 186,000 km^2, or 46 per cent of the area, while a level of 450 roentgens after forty-eight hours would have covered the entire area. Once again, damage would have been very extensive, and the overlapping of the fallout plumes would have made it impossible to escape from at least the less serious (450 roentgens after forty-eight hours) contour.

ATTACKS ON CITIES

A further JIGSAW report concerned a nuclear attack on the British city of Birmingham, a highly industrialized urban area, with a population of approximately 1,800,000 people. A 1 MT airburst* weapon exploded over

---

* This would have been some *eighty* times more powerful than the weapons dropped on Hiroshima and Nagasaki.

the centre of the city would have damaged virtually every building in the city, half of which would have been demolished or burnt out, the intensity of the damage decreasing with distance from ground zero. The normal functions of the city – such as transport, gas, electricity, food supplies and sewage disposal – would have been severely disrupted. There would also have been a serious local fallout hazard, extending over part of the city and for about 400–500 km² in the neighbourhood. Birmingham would to all intents and purposes have ceased to exist.

JIGSAW assessed that only cities with populations greater than several million would have required more than one 1 MT weapon to inflict a similar level of damage. London, for example, might have required six weapons, New York five, and Moscow four.

In 1980 the US Office of Technology Assessment published a study, which compared the effects of a single 1 MT weapon targeted on the US city of Detroit and on the Soviet city of Leningrad, both of which had a population of 4,300,000. The estimated casualties were 470,000 killed and 630,000 seriously wounded in Detroit, while Leningrad would have suffered 890,000 killed and 1,260,000 seriously wounded. The reason for the difference was the population density: in the US city the population was widely dispersed, whereas in the Soviet city the population was much more heavily concentrated, with the majority being housed in high-rise blocks.

All the examples given above were well within the capacity of both the superpowers.

CASUALTIES

One of the most chilling elements of these studies is the discussion of casualties of almost incomprehensible magnitude. Massive numbers of people had been killed in previous wars, and most estimates agree that the Soviet Union lost some 20 million people in the years 1941–5. These, however, were lost over a period of four years in a large number of individual actions.

Air power inflicted the four most devastating attacks in the Second World War – two with conventional bombs and two with atomic bombs. The attack on Dresden, Germany, took place on 13–14 February 1945 and involved several hundred bombers of the British and United States air forces; at least 100,000 people died. Probably the most costly attack of the war, however, was the USAAF raid on Tokyo on 9–10 March 1945, in which 334 B-29 bombers dropped 1,600 tonnes of incendiaries and the resulting firestorm killed 83,000, with a further 100,000 injured. Then came the two atomic bombs: on Hiroshima, on 6 August 1945, with 78,150 killed and over 70,000 injured, and on Nagasaki, on 9 August, with 40,000 killed ard 25,000 injured.

In terms of casualties incurred during the attack, the conventional attacks on Dresden and Tokyo were actually more destructive than the atomic attacks on Hiroshima and Nagasaki. The former attacks, however, required many hundreds of bombers dropping thousands of bombs, while the latter each needed only one bomber and one bomb. The atomic attacks also introduced a new and invisible killer: radiation. This ability of nuclear warheads to carry destructive power equivalent to hundreds (and later to hundreds of thousands) of conventional bombs, allied to the residual, invisible killer, was the spectre that was to haunt the planners of both sides throughout the Cold War.

One of the major problems in discussing casualties is that, not surprisingly, estimates varied wildly, not least because they were assessing something for which not even the A-bomb attacks on Hiroshima and Nagasaki provided a precedent. In addition, there were a large number of variables and uncertainties:

- US planners could plot population density in the USA accurately, but could only hazard guesses at the density in the USSR.
- Meteorological conditions over the target would have had a direct effect on accuracy, as well as on the direction and extent of the blast effect and of fallout plumes.
- Cities were obviously the most vulnerable targets, but an active and timely civil-defence policy of evacuation to rural areas could have substantially reduced casualties. Whether or not such a policy could have been successfully implemented was another matter.
- In addition to evacuation, civil-defence fallout shelters in the cities, coupled with timely warning to the populace to take cover, would also have reduced casualties.

In the mid-1970s one assessment of US deaths varied from 200,000 in a first-strike Soviet missile attack aimed specifically at US ICBM fields, to 20 million for an attack on all strategic forces and the related command-and-control facilities. Ten years later, another two studies showed that matters had moved on considerably. The first study analysed the civilian casualties likely to be incurred in the USA from a Soviet counter-force attack involving approximately 3,000 individual weapons. It was found that:

12–27 million Americans would die and that altogether 23–45 million would suffer lethal or serious non-lethal injuries from the short-term, direct effects of the nuclear explosions. In the longer term, an additional 2–20 million might develop radiation-caused cancers. The variation was due to different assumptions concerning winds and casualty models.[8]

The same authors then conducted a study of a similar attack on the USSR, and concluded that:

– A major US attack on strategic nuclear facilities in the Soviet Union might kill 12–27 million people, kill or injure a total of 25–54 million people in the short term and cause 2–14 million people to suffer radiation-induced cancers in the longer term.

– A worst-case attack on Soviet urban areas with one hundred one-MT airbursts would kill 45–77 million people and cause a total of 73–93 million to suffer lethal and non-lethal injuries.[9]

In other words, a counter-value attack would have involved up to 93 million casualties, but even an attack on counter-force targets would have involved at least 12 million and possibly as many as 27 million deaths.

A BATTLE IN EUROPE

The Setting

The setting devised by JIGSAW for its European study started with a ground battle in which the Warsaw Pact forces advanced into West Germany, with NATO forces' role being to delay and hold the main thrusts until the strategic nuclear strike on the Soviet Union had taken its full effect. In the area of interest to the British (i.e. that part of northern Germany where 1 (BR) Corps would be fighting), the Warsaw Pact thrust was considered to have two main axes: one in the north, on a frontage of some 160 km across the North German Plain, against Belgian, British and West German forces; the second, in the south, through the Fulda Gap and towards Frankfurt am Main, against West German and US forces. There would, of course, have been other thrusts in the Central Region from Czechoslovakia into southern Germany and along the Baltic coast to Hamburg and Denmark, as well as in Norway and southern Europe.

The JIGSAW team prefaced its assessments by drawing attention to one of the unusual characteristics of the German rural areas, which is the very large number of relatively small villages, which are laid out as if on a grid, some 3–5 km from each other. This meant that, even if the tactical weapons were very low-yield and aimed at military targets, they would inevitably include several of these villages within their lethal area.

The nuclear battle had three elements.* The first was the exchange actually on the battlefield in support of operations at the operational and tactical

---

* The European battle was based on the following assumptions:

1 The prevailing wind was 37km/h knots from the west.
2 In tactical areas and on the interdiction lines, the weapons were uniformly spaced and burst simultaneously.
3 Where blast pressures from separate explosions overlapped, the damage done was that caused by the higher overpressure only.

level. The study assumed exchanges of 500 weapons in the north and 250 in the south, with an average yield of 30 kT each.

The second was a series of interdiction strikes, aimed at bridges, ferries and other crossing points, which were designed to prevent reinforcements and supplies reaching the enemy's forward troops. The NATO interdiction strikes would have consisted of some 250 nuclear weapons, each of 300 kT yield, on a north–south line generally following the line of the river Elbe and extending from the Baltic to Prague – a distance of some 560 km. The Soviet interdiction strike would have been along a line running from Strasbourg in the south northward along the Rhine to Nijmegen and then north to the Ijselmeer, and would have been intended to prevent reinforcements and supplies reaching NATO forces in the forward area, and also to prevent those forward troops from withdrawing across the Rhine. This strike would have been of the same size as the NATO strike: i.e. 250 weapons, each with a 300 kT yield.

The third element consisted of two counter-air strikes, in which NATO would launch attacks against 115 Warsaw Pact airfields in Czechoslovakia, East Germany and Poland. The Warsaw Pact air forces would launch a concurrent attack on 100 NATO airfields: forty in Belgium, France and the Netherlands, and sixty in West Germany.

Although none of these attacks was specifically aimed at cities, some of the bridges and airfields were inevitably located in such urban concentrations.

The Outcome

The predicted outcome of such a battle is shown in Table 35.2. The boxed entries represent the unavoidable minimum effects. Thus, under airburst weapons (columns (d) and (e)), the figures show the area of severe blast damage in which the population would suffer some 80 per cent deaths in the inner zone, reducing to 10 per cent in the outer zone. In the groundburst case (columns (f) and (g)), the boxed entries represent the 'Z-zone', where it would have been necessary to evacuate immediately those people who had survived the effects of blast and fire to areas with a small risk of fallout.

If all the nuclear weapons used in this battle had been groundburst, there would have been a serious fallout hazard over 138,000 km² of the total land mass of West Germany, of which 36,000 km² would have been the Z-zone, from which any survivors would have had to be evacuated if they were not to die. In addition, 3.6 million people would have been homeless, with another 3 million homes damaged.

If, however, the battle had been conducted using airbursts alone, there would have been no residual radiation, but the immediate radiation dose (3,000 roentgens) would have been delivered over an area which, in peacetime, housed some 2 million people.

Table 35.2 Summary of Effects of a Nuclear Attack on West Germany (area 248,640 km²; population (1960) 54.5 million)

Criteria			Airburst Weapons		Groundburst Weapons	
Effect	Definition	Parameter	Area*	Population†	Area*	Population†
(a)	(b)	(c)	(d)	(e)	(f)	(g)
1 Radiation	Immediate gamma and neutron radiation	Immediate dose of 3,000 roentgens	4,533 km²	2,000,000	—	—
2		Z-zone	Cumulative dose of 3,000 roentgens in 48 hours	—	—	36,000 km²‡	11,800,000‡
3		Serious fallout hazard	Cumulative dose of 450 roentgens in 48 hours	—	—	102,000 km²	22,000,000
4 Blast	Devastation	<0.4 kgf/cm²	15,500 km²	5,900,000	8,500 km²	3,600,000
5	Severe blast damage	0.2–0.4 kgf/cm²	34,400 km²‡	6,600,000‡	9,500 km²	3,200,000
6 Burns§	Third-degree burns		36,000 km²	10,700,000	13,600 km²	5,700,000
7	Second-degree burns		43,000 km²	5,100,000	5,800 km²	1,600,000

* The figures in Columns (d) and (f) represent the geographical area exposed to the effect in Column (c). The figures in Columns (e) and (g) represent the civilian population normally resident in those areas, and thus the maximum potentially exposed to the effects in Column (c).

† The population figures are not cumulative, for two reasons:

(a) Protective measures would have reduced the casualties (e.g. people indoors would escape burns and, in some cases, radiation).
(b) People near ground zero would have been within the lethal area for more than one effect, but could only die once.

‡ The boxed entries represented the unavoidable minimum effect.

§ The numbers of people shown in Lines 6 and 7 are those at risk from burns, but the numbers actually receiving such burns would be very much fewer, since this would be the easiest effect to guard against.

It is important to note that these figures represented the areas affected by the stated hazard and the population within those area. Thus the population figures would not necessarily have been the total casualty figures, particularly in the case of immediate radiation, where a proportion of the population would have been indoors or possibly in shelters. Similarly, many people at risk from burns might have been protected by being indoors or even, if in the open, by being in the shadow of a building. Where blast is concerned, however, the case would have been different, since in the 'blast devastation' area (Lines 4–5) the homes of some 5.9 million people would have been reduced to rubble and those of a further 6.6 million severely damaged.

During the Second World War the German homeland was subjected to bombing attacks during a period of some five years, in which some 400,000 civilians were killed and a further 600,000 were injured. Cities were the main targets, and across the country as a whole some 10 per cent of the residential housing stock was destroyed and a further 10 per cent was damaged. In a nuclear war, far worse damage would have been caused in a matter of minutes than during the five years of the Second World War.

Whether the campaign had been conducted using airburst or ground-burst weapons the damage would have been massive. In the airburst case the damage would have been wrought mainly by blast, with the destruction of a large number of houses and factories, and with the probability of the death of many millions of people. In the groundburst case the blast effects would have been somewhat less, but the area of the Z-zone would have been about the same as for the airburst case and almost all the 11.8 million people within that zone would have died unless rapidly evacuated. In short, airbursts would have damaged more buildings, groundbursts would have caused more casualties to people.

36

The Financial Cost

If actual physical combat never broke out, there were nevertheless some real battlegrounds on which the Cold War was fought, among them those of equipment and of technology. But these depended upon the resources made available to finance them, and the management systems which controlled them. Indeed, there are good grounds for believing that NATO eventually priced the Warsaw Pact, and in particular the Soviet Union, out of business.

EQUIPMENT

All nations expended a substantial proportion of their defence budgets on equipment, and the Cold War was a 'happy time' for military men on both sides of the Iron Curtain, even though they constantly complained that they were short of money and starved of resources. The fact was that public funds had never been so generously lavished on military forces in peacetime, and many of the shortages were more apparent than real.

The naval, general and air staffs and the government procurement agencies alike faced many challenges, of which the most fundamental was that, in the worst case, the Third World War might have broken out very suddenly and then been both extremely violent and very short. This would have been quite unlike the First and Second World Wars, where there had been time to mobilize national industries, to develop new equipment, and to produce it all in sufficient quantities. But, whereas those wars had lasted four and six years respectively, the indications were that, in the worst case, the Third World War would have been over in a matter of months, perhaps even of weeks. Such a conflict would therefore have been fought with whatever was available at the time – a 'come as you are' war, as it was described at the time. In consequence, armed forces had to be constantly maintained at a state of high readiness, with their weapons, ammunition and equipment to hand – a

379

process which proved difficult to sustain for forty years. A second problem was that the accelerating pace of science and technology, coupled with the lengthy development time for new equipment, meant that many weapons systems were obsolescent before they had even entered service.

Inside their respective pacts, the two superpowers enjoyed many advantages: their financial and industrial resources were huge in comparison to those of their allies, and their own forces were so large that they guaranteed a major domestic market for any equipment that was selected. They thus dominated their partners, and it proved a struggle for their European allies on either side of the Inner German Border to avoid being overwhelmed.

Even for the USA, however, military procurement was by no means smooth sailing. Enormous amounts of money were expended on systems which, for one reason or another, were cancelled before they reached service. One prime example was the effort devoted by the US air force to finding a successor to the Boeing B-52, to maintain its manned strategic bomber force. First there was the XB-70 Valkyrie hypersonic aircraft, which was followed by the B-1, the B-1A (which was virtually a new aircraft) and then the B-2. The sums expended on these aircraft for what was, in the end, very little return are almost incalculable. Further, quite what purpose such aircraft would have served in a nuclear war, apart from dropping H-bombs in gaps left by ICBMs and SLBMs, is not clear. The US army had some dramatic failures, too, such as the Sergeant York divisional air-defence system and the MBT-70 tank.

The US forces were certainly not alone in having problems. The Canadians, who had little enough money for defence, undertook three massive projects, which many contemporary observers warned were over-ambitious. The first was the all-Canadian Arrow fighter of the late 1950s, which reached the prototype stage before cancellation. The second, in the 1980s, was the submarine project which grew from three replacement diesel-electric submarines to twelve nuclear-propelled attack submarines; this reached an advanced stage, though short of orders being placed, before it was cancelled. The third, in the 1990s, was an order for over fifty Westland helicopters to replace ageing anti-submarine and general-purpose helicopters; this was summarily cancelled by a new government, and large compensation payments had to be made. These three projects incurred expenditure totalling hundreds of millions of dollars, but, in the end, there was not a single aircraft, submarine or helicopter to show for any of them.

The British suffered from two problems. The first was projects reaching an advanced stage and then being cancelled. This affected numerous aircraft, such as the Nimrod AWACS, the Vickers-Supermarine Swift fighter and the TSR-2 strike aircraft, while the navy suffered a similar fate with the CVA-01 aircraft carrier, as did the army with the SP70 self-propelled gun and the Blue Water battlefield missile. In addition, some of the projects that did reach service did so only after many years in development and the expenditure of great sums of money, when a viable foreign alternative was readily available at much lower cost.

This is not to deny that some excellent equipment was produced. In the USA, the Los Angeles-class SSNs and aircraft such as the B-52 bomber, F-86 Sabre, F-4 Phantom, F-15 Eagle and F-16 Fighting Falcon were world leaders in their day. Among British successes were the Canberra and Vulcan bombers, the Hunter fighter and the Harrier V/STOL aircraft, the Leander-class frigates and the Centurion tank. The Germans bought most of their aircraft from abroad, but on land their Leopard 1 and Leopard 2 tanks were outstandingly successful. The French produced some outstanding fighter aircraft in the Mirage series, which sold around the world.

Indeed, some European equipment was so good that it even found a market in the United States. The US air force, for example, purchased the British Canberra bomber, while the Marines ordered hundreds of Harrier V/STOL aircraft. In the 1980s the US army bought its most important communications system, RITA, from France, while its tank guns came first from the UK (105 mm) and subsequently from Germany (120 mm).

MANAGEMENT

All equipment-producing countries knew that their procurement processes were slow, overbureaucratic and inefficient, but, while all tried a considerable number of alternative methods, none of them ever found a real solution. Projects conducted with extreme speed and then rushed into production, such as the US army's M47 and M48 tanks and the US air force's F-100 Supersabre fighter in the 1950s, tended to result in equipment which was simply not ready for operational use and which required years of additional work to sort out the problems. On the other hand, projects which were conducted with extreme care could take over a decade to complete, by which time the technology was out of date, and the time taken ensured that they were very expensive.

Some observers advocated an escape from this by using an incremental approach, whereby a new weapons system was created by bringing together various in-service components. Using this approach, the Soviet army achieved a major success with its ZSU-23-4 air-defence gun, but when the US army tried to do the same thing with the Sergeant York system it proved to be a time-consuming and costly failure.

It should not, however, be thought that the USSR had a better system. Because of the secrecy which was inherent in Soviet equipment procurement, the West only ever saw the equipment which had passed through the development system and had been put into service, where it could no longer be hidden. There were, however, many projects which, despite considerable expenditure, never reached service status.

DEFENCE COSTS

The true costs of defence equipment were virtually impossible to calculate. First, the budgeting systems were complex and the costs of various elements of a programme were spread over so many individual budgets that it was difficult (as legislators in many countries discovered) to track them all down. Second, the declared cost of getting a weapons system into service was seldom the real cost of the project, since early production models frequently either fell well short of performance criteria or only just met them, as a result of which much effort had to be devoted to resolving the problems. Third, belated admissions showed that even in the most democratic of countries, such as the USA and the UK, large hidden programmes had been undertaken without any authority from the legislature.

The original British A-bomb programme and the early part of the Chevaline warhead development were hidden from Parliament for many years, and numerous 'black' air-force programmes, such as the F-117 'stealth' fighter, were concealed from Congress in the United States. In addition, governments used differing methods and conventions for arriving at defence costs, thus making it virtually impossible to compare like with like. Some governments also had defence commitments outside the European area, the costs of which were difficult to extract from Cold War costs.

On the Soviet side, it is doubtful that even the Soviet government had any real idea of just how much its defence programmes cost, and estimates made in the West were essentially best guesses. What was certain, however, as judged by the eventual collapse of the USSR, was that the cost proved to be unaffordable.

37

The Cold War in Retrospect

The greatest single spectre haunting the political and military leaders throughout the Cold War was that of nuclear war, and it was a threat that influenced every decision of any significance. Equally, it was a threat which only a very few really understood, and it was a subject about which a great deal of nonsense was spoken.

Both NATO and the Warsaw Pact regularly rehearsed the use of tactical nuclear weapons in their exercises, treating them as some superior form of artillery. The fact was, however, that had even one nuclear weapon been used it would have created a totally new situation. And, since there was no known method of making a clandestine nuclear explosion, it must be supposed that when the first weapon was used there would have been no doubt as to what had happened. This was foreseen by the Cold War strategist Herman Kahn, who, in the early days of potential nuclear warfare, described the situation thus:

> once war has started, no other line of demarcation is at once so clear, so sancti-
> fied by convention, so ratified by emotion, so low on the scale of violence, and –
> perhaps, most important of all – so easily defined and understood as the line
> between using and not using nuclear weapons . . . Even though the distinction
> between nuclear and non-nuclear war may have defects from some technical
> point-of-view, it possesses a functional meaning or utility that transcends any
> purely technical question.[1]

That was written in the 1950s, but it remained true throughout the Cold War, and therein lay the danger of tactical nuclear weapons.

TACTICAL NUCLEAR WEAPONS

Discussions on removing intermediate-range nuclear forces took some years, but, when these weapons were eventually discarded under the INF Treaty, they all went.

These discussions did not cover the shorter-range battlefield nuclear weapons, but once the Cold War had ended these were then disposed of by mutual agreement and without either side bothering with the formalities of a treaty. Thus President George Bush announced on 27 September 1991 that all US Lance and nuclear artillery shells would be eliminated, including those nuclear warheads supplied to allies. On 5 October 1991 this was quickly followed by an announcement by President Gorbachev, who said that all Soviet nuclear artillery projectiles, nuclear landmines and nuclear warheads for non-strategic missiles (Frog, Scud and SS-21) would also be destroyed. The process was endorsed by NATO's Nuclear Planning Group, which declared on 18 October 1991 that 'We will therefore continue to base effective and up-to-date sub-strategic nuclear forces in Europe, but they will consist solely of dual-capable aircraft.'[2] That left only the French, but in 1992 President Mitterrand announced, first, that the readiness of all his country's nuclear forces was being reduced and, subsequently, that he had decided to disband the Pluton regiments totally; the last went in 1993.

Tactical nuclear weapons created two major areas of difficulty. First, had even one been used the 'nuclear threshold' would have been crossed. Second, it would have been extremely difficult to differentiate between strategic and tactical weapons. The US Pershing II, for example, had a range of 1,800 km – sufficient for it to reach targets well inside the Soviet Union's western border – while the Soviet SS-12, with a range of 900 km, could have reached targets in south-east England or eastern France from launch sites east of the Elbe. France, the USSR and the UK would all have regarded such strikes as 'strategic'. There was therefore a very real danger – possibly even an inevitability – that, while the side launching nuclear weapons might have classified them as being 'tactical', they would have led seamlessly into global nuclear war.

NUCLEAR WARFIGHTING

There was a school of thought, particularly in the United States, which considered that 'nuclear warfighting' (i.e. a protracted conflict using nuclear weapons) would be possible. It is, however, highly questionable whether the military forces could have continued to fight under nuclear conditions for long. Indeed, it seems not unlikely that fighting would simply have become impossible, and that at least some elements of the surviving military forces of both sides would have ceased to function as rational military organizations.

One of the features of battlefield nuclear weapons was that their use formed part of every major NATO field exercise in the 1970s and 1980s. The customary pattern was that the exercise would steadily build up to a climax, which duly arrived with 'nuclear release' and the launching of the battlefield nuclear weapons. Staff officers and troops always welcomed this, since experience showed that this was the certain signal that the exercise would end within the next two to three hours. Thus, not only did the situation of being under prolonged nuclear attack not form part of the exercises, but it appeared that the exercise planners found it simply unimaginable.

THE PLANS

There is little value in seeking to assess whether any of the strategic or tactical plans made by either side would have been successful. One of the major lessons to be derived from a study of military history is that, while a very few battles have proceeded according to the generals' or admirals' plan, most battles and virtually all wars have not.

The major problem in trying to predict the possible progress of battles or campaigns is that the outcome of each constituent event must be decided before progressing to consider the next event. But to arrive at such decisions involves a series of judgements about how various participants might have reacted. For example, one of the events considered by the book *The Third World War*[3] was a Soviet attack, using one SS-17 ICBM, on the British city of Birmingham, which was totally devastated. In the book, the response by the UK and the USA (with French agreement) was for four SSBN-launched weapons, two from each country, to be delivered on the Soviet city of Minsk. While such a scenario is not totally impossible, it seems unlikely. This is not to say that the authors were wrong to consider a 'demonstrative' first strike by the USSR, followed by a 'response-in-kind' by the UK and the USA; it means only that the authors had to presuppose a sequence of actions and reactions in the USSR and subsequently in France, the UK and the USA which in real life either might not have happened at all or might have happened in a different way.*

Thus, it is simply impossible to estimate whether the Soviet attack plans described in *this* book would have succeeded, or whether NATO's conventional defences, described in previous chapters, would have held out, either in whole or in part. It is similarly impossible to predict whether either side would have authorized nuclear release and, if so, when and under what circumstances. During the public debate on enhanced-radiation weapons, for example, President Jimmy Carter stated that:

---

* I would like to make it clear that this is not meant to be a criticism of a valuable and carefully written book. My only wish is to draw attention to the problems associated with depicting scenarios and the danger inherent in making assumptions.

The decision to use nuclear weapons of any kind, including enhanced radiation weapons, would remain in my hands, not in the hands of local theater commanders. A decision to cross the nuclear threshold would be the most agonizing decision to be made by any President. I can assure you that these weapons, that is to say, low-yield, enhanced radiation weapons, would not make that decision any easier.[4]

It would be easy to suggest that, judging by their performance over other issues, President Ronald Reagan might have been more prepared to issue the orders to go to war or to launch ICBMs than President Jimmy Carter, and that Prime Minister Margaret Thatcher would have been more willing to launch the British SLBMs than Prime Minister Harold Wilson. But it is impossible to assess how any of those four might have behaved if they had been forced to come face to face with the awful reality.

It is also debatable whether the Soviets would have used nuclear weapons. There is no doubt that the Soviet forces regarded 'weapons of mass destruction' as an integral part of their operational doctrine, and that their plans assumed their use at a very early stage. That is not to say, however, that they would actually have used them; indeed, since they would presumably have attacked western Europe in order to capture it intact rather than to overrun a nuclear wasteland, it could be argued that they had every incentive not to use them. Thus, if their prospect of success in a conventional battle looked good, they might well have publicly eschewed their use, thus forcing NATO either to follow suit or to order 'first use'.

There is equally no doubt that, at least in public, NATO regarded battlefield nuclear weapons either as a reasonable response to Soviet first use or as a last resort in the face of imminent conventional defeat. In addition, the West had plans to use a very small number of nuclear weapons in a demonstrative capacity.* French plans also included a *pre-stratégique* strike, which was in effect a 'demonstrative' strike. As always, however, the fact that such contingency plans had been prepared did not mean that they would be implemented.

Two factors which would have been of overwhelming importance were time and communications. Leaders would have been under the most intense pressure to make decisions upon which depended the fate of their country and – this is not an overdramatization – that of the world. Not only would such decisions have had to be made, but they would have had to be made very quickly. If either the United States or the USSR had detected a massive incoming strategic strike, then, given the time taken for the news to reach the national command authorities and for any subsequent decision for a counter-attack to be transmitted (and verified) in time to be of any use,

---

* The Berlin contingency plans certainly included 'demonstrative' use of nuclear weapons – see Chapter 32.

perhaps ten minutes at most was all that would have been available to make a decision.

Human history contains many examples of new weapons – such as long-bows, gunpowder, artillery, machine-guns, chemical gas, airplanes and missiles – which have struck terror into an enemy, but they have never prevented subsequent conflict. Until, that is, the nuclear weapon. Nuclear weapons were capable of inflicting more casualties and more damage in minutes than had been achieved in all the six years of the Second World War. Great cities such as Detroit, Birmingham, Paris and Leningrad could have been laid waste by just one 1 MT weapon each; sprawling megalopolises such as Greater London or the German Ruhr might have required up to six. As the tables in earlier chapters have shown, however, the two superpowers possessed sufficient warheads to devastate not only each other but many other countries as well.

Both sides in the Cold War seem to have realized that a conflict between them would almost certainly have escalated from conventional to nuclear, whether the original aggressor had intended it or not. In consequence, they kept their heads, and for forty years they kept the arms race within reason – just.

The outcome of the Cold War certainly appears to have been more propitious for NATO than for the Warsaw Pact, at least in the short term, but the fact that there is a long term to look forward to is a tribute to men of goodwill, sound judgement and common sense on *both* sides. There certainly were moments in the Cold War when some on one side or the other might have considered an attack to have been a worthwhile gamble, but, when that happened, colleagues with good sense held them back.

Even if a war in central Europe had been fought with conventional weapons, the conflict would have been extremely bloody for both sides, with a degree of devastation far exceeding any previously seen. It is highly probable that it did not happen because of the existence of nuclear weapons, the uncertainty over whether or not they would be used, and the certainty that, if they were used, the result would in all likelihood have been cataclysmic. Thus, despite its critics, the nuclear weapon did have a utility, after all.

The final word, as usual, belongs to Sun Tzu, who said that:

> . . . to win one hundred victories in one hundred battles is not the acme of skill. To subdue the enemy without fighting is the acme of skill.[5]

APPENDICES

Western Union Defence Organization

Under the Brussels Treaty the Five Powers agree to collaborate in the defence field as well as in the political, economic and cultural fields.

Defence Organization
The object of the Western Union defence organization is to provide for the co-ordination of defence between the Five Powers in the military and supply fields and for the study of the tactical problems of the defence of Western Europe; in addition, to provide a framework on which, in the event of any emergency, a command organization could be built up. It can be compared with the defence organization in the United Kingdom . . .

Western Union Defence Committee
First, Government direction and control is provided by the Western Union Defence Committee which, in peacetime, is composed of the Defence Ministers of the Five Powers.

The Defence Committee are served by the Western Union's Chiefs-of-Staff Committee and the Western Union Military Supply Board meeting regularly in London. These bodies are analogous to [the UK's] Chiefs-of-Staff Committee and Joint War Production Staff, respectively.

Western Union Chiefs-of-Staff Committee
The Western Union Chiefs-of-Staff Committee advise the Defence Committee on all matters affecting the defence of Western Europe, taking account of commitments in other parts of the world. Within this broad direction its special tasks are to ensure that within Western Europe questions such as:

(a) The military resources of the five countries are organized to meet the strategic requirements of the Allies.
(b) The forces of the various nations are welded into an effective fighting machine.
(c) The combined resources of the five nations are allotted in the best way.
(d) A proper balance is maintained between the conflicting requirements of internal security and home defence on the one hand, and the European battle on the other.

(e) The evaluation, preparation and distribution of the necessary resources, in particular to the Commander of the European battle, whose special task will be to make the necessary operational plans and to put them into operation.

(f) The exact area of the responsibility of the command of the European battle in war is to be defined. It will be necessary to keep this constantly under review.

Their relationship with the Combined Chiefs-of-Staff in Washington has yet to be decided.

The Military Committee organization which has been working since May and has been largely responsible for formulating the new organization, now becomes, with slight adjustment, the permanent staff serving the Western Union Chiefs-of-Staff Committee. It is organized to deal with all interservice subjects as well as subjects affecting only one of the three Services. These latter single service bodies deal direct with the respective service departments for executive action.

Representatives of the United States and Canadian Chiefs-of-Staff participate as non-members.

Western Union Military Supply Board
In parallel with this Chiefs-of-Staff organization, the establishment of a Supply Board has now been agreed, to advise the Defence Committee on all questions affecting military supplies and to make recommendations as to how the requirements of the Five Powers for Military Supplies can be met.

The Supply Board is on a high level and is composed of one representative from each country. The British representative, who is to be chairman for the first year, is also Chairman of the British Joint War Production Staff. Meetings of the Board itself will not be frequent but it will be served by a permanent Executive Committee working in London, composed of representatives from each country. The detailed organization below this has not yet been decided but it is expected that expert working parties will be formed ad hoc.

Secretariat
The secretariat work for all the above bodies is co-ordinated through a Five-Power Secretariat having a British Secretary-General.

Western Union Commanders-in-Chief Committee
The *Western Union Commanders-in-Chief Committee* has been set up, responsible to the Western Union Chiefs-of-Staff Committee. It is composed of:

(a) Chairman. Field Marshal Lord Montgomery.
(b) Commander-in-Chief Western Europe Land Forces. General de Lattre de Tassigny.
(c) Commander-in-Chief Western Europe Air Forces. Air Chief Marshal Sir James Robb.
(d) Flag Officer Western Europe. Vice-Admiral Jaujard.

Their immediate task is to study the tactical problems of the defence of Western Europe, that is to say, to make plans to meet a Russian armed threat in Western Europe. They will not assume executive command of any forces in peacetime, although they will be in close touch with Military Governors of the occupation zones, and it is hoped that it may be possible, to a limited extent, to adjust peacetime dispositions to meet the needs of defence.

The committee forms a nucleus command organization which, in war, would be capable of commanding all land forces and supporting air forces to meet a Russian armed threat. The Committee will not be concerned with home defence.

It is the intention at present that the Flag Officer Western Europe should advise the Commanders-in-Chief on naval matters and co-ordinate naval operations in their support. The questions of naval command in the event of an emergency and the tactical problems of naval warfare are being studied separately.

It is probable that the permanent headquarters of this organization will be on the continent of Europe, although the Chairman proposes to maintain a small echelon of his own headquarters in London, in order to keep contact with the Western Union Chiefs-of-Staff Committee and the Military Committee.

APPENDIX 2

The North Atlantic Treaty

Washington DC, 4 April 1949

The Parties to this Treaty reaffirm their faith in the purposes and principles of the Charter of the United Nations and their desire to live in peace with all peoples and all governments.

They are determined to safeguard the freedom, common heritage and civilization of their peoples, founded on the principles of democracy, individual liberty and the rule of law.

They seek to promote stability and well-being in the North Atlantic area.

They are resolved to unite their efforts for collective defence and for the preservation of peace and security.

They therefore agree to this North Atlantic Treaty:

Article 1
The Parties undertake, as set forth in the Charter of the United Nations, to settle any international dispute in which they may be involved by peaceful means in such a manner that international peace and security and justice are not endangered, and to refrain in their international relations from the threat or use of force in any manner inconsistent with the purposes of the United Nations.

Article 2
The Parties will contribute toward the further development of peaceful and friendly international relations by strengthening their free institutions, by bringing about a better understanding of the principles upon which these institutions are founded, and by promoting conditions of stability and well-being. They will seek to eliminate conflict in their international economic policies and will encourage economic collaboration between any or all of them.

Article 3
In order more effectively to achieve the objectives of this Treaty, the Parties, separately and jointly, by means of continuous and effective self-help and mutual aid,

will maintain and develop their individual and collective capacity to resist armed attack.

Article 4
The Parties will consult together whenever, in the opinion of any of them, the territorial integrity, political independence or security of any of the Parties is threatened

Article 5
The Parties agree that an armed attack against one or more of them in Europe or North America shall be considered an attack against them all and consequently they agree that, if such an armed attack occurs, each of them, in exercise of the right of individual or collective self-defence recognized by Article 51 of the Charter of the United Nations, will assist the Party or Parties so attacked by taking forthwith, individually, and in concert with the other Parties, such action as it deems necessary, including the use of armed force, to restore and maintain the security of the North Atlantic area.

Any such armed attack and all measures taken as a result thereof shall immediately be reported to the Security Council. Such measures shall be terminated when the Security Council has taken all the measures necessary to restore and maintain international peace and security.

Article 6
For the purpose of Article 5, an armed attack on one or more of the Parties is deemed to include an armed attack:

– on the territory of any of the Parties in Europe or North America, on the Algerian Departments of France, or on the islands under the jurisdiction of any of the Parties in the North Atlantic area north of the Tropic of Cancer;
– on the forces, vessels, or aircraft of any of the Parties, when in or over these territories or any other area of Europe in which occupation forces of any of the Parties were stationed on the date when the Treaty entered into force or the Mediterranean Sea or the North Atlantic area of the Tropic of Cancer.

Article 7
This Treaty does not affect, and shall not be interpreted as affecting, in any way the rights and obligations under the Charter of the Parties which are members of the United Nations, or the primary responsibility of the Security Council for the maintenance of international peace and security.

Article 8
Each Party declares that none of the international engagements now in force between it and any other of the Parties or any third State is in conflict with the provisions of this Treaty, and undertakes not to enter into any international engagement in conflict with this Treaty.

Article 9

The Parties hereby establish a Council, on which each of them shall be represented, to consider matters concerning the implementation of this Treaty. The Council shall be so organized as to be able to meet promptly at any time. The Council shall set up such subsidiary bodies as may be necessary; in particular it shall establish immediately a defence committee which shall recommend measures for the implementation of Articles 3 and 5.

Article 10

The Parties may, by unanimous agreement, invite any other European State in a position to further the principles of this Treaty and to contribute to the security of the North Atlantic area to accede to this Treaty. Any State so invited may become a Party to the Treaty by depositing its instrument of accession with the Government of the United States of America. The Government of the United States of America will inform each of the Parties of the deposit of each such instrument of accession.

Article 11

This Treaty shall be ratified and its provisions carried out by the Parties in accordance with their respective constitutional processes. The instruments of ratification shall be deposited as soon as possible with the Government of the United States of America, which will notify all the other signatories of each deposit. The Treaty shall enter into force between the States which have ratified it as soon as the ratification of the majority of signatories, including the ratification of Belgium, Canada, France, Luxembourg, the Netherlands, the United Kingdom and the United States, have been deposited and shall come into effect with respects to other States on the date of the deposit of their ratification.

Article 12

After the Treaty has been in force for ten years, or at any time thereafter, the Parties shall, if any of them so requests, consult together for the purpose of reviewing the Treaty, having regard for the factors then affecting peace and security in the North Atlantic area, including the development of universal as well as regional arrangements under the Charter of the United Nations for the maintenance of international peace and security.

Article 13

After the Treaty has been in force for twenty years, any Party may cease to be a Party one year after its notice of denunciation has been given to the Government of the United States of America, which will inform the Governments of the other Parties of the deposit of each notice of denunciation.

Article 14

This Treaty, of which the English and French texts are equally authentic, shall be deposited in the archives of the Government of the United States of America. Duly certified copies will be transmitted by that government to the governments of other signatories.

SUBSEQUENT CHANGES

Accession of Greece and Turkey
In the protocol signed in London on 22 October 1951, admitting Greece and Turkey to the Treaty, Article 6 was amended to read:

> For the purposes of Article 5, an armed attack on one or more of the Parties is deemed to include an armed attack:
>
> i. on the territory of any of the Parties in Europe or North America, on the Algerian Departments of France, on the territory of Turkey or on the islands under the jurisdiction of any of the Parties in the North Atlantic area north of the Tropic of Cancer;
> ii. on the forces, vessels, or aircraft of any of the Parties, when in or over these territories or any other area in Europe in which occupation forces of any of the Parties were stationed on the date when the Treaty entered into force or the Mediterranean Sea or the North Atlantic area north of the Tropic of Cancer.

Accession of the Federal Republic of Germany
The protocol was signed in Paris on 23 October 1954, but did not amend the basic Treaty in any way.

Inapplicability of the 'Algerian Departments of France'
As a result of Algerian independence on 3 July 1962, the French representative informed the North Atlantic Council (16 January 1963) that, since the 'Algerian Departments of France' had ceased to have any legal existence, any mention of them in the treaty was no longer relevant. This was noted by the North Atlantic Council.

Accession of Spain
The protocol was signed in Brussels on 10 December 1981, but did not amend the treaty in any way.

The Warsaw Treaty of Friendship, Co-operation and Mutual Assistance

Warsaw, Poland, 14 May 1955

Between the People's Republic of Albania, the People's Republic of Bulgaria, the Hungarian People's Republic, the German Democratic Republic, the Polish People's Republic, the Romanian People's Republic, the Union of Soviet Socialist Republics, and the Czechoslovak Republic.

[Preamble]*

Article 1
The contracting Parties undertake, in accordance with the Charter of the United Nations Organization, to refrain in their international relations from the threat or use of force, and to settle their international disputes by peaceful means so as not to endanger peace and security.

Article 2
The contracting Parties declare their readiness to take part, in the spirit of sincere co-operation, in all international undertakings intended to safeguard international peace and security and they shall use all their energies for the realization of these aims.

Moreover, the contracting Parties shall work for the adoption, in agreement with other States desiring to co-operate in this matter, of effective measures towards a general reduction of armaments and prohibition of atomic, hydrogen or other weapons of mass destruction.

Article 3
The contracting Parties shall take council among themselves on all important international questions relating to their common interests, guided by the interest of strengthening international peace and security.

---

* The Preamble has been omitted; it sets out the overlying principles and identifies the national representatives at the meeting.

They shall take council among themselves immediately, whenever, in the opinion of any of them, there has arisen the threat of an armed attack on one or several States that are signatories of the Treaty, in the interests of organizing their joint defence and of upholding peace and security.

Article 4

In the event of an armed attack in Europe on one or several States that are signatories of the Treaty by any State or group of States, each State that is a Party to this Treaty shall in the exercise of the right to individual or collective self-defence in accordance with Article 51 of the Charter of the United Nations Organization, render the State or States so attacked immediate assistance, individually and in agreement with other States that are partners to this Treaty, by all the means it may consider necessary, including the use of armed force. The States that are Parties to this Treaty shall immediately take council among themselves concerning the necessary joint measures to be adopted for the purpose of restoring and upholding international peace and security.

In accordance with the principles of the Charter of the United Nations Organization, the Security Council shall be advised of the measures taken on the basis of the present article. These measures shall be adopted as soon as the Security Council has taken the necessary measures for restoring and upholding international peace and security.

Article 5

The contracting Parties have agreed on the establishment of a joint command for their armed forces, which shall be placed, by agreement among these Parties, under this command, which shall function on the basis of jointly defined principles. They shall also take other concerted measures necessary for strengthening their defence capacity, in order to safeguard the peaceful labour of their peoples, to guarantee the inviolability of their frontiers and territories and to provide safeguards against possible aggression.

Article 6

For the purpose of holding the consultations provided for in the present Treaty among the States that are Parties to the Treaty, and for the purpose of considering problems arising in connection with the implementation of this Treaty, a political consultative committee shall be formed in which each State that is a Party to this Treaty shall be represented by a member of the government, or any other specially appointed representative.

The committee may form the auxiliary organs for which the need may arise.

Article 7

The contracting Parties undertake not to participate in any coalition and alliances, and not to conclude any agreements the purposes of which would be at variance with those of the present Treaty.

The contracting Parties declare that their obligations under existing international treaties are not at variance with the provision of this Treaty.

Article 8

The contracting Parties declare that they will act in the spirit of friendship and co-operation with the object of furthering the development of and strengthening the economic and cultural relations between them, adhering to the principles of mutual respect for their independence and sovereignty, and of non-interference in their internal affairs.

Article 9

The present Treaty is open to the accession of other States – irrespective of their social and State systems – which may express their readiness to assist in the present Treaty, in combining the efforts of peace-loving States for safeguarding the peace and security of the peoples. This act of acceding to the Treaty shall become effective with the consent of the States which are a Party to the Treaty, after the instrument of accession has been deposited with the Government of the Polish People's Republic.

Article 10

The present Treaty is subject to ratification, and the instruments of ratification shall be deposited with the Government of the Polish People's republic.

The Treaty shall take effect on the date on which the last ratification instrument is deposited. The Government of the Polish People's Republic shall advise the other States that are Party to the Treaty of each ratification instrument deposited with it.

Article 11

The present Treaty shall remain in force for twenty years. For the contracting Parties which will not have submitted to the Government of the Polish People's Republic a statement denouncing the Treaty a year before the expiration of its term, it shall remain in force throughout the following ten years.

In the event of a system of collective security in Europe, and the conclusion of a general European Treaty of collective security to that end, which the contracting Parties shall unceasingly seek to bring about, the present Treaty shall cease to be effective on the date the general European Treaty comes into force.

SUBSEQUENT CHANGES

There were no new accessions to the treaty.

There were no known amendments to the treaty.

Albania severed all relations with the USSR in December 1961, which implicitly included leaving the Warsaw Pact. It is doubtful that it complied with Article 11.

The Warsaw Treaty was not formally discontinued; it ceased to exist.

Equivalent Ranks and the 'Star' System

The military method used within NATO was to refer to senior appointments by their 'star' equivalent (which was also used to denote passengers' rank on staff-car plates). This saved repeated cross-references to naval, land and air equivalents. The corresponding national ranks were as follows:

'Stars'	Army and air force (except UK air force)	Navy	UK air force	Soviet army*
Five star	Marshal of France; General of the Army (US); Field Marshal (UK)	Admiral of the Fleet (UK); Fleet Admiral (US)	Marshal of the RAF (UK)	Marshal of the Soviet Union[†]
Four star	General	Admiral	Air Chief Marshal	General[‡]
Three star	Lieutenant-General	Vice-Admiral	Air Vice-Marshal	Colonel-General
Two star	Major-General	Rear-Admiral	Air Marshal	Lieutenant-General
One star	Brigadier-General[§]	Commodore	Air Commodore	Major-General

* These are approximate equivalents.
† There were three grades of marshal: Marshal of the Soviet Union, Senior Marshal and Marshal.
‡ All grades of general officer could be either army ranks (in effect, general staff) or in their 'arm of service', i.e. artillery, engineers, communications, and so on.
§ In the British army (and the Canadian army until 'unification' in the 1960s) the 'one-star' rank was *brigadier* and not *brigadier-general*.

Senior Appointments 1949–89: NATO and the Warsaw Pact

NATO

Secretary-General

1952–57	Lord Ismay	UK
1957–61	P.-H. Spaak	Belgium
1961–64	D. U. Stikker	Netherlands
1964–71	M. Brosio	Italy
1971–84	J. M. A. H. Luns	Netherlands
1984–88	Lord Carrington	UK
1988–	M. Wörner	Germany

Chairman of the NATO Military Committee in Permanent Session*

1958–61	General B. R. P. H. Hasselman	Netherlands
1961–63	General A. Heusinger	Germany

Chairman of the NATO Military Committee†

1963–64	General A. Heusinger	Germany
1964–68	Lieutenant-General C. P. de Cumont	Belgium
1968–71	Admiral Sir N. Henderson	UK
1971–74	General J. Steinhoff	Germany
1974–77	Admiral of the Fleet Sir P. Hill-Norton	UK
1977–80	General H. F. Z. Gundersen	Norway
1980–83	Admiral R. H. Falls	Canada

---

* From 1949 to 1963 the NATO Military Committee in Chiefs-of-Staff Session was chaired by one of its members for a year each, rotating in order of the initial letters of the countries' English names. From 1963 onwards it was chaired by the chairman of the NATO Military Committee.

† The Military Committee in Permanent Session and (from 1963) the NATO Military Committee are constituted from officers representing their chiefs-of-staff and who are permanently located in Brussels. The NATO Military Committee in Chiefs-of-Staff Session still meets and is chaired by the chairman of the Military Committee.

1983–86	General C. De Jager	Netherlands
1986–89	General W. Altenburg	Germany
1989–	General V. Eide	Norway

Major NATO Commanders (MNCs)

SUPREME ALLIED COMMANDER EUROPE (SACEUR)

1950–52	General of the Army D. D. Eisenhower, US Army
1952–53	General M. T. Ridgway, US Army
1953–56	General A. B. Gruenther, US Army
1956–63	General L. Norstad, USAF
1963–69	General L. L. Lemnitzer, US Army
1969–74	General A. J. Goodpaster, US Army
1974–79	General A. M. Haig, US Army
1979–87	General B. W. Rogers, US Army
1987–	General J. R. Galvin, US Army

SUPREME ALLIED COMMANDER ATLANTIC (SACLANT)

1950–54	Admiral L. D. McCormick, USN
1954–59	Admiral J. Wright, USN
1959–63	Admiral R. L. Dennison, USN
1963–65	Admiral H. P. Smith, USN
1965–67	Admiral T. H. Moorer, USN
1967–70	Admiral E. P. Holmes, USN
1970–72	Admiral C. K. Duncan, USN
1972–75	Admiral R. W. Cousins, USN
1975–78	Admiral I. C. Kidd, USN
1978–82	Admiral H. D. Train, USN
1982–85	Admiral W. C. McDonald, USN
1985–88	Admiral L. Baggett, Jr, USN
1988–	Admiral F. B. Kelso, USN

ALLIED COMMANDER-IN-CHIEF CHANNEL (CINCHAN)

1952	Admiral of the Fleet Sir A. J. Power, RN
1952–54	Admiral Sir J. H. Edelsten, RN
1954–57	Admiral of the Fleet Sir G. E. Creasey, RN
1957–59	Admiral Sir G. Grantham, RN
1959–61	Admiral Sir M. L. Power, RN
1961–63	Admiral Sir A. N. C. Bingley, RN
1963–65	Admiral Sir W. J. Woods, RN
1965–66	Admiral Sir V. Begg, RN
1966–67	Admiral Sir J. B. Frewen, RN
1967–70	Admiral Sir J. Bush, RN
1970–71	Admiral Sir W. O'Brien, RN
1971–73	Admiral Sir E. Ashmore, RN
1973–75	Admiral Sir T. Lewin, RN
1975–77	Admiral Sir J. Treacher, RN
1977–79	Admiral Sir H. Leach, RN

1979–81	Admiral Sir J. Eberle, RN
1981–82	Admiral Sir J. Fieldhouse, RN
1982–85	Admiral Sir W. Staveley, RN
1985–87	Admiral Sir N. Hunt, RN
1987–89	Admiral Sir J. J. R. Oswald, RN
1989–	Admiral Sir J. Bathurst, RN

WARSAW PACT

Commander-in-Chief Joint Warsaw Pact Armed Forces

1955–69	Marshal of the Soviet Union I. S. Konev
1960–67	Marshal of the Soviet Union A. A. Grechko
1967–76	Marshal of the Soviet Union I. I. Yakubovsky
1976–89	Marshal of the Soviet Union V. G. Kulikov
1989–	Army General P. G. Lushev (USSR)

Commander-in-Chief Group of Soviet Forces Germany

1955–57	Army General A. A. Grechko (USSR)
1957–60	Army General M. V. Zakharov (USSR)
1960–61	Army General I. I. Yakubovsky (USSR)
1961–62	Marshal of the Soviet Union I. S. Konev*
1962–65	Army General I. I. Yakubovsky (USSR)
1965–69	Army General P. K. Koshevoi (USSR)
1969–71	Colonel General V. G. Kulikov† (USSR)
1971–72	Colonel General S. K. Kurotkin (USSR)
1972–80	Colonel General E. F. Ivanovsky‡ (USSR)
1980–85	Army General M. M. Zaitsev (USSR)
1985–86	Army General P. G. Lushev (USSR)
1986–87	Army General V. A. Belikov (USSR)
1987–	Army General B. V. Snetkov (USSR)

---

* Marshall Konev assumed command of GSFG from General Yakubovsky in 1961 at the start of the Berlin crisis and handed it back to Yakubovsky in 1962 when the crisis was over.
† Promoted Army General in post in 1970.
‡ Promoted Army General in post in 1972.

Nuclear Weapons 'Firsts'

Event	USA	USSR	UK	France	China
First atomic explosion	16 July 1945	23 September 1949	3 October 1952	2 March 1960	16 October 1964
First strategic nuclear bomber operational	Boeing B-29: 6 August 1945	Myasishchev M-4 (Bison): 1956	Vickers Valiant: July 1955	Dassault Mirage IVA: 1 October 1964	Hong 7: c. 1970
First SSBN operational	*George Washington*: 15 November 1960	Hotel class: 1960	*Resolution*: June 1968	*Redoutable*: 28 January 1972	*Daqingyu*: 1987
First ICBM operational	Atlas: 1960	SS-6 (Sapwood): 1959	–	SSBS S-2: 1971	DF-3 CSS-3: 1971
First thermo-nuclear explosion	31 October 1952	12 August 1953	28 April 1958	24 August 1968	17 June 1967
First H-bomb in service	B21: December 1955	c. 1956	March 1958	TN 60: early 1976	c. 1968

German and US Land-Based Strategic Missiles: 1944–1990

Missile	In service	Maximum number deployed	Basing mode*	Fuel	Range (km)	Warhead	Launch weight (kg)	Accuracy (CEP)
A-4 (V-2)	1944–45	c. 4,000	A	Liquid	354	976 kg HE	12,988	n.k.
Jupiter PGM-19A†	1958–65	60	A	Liquid	2,400	1×1.44 MT	49,885	1.8 km
Thor SM-75‡	1959–64	60	B	Liquid	2,700	1×1.44 MT	49,900	3.2 km
Atlas SM-65D	1960–65	42	B	Liquid	14,000	1×1.4 MT	120,200	c. 4 km
Atlas SM-65E	1960–65	9	C	Liquid	14,000	1×3.75 MT	122,470	3.7 km
Atlas SM-65F	1961–7	60	D	Liquid	14,000	1×3.75 MT	122,470	3.7 km
Titan I HGM-25A	1961–6	54	D	Liquid	10,000	1×4 MT	99,970	1.4 km
Titan II SM-68B	1963–90s	54	E	Storable liquid	15,000	1×9 MT	149,700	830 m
Minuteman I LGM-30A/B	1962–9	800	F	Solid	10,000	1×1 MT	29,500	560 m
Minuteman II LGM-30F	1965–90s	450	F	Solid	12,500	1×1.2 MT	31,746	560 m
Minuteman III LGM-30G	1970–2008	550	F	Solid	13,000	3×335 kT MIRV	34,467	220 m
Peacemaker LGM-118	1986–	50	G	Solid	9,600	10×500 kT MIRV	88,450	100 m

* Basing mode:

A – mobile trailer
B – above-ground shelter
C – ground recesses ('coffins')
D – silos with lift to above-ground launch
E – silo with side vents
F – silo without side vents – hot launch
G – silo without side vents – cold launch

† Operated by Italian and Turkish air forces.
‡ Operated by UK air force.

APPENDIX 8

Soviet Land-Based Strategic Missiles: 1955–1990

Missile	In service	Maximum number deployed	Basing mode*	Fuel	Range (km)	Warhead	Launch weight (kg)	Accuracy (CEP)
SS-1B (Scud)	1955–	Several thousand	A	Liquid	300	70 kT or HE	6,370	450 m
SS-2 (Sibling)	1952–60	Few	A	Liquid	600	HE	20,400	n.k.
SS-3 (Shyster)	1956–70	28	A	Liquid	1,200	40 kT or HE	28,600	n.k.
SS-4 (Sandel)	1957–91	65 + 105 in reserve	A/F	Liquid	2,000	1 MT or HE	42,000	2.4 km
SS-5 Mod 3 (Skean)	1961–84	100	B/F	Liquid	4,100	3×300 kT (MRV)	35,000	1 km
SS-6 (Sapwood)	1959–68	4	B	Liquid	6,200	1×3 MT	300,000	8 km
SS-7 (Saddler)	1961–79	186	B/C/F	Storable liquid	11,500	1×5 MT	140,900	2.8 km
SS-8 (Sasin)	1965–77	23	F	Storable liquid	12,500	1×5 MT	80,000	2.8 km
SS-9 (Scarp) Mod 2	1966–79	255	F	Storable liquid	12,000	1×25 MT	190,000	1.8 km
SS-11 Mod 1 (Sego)	1966–88 ⎫		F	Storable liquid	10,000	1×950 kT	50,100	1.8 km
SS-11 Mod 2 (Sego)	1972–94 ⎬ 1,030		F	Storable liquid	13,000	1×1 MT	50,100	1.1 km
SS-11 Mod 3 (Sego)	1972–89 ⎭		F	Storable liquid	10,600	3×200 kT	50,100	1.1 km
SS-13 Mod 2 (Savage)	1972–96	60	F	Solid	9,400	1×750 kT	51,000	1.8 km
SS-16 (Sinner)	1971	50	A/F	Solid	9,000	1×1 MT	44,000	c. 400 m
SS-17 Mod 1 (Spanker)	1975–90	120	G	Storable liquid	10,000	4×200 kT MIRV	71,000	400 m
SS-17 Mod 2 (Spanker)	1975–90	20	G	Storable liquid	11,000	1×3.6 MT	71,100	400 m

407

Table continued

Missile	In service	Maximum number deployed	Basing mode*	Fuel	Range (km)	Warhead	Launch weight (kg)	Accuracy (CEP)
SS-17 Mod 3 (Spanker)	1975–	47	G	Storable liquid	10,000	4×200 kT MIRV	71,100	400 m
SS-18 Mods 1, 3 (Sickle)	1975		F	Storable liquid	10,000	1×20 MT	211,100	430 m
SS-18 Mod 2 (Sickle)	1976	308	F	Storable liquid	11,000	10×500 kT MIRV	211,100	350 m
SS-18 Mod 4 (Sickle)	1982		F	Storable liquid	11,000	10×500 kT MIRV	211,100	350 m
SS-19 Mod 3 (Stiletto)	1975–	360	F	Storable liquid	10,000	6×550 kT MIRV	105,600	400 m
SS-20 (Saber)	1975–	405	A	Solid	5,000	3×150 kT MIRV	36,000	400 m
SS-24 Mod 1 (Scalpel)	1987–	33	H	Solid	10,000+	10×500 kT MIRV	104,500	200 m
SS-24 Mod 2 (Scalpel)	1989–	57	F	Solid	10,000+	10×500 kT MIRV	104,500	200 m
SS-25 Mod 1 (Sickle)†	1985–	288	A	Solid	10,500	1×500 kT	45,100	200 m

* Basing mode:

  A – mobile trailer
  B – above-ground shelter
  C – ground recesses ('coffins')
  D – silos with lift to above-ground launch
  E – silo with side vents
  F – silo without side vents – hot launch
  G – silo without side vents – cold launch
  H – rail mobile

† Further missiles were deployed after 1990.

APPENDIX 9

Sea-Launched Strategic Missiles

USA

Missile	In service	Range (km)	Warhead	Launch weight (kg)	Throw weight (kg)	Accuracy (CEP)
Rigel	–	930	HE (1,361 kg)	5,670	1,361	549 m
Regulus I	1954–64	650	1×120 kT	6,587	1,500	c. 200 m
Regulus II	–	1,610	1×120 kT	10,433	1,325	n.k.
Polaris A-1	1960–65	2,600	1×500 kT	12,700	408	1,830 m
Polaris A-2	1961–74	2,800	1×800 kT or 3×200 kT MRV	13,608	500	1,200 m
Polaris A-3*	1964–81	4,630	3×200 kT MRV	13,600	500	850 m
Poseidon (C-3)	1971–94	4,600	10×40 kT MIRV	29,500	1,497	460 m
Trident I (C-4)	1979–	7,400	8×100 kT MIRV	32,850	1,500	463 m
Trident II (D-5)	1988–	12,000	8×475 kT or 8×100 kT MIRV	59,090	2,800	90 m

* Polaris A-3TK remained in service with the British navy until the mid-1990s.

USSR*

Missile	Mods	In service	Range (km)	Warhead	Launch weight (kg)	Throw weight (kg)	Accuracy (CEP)
SS-N-1 (Scud)	–	1959–60	150	HE/nuclear	3,100	800	8,000 m
SS-N-4		1961–73	650	1×1 MT	13,750	1,598	4,000 m
SS-N-5 (Sark)	Mod 1	1961–91	1,400	1×2 MT	19,650	1,179	3,000 m

USSR* (*continued*)

Missile	Mods	In service	Range (km)	Warhead	Launch weight (kg)	Throw weight (kg)	Accuracy (CEP)
SS-N-6 (Serb)	Mod 1	1967–90	2,400	1×1 MT	14,200	650	2,400 m
	Mod 2	1973–94	3,000	1×1 MT	14,200	650	2,400 m
	Mod 3	1975–90	3,000	2×350 kT MRV	14,200	650	1,300 m
SS-N-8 (Sawfly)	Mod 1	1971	7,800	1×800 kT	33,300	1,100	2,400 m
	Mod 2		9,100	1×800 kT	33,300	1,100	1.6 km
SS-N-17 (Snipe)		1977–91	3,900	1×500 kT	26,900	450	1,400 m
SS-N-18 (Stingray)	Mod 1	1977–	6,500	3×200 kT MIRV	35,300	1,650	800 m
	Mod 2	1978–	8,000	1×450 kT	35,300	1,650	1,400 m
	Mod 3	1979–	6,500	7×100 kT MIRV	35,300	1,650	1,400 m
SS-N-20 (Sturgeon)		1981	8,300	6–10×100 kT MIRV	84,000	2,550	500 m
SS-N-23 (Skiff)		1985	8,300	4×100 kT MIRV	40,300	2,800	500 m

* Source: *Conway's All The World's Fighting Ships: 1947–1995* (Conway Maritime Press, London, 1995).

Ballistic-Missile Submarines

USA

Class	In service	Number built	Submerged displacement (tonnes)	Missiles	Torpedo tubes	Crew
George Washington	1960–81	5	6,086	16×Polaris A-1 or 16×Polaris A-3	6×533 mm	112
Ethan Allen	1961–81	5	7,152	16×Polaris A-2 or 16×Polaris A-3	6×533 mm	110
Lafayette	1963–94	31	7,485	16×Polaris A-3 or 16×Poseidon C-3 or 16×Trident I C-4	4×533 mm	140
Ohio	1981–	18	16,964	24×Trident II D-5	4×533 mm	133

USSR

Class	In service	Number built	Submerged displacement (tonnes)	Missiles	Torpedo tubes	Crew
Zulu V*	1958–72	5	2,350	2×SS-N-1 or 2×SS-N-4	10×533 mm	70
Golf I*†	1959–90	15	2,900	3×SS-N-4	10×533 mm	59
Hotel	1960–89	6	6,000	3×SS-N-4	6×533 mm 2×406 mm	80
Yankee I	1967–93	34	9,600	16×SS-N-6	2×406 mm	120
Yankee II	1971–8	1	10,500	12×SS-N-17	2×406 mm	120
Delta I	1972–94	18	11,750	12×SS-N-8	4×533 mm 2×406 mm	120

411

USSR (*continued*)

Class	In service	Number built	Submerged displacement (tonnes)	Missiles	Torpedo tubes	Crew
Delta II	1975– late 90s	4	12,750	16×SS-N-8	4×533 mm 2×406 mm	126
Delta III	1976–	14	13,250	16×SS-N-18	4×533 mm 2×406 mm	126
Delta IV	1985–	7	13,500	16×SS-N-23	6×533 mm	130
Typhoon	1982–	6	25,000	20×SS-N-20	4×650 mm	150

* Zulu V and Golf class were diesel-electric-powered; all others in the table were nuclear-powered.
† Thirteen Golf Is were converted to Golf II, armed with three SS-N-5 missiles.

Strategic Bombers

USA*

Aircraft	Entered service	Number built	Engines	Range (unre-fuelled) (km)	Bombload	Maxi-mum speed (km/h)	Comments
Boeing B-29	1943	3,000+	4×piston	5,250	9,072 kg	575	Also used by RAF (Washington B.1) and copied by USSR (Tupolev Tu-4)
Boeing B-50	1948	371	4×piston	7,900	12,700 kg	640	Upgraded B-29
Convair B-36	1947	385	6×piston+ 4×turbojet	13,000	38,140 kg	707	Largest bomber to enter service
North American B-45	1948	140	4×turbojet	3,100	9,980 kg	933	First USAF jet bomber
Boeing B-47	1950	n.k.	6×turbojet	5,800	9,980 kg	994	1,260 in service with SAC in 1950s
Boeing B-52	1955	744	8×turbojet	12,900	8×nuclear bombs	925	Still in front-line service at the end of the Cold War
Convair B-58	1960	116	4×turbojet	8,250	3,175 kg	2,215	First supersonic bomber
General Dynamics FB-111	1967	437	2×turbojet	1,300	6×nuclear bombs	1,320	Swing-wing bomber
Rockwell B-1B	1985	100	4×turbojet	12,000	24×ALCM or SRAM; or 28×B61; or B83 gravity bombs	1,330	Swing-wing bomber with limited 'stealth'

USSR*

Aircraft	NATO name	Entered service	Engines	Range (unre-fuelled) (km)	Bombload	Max-mum speed (km/h)	Comments
Tupolev Tu-4	Bull	late 1940s	4×piston	5,230	9,072 kg	575	Reverse-engineered copy of US B-29
Tupolev Tu-16	Badger	1954	2×turbojet	4,800	9,000 kg	945	Also carried nuclear missiles
Myasishchev M-6	Bison	1955	4×turbojet	11,000	4,500 kg	900	Soviet air force only
Tupolev Tu-20	Bear	1956	4×turboprop	14,800	11,340 kg	870	World's only swept-wing turboprop bomber
Tupolev Tu-22	Blinder	1963	2×turbojet	2,250	9,070 kg	1,480	Also carried one large nuclear missile
Tupolev Tu-26	Backfire-B	1974	2×turbojet	5,745	9,500 kg	2,450	
Tupolev Tu-160	Blackjack	1987	4×turbojet	14,000	16,330 kg	Mach 1.9	Probably the finest bomber ever built; 18 were produced

* All data in this table refer to the initial service version of each type. Virtually all types went through many modifications, which resulted in increases in speed, range or payload.

Strategic Tanker Aircraft

Tanker aircraft	Country	Entered service	Transferable fuel carried (kg)	Refuelling system	Comments
Boeing KC-97 Stratotanker	USA	1950	c. 20,000	1×flying-boom	New-build based on C-97 military transport
Boeing KC-135A	USA	1957	37,650	1×flying-boom	New-build based on C-135 military transport. Also in service with French air force
Boeing KC-135R	USA	1984	56,500	1×flying-boom	Upgraded KC-135A
McDonnell Douglas KC-10 Extender	USA	1981	90,000	3×probe-and-drogue 1×flying-boom	New-build based on DC-10 airliner
Tupolev Tu-16 (Badger)	USSR	c. 1960	19,000	wingtip–wingtip; later probe-and-drogue	In-service conversion of Tu-16. Used for other Tu-16s only
Myasishchev M-4 (3MS-2) (Bison-B)	USSR	c. 1965	40,000	1×probe-and-drogue	In-service conversion based on M-4 bomber
Ilyushin Il-78M (Midas)	USSR	c. 1990	35,000	3×probe-and-drogue	New-build, based on Il-76 (Candid) transport
Vickers Valiant K.Mk 1	UK	1959	20,000	1×probe-and-drogue	In-service conversion from Valiant B.1 bomber
Handley-Page Victor K.Mk 1	UK	1965	24,000	3×probe-and-drogue	In-service conversion from Victor B.1 bomber
BAC VC-10 K.Mk 3	UK	1984	26,037	3×probe-and-drogue	In-service conversion from VC-10 airliner
Lockheed Tristar K.Mk 1	UK	1986	45,387	1×probe-and-drogue	In-service conversion from Tristar transport/airliner

415

Strategic Nuclear Bombs and Bombers: UK

BOMBS

Weapon	Source	Yield	Weight (kg)	Years in service	Carrier	Comments
Blue Danube	UK	20 kT	4,535	1953–62	Valiant Vulcan B.Mk 1/1A	
Blue Steel/ Red Snow	UK	1 MT	6,800	1963–8 1963–70	Victor B.Mk 2R Vulcan B.Mk 2A	57 ordered
Red Beard	UK	15 kT	910	1961–71	Canberra Valiant Vulcan B.Mk 1	
Violet Club	UK	1 MT	4,080	1958	Vulcan B.Mk 1	Also known as the 'interim megaton weapon'; 12 made
Yellow Sun Mk 1/ Green Grass	UK	500 kT	3,180	1960–63 1960–63	Vulcan B.Mk 1/1A Victor B.Mk 1	
Yellow Sun Mk 2/ Red Snow	UK	1 MT	3,290	1961–6	Vulcan B.Mk 1/1A Vulcan B.Mk 2	
Mark 7	USA	1 MT	770	1960–66	Canberra	
Mark 28	USA	60–100 kT	860	1960–65	Valiant	
B 43	USA	1 MT	950	1966–72	Canberra	

AIRCRAFT

Aircraft	Strategic service	Number built	Speed (high level)	Range (km)	Weight (kg)	Comments
English Electric Canberra: bomber version	1956–72	175 (see comments)	Mach 0.87	4,930	20,865	One nuclear weapon; many others built for non-nuclear role
Short Sperrin	–	2	Mach 0.86	7,150	52,164	(a) Did not enter service (b) Bombload 9,000 kg
Vickers Valiant	1955–64	104	Mach 0.86	8,340	79,000	Retired prematurely
Avro Vulcan B.Mk 1/ 1A	1957–65	45	Mach 0.95	6,490	77,300	
Avro Vulcan B.Mk 2	1960–82	89	Mach 0.98	8,520	91,000	Could carry maximum of four nuclear bombs
Avro Vulcan B.Mk 2A	1963–70	33	Mach 0.98	8,520	91,000	Converted from B.Mk 2 to carry Blue Steel
Handley-Page Victor B.Mk 1/1A/2	1958–64	83	Mach 0.90	4,020	82,000	Maximum two nuclear gravity bombs
Victor B.Mk 2R	1963–8	23	Mach 0.92	5,630	101,150	Converted from B.Mk 2 to carry Blue Steel

Ballistic–Missile Submarines: China, France, UK

Class	In service	Number built	Submerged displacement (tonnes)	Strategic missiles	Torpedo tubes	Crew	Comments
China							
Daqingyu	1987–	1	6,500	12×JL-1	6×533 mm	140	
France							
Redoutable	1972–	5	9,144	16×MSBS M1 (1972–5) 16×MSBS M2/M20 (1977–87) 16×MSBS M4B (1987–)	6×533 mm	130	First boat not fitted with M4 and retired in 1991
L'Inflexible	1985–	1	8,780	16×MSBS M4A/B (1985–)	6×533 mm	127	Improved Redoutable design
UK							
Resolution	1968–92/96	4	8,636	16×Polaris A-3 (1968–82/88) 16×Polaris A-3TK Chevaline (1982/8–1992)	6×533 mm	144	Retired in early 1990s

APPENDIX 15

French Nuclear Weapons

WEAPONS

Weapon		Yield	Weight (kg)	Accuracy (m)	Years in service	Carrier	Comments
AN 11	Bomb	60 kT	1,500	<200	1963–8	Mirage IVA	High-level delivery only
AN 22	Bomb	60–70 kT	750	<200	1967–88	Mirage IVA	Retarding system for low-level delivery
MR 31	RV	120 kT	700	c. 1,000	1970–80	SSBS S2	
MR 41	RV	500 kT	700	c. 1,000	1971–79	MSBS M1/M2	
TN 60/61	RV	1 MT	375	800	1976–91	MSBS M20 SSBS S3	
TN 70/71	MIRV	150 kT	250	480	1983–	MSBS M4A/M4B	
TN 80/81	ALCM	300 kT	200	400	1985–	ASMP on Mirage IVP	

AIRCRAFT

Aircraft	Strategic service	Number built	Speed (high level)	Range (unrefuelled) (km)	Weight (kg)	Weapons load	Comments
Mirage IVA	1964–88	62	Mach 2.2	2,500	33,000	1×AN 11/AN 22	
Mirage IVP	1986–97	19	Mach 2.2	2,500	33,000	1×ASMP	Converted from Mirage IVA

MISSILES

Type	Designation	Strategic service	Range (km)	Warhead	Launch weight (kg)	Throw weight (kg)
SSBS	S2	1971–83	3,300	1×120 kT	31,900	n.k.
	S30	1980–	3,500	1×1 MT	25,800	1,800
MSBS	M1	1971–4	2,500	1×500 kT	18,000	n.k.
	M2	1974–7	3,000	1×500 kT	20,000	n.k.
	M20	1977–91	3,000	1×1 MT	20,000	2,200
	M4A	1985–	4,000	6×150 kT (TN 70)	35,000	1,200
	M4B	1987–	5,000	6×150 kT (TN 71)	35,000	1,200
ASMP		1986–	300	1×300 kT (TN 80/TN 81)	840	

Chinese Ballistic Missiles

Missile*	In service	Range (km)	Warhead	Launch weight (kg)	Throw weight (kg)	Accuracy (CEP)
Dong Feng 2A (CSS-1)	1966–84	1,250	1×20 kT	32,000	1,550	2–3 km
Dong Feng 3/3A (CSS-2)	1971–	2,650	1×3 MT	64,000	2,150	1,000 m
Dong Feng 4 (CSS-3)	1981–	4,500	1×3 MT	82,000	2,200	1,500 m
Dong Feng 5 (CSS-4)	1981–	13,000	1×5 MT	183,000	3,200	500 m
Ju Lang 1 (CSS-N-3)	1983–	1,700	1×250 kT	14,700	600	n.k.

* Dong Feng (= East Wind) and Ju Lang (= Great Wave) are the Chinese names; CSS-/CSS-N- are the US designations (= Chinese Surface-to-Surface-/Chinese Surface-to-Surface – Naval-).

Strategic Missile Balances: 1970, 1980, 1990

1970 – USA

Missile	Warhead yield (MT)	CEP (n.m.)	CMP*	RVs per missile[†]	Number of ICBMs	SSBNs	Submarines Missiles per SSBN	Total SLBMs	Total RVs	Total CMP[‡]
(a)	(b)	(c)	(d)	(e)	(f)	(g)	(h)	(i)	(j)	(k)
Minuteman I	1	0.3	11.11	1	550	–	–	–	550	6,111
Minuteman II	1.2	0.3	12.54	1	450	–	–	–	450	5,646
Titan II	9	0.45	21.34	1	54	–	–	–	54	1,152
Polaris A-2	0.2	0.64	0.84	1	–	13	16	208	208	175
Polaris A-3	0.2	0.455	1.65	3 (MRV)	–	28	16	448	448	739
Totals					1,054	41		656	1,710	13,823

1970 – USSR

Missile	Warhead yield (MT)	CEP (n.m.)	CMP*	RVs per missile[†]	Number of ICBMs	SSBNs	Submarines Missiles per SSBN	Total SLBMs	Total RVs	Total CMP[‡]
(a)	(b)	(c)	(d)	(e)	(f)	(g)	(h)	(i)	(j)	(k)
SS-7	5	1.5	1.3	1	187	–	–	–	187	243
SS-8	5	1.5	1.3	1	23	–	–	–	23	30
SS-9	25	1.0	8.55	1	255	–	–	–	255	2,180
SS-11	0.95	1.0	0.967	1	1,000	–	–	–	1,000	967
SS–N–5[§]	2.0	1.5	0.7	1	–	7	3	21	21	15
SS–N–6	1.0	1.3	0.59	1	–	13	16	208	208	123
Totals					1,465	20		229	1,694	3,558

* CMP = Yield^n ÷ CEP^2, where $n = 2/3$ except when yield is less than 200 kT, when $n = 4/5$.
[†] MIRVs are treated as individual warheads; MRVs are treated as one warhead.
[‡] Total CMP = CMP (column (d))×number of RVs (column (e))×number of missiles (column (f) or column (i)).
[§] SALT II excluded SS-N-5 on Golf-class SSBNs, but included Hotel-class SSBNs, as shown here.

Strategic Missile Balances: 1970, 1980, 1990

1980 — USA

Missile	Warhead yield (MT)	CEP (n.m.)	CMP	RVs per missile	Number of ICBMs	SSBNs	Submarines Missiles per SSBN	Total SLBMs	Total RVs	Total CMP
(a)	(b)	(c)	(d)	(e)	(f)	(g)	(h)	(i)	(j)	(k)
Minuteman II	1.2	0.3	12.54	1	440	–	–	–	440	5,478
Minuteman III										
Mk 12 RV	0.17	0.12	16.8	3	250	–	–	–	750	12,600
Mk 12A RV	0.335	0.12	33.74	3	300	–	–	–	900	30,366
Titan II	9.0	0.45	21.34	1	49	–	–	–	49	1,046
Polaris A-3	0.2	0.455	1.65	3 (MRV)	–	5	16	80	80	132
Poseidon C-3	0.4	0.25	8.69	10 (MIRV)	–	26	16	416	4,160	36,150
Trident C-4	0.1	0.25	2.53	8 (MIRV)	–	5	16	80	640	1,619
Totals					1,039	36		576	7,019	87,391

1980 — USSR

Missile	Warhead yield (MT)	CEP (n.m.)	CMP	RVs per missile	Number of ICBMs	SSBNs	Submarines Missiles per SSBN	Total SLBMs	Total RVs	Total CMP
(a)	(b)	(c)	(d)	(e)	(f)	(g)	(h)	(i)	(j)	(k)
SS-11	0.95	1.0	0.97	1	650	–	–	–	650	631
SS-13	0.75	1.0	0.83	1	60	–	–	–	60	50
SS-17										
Mod 1	0.2	0.24	5.94	4 (MIRV)	120	–	–	–	480	2,851
Mod 2	3.6	0.23	44.4	1	20	–	–	–	20	888
SS-18										
Mod 2, 4	0.5	0.23	17.6	10	214	–	–	–	1,712	30,131
Mod 1, 3	25.0	0.19	237	1	26	–	–	–	26	6,162
SS-19	0.55	0.21	15.3	6 (MIRV)	240	–	–	–	1,440	22,032
SS-N-5	2.0	1.5	0.7	1	–	6	3	18	18	13
SS-N-6	1.0	1.3	0.59	1	–	29	16	464	464	274
SS-N-8	0.8	1.3	0.51	1	–	18	12	216	216	144
						4	16	64	64	
						1	3	3	3	
SS-N-17	0.5	0.75	1.12	1	–	1	12	12	12	13
SS-N-18	0.1	0.43	0.86	7 (MIRV)	–	10	16	160	1,120	963
Totals					1,330	69		937	6,285	64,152

1990 – USA

Missile	Warhead yield (MT)	CEP (n.m.)	CMP	RVs per missile	Number of ICBMs	SSBNs	Missiles per SSBN	Total SLBMs	Total RVs	Total CMP
(a)	(b)	(c)	(d)	(e)	(f)	(g)	(h)	(i)	(j)	(k)
Minuteman II	1.2	0.3	12.53	1	440	–	–	–	440	5,513
Minuteman III	0.335	0.12	33.74	3	500	–	–	–	1,500	50,610
Peacekeeper	0.5	0.05	252	10 (MIRV)	50	–	–	–	500	126,000
Poseidon C-3	0.4	0.25	8.68	10 (MIRV)	–	12	16	192	1,920	16,685
Trident I C-4	0.1	0.25	2.53	8 (MIRV)	–	8	24	192	1,536	3,886
						12	16	192	1,536	3,886
Trident II D-5	0.475	0.06	170	8	–	2	24	48	384	65,280
Totals					990	34		624	7,816	271,860

1990 – USSR

Missile	Warhead yield (MT)	CEP (n.m.)	CMP	RVs per missile	Number of ICBMs	SSBNs	Missiles per SSBN	Total SLBMs	Total RVs	Total CMP
(a)	(b)	(c)	(d)	(e)	(f)	(g)	(h)	(i)	(j)	(k)
SS-11	0.95	1.0	0.97	1	650	–	–	–	650	631
SS-13	0.75	1.0	0.83	1	60	–	–	–	60	50
SS-17 Mod 3/4	0.2	0.2	6.9	4 (MIRV)	75	–	–	–	300	2,070
SS-18 Mod 4	0.5	0.18	19.5	10 (MIRV)	320	–	–	–	3,200	62,400
SS-19 Mod 3	0.55	0.22	13.9	6 (MIRV)	320	–	–	–	1,920	26,688
SS-24	0.5	0.1	63.0	10 (MIRV)	60	–	–	–	600	37,800
SS-25	0.5	0.1	63.0	1	225	–	–	–	225	14,175
SS-N-5	2	1.5	0.7	1	–	2	3	6	6	4
SS-N-6	1.0	1.3	0.6	1	–	12	16	192	192	115
SS-N-8	0.8	0.86	1.2	1	–	18	12	216	216	336
						4	16	64	64	
SS-N-17	0.5	0.76	1.1	1	–	1	12	12	12	13
SS-N-18	0.1	0.43	0.86	7 (MIRV)	–	14	16	224	1,568	1,348
SS-N-20	0.1	0.27	2.2	6 (MIRV)	–	6	20	120	720	1,584
SS-N-23	0.1	0.27	2.2	4 (MIRV)	–	6	16	96	384	845
Totals					1,410	61		924	10,117	148,059

424

NATO and Soviet Naval Strengths: 1950

	Belgium	Canada	Denmark	France	Italy	Netherlands	Norway	Portugal	UK	USA	All NATO	USSR
Battleships				2	4				5	18	29	2
Aircraft carriers									10	25	35	
Light carriers		1		1						9	11	
Escort carriers				1		1				66	68	
Cruisers		2		4	2				27	41	76	16
Light cruisers										84	84	
Destroyers		11	8	35	20		8	5	98	341	526	15
Escorts/ frigates	3	21	13		21	6	8	8	154	244	478	
Submarines			2	12		6	5	3	61	167	256	360*
Mine counter-measures	9	30	40		16		2		47	175	319	150*

* Estimates

Notes:
1 Source: *Janes Fighting Ships: 1951* (Jane's, London, 1951).
2 Note that a proportion of ships in most countries were in reserve; for example in the US navy 16 battleships, 7 heavy and 7 light/escort carriers were in reserve.
3 These figures give force totals, but note that Soviet ships were split between Northern, Baltic, Black Sea and Pacific fleets. Similarly, US ships were split between Atlantic and Pacific fleets.
4 This table uses the traditional classifications of 'cruiser', 'destroyer' etc.

Nuclear Submarine Accidents: USSR

Date	Submarine	Nature of accident	Place	Remarks
4 July 1961	November class (K-19)	Lost pressure in primary coolant loop	n.k.	10 deaths; towed back to base. This boat was nicknamed 'Hiroshima' in the Soviet navy
12 February 1965	November class (K-11)	Radiation leakage in reactor area	Polyarny	Unknown number of crew hospitalized for radiation sickness
20 November 1965	Echo II (K-74)	Turbine failure	Atlantic	
September 1967	November class (K-3) (*Leninsky Komsomol*)	Internal fire	Near North Pole	39 died
1968	Echo II	Sank with all hands	Kolsky Zaliv off Severomorsk	90-man crew perished
23 August 1968	Yankee I (K-140)	Reactor ran out of control	In port	Later rebuilt as sole Yankee II
15 November 1969	November (K-19)	Collided with USS *Gato* (SSN-615)	Entrance to White Sea	
8 April 1970	November class (K-8)	Internal fire	Off Cape Finisterre	Boat sank; crew rescued
April–May 1970	Unknown	Internal fire	Near Faroes	Scuttled by crew to prevent fire reaching reactor
20 June 1970	Echo II (K-557)	Collided with USS *Tautog* (SSN-639)	Pacific	Nearly sank
February 1972	Hotel II	Lost all power	600 n.m. NE of Newfoundland	Several deaths; towed back to USSR
24 February 1972	November (K-19)	Unknown accident	n.k.	29 deaths

Table continued

Date	Submarine	Nature of accident	Place	Remarks
December 1972	Unknown	Radiation leakage in nuclear-tipped torpedo	Off US coast	Towed to Severomorsk; several deaths
14 June 1973	Echo II (K-56)	Collided with Soviet ship *Akademik Berg*	Near Nakhoda	27 killed
31 August 1973	Yankee I (K-219)	Accident in missile tube	At sea	
1973	November	Disabled; unable to proceed	Off Newfound-land	Towed back to USSR
October 1976	Unknown	Fire in missile launch compartment	Atlantic	Unknown; returned to port under own power
1977	Unknown	Internal fire	Indian Ocean	Unknown number of deaths; towed to Vladivostok
28 August 1977	Echo	Surface collision with USS *Voge* (FF 1047)	Mediterranean	Hull damage
19 August 1978	Echo	Engineering casualty in nuclear section	140 n.m. NW of Scotland	Casualties not known; towed to Severomorsk
July 1979	Echo II (K-116)	Reactor meltdown at sea	n.k.	
1979/80	Echo II (K-10)	Underwater collision	Pacific	Nearly lost
21 August 1980	Echo I (K-45)	Internal fire	290 n.m. E of Okinawa	Towed to Vladivostok
September 1981	Unidentified	Series of strong physical shocks	Baltic	Unknown number of crew hospitalized for radiation burns; submarine towed to Kaliningrad
23 June 1983	Charlie I (K-429)	Believed to be ventilator not closed	Off Petropavlovsk, Kamchatka Peninsula	Boat was on post-refit dive. Casualties unknown. Salvaged refitted, sank in dock. Salvaged, refitted, used as training hulk
September 1983	Echo I (K-122)	Internal fire	Pacific	Nine deaths
31 October 1983	Victor III	Propeller entangled in array of USS *McCloy* (FF 1038)	Off South Carolina US coast	Towed to Cuba by Soviet tug
21 March 1984	Victor I	Collision with USS *Kitty Hawk* (CV 63)	Sea of Japan	Damage unknown
18 June 1984	Echo II (K-131)	Fire	n.k.	13 dead
10 August 1984	Echo II (K-431)	Reactor exploded during refuelling	Vladivostok	10 dead

Table continued

Date	Submarine	Nature of accident	Place	Remarks
21 September 1984	Victor I	Collision with Soviet merchant ship	Strait of Gibraltar	Damage to bow sonar dome
10 August 1985	Victor I (K-371)	Severe damage while being recored	In dock, Far East	Stricken
December 1985	Charlie I	Nuclear accident (possibly reactor meltdown)	–	
1986	Echo II (K-175)	Reactor accident	Cam Ranh Bay	
13 January 1986	Echo II	Unknown	280 n.m. NW of Okinawa	Towed to Vladivostok
6 October 1986	Yankee I (K-219)	Internal explosion in missile tube	East of Bermuda	Three dead, others injured; sank 6 October, 763 n.m. SE of New York
7 April 1989	Mike (K-728)	Fire	Norwegian Sea	All crew (57) lost
26 June 1989	Echo II (K-154)	Serious reactor accident		Led to retiring all HEN-powered nuclear boats
7 December 1989	Delta IV (K-89)	Tried consecutive launch of 16 missiles; third failed and fell back on submarine	White Sea	Injured 13 men

Soviet Nuclear-Powered Attack Submarines

Class	Entered service	Number built	Displacement (submerged) (tonnes)	Max. speed (knots)	Crew	Torpedo tubes (total carried)	Comments
November	1960	15	5,300	28	80	10 (32)	
Victor I (Project 671)	1965	16	5,100	30	94	6 (18)	
Victor II (Project 671RT)	1972	7	5,700	30	94	6 (18)	
Victor III (Project 671RTM)	1978	26	6,000	30	94	6 (18)	
Alfa (Project 705)	1972	7	3,680	45	31	6 (18)	
Sierra (Project 945)	1984	4	7,900	35	60	2×533 mm 4×650 mm	Three more scrapped before completion
Akula (Project 971)	1984	16	9,100	35	73	2×533 mm 4×650 mm	
Mike (Project 685)	1983	1	8,500	31	57	6×533 mm (12)	Lost April 1989
Echo I (Project 659T)		5	5,500	25	75	6×533 mm 4×406 mm	Converted from SSGN
Total		97					

Soviet Diesel-Electric Submarines

Class	In service	Number built*	Displacement (submerged) (tonnes)	Max. speed (submerged) (knots)	Crew	Torpedo tubes (total carried)	Comments
Whiskey (Project 613)	1951–93	215	1,340	13	52	6 (12)	
Zulu (Project 611)	1952–	18	2,350	16	70	10 (22)	Many converted for other uses
Quebec (Project 615)	1954–60s	30	540	16	30	4 (8)	Closed-cycle propulsion system
Romeo (Project 633)	1957–87	21	1,700	13	56	8 (14)	Improved Whiskey
Foxtrot (Project 641)	1963–90s	62	2,484	16	75	10 (22)	
Tango (Project 641 Buki)	1972–	19	3,900	16	72	6	
Kilo (Project 877)	1980–	28	3,076	17	53	6 (18)	
Total		393					

* This table includes submarines built for the Soviet navy only.

US Navy Carrier Air Wing: 1980

	Role	Aircraft	Crew	Maximum speed	Range (n.m.)	Total in carrier air wing
Fixed wing	Interceptor/air-superiority fighter	Grumman F-14A Tomcat	2	Mach 2.34	1,700 (fighter)	24
	Fighter-bomber	Vought A-7E Corsair	1	Mach 0.9	700 (1,810 kg weapons)	24
	All-weather bomber	Grumman A-6E Intruder	2	Mach 0.9	920 (2,720 kg weapons)	10
	Electronic warfare	Grumman EA-6B Prowler	2	1,060 km/h (sea level)	710 (4×ECM pods)	4
	Airborne early warning	Grumman E-2C Hawkeye	5	600 km/h	200 (6 h on station)	4
	Anti-submarine warfare	Lockheed S-3A Viking	4	810 km/h	2,300 (patrol)	10
Tankers	Air-to-air refuelling	Grumman KA-6D Intruder	2	Mach 0.9	920	4
	Photo reconnaissance	Vought RF-8G Crusader	1	1,080 km/h	640	3
Helicopters	Anti-submarine warfare	Sikorsky SH-3D Seaking	4	270 km/h	625	4
	Search and rescue	Sikorsky SH-3D Seaking	4	270 km/h	625	2
Total						89

Sea Mines Laid and Damage Caused in the Second World War

MINES LAID

Axis powers		Allied powers	
Country	Number	Country	Number
Germany	223,000	UK	263,376
Japan	51,000	USA	44,000
Italy	54,457	USSR	40,000
Finland	5,500	Norway	5,000
Bulgaria	1,000	Poland	110
Romania	6,500	France	some
		Greece	some
Total	341,457		*c.* 352,486

DAMAGE CAUSED

Ship type	Total losses from all weapons	Losses caused by mines	
		Number	% of total losses
Battleships	10	0	0
Commerce raiders	7	0	0
Destroyers, torpedo boats	96	20	21
Submarine chasers	601	33	5
Submarines	974	38	4
Minelayers	12	2	17
Minesweepers	213	72	34
MTBs/PT boats, E-boats	84	5	6
Supply ship/auxiliary/ miscellaneous	853	354	42
Merchant ships	1,563	496	32
Totals	4,413	1,020	23

NATO's 1950s Mine Countermeasures Programme*

Country	Class	Number	built	Entered service	Funded	Comments
Belgium	Agile	5	USA	1956	MDAP	
	Bluebird[†]	18	USA		MDAP	
		8	Belgium		National	
	Herstal	16	Belgium	1956	MDAP – 8 National – 8	British Ham class
Canada	Bay	10	Canada	1951	National	Based on British Ton class
Denmark	Bluebird[†]	8	USA	1955	MDAP	
	Asvig	4	Denmark	1960	National	Danish design
	Cove	4	USA	1959	MDAP	
France	Agile	15	USA	1954	MDAP	
	Bluebird[†]	30	USA	1953	MDAP	
	Bay	6	Canada	1954	MDAP	British Ham class
	Ham	15	UK	1954	MDAP	All built in UK
	Sirius	34	France	1952	MDAP – 28 National – 6	Closely based on UK Ton
	Mercure	1	France	1957	MDAP	Based on US Bluebird design
Germany	Lindau	18	Germany	1957	MDAP	Based on US Bluebird design
	Vegesack	6	France	1959	National	
	Schutze	30	Germany	1959	National	
Greece	Bluebird[†]	9	USA	1950s	MDAP	
	Cove	4	USA	1959	MDAP	
Italy	Agile	4	USA	1956	MDAP	
	Bluebird[2]	17	USA	1953	MDAP	
	Agave	19	Italy	1955	MDAP	US Bluebird class
	Aragosta	20	Italy	1955	MDAP	British Ham class
Netherlands	Bluebird[†]	14	USA	1953	MDAP	
	Agile	6	USA	1954	MDAP	
	Dokkum	18	Netherlands	1954	MDAP	UK Ton class

BUILDING PROGRAMMES (*continued*)

Country	Class	Number	built	Entered service	Funded	Comments
Netherlands	Wildervank	14	Netherlands	1955	Netherlands	UK Ton class
(*continued*)	Van Straelen	16	Netherlands	1959	MDAP – 8 National – 8	UK Ham class
Portugal	Agile	4	USA	1955	MDAP	
	Bluebird[†]	8	USA	1953	MDAP	
	Sao Roque	4	Portugal	1954	MDAP – 2 National – 2	UK Ton class
Turkey	Bluebird[†]	4	USA	1958	MDAP	More were supplied later
	Bay	4	Canada	1958	MDAP	Based on British Ton class
	Cove	4	USA	1958	MDAP	
UK	Ton	115	UK	1952	National	
	Ham	93	UK	1953	National	
	Ley	11	UK	1950	National	
USA	Agile	62	USA	1952	National	
	Ability	3	USA	1956	National	No exports
	Bluebird[†]	20	USA	1953	National	
	Cove	2	USA	1958	National	
Total		703				

* This covers only the new-construction ships produced as part of the NATO programme. It does not include:

(a) Second World War ships transferred between NATO countries (e.g. British Algerine class to Belgium);

(b) former *Kriegsmarine* vessels refitted and returned to service with the newly created *Bundesmarine*;

(c) ships built for export to non-NATO countries.

[†] The US-designed inshore minesweepers are variously known as the 'Bluebird', 'Redwing' and 'Adjutant' classes, as a result of minor differences between the three groups. They are, however, essentially the same design and are treated as all belonging to the 'Bluebird' class for the purposes of this table.

SPECIFICATIONS

Class	Country of origin	Displacement (full load) (tonnes)	Length (m)	Max. speed/range	Crew
Agile	USA	667	52.4	15.5 kt/3,300 n.m. at 10 kt	72
Bluebird	USA	363	44.3	13 kt/2,500 n.m. at 10 kt	39
Ton	UK	432	46.3	15 kt/3,000 n.m. at 8 kt	29
Ham	UK	162	32.75	14 kt/2,350 n.m. at 9 kt	15
Ley	UK	167	32.5	13 kt/2,350 n.m. at 9 kt	15

Main Battle Tanks: NATO and Warsaw Pact

Country of origin	Tank*	Entered service	Weight (tonnes)	Main gun (mm)	Rounds carried	Anti-tank rounds†	Engine	Power: weight ratio (kW/tonne)	Max. road speed (km/h)	Road range (km)	Crew
France	AMX-30	1967	37	105	47	HEAT	Diesel	13	65	520	4
Germany	Leopard 1	1965	40	105	60	APDS APFSDS	Diesel	14	68	560	4
	Leopard 2	1980	55	120	42	APFSDS MP	Turbo-charged diesel	20	72	550	4
UK	Centurion	1947	49	76	70	APDS HESH	Petrol	12.3	35	184	4
	Conqueror	1955	65	120	35	APDS HESH	Petrol	10	34	100	4
	Chieftain	1967	55	120	64	APDS	Diesel	10	48	450	4
	Challenger	1983	62	120	52	APDS	Diesel	14	56	600	4
USA	M4 Sherman	1942	32	75	97	APCBC HVAP	Petrol	16	42	160	5
	M26 Pershing	1945	42	90	n.k.	APCBC HVAP	Petrol	9	48	160	5
	M47	1952	47	90	71	APCBC HVAP	Petrol	16	48	130	5
	M48 Patton	1953	48	90	62	APFSDS HEAT	Diesel	12	48	112	4
	M60	1959	48	105	63	APFSDS HEAT	Diesel	10	48	480	4
	M1A1 Abrams	1985	57	120	40	APFSDS MP	Gas turbine	19	66	465	4
USSR	T-34/85	1940	32	85	55	AP APCBC	Diesel	11.6	50	370	4
	JS-3	1945	46	122	28	AP APCBC	Diesel	11.3	40	150	4
	T-10	1957	51	122	30	AP APCBC	Diesel	10	28	200	4

Table continued

Country of origin	Tank*	Entered service	Weight (tonnes)	Main gun (mm)	Rounds carried	Anti-tank rounds†	Engine	Power: weight ratio (kW/tonne)	Max. road speed (km/h)	Road range (km)	Crew
USSR (*continued*)	T-54/55	1954	36	100	43	HVAP AP	Diesel	12	48	400	4
	T-62	1962	37	115	40	APFSDS HEATFS	Diesel	11	50	450	4
	T-64B	1967	38	125	40	APFSDS HEATFS	Diesel	15	75	450	3
	T-72M	1975	43.5	125	40	APFSDS HEATFS	Diesel	13	60	460	3
	T-80	1979	42	125	40	APFSDS HEATFS	Gas turbine	20	75	400	3

* This table shows only the initial service version of each tank. All were subsequently improved.
† Types of anti-tank round:

AP – armour-piercing
APCBC – armour-piercing, capped, ballistic-capped
APDS – armour-piercing, discarding sabot
APFSDS – armour-piercing, fin-stabilized, discarding sabot
HEAT – high-explosive, anti-tank
HEATFS – high-explosive, anti-tank, fin-stabilized
HESH – high-explosive, squash-head
HVAP – high velocity, armour-piercing
MP – multi-purpose

Artillery: NATO and Warsaw Pact

Country	Type	Calibre (mm)	Entered service	Wheeled/ tracked*	Range (km)	Max. rate of fire (rounds per min)	HE projectile weight (kg)	Nuclear capable
Czechoslovakia	DANA	152	1980	SP – wheeled	20.0	6	43.5	No
France	TR	155	1984	Towed – wheeled	24.0	6	43.2	No
	GCT	155	1979	SP – tracked	23.5	8	43.2	No
International (Germany/ Italy/UK)	FH70	155	1975	Towed – wheeled	24.0	6	43.5	No
USSR	D-30	122	1967	Towed – wheeled	15.3	8	21.8	No
	M-46	130	1954	Towed – wheeled	27.5	6	33.4	No
	S-23	180	1955	Towed – wheeled	30.0	1	84.1	Yes
	SAU-122 (2S1)	122	1974	SP – tracked	15.3	6	21.8	No
	SAU-152 (2S3)	152	1974	SP – tracked	24.0	6	43.6	Yes
	SO-203 (2S7)	203	1975	SP – tracked	30	2	n.k.	Yes
UK	25-pdr	88	1940	Towed – wheeled	12.3	5	11.34	No
	5.5 inch	140	1942	Towed – wheeled	14.6	2	41.0	No
	Abbot	105	1964	SP – tracked	17.0	12	16.1	No
USA	M110	203	1961	SP – tracked	16.8	2	92.5	Yes
	M107	175	1963	SP – tracked	32.7	2	66.8	No
	M109	155	1963	SP – tracked	14.6	3	42.9	Yes
	M108	105	1963	SP – tracked	11.5	3	18.1	No
	M44	155	1953	SP – tracked	14.6	2	42.9	No

* SP = self-propelled.

Tactical Nuclear Weapons Systems

USA

	System	Type	Entered service	Accuracy (CEP)	Approx. yields	Range (km)	Comments
Ballistic missiles	Corporal	Liquid-fuel, single-stage missile	1953	n.k.	60 kT	138	(a) Served with US and UK armies only (b) Required 15 vehicles; took 7 hours to bring into action
	Honest John	Solid-fuel, truck-launched (wheeled) missile	1954	1,850 m	1–20 kT	6–38	(a) Widely used by NATO. Replaced by Lance (b) Dual-capable*
	Redstone	Liquid-fuel, vertically launched missile	1958	n.k.	W29Y1 – 1 MT W29Y2 – 2 MT	400	
	Sergeant	Road-mobile, solid fuel	1961	n.k.	60 kT	45–140	(a) Used by US and West Germany only
	Pershing I/IA	Road-mobile, vertically launched, solid-fuel, two-stage missile	1962	400 m at max. range	60, 200, 400 kT	740	(a) Pershing IA featured upgraded launch and tracking; missile was unchanged from Pershing I. (b) Served with US Army and West German *Luftwaffe*
	Pershing II	Road-mobile, vertically launched, two-stage missile	1983	45 m at max. range	5–50 kT	1,800	

Tactical Nuclear Weapons Systems

USA (*continued*)

	System	Type	Entered service	Accuracy (CEP)	Approx. yields	Range (km)	Comments
	Lance	Storable-liquid-fuel, truck-launched (tracked) missile	1972	375 m at max. range	Fission: 1–100 kT ER: 1 kT	5–125	(a) Replaced Honest John and Sergeant (b) Dual-capable* (c) Fission version widely used by NATO (d) ER version US only
Cruise missiles	Tomahawk (BGM-109)	Ground-launched cruise missile (GLCM)	1983	80 m at max. range	1×200 kT	2,500	Deployed in various NATO countries; all operated by USAF
Howitzers	Gun, Heavy, Motorized, 280 mm, M65	Wheeled-gun system	1952	n.k.	1×15 kT or 1×10–15 kT	30.3	
	203 mm howitzer	M110 tracked howitzer	1961	Short-range – 40 m Medium-range – 100 m Long-range – 172 m	12 kT	20.6 (M110A) 29.0 (M110A2)	
	155 mm howitzer	M109 tracked howitzer	1963	n.k.	0.1 kT	18.1 (M109A1) 30.0 (M109A3)	Used by most NATO armies
Atomic demolition mines	SADM	Atomic demolition mine	1964	n.k.	0.01–1 kT	–	(a) Deployed with US and some NATO armies (b) Carried in backpack by one soldier
Rocket launcher	Davy Crocket	Tube-launched, vehicle-mounted (Jeep) missile	1960	n.k.	0.25 kT	2.0	(a) Deployed with US army only (b) Lethality alleged to have been greater than its maximum range

* Dual-capable missiles could carry either a nuclear or a conventional (high-explosive) warhead.

USSR

	System	Type*	Entered service	Accuracy (CEP)	Approx. yields	Range (km)	Comments
Missiles	Frog-1	Liquid-fuel, vehicle-mounted (tracked) missile	1957	n.k.	n.k.	32	(a) Mounted on JS-3 tank chassis (b) Served with Soviet army (nuclear) and other Warsaw Pact armies (non-nuclear)
	Frog-3	Liquid-fuel, vehicle-mounted (tracked) missile	1960	n.k.	n.k.	40	(a) Mounted on PT-76 chassis
	Frog-7	Solid-fuel, vehicle-mounted (wheeled) missile	1965	500 m	25 kT	70	(a) Mounted on ZIL-135 chassis
	SS-1 (Scud-A)	Liquid-fuel, vehicle-mounted (tracked) missile	1955	3,000 m	50 kT	150	(a) Mounted on JS-3 tank chassis
	SS-1 (Scud-B)	Liquid-fuel, vehicle-mounted (tracked) missile	1965	450 m	5–70 kT	300	(a) Mounted on MAZ-543 8-wheel truck
	SS-12A (Scaleboard)	Liquid-fuel, vehicle-mounted (wheeled) missile	1962	100 m (estimate)	500 kT	900	
	SS-12B	Solid-fuel, vehicle-mounted (wheeled) missile	1979	30 m	500 kT	900	Originally designated SS-22 by NATO
	SS-20	Solid-fuel, vehicle-mounted cruise missile	1975	400 m	3×150 kT MIRV	5,000	
Howitzers	S-23	Towed	1955	n.k.	0.2 kT	30	
	2S3 152 mm M-1973	Tracked SP howitzer	1971	n.k.	2 kT	24	
	2S5 152 mm	Tracked SP gun	1981	n.k.	2 kT	27	
	2S7 203 mm	Tracked SP howitzer	1975	n.k.	2 kT	30	

* SP – self-propelled.

A Hypothetical US Counter-Force Attack on Soviet Strategic Forces in 1986

Target category	Target type	Number of targets	Attack assumptions (MT)		Comments
			Groundburst	Airburst	
Missile silos (See Note 2.)	SS-4	112	0.1	0.1	Included to prevent use against NATO Europe
	SS-11	448	0.1	0.1	
	SS-13	60	0.1	0.1	
	SS-17	150	0.35	0.17	
	SS-18	308	0.35	0.17	
	SS-19	360	0.35	0.17	
Missile launch-control centres	SS-4, SS-11, SS-13	66	1.2	0.17	Assumed one site per 10 missiles
	SS-17, SS-18	48	0.35	0.17	
	SS-19	36	0.35	0.1	
ICBM test silos	All types	27	0.1	0.1	Located at test sites – e.g. Plesetsk
Bases for mobile missiles	SS-25	3	1.2	16×0.1	See Note 3.
	SS-20	16	1.2	16×0.1	(a) Five SS-20 bases included in ICBM/IRBM fields (b) See Note 3.
ABM launcher sites	Exo-atmospheric interceptors	2	0.1	0.1	
	Endo-atmospheric interceptors	7	0.1	0.1	
Nuclear navy bases	SSBNs	8	1.2	1.2	

Table continued

Target category	Target type	Number of targets	Attack assumptions (MT)		Comments
			Groundburst	Airburst	
Nuclear navy bases (*continued*)	Other nuclear-capable ships	8	1.2	1.2	
	Naval yards	5	1.2	1.2	
Bomber bases	Long-range (Bison/Bear)	3	1.2	16×0.1	See Note 3.
	Arctic staging	5	1.2	16×0.1	See Note 3.
	Intermediate-range (Backfire)	10	1.2	16×0.1	See Note 3.
	Medium-range (Badger/Blinder/Fencer)	6	1.2	16×0.1	See Note 3.
National and strategic rocket forces HQs	Underground	19	0.1	0.1	
	Base for airborne command post	1	1.2	16×0.1	See Note 3.
Communications facilities	Early-warning and ABM radars	13		0.1	Three further radars collocated with other sites
	Radio transmitters	19		0.1	Six further transmitters collocated with other sites
Total targets		1,740			

Notes

1 This attack plan is taken from Barbara G. Levi, Frank N. von Hippel and William H. Dogherty, 'Civilian Casualties from "Limited" Nuclear Attacks on the USSR', *International Security*, vol. 12, no. 3 (winter 1987/88), pp. 168–89.

2 It was assumed that each target would be attacked by two nuclear warheads – one groundburst, one airburst – in order to increase the probability of their destruction.

3 Area targets such as bomber airfields and bases for road/rail-mobile ICBMs were attacked using a single 1.2 MT groundburst at the centre of the target plus a pattern of sixteen 0.1 MT airbursts delivered around the target at a sufficient distance to destroy aircraft which had taken off or mobile missile launchers which had left their garage but were not yet clear of the area. Such a pattern would have required sufficient spacing between individual bursts to avoid 'fratricide'.

Glossary

Note   Italic type indicates that there is a glossary entry for the word italicized.

ABM   Anti-ballistic missile – a missile capable of destroying incoming *ballistic missiles* or their warheads before they impact on their target.

ABM Treaty   The ABM Treaty, signed on 3 October 1972, limited both the USA and the USSR to two *ABM* sites. One allowable site was the national capital; the other was at an *ICBM* field. Not more than 100 launchers and 100 missiles were allowed at each site.

ACE   Allied Command Europe (NATO).

AFCENT   Allied Forces Central Europe (NATO).

ALCM   Air-launched *cruise missile*.

APC   Armoured personnel carrier. A tracked or wheeled vehicle designed to carry *infantry*men.

Army formations and units   Armies used the same terms to describe their constituent elements, but with widely differing meanings. In general, the following meanings apply.

BATTALION   The smallest permanent tactical unit, made up of a number of companies, each consisting of a number of platoons. A battalion was commanded by a lieutenant-colonel in some armies and by a major in others. Battalions varied in size from about 500 to 1,000 men. There were various types of battalion, their role normally being indicated in their title – e.g. 234 Motor Rifle Battalion, 2 Armoured Battalion, 24 Infantry Battalion, etc. Most British battalions had names – e.g. 1st Battalion, Green Howards – and did not have an indicator of their role.

REGIMENT   'Regiment' had four rather different meanings:

- In some armies a regiment was a permanent tactical formation consisting of two to four battalions, but without integral supporting arms such as armour and artillery.

443

- In the Soviet army a regiment was a permanent tactical unit, consisting of a number of battalions with integral all-arms support. There were three *motor-rifle* regiments and one tank regiment in a motor-rifle division. The Soviet regiment was thus equivalent in most respects to a NATO brigade.
- In some armies a regiment was an administrative and historical entity, composed of a number of battalions, each of which operated as a totally independent tactical unit. For example, the Queen's Regiment in the UK consisted of a number of battalions which operated independently of each other – thus, 1/QUEENS, 2/QUEENS, etc.
- Some armies designated battalion-sized units with a cavalry history as a regiment. Thus, in the British army units designated as tank, artillery and engineer regiments were, in fact, the same size as battalions.

BRIGADE   A brigade was composed of a number of battalions – usually three tank battalions and one infantry battalion (armoured brigade) or one tank battalion and three infantry battalions (infantry brigade):

- In most armies a brigade was an all-arms force, which included integral artillery, engineer, aviation, communications and logistics units.
- In some armies brigades could be reinforced, when they were usually known as 'brigade groups'.
- The brigade commander was usually a brigadier-general, a brigadier (British army) or a colonel.

DIVISION   Both NATO and the Warsaw Pact had divisions, composed of between two and five brigades (regiments in the Soviet army). These were designated as either 'tank' or 'infantry', depending upon which arm predominated. In most armies a division was commanded by a major-general, or equivalent. It is important to note that there were wide variations in numerical strength and capability between the divisions of different nations.

CORPS (NATO)   A corps was the highest national formation and was made up of a number of divisions, plus a large number of corps troops (additional artillery, engineers, signals, logistics troops, etc.). Corps were not, however, designated 'tank' or 'infantry', but the national designator was always used (e.g. 3 (US) Corps). A corps was commanded by a general or lieutenant-general.

ARMY (WARSAW PACT)   In the Warsaw Pact an army was approximately equivalent in size to a NATO corps and included its predominant arm in its title – e.g. 'Tank Army' or 'Combined-Arms Army'.

ARMY GROUP (NATO)   Originally used to designate a collection of armies (e.g. 21st Army Group), but in NATO the term was used to describe a collection of corps (e.g. CENTAG = Central Army Group). A NATO army group was commanded by a general.

Assured destruction   Strategic term, describing the ability to inflict unacceptable damage on an enemy.

ASW   Anti-submarine warfare.

AWACS Airborne warning and control system – an aircraft-mounted radar system designed to detect and track enemy aircraft and land vehicles, and to direct action against them.

Ballistic missile A projectile, propelled into space by a rocket motor, which then follows a ballistic trajectory – i.e. one governed mainly by gravity and drag.

Battalion See *Army formations and units.*

Bias The distance between the aiming point for one or more warheads directed at the same target and the mean point of impact.

Booster A self-contained rocket motor attached to a missile to give extra thrust for take-off, after which it was usually jettisoned.

Brigade See *Army formations and units.*

Brigade group See *Army formations and units.*

Bundeswehr The armed forces of the Federal Republic of Germany, comprising the *Bundesmarine* (navy), *Bundesheer* (army) and *Luftwaffe* (air force).

Bus See *Post-boost vehicle.*

C³ Command, control and communications – equipment, personnel and procedures used to acquire, process and disseminate data needed by decision-makers to plan and control operations.

CENTAG Central Army Group (NATO).

CEP Circular error probable – a term used to describe the delivery precision of a weapon, particularly a missile *warhead.* The CEP is the radius of a circle, centred upon the mean point of impact, within which 50 per cent of the warheads aimed at the target will fall. The CEP is normally assessed at the missile's maximum range; at less than maximum range the CEP reduces in proportion.

Civil defence (CD) Passive measures taken to minimize the effects of enemy action upon all aspects of civil life, and to restore utilities and facilities following an attack.

CIWS Close-in weapons system – naval gun systems designed to give last-ditch defence against incoming aircraft and missiles.

CMP Counter-military potential – a static measure of the ability of nuclear weapons to damage hard targets such as missile silos.

Cold launch A method of expelling a missile from a launch tube using compressed air. The missile main motor fires once the missile is clear of the tube, which is therefore not damaged and can be reused. See also *Hot launch.*

Conventional power A propulsion or generating system which does not use nuclear power. Usually applied to ships and submarines.

Conventional war A war in which nuclear weapons are not used.

Conventional warhead A non-nuclear *warhead*, normally high-explosive.

Corps See *Army formations and units.*

Counter-force Describes strategic attacks using nuclear weapons directed against enemy weapons and military forces, especially nuclear-weapon delivery systems.

Counter-value Describes the use of strategic forces to attack selected enemy population centres, industries and other resources which constitute the essential fabric of the nation.

CPSU Communist Party of the Soviet Union.

Cruise missile A missile which flies for long distances supported by lift from the wings and/or body. Power is provided by an air-breathing engine, such as a turbo-jet. Cruise missiles could be launched from aircraft (ALCM = air-launched cruise missile), the ground (GLCM), ships or submarines (SLCM).

Deterrence A political and military strategy designed to prevent potential enemies from taking armed action, or, if conflict should break out, to prevent it from escalating.

Displacement The displacement of a warship is the mass of water displaced by a ship's hull when floating. In this book the displacement given for surface warships is the 'standard' figure – i.e. when the ship is fully manned and stored, but without fuel or reserve feed-water for boilers. The figure is expressed in tonnes, using published figures for navies using the metric system and imperial tons or US short tons converted to metric tonnes in the case of British and US warships. For submarines the displacement is given for the submarine when submerged.

Division See *Army formations and units.*

Dual capable Able to carry either nuclear or conventional bombs/missiles (aircraft) or *warheads* (missiles/guns).

ECCM Electronic counter-countermeasures – a form of electronic warfare designed to overcome enemy use of *ECM* and thus permit continued use of the electromagnetic spectrum.

ECM Electronic countermeasures – a form of electronic warfare designed totally or partially to prevent effective use by the enemy of the electromagnetic spectrum.

ELINT Electronic intelligence – intelligence derived from enemy electronic emissions other than telecommunications (e.g. radar). See also *SIGINT.*

EMP Electromagnetic pulse – a sharp pulse of radio-frequency electromagnetic radiation produced by a nuclear explosion.

EMT Equivalent megatonnage – a measure of damage by nuclear weapons against 'soft targets' such as cities.

Enhanced radiation (ER) – describes a nuclear weapon designed to release about 80 per cent of its *yield* in high-energy neutrons, resulting in a weapon more dangerous to people than to military equipment or structures. Also known as the 'neutron bomb'.

ER See *Enhanced radiation.*

First strike The first offensive move in a conflict. As applied to nuclear warfare, it implies an attempt to eliminate effective retaliation by the enemy.

Flexible response A strategy based on the capability to act effectively across the entire spectrum of war, at the time, place and manner of the user's choosing.

FOBS Fractional Orbital Bombardment System – a nuclear warhead delivered by a partial orbit, enabling the approach to be made from any direction.

Fratricide The situation when more than two nuclear warheads arrive nearly simultaneously at the same target, and the first warhead to explode therefore either destroys or diverts the following warhead(s).

FRG Federal Republic of Germany – during the period covered by this book, West Germany (Bundesrepublik Deutschland).

Front end The forward part of a missile, containing the *post-boost vehicle, warheads, penetration aids,* etc.

GDR German Democratic Republic – East Germany (Deutsche Demokratik Republik).

General war Armed conflict involving the two superpowers.

GLCM Ground-launched *cruise missile.*

GSFG Group of Soviet Forces Germany.

GZ Ground zero – the point on the earth's surface upon, above or below which a nuclear explosion takes place. All effects of the explosion are expressed at distances from GZ.

Hardened Protected against the effects of nuclear weapons. This term was usually applied to 'hardened aircraft shelters' (HAS), 'hardened equipment shelters' (HES), pilot briefing facilities (PBF), etc.

Hardness The ability of a target to withstand a nuclear explosion and its effects of shock, heat, radiation and *EMP.* Normally expressed in terms of overpressure withstood in kgf/cm^2.

HE High explosive.

Hot launch A launch in which a missile is expelled from the launch tube using the missile's main motor. See also *Cold launch.*

IBM See *IRBM.*

ICBM Intercontinental [range] ballistic missile – a land-based missile with a range in excess of 3,000 nautical miles (5,560 km).

ICV Infantry combat vehicle – an armoured vehicle designed to carry between six and ten infantrymen, who were able to fire their weapons from within the vehicle. Sometimes also known as 'mechanized-infantry combat vehicle' (MICV).

447

INF   Intermediate-range nuclear forces – e.g. *IRBMs*.

Infantry   Infantry are troops who, traditionally, capture ground in the attack and hold ground in the defence. In the Cold War the designation 'infantry' was frequently qualified to indicate their method of transportation:

- Mechanized infantry. Troops whose basic means of transport was infantry combat vehicles.
- Motorized infantry. Troops which moved in wheeled vehicles.
- Motor-rifle. English translation of the Russian designation of mechanized infantry; applied to Warsaw Pact forces only.
- Panzer grenadiers. West German designation for troops mounted in infantry combat vehicles and who were capable of fighting from those vehicles.

INR   Initial nuclear radiation.

IRBM   Intermediate-range ballistic missile – a land-based missile with a range between 1,500 nautical miles (2,780 km) and 3,000 nautical miles (5,560 km). In about 1980 this term changed to 'IBM'.

Knot   A speed of one *nautical mile* per hour.

KT   Kiloton – see *Yield*.

LANDJUT   Land Forces Jutland (NATO).

Launch-on-warning   Strategic retaliation using *ICBMs* on receiving information of incoming hostile *ballistic missiles*. The aim was for the retaliating ICBMs to be clear of their silos before the hostile missiles arrived, thus ensuring their survival and continued flight to their targets.

Launch-under-attack   Strategic retaliation using *ICBMs* in which the missiles would be launched while actually under attack. This implies that the executive decision to launch has not been given in sufficient time to achieve *launch-on-warning*.

Launch weight   The total weight of a fully loaded missile at the time of launch, including *boosters*, *post-boost vehicle* and *warheads*.

Limited war   A conflict in which the participants exercise some form of geographical or escalatory restraint, either voluntarily or under pressure from outside powers.

LRTNF   Long-range tactical nuclear forces.

Mach number   Speed expressed as multiples of the speed of sound (Mach 1), which at sea level is approximately 1,200 km/h, but varies with temperature and pressure.

MAD   Mutually assured destruction – the ability of the two superpowers to impose unacceptable destruction on their opponent at any time during the course of a nuclear war, even following a surprise attack.

MCMV   Mine-countermeasures vessel.

Mechanized infantry See *Infantry*.

MICV See *ICV*.

MIRV Multiple independently targeted re-entry vehicle – one of several *warheads* mounted on *ICBMs* or *SLBMs* which can be targeted on separate targets up to several hundred kilometres apart.

MNC Major NATO command/commander.

Motorized infantry See *Infantry*.

Motor-rifle See *Infantry*.

MRBM Medium-range ballistic missile – a land-based missile with a range between 600 nautical miles (1,110 km) and 1,500 nautical miles (2,780 km).

MRV Multiple re-entry vehicle – one of several separate *warheads* mounted on *ICBMs* or *SLBMs* which can be targeted on the same target or on a number of targets sited very close to each other. In principle, this is similar to firing pellets from a shotgun.

MSBS *Mer–Sol Balistique Stratégique* – the French designation for France's submarine-launched *ballistic missile*.

MSC Major subordinate command/commander (NATO).

MT Megaton – See *Yield*.

NATO North Atlantic Treaty Organization.

NATO designations During the Cold War, NATO seldom knew the correct Soviet names for Warsaw Pact equipment. Such equipment was therefore assigned 'reporting names' and designations.

Missile designations consisted of a type identifier (usually two letters) and a unique number. The type identifier could be suffixed by 'N' for a naval system and by 'X' for an experimental system. The type numbers were allocated sequentially, and sub-types were indicated by 'Modification' numbers (the original version being 'Mod 0'). The most common type designators were:

- SS – surface-to-surface (e.g. SS-18, SS-N-20);
- SA – surface-to-air. (e.g. SA-16 Mod 1).

A different system applied to Soviet tanks, which were designated by the letter 'T' followed by the year that production began (e.g. T-54, T-55, T-72, etc.).

Soviet submarine classes were given nicknames, which were supposed to be applied in alphabetical order (e.g. Whiskey class, Alfa class, etc.). The exception to this system was when NATO allocated the name 'Typhoon class' to a type known to be named '*Taifun*' by the Soviets. The system became confused, however, when NATO ran out of letters and designated a new class the Akula class (*akula* is the Russian word for shark), following which the Soviets named a different class the *Akula* class.

Naval Infantry Soviet marines.

NBC Nuclear, biological, chemical (weapons).

nm Nautical mile. 1 nm = 1.853 km.

NORTHAG Northern Army Group (NATO).

Nuclear propulsion/power A system using nuclear energy – usually applied to ships and submarines.

Nuclear war A war in which nuclear weapons are used.

Panzer grenadiers See *Infantry*.

PBV See *Post-boost vehicle*.

Penaid See *Penetration aid*.

Penetration aid A device, carried on the *post-boost vehicle* on an *ICBM* or *SLBM*, which is designed to confuse the enemy as to the number and trajectory of the real *warheads*.

Post-boost vehicle (PBV) A device carried on the *front end* of a missile, upon which are mounted the *re-entry vehicles* (RVs), plus guidance and propulsion packages and *penetration aids*, which dispenses the RVs sequentially towards their targets. Also known as a 'bus'.

PSC Principal subordinate command/commander (NATO).

Regiment See *Army formations and units*.

Re-entry vehicle (RV) A body carried on the front end of a missile to protect a nuclear warhead when the missile re-enters the earth's atmosphere.

RV See *Re-entry vehicle*.

SAC Strategic Air Command (US).

SACEUR Supreme Allied Commander Europe (NATO).

SACLANT Supreme Allied Commander Atlantic (NATO).

SALT Strategic Arms Limitation Talks (or Treaty). There were two SALT treaties:

- SALT I. Signed in Moscow on 26 May 1972; came into effect on 3 October 1972.
- SALT II. Signed in Vienna on 18 June 1979. Not ratified by the US Senate, but the USA and the USSR tacitly agreed to adhere to its terms.

SAM Surface-to-air missile.

Second strike A strategic concept in which the victim of a surprise *first strike* retains sufficient nuclear capability to launch a strike which will attempt to inflict unacceptable damage on the aggressor.

SHAPE Supreme Headquarters Allied Powers Europe (NATO).

Ship designation The system of ship designation developed by the US navy in the 1920s was adopted first by NATO and subsequently by the majority of navies around the world. The main designations relevant to this book are:

Aircraft carriers	CV (general); CVN (nuclear-powered); CVA (attack); CVS (anti-submarine)
Amphibious	LSD (dock landing ship); LST (tank landing ship)
Battleship	BB
Battlecruiser	BC
Cruiser	CC (general); CA (with guns); CG (with missiles)
Destroyer	DD (general); DDG (with missiles)
Frigate	FF (general); FFG (with missiles)
Intelligence collector	AGI
Mine countermeasures	MCMV (general); MH (minehunter); MS (minesweeper); MSC (coastal minesweeper); MSI (inshore minesweeper); MSO (ocean-going minesweeper)
Submarine	SS (general); SSN (nuclear-powered); SSBN (with ballistic missiles, nuclear-powered)

SIGINT Signals intelligence – intelligence derived from monitoring enemy telecommunications systems. See also *ELINT*.

SIOP Single Integrated Operational Plan – the US master plan for strategic nuclear attack on the Soviet Union. Specific versions were identified by the year, which was added as a suffix – e.g. 'SIOP-68'.

SLBM Submarine-launched *ballistic missile*. (Note that, unlike land-based missiles, SLBMs were not subdivided according to range.)

SLCM Ship/submarine-launched *cruise missile*.

Soft In strategic terms, describes an unprotected (as opposed to a '*hardened*') target.

SRAM Short-Range Attack Missile.

SS Submarine, conventionally (i.e. diesel-electric) powered.

SSBN Submarine, ballistic, nuclear – i.e. a nuclear-powered *ballistic-missile* submarine.

SSBS *Sol–Sol Balistique Stratégique* – the French designation for France's land-based *ballistic missiles*. Note that, although designated 'strategic' by France, SSBSs were intermediate-range (*IRBM*s) according to the US/Soviet definition agreed in *SALT*.

SSM Surface-to-surface missile.

SSN Submarine, nuclear – i.e. a nuclear-powered attack submarine.

Stage A self-contained rocket motor and fuel tank which is an integral part of the missile structure and which drops away when its fuel has been used up.

Surface zero The point on the sea's surface vertically above or below the centre of a nuclear explosion – equivalent to *ground zero* for an explosion on land.

TEL Transporter–erector–launcher. A wheeled or tracked device which carried a missile, raised it into the firing position, and then launched it.

Throw weight The useful weight which can be placed on a trajectory towards the target by the main or boost stage of a missile. In *SALT* II, throw weight was defined as the sum of the weights of the *re-entry vehicle(s)*, plus any *post-boost vehicle*, plus *penetration aids*, and their releasing mechanisms.

TREE Transient radiation effects on electronics.

USAF United States Air Force.

V/STOL Vertical/short take-off and landing.

Warhead The explosive device of a weapon, either nuclear or conventional. In a *ballistic missile* the warhead was carried inside a *re-entry vehicle*.

Yield The energy released in a nuclear explosion, expressed in terms of the equivalent number of tons of TNT (high explosive) releasing the same energy. It is normally expressed in terms of thousands of tons of TNT (kilotons) or millions of tons (megatons). The energy is principally released as nuclear radiation, thermal radiation and blast energy, the proportions of each depending upon the medium in which the explosion occurs – i.e. whether the explosion is an air, surface or subsurface burst.

Notes

CHAPTER 1

1 Former British prime minister Winston Churchill in a letter to US president Harry S. Truman, November 1945; quoted in D. Cook, *Forging the Alliance: NATO 1945–1950* (Secker & Warburg, London, 1989), p. 50.

CHAPTER 2

1 Cook, *Forging the Alliance*, p. 163.
2 *Keesing's Contemporary Archives*, 1949.

CHAPTER 3

1 NATO Communiqué, Ministerial Meeting, 13–14 December 1967, paragraph 12.
2 Ibid., Annex, paragraph 14.
3 *Soviet Military Power* was issued by the US Department of Defense, Washington DC, in 1981, 1983, 1984, 1985, 1986, 1987, 1988, 1989 and 1990. A successor titled *Military Forces in Transition*, which perhaps significantly was printed in monochrome, was issued in 1991, but proved to be the final document in the series.
4 *Whence The Threat To Peace?* was issued by the Military Publishing House of the USSR Ministry of Defence, Moscow, in 1982 (1st edn), 1982 (2nd edn (supplemented)) and 1984 (3rd edn).
5 *NATO and the Warsaw Pact: Force Comparisons* was issued by the NATO Information Services, Brussels, in 1982, 1983 and 1984.

CHAPTER 4

1 North Atlantic Council Meeting, 11–14 December 1956, Final Communiqué, paragraph 7.

Notes

2 Tony Geraghty, *Beyond the Front Line* (HarperCollins, London, 1996), p. 159.
3 North Atlantic Council in Ministerial Session, Brussels, 15–16 November 1968, Final Communiqué, paragraph 2.
4 NATO Special Meeting of Foreign and Defence Ministers, Brussels, 12 December 1979, Final Communiqué, paragraph 7.
5 Ibid., paragraph 9.
6 NATO Communiqué, Defence Planning Committee Meeting, 1–2 June 1983.
7 NATO Nuclear Planning Group Meeting, 29–30 October 1985, Final Communiqué, paragraph 6.

CHAPTER 5

1 NATO Communiqué, Defence Planning Committee, 14 June 1974, paragraph 12.

CHAPTER 6

1 Geraghty, *Beyond the Front Line*, p. 334.
2 'Warsaw Pact and the Polish Crisis in 1980–81' (SED-State Research Group, Internet).
3 Raymond L. Garthoff (former US ambassador and fellow of the Brookings Institute), 'When and Why Romania Distanced Itself from the Warsaw Pact' (Internet: http://www.brook.edu).
4 Jonathan Eyal, 'Romania: Looking for Weapons of Mass Destruction?' *Jane's Soviet Intelligence Review*, vol. 1, no. 8 (August 1989), pp. 378–82.

CHAPTER 7

1 T. B. Cochrane, W. M. Arkin, R. S. Norris and M. M. Hoenig, *Nuclear Weapons Databook, Volume II: US Nuclear Warhead Production* (Ballinger, Cambridge, Mass., 1987), p. 154.
2 S. Glasstone and P. J. Dolan, *The Effects of Nuclear Weapons* (US Department of Defense, Washington DC, 1977).
3 Ibid., pp. 522–3.
4 SIPRI, *World Armaments and Disarmament Yearbook 1991* (SIPRI, Stockholm, Sweden), pp. 46–7.

CHAPTER 8

1 *Annual Report to Congress: Fiscal Year 1987* (US Department of Defense, Washington DC, 1986).
2 V. D. Sokolovskiy, *Soviet Military Strategy*, 3rd edn, ed. H. F. Scott (Macdonald and Jane's, London, 1975), p. 288.
3 Ibid., p. 289.

Notes

4 Sir John Hackett et al., *The Third World War: August 1985* (Sidgwick & Jackson, London, 1978).
5 Lieutenant-Colonel G. T. Rudolph, 'Assessing the Strategic Balance' (paper submitted to the International Institute for Strategic Studies, London, June 1976), p. 16.

CHAPTER 9

1 *Soviet Military Power: 1987* (US Department of Defense, Washington DC), p. 29.
2 Ibid.
3 D. Hölsken, *V-Missiles of the Third Reich: The V1 and V2* (Monogram Aviation Publications, Sturbridge, Mass., 1994), pp. 260–61.
4 *Armed Forces Journal*, January 1980, p. 35.

CHAPTER 10

1 *Conway's All the World's Fighting Ships: 1947–1995* (Conway Maritime Press, London, 1995), p. 199, and Admiral A. Baldini, 'The Missile Systems of the Italian Navy', *International Defense Review*, IV (1969), p. 357. According to the latter, 'This proved to be an ingenious and interesting solution which gave completely positive results when tested.' It is possible, although there is no evidence for this, that the planned Polaris missiles for Italy were cancelled as part of the Cuban Missiles Crisis deal, in which Jupiter land-based missiles were withdrawn from Italy and Turkey. No evidence has been found of any other NATO ships of this era actually being fitted with Polaris tubes.
2 *Conway's All the World's Fighting Ships: 1947–1995*, p. 342.

CHAPTER 11

1 H. Wynn, *The RAF Strategic Deterrent Forces: 1946–1969* (Her Majesty's Stationery Office, London, 1994), pp. 337–9.
2 A. Cave Brown (ed.), *Operation World War III: The Secret American Plan 'Dropshot' for War With the Soviet Union, 1957* (Arms and Armour Press, London, 1979), pp. 208–9.
3 Bill Gunston, *An Illustrated Guide to Modern Bombers* (Salamander Books, London, 1988), p. 48.

CHAPTER 12

1 Wynn, *The RAF Strategic Deterrent Forces: 1946–1969*, p. 12.
2 Ibid., p. 273.
3 Ibid., p. 276.

4 Admiral Sir Ian Easton, formal statement to the 'Polaris Successor' seminar held at the Royal United Services Institute for Defence Studies on 30 April 1980; reported in *Journal of the Royal United Services Institute for Defence Studies*, vol. 125, no. 3 (September 1980), p. 19.

5 David S. Yost, *France's Deterrent Posture and Security in Europe, Part I: Capabilities and Doctrine* (International Institute for Strategic Studies, London, Adelphi Paper No. 194, winter 1984/85), p. 14.

6 R. S. Norris, et al., *Nuclear Weapons Databook, Volume V: British, French and Chinese Nuclear Weapons* (Westview Press, Boulder, Col., 1994), p. 385.

7 *United States Military Posture for FY 1983* (The Organization of the Joint Chiefs-of-Staff, Washington DC, 1982), p. 117.

CHAPTER 13

1 Barbara G. Levi, Frank N. von Hippel, William H. Dogherty, 'Civilian Casualties from "Limited" Nuclear Attacks on the USSR', *International Security*, vol. 12, no. 3 (winter 1987/88), pp. 168–9. The strike plan on which their study was based is given in Appendix 28.

2 *NATO: Facts and Figures*, 11th edn (NATO Information Service, Brussels, 1989), p. 259.

3 *Norwegian Defence: Facts and Figures* (Royal Ministry of Defence, Oslo, 1995), p. 37.

CHAPTER 14

1 Norris et al., *Nuclear Weapons Databook, Volume V*, p. 363.

2 Cochrane et al., *Nuclear Weapons Databook, Volume II*, pp. 50–51.

3 Max Walmer, *An Illustrated Guide to Strategic Weapons* (Salamander Books, London, 1988), p. 67.

4 *Conway's All the World's Fighting Ships: 1947–1995*, p. 356.

CHAPTER 19

1 Sokolovskiy, *Soviet Military Strategy*, p. 300.

CHAPTER 23

1 NATO Military Committee Document MC-14/2 (NATO Headquarters, Fontainebleau, 1956).

2 *The Falklands Campaign: The Lessons* (Cmnd 8758, Her Majesty's Stationery Office, London, 1982), paragraph 243.

3 UK Royal Navy, *General Statistics* (D/DPR/129/3/11/9, dated 17 April 1991).

Notes

CHAPTER 24

1 Sokolovskiy, *Soviet Military Strategy*, p. 250.
2 *NATO and the Warsaw Pact: Force Comparisons* (NATO Information Services, Brussels, 1984).

CHAPTER 25

1 A. J. Alexander, *Armor Development in the Soviet Union and the United States* (Rand Corporation, Santa Monica, 1976), p. 127.

CHAPTER 31

1 Sokolovskiy, *Soviet Military Strategy*, p. 141.
2 Sun Tzu, *The Art of War*, trans. and intro. Samuel B. Griffith (Oxford University Press, London, 1963), p. 69.
3 Details of the NATO Alert Systems are contained in PRO DEFE 5/166 (Chiefs-of-Staff Paper 27/66) and in PRO FO371/190667.

CHAPTER 32

1 'Declaration Regarding the Defeat of Germany and the Assumption of Supreme Authority by the Allied Powers', signed in Berlin at 1800 hours Central European Time, 5 June 1945, by General of the Army Dwight D. Eisenhower (USA), Marshal of the Soviet Union G. Zhukov (USSR), Field Marshal Sir Bernard Montgomery (UK) and General J. de Lattre de Tassigny (France).
2 Paper JP(62)6 (Final), dated 19 June 1962, in PRO/DEFE 11/489.
3 J. J. Sokolsky, *Seapower in the Nuclear Age: The United States Navy 1949–80* (Routledge, London, 1991), pp. 61, 74.
4 PRO/DEFE 11/491.
5 R. J. S. Corbett, *Berlin and the British Ally: 1945–1990* (published privately, 1992), p. 62.
6 Ibid., p. 94.

CHAPTER 33

1 T. B. Cochrane, W. M. Arkin, and M. M. Hoenig, *Nuclear Weapons Databook, Volume I: US Nuclear Forces and Capabilities* (Ballinger, Cambridge, Mass., 1984), pp. 30–31.
2 News Conference, 3 January 1955.
3 *Annual Report to Congress: Fiscal Year 1975* (US Department of Defense, Washington DC, 1974), p. 82; quoted in W. van Cleave and S. T. Cohen, *Tactical Nuclear Weapons: An Examination of the Issues* (Macdonald and Jane's, London, 1978).

4 *Annual Report to Congress: Fiscal Year 1982* (US Department of Defense, Washington DC, 1981), p. 129.

5 *United States Military Posture for FY 1983* (The Organization of the Joint Chiefs-of-Staff, Washington DC, 1982).

6 Sir Solly Zuckerman to the British minister of defence, 7 August 1962 (PRO DEFE 13/254).

CHAPTER 34

1 This is based on information contained in the Federal German government document *Militärische Planungen des Warschauer Paktes in Zentraleurope – Eine Studie (Warsaw Pact Military Plans in Central Europe: A Study)*, issued by the Federal Ministry of Defence Press Office, Bonn, Germany, in February 1992.

CHAPTER 35

1 D. Ball, *Targeting for Strategic Defence* (International Institute for Strategic Studies, London, Adelphi Paper No. 185, summer 1983), p. 5.

2 Cochrane et al., *Nuclear Weapons Databook, Volume I*, p. 6.

3 Cave Brown (ed.), *Operation World War III*, p. 24.

4 Ball, *Targeting for Strategic Defence*, p. 8.

5 Ibid., p. 9.

6 Glasstone and Dolan, *The Effects of Nuclear Weapons*.

7 The JIGSAW reports are in PRO/DEFE 11/436.

8 'The Consequences of "Limited" Nuclear Attacks on the United States', *International Security*, vol. 10, no. 4 (spring 1986), pp. 3–45.

9 Levi et al., 'Civilian Casualties from "Limited" Nuclear Attacks on the USSR', pp. 168–89.

CHAPTER 37

1 Herman Kahn, *On Escalation* (Pall Mall Press, London, 1965 (reprint of earlier US edn)), pp. 95, 97.

2 Nuclear Planning Group, Final Communiqué, Taormina, Italy, 17–18 October 1991, paragraph 6.

3 Hackett et al., *The Third World War*.

4 President Jimmy Carter in a letter to Senator John C. Stennis dated 11 July 1977; quoted in van Cleave and Cohen, *Tactical Nuclear Weapons*, p. 8.

5 Sun Tzu, *The Art of War*, p. 76.

Bibliography

BOOKS

Alexander, A. J., *Armor Development in the Soviet Union and the United States* (Rand Corporation, Santa Monica, 1976)

Alexander, J. H., and Bartlett, M. L., *Sea Soldiers in the Cold War – Amphibious Warfare: 1945–1991* (Naval Institute Press, Annapolis, Md., 1995)

Archer, C. (ed.), *The Soviet Union and Northern Waters* (Routledge, London, 1988)

Ball, D., *Targeting for Strategic Defence* (International Institute for Strategic Studies, London, Adelphi Paper No. 185, summer 1983)

Bellany, I., *Nuclear Vulnerability Handbook* (Centre for the Study of Arms Control and International Security, Lancaster, 1981)

Campbell, D., *The Unsinkable Aircraft Carrier* (Paladin Grafton Books, London, 1986)

Cave Brown, A. (ed.), *Operation World War III: The Secret American Plan 'Dropshot' for War with the Soviet Union, 1957* (Arms and Armour Press, London, 1979)

Cochrane, T. B., Arkin, W. M., and Hoenig, M. M., *Nuclear Weapons Databook, Volume I: US Nuclear Forces and Capabilities* (Ballinger, Cambridge, Mass., 1984)

Cochrane, T. B., Arkin, W. M., Norris, R. S. and Hoenig, M. M., *Nuclear Weapons Databook, Volume II: US Nuclear Warhead Production* (Ballinger, Cambridge, Mass., 1987)

Collins, J. M., *American and Soviet Military Trends since the Cuban Missile Crisis* (Center for Strategic and International Studies, Georgetown University, Washington DC, 1978)

——*Imbalance of Power: Shifting US–Soviet Military Strengths* (Macdonald and Jane's, London, 1978)

——*US–Soviet Military Balance: Concepts and Capabilities* (McGraw-Hill, New York, 1980)

Cook D., *Forging the Alliance: NATO 1945–1950* (Secker & Warburg, London, 1989)

Corbett, Sir Robert, *Berlin and the British Ally: 1945–1990* (published privately, 1992)

Cordesman, Anthony H., *NATO's Central Region Forces* (Royal United Services Institute for Defence Studies, London, 1988)

Davis, J. K., et al., *SALT II and US–Soviet Strategic Forces* (Institute for Foreign Policy Analysis, Cambridge, Mass., 1979)

Douglass, J. D., and Hoeber, A. M., *Soviet Strategy for Nuclear War* (Hoover Institution Press, Stanford, Cal., 1979)

Fursenko, A., and Naftali, T., *The Secret History of the Cuban Missile Crisis: 'One Hell of a Gamble'* (John Murray, London, 1997)

Geraghty, Tony, *Beyond the Front Line* (HarperCollins, London, 1996)

Gunston, Bill, *The Illustrated Encyclopedia of the World's Rockets and Missiles* (Salamander Books, London, 1979)

——*An Illustrated Guide to Modern Bombers* (Salamander Books, London, 1988)

Hackett, Sir John, et al., *The Third World War: August 1985* (Sidgwick & Jackson, London, 1978)

Hanks, R. J., *The Unnoticed Challenge: Soviet Maritime Strategy and the Global Choke Points* (Institute for Foreign Policy Analysis, Cambridge, Mass., 1980)

Hölsken, D., *V-Missiles of the Third Reich: The V-1 and V-2* (Monogram Aviation Publications, Sturbridge, Mass., 1994)

Isby, D. C., *Weapons and Tactics of the Soviet Army* (Jane's, London, 1981)

Lashmer, Paul, *Spy Flights of the Cold War* (Sutton Publishing, Stroud, 1996)

Maloney, S. M., *Securing Command of the Sea: NATO Naval Planning 1948–1954* (Naval Institute Press, Annapolis, Md., 1995)

Norris, R. S., et al., *Nuclear Weapons Databook, Volume V: British, French and Chinese Nuclear Weapons* (Natural Resources Defense Council, Boulder, Col., and Westview Press, Oxford, 1994)

Reznichenko, V. G. (ed.), *Tactics: A Soviet View* (English edition published by United States Air Force, Washington DC, 1984)

Rudolph, Lieutenant-Colonel G. T., 'Assessing the Strategic Balance' (paper submitted to the International Institute for Strategic Studies, London, June 1976)

Senger und Etterlin, F. von, *Taschenbuch der Panzer* (Bernard & Graefe Verlag, Koblenz, 1990)

Simon, J. (ed.), *NATO–Warsaw Pact Force Mobilization* (National Defense University Press, Washington DC, 1988)

Sokolovskiy, V. D., *Soviet Military Strategy*, 3rd edn, ed. H. F. Scott (Macdonald and Jane's, London, 1975)

Sokolsky, J. J., *Seapower in the Nuclear Age: The United States Navy 1949–80* (Routledge, London, 1991)

Staercke, A. de, et al., *NATO's Anxious Birth: The Prophetic Vision of the 1940s* (C. Hurst & Co., London, 1985)

Sun Tzu, *The Art of War*, trans. and ed. Samuel B. Griffith (Oxford University Press, London, 1963)

Twigge, S. R., *The Early Development of Guided Weapons in the United Kingdom: 1940–1960* (Harwood Academic Publishers, Chur, Switzerland, 1993)

van Cleave, W., and Cohen, S. T., *Tactical Nuclear Weapons: An Examination of the Issues* (Macdonald and Jane's, London, 1978)

Walmer, Max, *An Illustrated Guide to Strategic Weapons* (Salamander Books, London, 1988)

Bibliography

Wiener, F., *Die Armeen der Warschauer-Pakt-Staaten* (Verlag Carl Ueberreuter, Vienna, 1974)

Woff, R. (ed.), *Warsaw Pact High Command* (Jane's Information Group, London, 1989)

Wynn, H., *The RAF Strategic Deterrent Forces: 1946–1969* (Her Majesty's Stationery Office, London, 1994)

Yost, David S., *France's Deterrent Posture and Security in Europe, Part I: Capabilities and Doctrine* (International Institute for Strategic Studies, London, Adelphi Paper No. 194, winter 1984/85)

OFFICIAL PUBLICATIONS

The Falklands Campaign: The Lessons (Cmnd 8758, Her Majesty's Stationery Office, London, 1982)

Glasstone, S., and Dolan, P. J., *The Effects of Nuclear Weapons* (US Department of Defense, Washington DC, 1977)

NATO: Facts and Figures, 11th edn (NATO Information Service, Brussels, 1989)

NATO and the Warsaw Pact: Force Comparisons (NATO Information Services, Brussels; issued in 1982, 1983, 1984)

Soviet Military Power (US Department of Defense, Washington DC; issued in 1981, 1983, 1984, 1985, 1986, 1987, 1988, 1989, 1990)

Soviet Naval Exercises: 1960–1984 (NATO Information Service, Brussels, 1985)

Texts of Final Communiques, 1949–74, 1975–80, 1981–5, 1986, 1987, 1988, 1989 (NATO Information Service, Brussels, published the following year)

United States Military Posture for FY 1983 (The Organization of the Joint Chiefs-of-Staff, Washington DC, 1982)

US Army, *Soviet Army Operations* (US Army Intelligence and Threat Analysis Center, Arlington, Wash., 1978)

US Army, *Handbook on the Satellite Armies* (Pamphlet 30-50-2, Department of the Army, Washington DC, 1958)

US Army, *History and Role of Armor* (US Army Armor School, Fort Knox, Ky., 1971)

Whence the Threat to Peace? (Military Publishing House, USSR Ministry of Defence, Moscow; issued in 1982 (1st edn), 1982 (2nd edn (supplemented)), 1984 (3rd edn))

MAGAZINES AND JOURNALS

International Defense Review
Jane's Defence Weekly
Journal of the Royal United Services Institute for Defence Studies
Proceedings of the US Naval Institute

REFERENCE BOOKS

Conway's All the World's Fighting Ships: 1947–1995 (Conway Maritime Press, London, 1995)

Bibliography

Jane's Armour and Artillery (Jane's, London, various years)
Jane's Fighting Ships (Jane's, London, various years)
Janes Strategic Weapons Systems (Jane's, London, various years)
The Military Balance (International Institute for Strategic Studies, London, various years)
World Armaments and Disarmament Yearbook (SIPRI, Stockholm, Sweden, various years)

OFFICIAL DOCUMENTS

Documents held in the British Public Record Office are acknowledged in the notes with the prefix 'PRO'.

Index